Fyffes and the Banana

To:

Harvey,

With every good wish.

Feb. 2017

By the same author
The Japanese Shipping and Shipbuilding Industries, Athlone 1990
(with Professor T. Chida)

Far and away the best banana

Fyffes and the Banana: Musa Sapientum

A Centenary History 1888–1988

PETER N. DAVIES

THE ATHLONE PRESS
London & Atlantic Highlands, NJ

First published 1990 by The Athlone Press Ltd
1 Park Drive, London NW11 7SG
and 171 First Avenue, Atlantic Highlands, NJ 07716

British Library Cataloguing in Publication Data

Davies, Peter N. (Peter Neville)
   Fyffes and the banana: musa sapientum: a centenary
history 1888–1988.
   1. Great Britain. Banana importers. Fyffes Group, history
I. Title
382.41477206541

ISBN 0–485–11382–1

Library of Congress Cataloging in Publication Data

Davies , Peter N.
   Fyffes and the banana: musa sapientum: a centenary history,
1888–1988/Peter N. Davies.
      p.   cm.
   Includes bibliographical references.
   ISBN 0–485–11382–1
   1. Fyffes Group—History.   2. Banana trade—Great Britain–
–History.   I. Title.
HD9259.B3G734   1990
382'.414772'06041—dc20

Typeset by J&L Composition Ltd, Filey, North Yorkshire
Printed in Great Britain by The Bath Press.

This book is dedicated to my wife, Maureen,
and to my son, Simon.

Contents

Foreword

It is now just over one hundred years since Edward Wathen Fyffe imported his first tiny cargo of bananas from the Canary Islands and thereby played a significant part in establishing the British banana industry. The subsequent growth of his enterprise and of the demand for what had previously been a rare and exotic fruit then led to an amalgamation with its greatest competitor so that Elders and Fyffes Ltd was formed in 1901. Under the leadership of A.H. Stockley and A.R. Ackerley and somewhat against the wishes of its principal shareholder, Sir Alfred Jones, the new company rapidly created its own fleet and a national distribution and ripening system. These developments then enabled Canary, Central American and particularly Jamaican bananas to be brought within the reach of every family in the land. More recent changes have seen the firm re-organised as the Fyffes Group and its entry into the fresh fruit and produce business. However, even today, as Fyffes commences its second century the banana remains as its largest, single, interest and the company continues to play a major role within the UK banana market.

Having been associated with Fyffes for over thirty-seven years I have always been interested to learn more about the antecedents of this remarkable concern. At a time of extensive change, such as the present, it is important to be able to pause and look back and to consider the firm's history. In many respects the future grows out of the past and can best be understood by examining the various influences and contributions which have brought the enterprise to its current position. The growth of Fyffes from tiny beginnings to a massive business with worldwide linkages illustrates this very clearly and provides a fascinating story which has been described and analysed in graphic detail in the following pages.

Peter Davies has been extremely diligent in seeking out every piece of written evidence and has also been most enthusiastic in interviewing many former and present members of staff. The result has been a study of high quality which I am happy to commend to all who would wish to learn more about this fascinating industry.

Everything that is now known suggests that Fyffes' second century will be quite as challenging as its first – it seems equally certain that its future response will be just as vigorous as it has been in the past.

A. John Ellis, CBE
Chairman and Chief Executive,
Fyffes Group Ltd

List of Tables in the text

List of Illustrations in the text

List of Tables in the Appendix

Preface by the author

The banana has been the subject of many publications which have ranged from the very serious to the extremely light-hearted. Its botanical background and evolution have been carefully studied and analysed and there are a number of works which have examined its cultivation and the scientific methods necessary to control the diseases with which it is all too frequently afflicted. Other studies have shown how the fruit was developed for human consumption and how it spread to form part of the basic diet in many parts of the tropical and sub-tropical worlds. The more recent addition of the banana to the food available to the peoples of the more temperate zones has also received some attention – principally in accounts of the three American multi-national corporations – United Fruit (now United Brands), Standard Fruit and Del Monte.

There are a number of parallels between the development of the banana market in North America and that in Europe. Both received small quantities of the fruit on an *ad hoc* basis through the enterprise of individual seafarers but nothing in the way of an organised trade was able to evolve until the second half of the nineteenth century. This was partly because of the particular qualities of the banana which required a speedy journey from producer to consumer. The provision of steam shipping was essential for this to be achieved but this and other necessary facilities were expensive and could only be justified if a large and reliable throughput could be guaranteed. Paradoxically, however, while Carl Frank began to import bananas from Panama to New York by utilizing the steam ships of the Pacific Mail Company in 1864, it was Captains George Busch and Dow Baker who employed small wooden sailing vessels to carry the fruit from Jamaica who were the real American pioneers.

The earliest attempt to establish a commercial trade in the UK would appear to have been in 1872 when a trial cargo of *prata* bananas was imported from St Michael's in the Azores.[1] Although stated to have been a success the experiment was not, apparently, repeated – perhaps because the growing shipments of pineapples and oranges from this island offered better financial returns! It was left, therefore, to Alfred Lewis Jones of the Elder Dempster Line and to Edward Wathen Fyffe to lay the real foundations of the British banana business. In Jones' case this was achieved by filling any spare capacity with the fruit when his own vessels called at the Canaries on their return from West Africa to Liverpool. These cargoes were carried on the ship's own account whereas Mr Fyffe acted as an agent for a number of Canary growers and employed any convenient steam ship which happened to call in the Archipelago while *en route* for London.

Unlike the American firms the emergence of these two British companies and their subsequent amalgamation to form Messrs Elders and Fyffes Limited has never been fully recorded and analysed. As the resultant business was to play a seminal role in creating and then developing the UK and, later, the European banana markets, this is a surprising and major omission which this work will attempt to redress. In addition, in view of the significance of what was to become the Fyffes' Group in 1969 and of its overwhelming importance in a British context, this study will not only be concerned with the history of a highly successful enterprise but will also be an account of the industry itself.

Any study of a commercial undertaking must necessarily consider how successful it has been in taking advantage of the opportunities available to it. Apart from this purely financial criterion, most business activities must also take cognizance of the economic, political and social environment in which they operate, and this is certainly true in the case of the banana industry. In addition the nature of the product itself places further, heavy demands upon those who wish to gain a full understanding of any specific enterprise, and the banana poses particular difficulties in this respect. The character of the fruit, the problems of its cultivation, its transport from producer to consumer including the need for specialized ocean shipping, the sophisticated arrangements necessary to handle, ripen and distribute it to the appropriate markets, and the way in which it must compete with other fruits and substitutes are all important aspects which must be carefully examined.

The widespread and diverse nature of the banana industry and of the many factors which have aided or retarded its progress over the past one hundred years has meant that the author of this current study has been obliged to rely very heavily upon the assistance provided by past and present members of the trade. Their willing co-operation has been an essential part in illuminating numerous obscure events but as all evidence from whatever source has been interpreted by the writer, he alone is responsible for any errors or misconceptions.

Mr A. J. Ellis, Chief Executive since 1969, has been of immense help in ensuring that all requests for information have been fully met. As the person concerned with all major decisions over the past twenty years, his great knowledge of both the Company and the trade have been invaluable and this work owes much to his personal support and active collaboration. Much of his former and present management team have been equally co-operative and I would wish to specially mention John A. Benns, G. L. Foster, Alan Hall, Dennis Martin and David Philp. On the general produce side of the business, I would also like to record my appreciation for the assistance given by Charles Penny (ex Francis Nichols and Geo. Monro) and John Priest (ex Geo. Jackson). The aid provided by David Bagshaw and Paul Shields in respect of the present situation must also be mentioned and I would also like to acknowledge the aid given by many other Fyffes' employees including Andy Anderson, Pat Caws, the late Stan Clements, the late Fred Darter, Clive Dury, the late E. J. Easterbrook, S. W. F. Johnson, W. H. Knight, Joe Lees, Tommy Tomkins, Ben Whaley and Vic Whiteley.

Individuals concerned with the production areas have also been extremely helpful. Information concerning the Cameroons (and Fernando Po) was supplied by the late P. J. Cochrane, Harold Goodwin, the late A. 'Sandy' Maclaurin, Gordon Miller and by S. 'Paddy' Watters. Company staff in Tenerife were equally helpful and I am most obliged to John Colville, Ray Hay and Tim Stickney. Former employees including Mr and Mrs Norton-Amor, Austin Baillon (a local historian) Sn Diaz (of CREPÉ), the late Mrs D. C. Moore (widow of Wilfred Moore) and the Pavillard family in Las Palmas, also made useful contributions to my understanding. My knowledge of the Jamaican business relied heavily upon C. V. Black and Herbert Hart and this was supplemented by David Read of Jamaican Producers, John Burlton (ex Fyffes and now Jamaica Producers), A. Jeffares (JAMCO) and Norman Ridge (ex Fyffes and currently JAMCO). Ray Hilborne of Geest Industries did much to clear my understanding of activites in the Windward Islands while the late J. G. Batten, D. H. Brown and Arthur Wadland did their best to supply a basic knowledge of the Company's intricate operations in Europe.

The movement of cargoes of bananas over long distances is a highly skilled and specialized business. I was fortunate, therefore, in receiving the advice and encouragement of a number of experts from the marine side. These included R. A. Peters and A. J. Walker at head office, Mr Brian Dawson of Messrs T. & J. Harrison, and Captains Bull, Kinsley and Leslie – the latter being also a maritime historian of considerable merit who has made every effort to assist me with this area of my study.

The lengthy research into such a broad topic and the subsequent writing of this substantial volume have been facilitated enormously by the enthusiastic collaboration of many of Fyffes' employees and pensioners, the support of its customers and the co-operation of its competitors. While it is not possible to list everyone who has contributed to this project I am most anxious to thank all concerned and trust that this completed book will provide at least some recompense for the effort involved. However, one further person must be acknowledged for throughout the long period of the work's gestation and during what could have been a difficult run towards publication I have been greatly sustained by the continued support provided by Fyffes' public relations manager, Mr Duncan Miller. His vast knowledge of the business and of its intricacies and ramifications has proved to be invaluable and he has undoubtedly played a vital role in bringing my study to completion.

My grateful thanks are also due to Mrs Gill Curtis who was responsible for the bulk of the typing, to Miss Val Dodd for her aid with corrections and to Dr Sheila Marriner, Mr T. L. Norton and Mr David Williams for their help wih many aspects of the basic research.

Peter N. Davies
University of Liverpool

Introduction: the banana – its geographic, botanic and historic background

The banana is now such a cheap and commonplace fruit that it may be hard to believe that it is just over one hundred years since it was first brought to Britain on a commercial scale. Yet the primitive banana occurred naturally over large areas of Southern Asia and what is now Indonesia and was gradually developed by early man to become a major subsistence crop throughout the Tropics. In many respects the banana occupied the role of a staple food plant in those areas that was comparable to that of wheat and barley in the temperate zones and to that of Indian corn in much of the New World.

The banana did not, of course, achieve this enormous status all at once. Its origins are lost in the mists of antiquity but it is clear that it took many thousands of years for it to be transformed from seed-bearing varieties of little nutritious value to seedless types with increasingly large quantities of pulp. The manner in which this was accomplished has been the subject of much speculation, but the correct explanation is probably that offered by William Fawcett:

As to the origin of seedless varieties of fruit, there are several species of *Musa* of which the fruit has no pulp, but consists merely of the outer shell and large seeds filling up the shell like a pea-pod and its seeds, the peas: other varieties have a small amount of pulp. The pulp is of greater value in this case as food than the seeds. Primitive man, whose food was precarious, was always keen in the matter of selecting food-plants and preserving varieties that were promising, and no doubt took care of the suckers of a banana which yielded pulpy fruit, just as the Arabs grow suckers from date palms that are known to bear good fruit. The selection would be continuous and whenever a variation occurred with a larger amount of pulp and a corresponding fewness of seeds, it would be carefully treasured and the suckers

1

planted instead of those with little pulp and many seeds. There is (thus) no difficulty whatever in understanding how the seedless banana has arrived, nor in understanding how varieties have occurred and been propagated from time to time.[1]

Many other writers who were contemporary with Fawcett agreed with this explanation and were convinced that it was the conscious work of incalculable generations of early man that was largely responsible for the gradual evolution of the seedless banana. However, some later authors have suggested that it was the mutations which were produced from time to time by the natural process of hybridization that was the key element in these developments.[2] In any event there can be no doubt that primitive man took advantage of the improved varieties which emerged and by following a policy of selection then completed the task of creating a fruit which was later to form the basis of the modern banana industry.

It will be appreciated from this analysis that the banana took many forms, although it was only those which were of value to man that were ultimately to be developed to satisfy his needs. However, the wide range of fruit which gradually emerged undoubtedly had a common botanical origin, and the resulting group has been scientifically described as the *family Musaceae*. This includes many subfamilies, or *genera*, which cover a wide range of plants such as arrowroot, canes, ginger, grasses, lilies and palms. Amongst these is the genus *Musa* and it is from one of its sub-divisions – that of *Eumusa* – that the edible banana has evolved. The 'genealogical tree' in Fig. 1 provides a schematic view of the complexity of this particular family.

From a commercial point of view the *Eumusa* genus provides three separate and distinct products. The first of these – *Musa textilis* – is the source of abaca fibre (commonly known as Manila hemp) which has traditionally been used to make the ropes and hawsers needed by ships of all types. Prior to the Second World War this was grown on a large scale only in the Philippines, but when these supplies were cut off by Japanese Occupation the plant was quickly cultivated in Panama, Costa Rica, Guatemala and Honduras.[3] As a fibre with unique qualities which have only recently been challenged by nylon and other artificial products, this is certainly an important crop, but as it does not bear edible fruit its history forms no part of the present work.

The second commercial crop produced by the *Eumusa* genus is the plantain, or more correctly, *Musa paradisiaca*. This was so named out of respect for a medieval belief which suggested that it was this green and starchy type of banana, and not the apple, which was the real forbidden fruit of paradise.[4] Another source of uncertainty was created by a

2

Fig. 1.1   Family tree of *Musaceae*

Source: Frontispiece to P. K. Reynolds, *The Banana, Its History, Cultivation and Place among Staple Foods* (1927).

number of pioneer writers who frequently confused the edible banana and the plantain:

> The latter is also a cultivated product, but it is purely a vegetable and not a fruit. The banana is both, but until recently it has had little utility save as a fruit.
>
> For centuries the plaintain has been the leading food staple of hundreds of millions of people. It has performed for them the double function which bread and potatoes do for us in the temperate zone. The plantain has the appearance of a very large banana, but does not resemble it in flavour, texture or uses.[5]

Another authority has confirmed these essential differences between the edible banana and the plantain:

> Plantains are a staple food of all people in hot, moist countries, and in some tropical regions are used as a substitute for potatoes and bread. They are never eaten raw, but are cooked in various ways. The green fruit, rich in starch, with a hard, dry flesh, is sliced and toasted, boiled, baked or fried as a vegetable or used for making soup and gruel. Nourishing and appetizing in all forms, plantains will doubtless be in greater demand in the temperate zones as they become better known.[6]

The last sentence, written in 1927, has not been justified by events, although there is some trade between the Caribbean and the southern United States and in recent years imports from the West Indies into Britain have also begun to rise. Thus, in spite of the fact that the plantain is cultivated more widely and extensively than the banana, it is not a major item in world commerce and it is produced almost entirely as a subsistence crop for personal or local consumption. For a variety of reasons, therefore, the plantain is obviously very different from the 'edible banana' and any attempt to include it in this current study would only add to the confusion which still, apparently, exists in some quarters.

The third of the products of the *Eumusa* family is *Musa sapientum* ('the fruit of the wise men'). It was given this distinctive name by Linnaeus, the famous Swedish botanist, because Pliny had reportedly stated that certain Indian sages had reposed in its shade and refreshed themselves with its fruit.[7] This sub-genus included most varieties of 'edible banana' (one of which was 'Gros Michel') and with the addition of the closely related *Musa cavendishii* (variously known as the Canary, Cavendish, Chinese or Dwarf) was eventually to provide practically all the bananas of commerce.[8] This, therefore, is the sub-division of *Eumusa* with which this study is concerned, but it should be clearly understood that much of the background applies equally well to virtually all of the other varieties of edible and non-edible bananas and plantains.

Thus, irrespective of the particular genus, a vast majority of authorities have concluded that the fruit had its origins somewhere in the South-East Asian region. Typical of this view is that provided in a later work by P. K. Reynolds:

> The first home of the edible banana was pretty clearly the humid tropical area of southern and especially south eastern Asia, together with Ceylon and the large islands of Indonesia and Malaysia up to, but not including, New Guinea. There is every reason to believe that the banana has been a staple food since prehistoric times in those moister parts of India lying generally east of Bombay, in Siam, Burma, Indo-China, and the district of Canton in China proper, and the same doubtless holds true of the large populous islands southeast of Asia, including Sumatra, Java, Borneo, Celebes and Formosa, running north to and including the Philippines.[9]

An opposing view has suggested that the banana evolved simultaneously in both Asia and America. This was originally based on the discovery of fossils from the Eocene period in the Rocky Mountains which were apparently similar to fossilized seeds that had been found in Java. Other fossils found in tertiary strata near Bogata in Colombia were thought to support this opinion as they closely resembled the seeds of the African *Musa ensete*.[10] Later research, however, identified the Rocky Mountain fossils as belonging to the *Heliconia* genus and not to *Musa*, and, although the Colombian seeds still cast a minor doubt, critics of their authenticity point out that not a single specimen or evidence of their existence has survived to form part of South America's flora.[11] On balance, therefore, scholarly opinion remains firmly convinced that it was the 'Old World' that was responsible for the emergence of the banana, with South-East Asia as the most likely centre for its original evolution. This, and its subsequent movement, can best be seen by reference to Fig. 2.

Over the course of many centuries some of the inhabitants of the original banana homelands were obliged to seek fresh areas to occupy. These movements were caused by a wide range of factors which included over-population, the expansion of stronger neighbours and the exhaustion of soils. Whatever the motivation it is inconceivable that the migrants would have travelled without their more important food crops, so the banana came to be established wherever the soil and climatic conditions were appropriate. The comprehensive nature of this movement can be seen from the eastward migration which carried what was to become the subspecies *Musa acuminata* far into the Pacific.

5

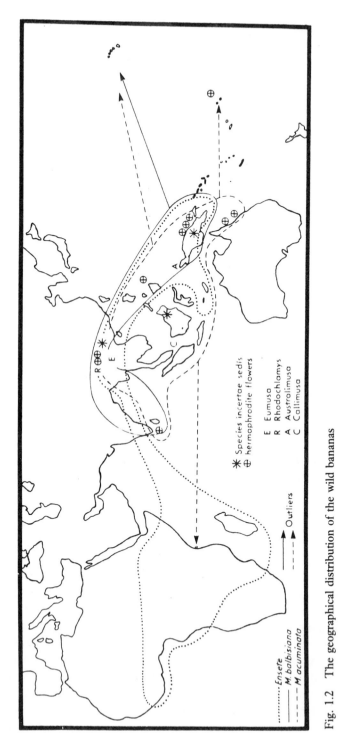

Fig. 1.2 The geographical distribution of the wild bananas
Source: N. W. Simmons, *The Evolution of the Banana.*

Indeed its cultivation was extended so that it not only included Hawaii and Australia but also reached Easter Island which lay nearly two thousand miles from the nearest point of human contact.[12]

The movement to the west was more complicated. As some areas of India were close to, or formed part of, the original homeland of the banana, it is not surprising that evidence of its cultivation there dates back to the dawn of its civilization. The earliest literary reference to the fruit is as far removed as 600 BC[13] and this has been supported by the 'stone pictures' revealed through the excavation of ancient Buddhist temples, although these do not go back much before 175 BC.[14] The partial conquest of India by Alexander the Great in 327 BC. provides yet another useful cross-reference, for it resulted in a contemporary description of four Indian fruit trees by the Greek philosopher, Theophrastus.[15] One of these was later to be identified by Pliny the elder as being a variety of banana:

There is another tree in India of still larger size, and even more remarkable for the size and sweetness of its fruit, upon which the sages (Brahmins) of India live. The leaf of this tree resembles in shape the wing of a bird, being three cubits in length and two in breadths. It puts forth its fruit from the bark, a fruit remarkable for the sweetness of its juice, a single one containing sufficient to satisfy four persons. The name of this tree is *pala* and of the fruit *ariena*. They are found in the greatest abundance in the country of the Sydraci, a territory which forms the extreme limit of the expedition of Alexander.[16]

As it is known from other sources that Alexander reached the Punjab, where bananas were certainly growing at that time, and as the name of *palan* was subsequently found by Portuguese explorers to be the Malayan word used for the fruit in East Africa, it is clear that the Greeks were quite familiar with *Musa sapientum*. Strangely enough neither the Greeks nor the Romans appear to have introduced the banana to any of the territories under their control in western Asia or eastern Africa. Consequently it is thought that the fruit did not reach either the Holy Land or northern Egypt prior to the Mohammedan Conquest in 650 AD when the plants were first imported by Arab traders.[17]

There is ample evidence to show that this was not the earliest occasion that the banana had reached Africa. At one stage it was believed that Arab merchants may have brought the *Musa* cultivars from India, for it is widely accepted that they were responsible for large quantities of trade between these two regions following a route via Arabia to the Horn of Africa.[18] More recent research has indicated, however, that this possibility was probably pre-dated by a direct link from Sumatra to Madagascar. The latter came into being when around the beginning of the first century the Hinduized Malays of Sumatra had colonized the island. As a voyage to East Africa could, under good conditions, be completed in only forty days it is clear that it would be quite feasible to transport a dried banana sucker over this distance. This latter view is supported by the subsequent spread of the plant within Africa which would have been difficult from the Horn. On the other hand a route from Madagascar via the Zambezi valley, the Great Lakes and down the Congo to the west country certainly provided ideal ecological conditions.[19] When this fact is added to the activities of Arab merchants who found it profitable to trade for slaves and ivory right across the continent, it will be readily understood how both banana and plantain were firmly established in West Africa when the Portuguese explored the Guinea Coast in the years 1469 to 1474.[20]

It is generally accepted that it was the Portuguese who then distributed banana plants to the offshore Canary Islands and to Madeira and the Azores. It was, however, the Spanish who had taken control of the Canaries by the end of the fifteenth century and it was under their authority that the banana secured a firm position in the islands as a major subsistence crop. It is against this background that the appointment of a new prior to the Dominican convent in the city of Santo Domingo was to result in the transportation of the banana across the Atlantic to begin a fresh era in the Americas. A contemporary account of this momentous incident has been left to us by a Spanish historian, Oviedo y Valdes, who was acting as the official supervisor of gold smelting at Santo Domingo at the time when the first cultivars arrived:

> There is a fruit here which is called 'Platanos' ... nor did they use to be in the Indies but were brought hither ... One hears on all sides that this special kind was brought from the Island of Gran Canaria in the year 1516 by the Reverend Father Tomas de Berlanga of the Order of Predicadores, to this city of Santo Domingo [now Trujillo] whence they spread to the other settlements of this island [Hispaniola or what is now the Dominican Republic] and to all other islands peopled by Christians. And they have been carried to the mainland and in every party they have flourished ... The first ones were brought, as has been said, from Gran Canaria, and I saw them there in the very monastery of San Francisco in the year 1520 ...[21]

Father Tomas de Berlanga was named Bishop of the newly established See of Panama in 1530. This diocese 'embraced everything discovered and to be discovered on what is now the west coast of South America',[22] and Berlanga made it his business to promote its economic well-being by encouraging the cultivation of a wide range of fruits which included oranges and lemons as well as bananas. One example of the very rapid spread of banana cultivation can be seen by a reference to its arrival in Mexico in 1531[23] and by the seventeenth century the existence of the fruit throughout tropical America is heavily documented.[24]

The reasons for this almost instant popularity of the banana and plantain are not hard to discover. Although the variety introduced by Tomas de Berlanga cannot now be identified, this is relatively unimportant as many other importations quickly followed and all shared the same characteristics. The fact that the plants could be easily transported and only required a rich soil in a warm and humid climate to grow rapidly was clearly of great advantage. In addition its attraction was enhanced by being a non-seasonal producer and by the numerous ways in which it could be prepared and eaten. However, its most significant asset was the very scale of its yield, for while the most that could be expected from a good acre of wheat would be about 1,300 pounds per year, and a similar acre of (Indian) corn would produce 2,800 pounds, the same area could be expected to deliver 18,000 pounds of bananas.[25] The plantain was, of course, even more productive than the banana, and Baron von Humboldt, the eminent German scientist, estimated that under ideal circumstances its yield per acre was up to forty times greater than that of the potato.[26]

Thus the attractions of both banana and plantain are abundantly clear. Unfortunately they both shared the same fault in being extremely perishable so could only be eaten in the immediate vicinity of where they were grown. For several hundred years, therefore, *Musa sapientum* and *Musa paradisiaca* were grown entirely as subsistence crops and, although surpluses must have arisen from time to time, the limitations on overseas trade imposed by the inadequacies of the transport system meant that there was no effective means of marketing this additional production. For this situation to be resolved required two fundamental changes: the first of these was the emergence of a potential market, and the second was the development of a cheap and efficient network of mass transport. These pre-conditions were not to be achieved until the second half of the nineteenth century, and as late as 1873 the *American Encyclopaedia*'s article on the banana did not even hint that it was ever available outside the tropics.[27]

1

The origins of the international fruit trade and the impact of changing maritime technology

Until the beginning of the eighteenth century the economic development of England and Wales was little different from that of its neighbours in western Europe. Like them its relatively small population was mainly engaged in rural pursuits or in agriculture-based industries. A minor distinction was that the country already enjoyed a long tradition of naval glory and its favoured geographic position was gradually encouraging a greater emphasis on overseas trade.

During the next hundred years or so this situation was to change dramatically for, while other nations made only slow progress, a series of fortuitous, though interconnected, events were to more than triple the size of the population and to see Britain emerge as 'the first industrial nation'.[1] One consequence of this development was that Britain evolved as the cheapest producer of most manufactures and, indeed, as the only source of many of the newer items. The combination of industrialization and of the growth of the population then led to a second consequence in that Britain became increasingly dependent upon imports of raw materials and food. The magnitude of these changes can be seen from the fact that in spite of the increase in the population from 9 million in 1801 to 36 million in 1911 the volume of foreign trade per head grew twenty-five-fold in the same period.

One major impact of these developments was that it became increasingly necessary to import larger and larger quantities of food. In practice the shortfall was principally made up by the purchase of grain which until 1850 was mainly acquired in France, the Baltic region and in Russia. Thereafter the introduction of steam shipping and of railways meant that new sources of supply were gradually opened up and by 1900 as much as 87 per cent of grain imports came from outside Europe. A similar pattern evolved more slowly in the case of meat. The transport of live animals was difficult and even after the adoption of refridgeration in

10

the 1880s the proportion that was imported remained relatively low. Other commodities such as sugar, tea and wine were, however, imported on an ever-increasing scale to satisfy the rising expectations of the working population.

It was a rise in real wages that made possible a change in the dietary habits of the working classes, and the consequence was that fewer families were obliged to rely quite so heavily on bread and potatoes for the bulk of virtually every meal. The result was that ordinary people wanted and could afford to pay for more fish and meat, and that the demand for dairy produce, green vegetables and for fruits gradually rose. This was partly satisfied by an increase in domestic production which took place in a wide range of favoured locations including Kent, the Vale of Evesham, the Lea Valley and Dundee – the main products being apples, cherries, damsons, pears and plums with rising quantities of 'small fruit', including currants, gooseberries, raspberries and straw-berries.[2] However, much of the additional demand needed to be filled by fruit which had been grown abroad, and from very small beginnings this had expanded to form a very substantial trade by the 1880s.

The importation of fruit into Britain has two separate and distinct origins. Dried fruit, principally currants, dates and figs, had been valued for many centuries and as they had good keeping qualities they presented no particular difficulties for even the slowest and most primitive methods of carriage. However, the very small scale of this trade should be kept in mind, for it has been estimated that the capacity of shipping required to cater for these imports from southern Europe and Turkey only amounted to 8 or 9 thousand tons per year in the first half of the eighteenth century.[3] By the nineteenth century this trade had grown to much larger proportions and the gradual popularization of the Christmas festivities added a considerable seasonal boost to the demand for currants from the Mediterranean, with raisins from Malaga and Alicante and figs from Portugal providing many of the cargoes.[4]

Fresh fruit was a very different matter, but the importation of oranges and lemons which possessed what would now be termed a 'long shelf-life' evolved alongside the trade in dried products. At first these items originated in many locations in southern Europe, but with the passage of time Spain came to dominate the supply of oranges while Sicily emerged as the principal source of lemons. According to the letterbook of a Liverpool merchant, Thomas Leyland, which covered the period 1786 to 1788 he obtained most of his 'China oranges' and 'sour oranges' from Seville. He also imported oranges from St Michaels in the Azores and attempted to bring in lemons from Portugal. As this last venture proved to be unprofitable owing to the poor quality of the fruit it was not repeated.[5] The Spanish did not make the mistake of allowing sub-standard oranges to ruin their reputation, and as early as 1788 the first regulations for the loading of the fruit had already been implemented.[6]

These imports of citrus fruits were supplemented by large quantities of apples, pears and cherries. Statistics published in 1839 indicate that in the previous two decades an average of over 37,000 bushels of apples, 330 bushels of pears and approximately 110 cwt. of cherries per year were imported. France was always the principal supplier of all of these three categories, with Holland and Belgium next and North America and Germany providing most of the balance.[7] An overall picture of the items imported in Great Britain and Ireland during 1840 is provided by Table 1.1.

TABLE 1.1   IMPORTS OF FRUITS AND VEGETABLES INTO GREAT BRITAIN AND IRELAND IN 1840[8]

				value
Almonds	(cwt.)		22,097	£86,211
Apples				33,627
Cherries				211
Currants	(cwt.)		221,119	589,651
Dates		(cwt.)	985	2,446
Figs		(cwt.)	30,063	42,444
Unenumerated fruit				2,665
Grapes				32,108
Nutmegs		(lb)	113,193	20,987
Coconuts				4,486
Chestnuts		(bushels)	25,124	8,793
Smallnuts		(bushels)	82,795	23,978
Walnuts		(bushels)	33,084	8,271
Onions		(bushels)	15,152	3,409
Oranges & lemons		(boxes)	26,752	150,137
Pears				265
Plums				21,873
Potatoes		(cwt.)	545,744	109,206
Raisins		(cwt.)	178,116	238,230

In addition to these major items a number of 'exotic' varieties were also imported and recorded under the heading of 'unenumerated' fruits. As these were inevitably very expensive, considerable attention was given to their production in glasshouses, and this activity was given a considerable boost when a system of hot water heating was devised in 1815. Thus importations of pickled mangoes which were looked upon as a special delicacy were complemented by fresh mangoes which had been grown in the forcing houses of Earl Powis at Walcot Hall. Grapes, peaches and tomatoes were also produced via this method, which

12

received a great impetus in 1842 when a magnificent range of hothouses was constructed at Frogmore. The removal of the duty on glass in 1845 gave a further push to these developments, and the growing of 'exotics' became quite fashionable as well as attracting commercial attention. The forcing of pineapples was especially popular and in June 1820 a specimen of over 9 lb. was grown in Glamorgan and presented to King George IV. This appears to have inspired many others to enter what became a fairly substantial, if high-cost, business, but it tended to peter out after about 1850 when regular shipments from the Azores led the price of home-produced pineapples to fall below the cost of production.[9]

When W. E. Gladstone abolished the duties on imported fruit in 1860 this gave an important boost to the consumption of lemons, figs, currants, raisins and especially oranges. In 1864 he also reduced the duty on sugar – this was finally ended altogether ten years later – and thus gave a further impetus to the trade, especially the domestic producer, as jam-making expanded on a grand scale. Thus the areas under cultivation grew steadily, year by year, as will be seen from the statistics in Tables 1.2 and 1.3.

TABLE 1.2   EXTENT OF ORCHARDS IN GREAT BRITAIN IN EACH YEAR, 1887–91[10]

Year	Acres	Year	Acres	Year	Acres
1887	202,234	1892	208,950	1897	224,116
1888	199,178	1893	211,664	1898	226,059
1889	199,897	1894	214,187	1899	228,603
1890	202,305	1895	218,428	1900	232,129
1891	209,996	1896	221,254	1901	234,660

TABLE 1.3   AREAS OF SMALL FRUIT IN GREAT BRITAIN, 1890–93

Year	Acres	Year	Acres	Year	Acres
1890	46,234	1894	68,415	1898	69,753
1891	58,704	1895	74,547	1899	71,526
1892	62,148	1896	76,245	1900	73,780
1893	65,487	1897	69,792	1901	74,999

From the 1880s until the turn of the century considerable progress was made by British fruit farmers, so that ever-larger quantities of apples, cherries, damsons, pears and plums were produced in their orchards while the cultivation of currants, gooseberries, raspberries and strawberries also continued to expand. However, the rise in the population together with the increase in real wages meant that demand for fruit rose at an even more rapid pace so that even more imports were attracted into the British market (see Table 1.4).

TABLE 1.4 IMPORTS OF RAW APPLES, PEARS, PLUMS, CHERRIES AND GRAPES INTO THE UNITED KINGDOM, 1892–1901[11]

Year	Quantities (in 1,000 bushels)				
	Apples	Pears	Plums	Cherries	Grapes
1892	4515	637	413	217	762
1893	3460	915	777	346	979
1894	4969	1310	777	311	833
1895	3292	407	401	196	865
1896	6177	483	560	219	883
1897	4200	1052	1044	312	994
1898	3459	492	922	402	1136
1899	3861	572	558	281	1158
1900*	2129	477	423	243	593
1901*	1830	349	264	213	680
	Values (in £1,000 sterling)				
1892	1354	297	200	135	394
1893	844	347	332	195	530
1894	1389	411	302	167	470
1895	960	167	166	96	487
1896	1582	207	242	106	443
1897	1187	378	498	178	495
1898	1108	222	435	231	550
1899	1186	266	294	154	588
1900	1225	367	393	308	595
1901	1183	296	244	214	695
1908	2079	515	428	235	728

* Figures for these years in 1,000 cwt.

TABLE 1.5 EXPORTACION DE NARANJA A INGLATERRA (THE EXPORT OF ORANGES TO ENGLAND) (BOXES)[12]

Campana	De Valencia	De Sevilla
1872–73	454,424	4,278
1873–74	422,256	6,495
1874–75	617,908	11,435
1875–76	652,462	7,016
1876–77	730,693	6,719
1877–78	869,005	25,256

Another major, external, beneficiary of this increased demand was the Spanish orange industry, and its exports to England more than doubled during the 1870s. Thereafter citrus fruits continued to grow in importance and the combined value of oranges and lemons imported from Spain into England grew from £805,890 in 1878 to £2,119,294 in 1913.[13]

The rising level of what might best be described as traditional fruit imports created many physical problems. The customary method of shipment was by the use of sailing vessels which were built for speed and which usually fell in the 80 to 160 tons category. In their day, from about 1825 to 1875, large numbers were constructed and it has been estimated that over 300 were engaged in the trade at one time.[14] The majority were owned and operated by firms and individuals based in the south-west, with the Scillies and Cornwall playing an important role in the business. These vessels were employed on routes from Spain, the Mediterranean, the Azores or, in some cases, the West Indies, and although subject to delay in adverse conditions were usually fast enough to be able to deliver their cargoes in reasonable condition. In the longer term, however, it is certain that their size and speed would have made this type of vessel less and less appropriate for the larger quantities of fruit being demanded and, in any case, they were not suitable for the carriage of the more perishable varieties that were increasingly becoming available in the tropical regions.

It was fortunate, therefore, that the gradual evolution of the iron steamship was to effectively revolutionize the transport of bulk cargoes over long distances. A great deal of pioneering work on the application of steam to the propulsion of small river craft was undertaken in the second half of the eighteenth century, but it was not until 1807 that it was used commercially. In that year the *Clermont*, built by Robert Fulton, began a regular service between New York and Albany, and five years later, in 1812, Henry Bell's *Comet* began to operate from Glasgow to Greenock and Helensburgh. Clearly the Americans were the first in this field but any claim to pre-eminence is usually contested on two grounds: Fulton is alleged to have been the son of an Ayrshire emigrant (so was really British!) and, of more importance, the engine which he used to power the *Clermont* had been made by Boulton and Watt in Birmingham, England.[15]

At this stage in their development steam vessels required enormous quantities of coal, and as they were still relatively unreliable they were unsuitable for long voyages on both counts. Nevertheless, their independence of wind and currant made them ideal as tugs and ferries and for providing cross-channel services. Thus in 1819 *Rob Roy* commenced what was probably the world's first regular sea service by steaming between Greenock and Belfast, and in the same year *Waterloo* began to operate in a similar way between Belfast and Liverpool. Two years later

Rob Roy was moved to the Dover–Calais route where she operated with great regularity – her 30 h.p. engine giving a speed of 7 knots and an average crossing time of approximately 2 hours and 45 minutes.[16]

The success of steamships on these shorter routes led to attempts to extend their services to more distant places, and by 1826 the General Steam Navigation Company was employing two steamers between London and Portugal. In 1828 the City of Dublin Steam Packet Company began to operate between Dublin and Bordeaux, but longer voyages were still regarded as non-viable propositions. More typical of the era was the activity on the Thames, where some 35 steam boats were placed into service between 1814 and 1828 – these were mainly to provide passenger services and eventually covered the river from Richmond to Margate. However, a few experimental voyages were completed over lengthy distances. These included: *Savannah*, New York to St Petersburg in 1819; *Rising Star*, England to Chile in 1821; and *Enterprise*, Falmouth to Calcutta in 1825. All of these journeys were made partly or mainly with the aid of sail – many technical advances were to become necessary before steam could be used as the sole means of propulsion over long distances.

Efforts to improve the efficiency of ocean-going vessels were directed on to a number of fronts simultaneously so that advances in engine performance and transmission were complemented by progress in the design and construction of the hull. The development of steam engines is very closely allied to improvements in boilers, and in the 1820s the safe pressure that could be achieved was rarely more than 5 lb. per square inch. This meant, in practice, that the consumption of coal could be as much as 10 lb. per horsepower per hour. By the 1840s boiler pressure had risen to 10 lb. and by the 1850s it was frequently used at 20 lb. per square inch. With pressure at this level a simple expansion engine, fitted with jet condensers, would require about 4 lb. of coal per indicated horsepower per hour.[17]

The introduction of the compound engine in which the steam is expanded in two stages, allied to ever-higher boiler pressures, then led to coal consumption being halved in many cases. This innovation also reduced the weight of the machinery and the space it occupied and opened the way for faster speeds to be achieved. The firm of Randolf and Elder fitted the first effective engine of this type to the *Brandon* in 1853, but the most impressive example of early compounding was that of Alfred Holt's *Agamemnon*, *Ajax* and *Achilles*. These vessels, constructed in 1864, operated with a boiler pressure of 60 lb. per square inch and at their service speed of 10 knots required only 2¼ lb. of coal per indicated horsepower. The consequence of this economical performance was that these ships could make the run of 8,500 miles from

England to Mauritius without refuelling, so this implied that just about all ocean routes were now open to steam navigation.

The advances in boilers and engines were aided by the almost universal, if gradual, replacement of paddle-wheels by screw propulsion. Other improvements in technology such as the surface condenser and the developments in hull design that ensured a free flow of water to the propellor also resulted in substantial gains to efficiency. Of even greater significance, however, was the adoption of iron for the construction of the hull. The first iron steamship was *Aaron Manby*, built in 1822, and she was to prove the forerunner of many such vessels designed for river and estuary work.

Many experts, however, thought that an iron vessel was an affront to nature and although these gradually gained acceptance for coastal work, it took a long time for them to be used for ocean voyages. The first sea-going vessel to be constructed of iron was *Alburkah* of 35 tons and her success in making her own way out to West Africa and up the River Niger helped to convince many sceptical shipowners and engineers that iron was a suitable medium for hulls. As a result, Lloyd's Register classified its first iron steamer, *Sirius*, of 180 tons in 1837. A second vessel, the sailing ship *Ironsides* of 270 tons was classified in 1838, but the Society did not lay down any rules for constructors until 1855. This is not to suggest that problems did not exist, for the rapid fouling of iron hulls by marine growths and the deviation of the compass needle due to iron in the ship obviously led to difficulties and expense.

Nevertheless, iron came rapidly into favour for the building of both steamers and sailing vessels during the 1860s, for in spite of its various defects it possessed two important advantages over wood. In the first place although iron is heavier than wood its greater tensile strength permits so large a reduction in thickness that an iron ship weighed about a quarter less than a wooden vessel of the same dimensions, so that she could carry considerably more cargo without diminishing her buoyancy. Secondly, whereas the structural limit of the length of a wooden ship was about 300 feet, there was practically no restriction on the size of an iron ship other than the ability of her owners to fill her and of ports to handle her. These two aspects of iron construction were of such value that they easily outweighed its disadvantages, but it should not be forgotten that in the 1850s and 60s the P.&O. Company had to spend some £70,000 a year to keep the bottoms of their vessels clear of fouling.[18]

The acceptance of iron for hull construction was not, of course, confined to steamships, and many sailing vessels benefited from its use. At first iron was substituted for wood in the framing only and wood continued to be used for the deck and the 'skin'. However, sailing ships

17

built entirely of iron gradually became more common especially for the larger craft and, with its aid, sail was able to slow down the advance of steam. Other factors which increased the efficiency of sail during this period included the alterations in the tonnage laws in 1836 and in 1854. These allowed changes in hull design, for owners were no longer constrained by penalties on breadth and, under pressure from the competition of steam, many labour-saving devices were installed. The work of M.F. Maury, who combined the experience of hundreds of voyages into sailing directions for all parts of the world also meant that significant savings in time could be achieved by taking advantage of favourable winds and currents.[19] Taken together these measures ensured that it was not until the 1880s that Britain's steam tonnage equalled her sailing tonnage.

It was the certainty of performance that finally secured the victory of steam over sail. Many clipper ships could log 15 knots under certain circumstances, whereas the average steamer in the 1880s would seldom have a service speed of over 10 knots. But while the clipper might be becalmed for days on end, the steamer was not subject to delays of this kind, and being less dependent on climatic conditions the power-driven vessel could take a direct course from port to port, whereas the sailing ship might have to tack many hundreds of extra miles in order to take advantage of the prevailing winds and ocean currents. The consequences of these factors were that the steamship could perform far more round voyages in the year than the sailing vessel and her annual carrying-power was therefore likely to be at least four times greater. The opening of the Suez Canal in 1869 was a further blow, for sailing ships (which could be towed through the canal) found it difficult to pass through the Red Sea and were obliged to continue to use the Cape route, while steamers saved between 3,000 and 4,000 nautical miles on the trading routes from Europe to Asia.[20] The subsequent replacement of iron by steel and the development of very high boiler pressures and of extremely fuel-efficient triple-expansion engines then completed the ascendancy of steam, and sail went into a rapid decline.

The increasing efficiency of ocean shipping, which may be characterized by the transition from sail to steam and wood to iron, then had a major effect on the size of the international market, for it was:

> ... a vital condition for industrial growth – according to the degree that goods are bulky relatively to their value ... The cheaper transport costs become the larger the area over which such cheap and bulky goods can get marketed. Areas with special advantages in processing costs – cheap coal, cheap power, cheap raw materials, good labour supplies – can thus expand their markets as 'transfer costs' decline.

And this chance of expanding markets makes possible and encourages more division of labour, innovation, all the economies of larger-scale production. Rising output and productivity will lower the average costs of the commodity – but only if the goods can be cleared to a widening market. Cheap transport thus becomes economically important according to the degree of its effects upon total costs.[21]

These theoretical considerations were to result in the development of ever-larger and consequently more expensive tonnage. The increase in scale can best be illustrated by examining the cargo and passenger capacity of three vessels of the Cunard Line. In 1840 *Britannia*, built of wood, with a simple side lever engine, had a gross tonnage of 1,139 and could carry only 225 tons of cargo and ninety passengers. *Persia*, an iron paddle steamer of 3,300 gross tons, constructed in 1855, had a capacity for 1,100 tons of cargo and 180 passengers, and *Bothnia*, an iron screw vessel fitted with compound engines, which went into service in 1874, had a gross tonnage of 4,556 and could carry 3,000 tons of cargo together with 1,140 passengers. In addition, the increase in speed from the 8.3 knots of *Britannia* to the 13 knots of *Bothnia* meant that annual capacity was much greater because of the larger number of voyages that could be completed in a year.[22]

From a commercial point of view the provision of such vast quantities of cargo and the arrangements that had to be made to deal with such enormous numbers of passengers meant that an entirely different form of organization had to be evolved. Another consequence of the increase in the size of the ships was on their cost. When Samuel Cunard negotiated with Robert Napier in 1839 for the construction of vessels for his proposed Atlantic service the price quoted for a ship of 960 tons was £32,000. Less than thirty years later Cunard purchased *Oregon* of 7,375 tons for the sum of £220,000. In these circumstances, demurrage (the cost of one day's operation), which had been of little account with smaller and inexpensive sailing vessels, assumed great significance and so speed of turn-round in port became a critical factor in determining profitability. In the final analysis all of these problems were of course overcome, for the economies of scale were so substantial that they offered very high real savings. Thus in spite of improvements in both the regularity of services and the quality of the ships, the level of freight rates fell steadily throughout the nineteenth century and the Isserlis Index which used 1869 as its base of 100 had fallen to only 49 by 1904.[23]

As this decline was far greater than the reduction in the price level, the real cost of transport was constantly being lowered, and as this was especially evident on the longer voyages, the scale and range of world

19

trade was significantly widened.[24] It was, of course, the carriage of cargoes with high bulk and low value that were affected most. This can be clearly seen by reference to Table 1.6, which shows a seven-fold increase in *value* in the cargoes carried by sea between 1840 and 1887.

TABLE 1.6 MERCHANDISE CARRIED BY SEA, ANNUAL TOTALS, 1840 AND 1887 (1,000 TONS)[25]

Commodity	1840	1887
Coal	1,400	49,300
Iron	1,100	11,800
Timber	4,100	12,100
Grain	1,900	19,200
Sugar	700	4,400
Petroleum	—	2,700
Cotton	400	1,800
Wool	20	350
Jute	—	600
Meat	—	700
Coffee	200	600
Wine	200	1,400
Salt	800	1,300
Sundries	9,180	33,750
Total	20,000	140,000

This tremendous increase in world trade should be seen against the background of a rising world population. This not only rose from an estimated 903 million in 1800 to an approximate 1,608 million in 1900, but also consisted of individuals whose purchasing power in real terms was significantly enhanced over the century.

Changes in income levels have much to do with changes in demand and consequently with changes in the structure of output and the composition of foreign trade ... Thus the shift in the diet of the United States and other Western nations from cereals towards meat and dairy products as the standard of living rose was important both for the domestic producers of these commodities and for the trade flows that existed between these countries. Another example associated with the rise in real income is the increased demand for colonial products. Items of trade, such as sugar, tobacco, tea, coffee and cocoa, largely unknown to previous generations, came to be regarded as necessities during the nineteenth century, while the consumption of tropical fruits also became important for the first time towards the end of this period.[26]

20

From the foregoing it is abundantly clear that the growth of world population together with an increase in the purchasing power of many individuals provided many fresh opportunities for trade during the nineteenth century. At the same time the technical advances made by the shipping industry made it possible to handle bulk cargoes on a large scale and, by reducing the cost of ocean transport, further expanded the potential for international exchange. At first, however, these developments had little real impact on the British fruit business which was probably influenced more by the spread of the railway network and by the extension of hothouse facilities than it was by a gradual reduction in maritime freight rates. The provision of cheaper and faster overseas services merely, it seems, enabled larger quantities of traditional crops to be imported. These cargoes of apples and soft fruit were then used to fill the gaps which the domestic producer was unable to satisfy but, apart from the oranges brought in from Spain, there was no significant increase in the importation of fresh items from the Tropics. Evidence to support this statement can be gleaned from the comprehensive description of the stock of a fruiterer's shop which was provided by Charles Dickens in *A Christmas Carol* which was first published in 1843. His account refers to the large quantities of chestnuts, pears, apples, grapes, filberts (hazelnuts), oranges and lemons that were being displayed at what was, and remains, a peak selling period. Surprisingly, perhaps, there was no mention of the banana or of any other 'exotic' fruits.

The banana had, in fact, been known in Britain since the seventeenth century but the irregularity and uncertainty of supply ensured that it was both rare and expensive. The first few bunches that were imported came as a result of the opening of trade with Africa, for this led to small numbers of ships calling at either the Canary Islands or Madeira while on their way home to Europe. These visits were primarily to replenish water and provisions, but officers and men would frequently take local products on board with a view to making a profit when they arrived home. These inevitably included some bananas and enough of these survived the rigours of an ocean voyage under sail for the fruit to become at least slightly known at a few British ports.

With the introduction of steam and the consequent reduction in voyage times, it became easier to carry these individually purchased bananas without deterioration. Consequently, by the mid-nineteenth century a tiny business had developed so that the London market was occasionally provided with what was regarded as an expensive luxury – a hand usually costing between 20 and 30 shillings depending upon availability and condition. It should be stressed, however, that there was no organized trade in bananas and the few bunches which arrived came entirely through the initiative of individual seafarers.

This situation was not to change even after regular steamship services between Liverpool and West Africa began in 1853. This can be seen by reference to the manifest of the s.s. *Faith* which called at both Madeira and Tenerife on her first homeward voyage. This shows that only lemons were collected at the former and that no fruit of any description was picked up at the latter. The explanation for this omission was that port and loading facilities were so primitive at this time that it was not possible to attract the larger types of steam vessels on a regular basis. In turn the lack of a cheap and reliable service meant that it was difficult for any trade, let alone one concerned with a delicate and perishable item, to become firmly established. As the Canaries lay nearly 2,000 miles from its potential market in Britain it was not possible to operate such a service with the sailing 'fruiterers' which carried the longer-lasting citrus fruits with reasonable success. Consequently the emergence of a substantial trade in bananas had necessarily to wait until a wide range of other pre-conditions were fully satisfied. As these facilities did not become available until the 1880s, the birth of the Canary Island banana business was to be delayed for a further thirty years after the *Faith* and her sister ships had made it technically feasible.

Somewhat paradoxically, while the modern vessels of the African Steam Ship Company were unable to initiate the carriage of bananas from the Canaries to Britain, an older form of technology was soon to succeed on the other side of the Atlantic. This was because the sources of supply in the Caribbean and Central America lay within a few hundred miles of their potential markets in the United States. As a result small, wooden sailing craft could, with reasonable weather, be expected to complete such a voyage in so short a time that the fruit would arrive in sound condition. As ships of this type required only the most basic of facilities and as the capital requirements for an enterprise of this kind were extremely low, it is not surprising that attempts to create a trade in bananas began at an early date. The success of at least some of these ventures was to mark the beginning of the modern banana industry.

2

The early development of the American banana market

Although a few of the original investigators considered that the banana was a natural American plant, this view is overwhelmingly opposed by a much larger group of academics. The latter argue that the banana was never mentioned by the first pioneers and it seems certain that it was not cultivated by the Indian before it was brought to their attention by the Europeans.[1] However, the most telling argument is that provided by Baron Erland Nordenskiöld:

> It is important to remember that if the banana had really existed in America it must have been universal. A fruit so easily cultivated *and so important as an article of food* could never have remained uncommon.[2]

If, therefore, it can be accepted that Father Thomas de Berlanga did indeed import the first banana plant into Santo Domingo in 1516, it must also be appreciated that it then spread extremely quickly. Thus by the seventeenth and eighteenth centuries practically every work on tropical America included references to the cultivation and use of the banana and the plantain.[3] By then, unlike in the earlier period, there were also many mentions of 'wild' bananas being discovered along the rivers in Central and South America. However it is generally considered that these are not evidence of indigenous fruits but rather that they were the survivors of plants which had drifted away from Spanish settlements before rooting downstream.

The wide geographic spread of both banana and plantain and their roles as subsistence crops throughout the hotter and more humid regions of the Americas is widely documented, and there can be no doubt that they proved to be of the utmost importance in the localities where they were grown. The extent to which small quantities of these and other tropical fruits were occasionally carried to the centres of population in North America cannot now be ascertained, but it seems very probable that at least some bananas may have been transported on an *ad hoc* basis when ships travelled from the warmer to the cooler regions. Details of how these voyages gradually evolved into regular trades must now be deduced from the remaining evidence, and this suggests that this was to be a process which took nearly two centuries before it was finally completed.

In a statement attributed to William H. Bennett, a shipping reporter, it was claimed that:

> ... an unnamed skipper of an unnamed merchantman first brought Caribbean-grown bananas to our shores in 1690. The shipment probably came from Panama, and it is said to have been delivered at Salem, where the Puritans boiled the bananas with pork to complement a boiled New England dinner. The citizens reported with great indignation that the bananas tasted like soap.[4]

This very imprecise claim could, no doubt, be repeated many times, for it appears very likely that vessels engaged in trade from the Caribbean may well have brought odd lots of bananas to colonial ports prior to the War of Independence (Revolutionary War). Unfortunately, no satisfactory report of any such landings has been preserved, and the first semi-authenticated account does not appear until 1804 when the schooner *Reynard* was stated to have brought thirty bunches from Cuba to New York.[5] Thereafter small consignments may well have followed this route from Cuba to the United States coastal ports, but these were isolated cases and nothing in the form of a regular trade had yet evolved.

Nevertheless, evidence is available to suggest that a gradual increase in imports did take place, and in May 1843 a New York commission dealer, John Pearsall, is reported to have brought in and auctioned 300 bunches of 'Cuban reds'. The same man is also credited with the importation of two further small cargoes in 1845, but this remained a risky enterprise which was heavily dependent upon favourable winds and weather. However, by 1850 somewhat larger 'clipper' schooners commenced to deliver more substantial cargoes of both yellow and red bananas from Cuba to a number of North American ports. Even then the trade remained extremely haphazard and the independent ship-masters engaged on this route used the banana simply as deck cargo as an adjunct to their normal business. These gentlemen:

> ... bartered for the fruit with whisky, rum, cheap jewelery, whips or firearms; and haggled for the lowest price or best swap. They knew that no matter how favorable the terms of purchase were, the trade remained a wild gamble, for even when the fruit was entirely green at the time it was laid on deck, it was likely that over-ripe bananas would

have to be pitched overboard before the ship reached a market port. If the shipments arrived at port in fairly good condition, prospective buyers went to the wharves or the ships and picked over the fruit. They bought small quantities, usually five to twenty bunches at a time. The early comers sometimes got a bargain, but the late comers got only 'shatters and leavin's' ...[6]

Many of these patterns of trade were disturbed by the outbreak of the American Civil War in 1861, but there are many reports which suggest that bananas continued to be imported into New Orleans from the Bay Islands and Honduras, even though this port was technically being blockaded. All of this fruit was carried in small wooden sailing vessels and was mainly handled by Italian immigrants. These included Salvatore Oteri, D. Cifalu and (later) the three Vaccaro Brothers who were to go on and establish the Standard Fruit Company.[7]

The ending of hostilities meant that all restrictions to navigation were quickly removed. Thus the traditional suppliers were free to continue or re-enter the trade, and numerous ship's captains carried deck cargoes of bananas as and when supplies were available and the weather seemed appropriate. Of more lasting significance was the employment of a steam vessel for the first time to transport the fruit. This came about in 1864 when Carl Augustus Frank (sometimes referred to as 'Franc'), a German-born ship's steward, became aware of the potential profits to be earned from the importation of the fruit. He had been working for the Pacific Mail Company which operated between New York and Colon in Panama (then part of Colombia) and during the turn-round of the ship he had an excellent opportunity to discover the ease with which the banana could be grown and purchased. According to one source he then acquired six dozen bunches of green bananas and, after an eleven-day voyage, sold them for a net profit of 100 per cent in New York.[8] Another account[9] suggests that Frank's activities did not begin until 1866, but in any event he and his brothers then entered into the business on a regular basis and in the summer of 1870 it is reported that they utilized three steamships to bring in over 3,000 bunches from Panama.[10]

Amongst those who entered the business after the ending of the Civil War and who continued to employ small wooden vessels was Captain George Busch. It is reported that in 1866 he loaded his schooner with 500 stems[11] at Oracabessa and Port Antonio and fourteen days later he successfully sold his bananas at a profit in Boston. This activity was to mark the beginning of Jamaica's export trade in bananas and Busch's activities proved to be so promising that he returned to Port Antonio and persuaded many small farmers to plant additional fruit with a view to its ultimate export. This policy was followed with such enthusiasm that within two years Busch was able to secure full cargoes at short notice; he then set himself up as an agent for a number of American fruit houses and in 1869 sent seven cargoes of bananas and coconuts to the United States.[12]

Busch's example was quickly followed by a native of New England, Captain Lorenzo Dow Baker. As the owner of the Cape Cod fishing schooner *Telegraph*, Baker frequently undertook trading voyages on his own account and in 1870 he accepted a commission to carry a number of gold miners and their equipment to a point 300 miles up the Orinoco River in Venezuela.[13] Once this had been successfully accomplished Baker headed for home, but as his vessel was leaking badly he put in at Port Antonio for repairs. Then during the ten days it took for re-caulking he looked to see if he could find a cargo that would help to increase the profits on his voyage. Unfortunately all that was on offer was Jamaican bamboo, ginger and allspice. Consequently he was greatly tempted when he was offered green bananas at one shilling a bunch and was assured that they would not ripen for a further fourteen days. Deciding to take a chance he purchased 160 bunches and after an eleven-day journey with the fruit stowed on deck he arrived safely at Jersey City and sold his cargo at a profit of two dollars a bunch.[14]

This favourable experience convinced Captain Baker that this trade warranted further investigation, so in March 1871 he loaded a mixture of flour, timber, pork, salted cod fish, shoes and textiles, and sailed from Provincetown for Port Antonio. After his arrival *Telegraph* was in such a poor condition that it took several weeks to make her seaworthy. During this period he was able to dispose of his cargo at a good price and was then able to use the proceeds to acquire large quantities of fruit. Thus by 11 May, when he began his return voyage, the schooner was fully laden with over 35,000 coconuts and perhaps a thousand bunches of bananas.[15] In spite of extremely bad weather Baker was alongside the Long Wharf in Boston by 29 May. Thus the fruit was still in excellent condition and sold without difficulty, so he achieved a high return on his investment.

The success of this venture encouraged Captain Baker to repeat the experiment, and by July he was back in Boston with a second substantial cargo. On this occasion one of the keenest buyers of his bananas was a young man named Andrew Woodbury Preston, who at that time was working as the representative for the Boston commission firm of Seaverns and Company. As this concern had never handled 'exotic' fruits before, and as Preston was acting on his own initiative, this transaction was a matter of some concern. However, as the bananas proved to be profitable all was well and so he was instructed to buy more as and when they became available.[16] Thus began Preston's long association with the banana which was to last for the remainder of his life and was to see him become President of one of the world's largest fruit corporations.[17]

Captain Baker's achievement in carrying bananas to Boston can be more readily appreciated by the knowledge that at this particular time only a few thousand bunches were imported into the whole of the United States. In addition Boston was one of the most difficult ports to supply as it lay between 1,400 and 2,000 miles from the source of the fruit.[18] Had Baker been able to utilize a steam vessel, which would have reduced voyage times and made the business less dependent upon favourable weather, his problems would have been great enough; the fact that he was actually employing a small schooner made the task highly speculative. Nevertheless, he was quickly convinced that the trade showed considerable promise as at least a supplementary source of income.[19] Consequently he continued in the business during the spring and summer of succeeding years, bananas then being thought of as a seasonal trade, and was gradually able to expand the scale of his operations. Thus, while he was obliged to spend more and more time in Jamaica securing and loading the fruit, he relied increasingly on Andrew Preston as his selling agent in Boston. Baker also involved Captain Jesse H. Freeman, an old associate from Cape Cod, to assist in the chartering and running of additional schooners and, with his aid, attempts were made to widen the scope of the business.

Unfortunately the uncertainty created by the continued use of sailing vessels led to a period of unprofitability and after a further three years he was obliged to return to sea to subsidize this side of his business. In 1874, therefore, Baker acted as master of the *Ruth N. Atwood* and in 1876 commanded the *Eunice P. Newcomb* (both schooners of 109 tons) using them to carry general goods out to Jamaica and returning with bananas for Boston.[20] This was, however, to be only a temporary setback and once he had restored his financial position he decided to concentrate all his energies on placing his irregular banana business on a sound basis. Captain Baker's previous experience had indicated that there was a strong demand for bananas and that they could be sold profitably providing that satisfactory arrangements could be made for supply and transport. He also knew that the Frank Brothers had solved these problems by establishing plantations in Panama and by using the regular steamship services which were operated between there and New York. In 1875 a bitter feud began between the Panama Railroad and the Pacific Mail shipping lines and this caused freight rates to decline dramatically.[21] The Franks took full advantage of this situation and were able to develop a growing market in New York. It appeared to be very possible at this stage that the Franks might well decide to expand still further and might even extend their activities to include Boston.

The need to counter this potential competition on equal terms was, perhaps, the final factor which led Baker to decide to risk all on an attempt to create a comparable system. As a first step he and his family moved to Jamaica and he then established a permanent home near to Port Antonio. His firm, L. D. Baker and Company, conducted all their activities from this base from 1877 and it was therefore well placed to encourage the production of better quality and larger quantities of bananas for export. It is reported that by the end of its first year the company had already made arrangements to purchase all fruit of an exportable quality from over 2,000 acres.[22] Thus one critical aspect of Baker's plans was quickly accomplished; the provision of satisfactory transport arrangements was to take a little longer.

Baker and his long-standing friend, J. B. Freeman, became partners in the newly established Standard Steam Navigation Company in 1876, but as this only operated sailing vessels, it was not the real answer to the carriage of perishable fruit. Indeed, throughout the 1870s Baker had based his business on the expectation that only two out of three of his cargoes would arrive in a saleable condition so he was extremely anxious to find a solution that would reduce these losses. The employment of steam vessels was, of course, the obvious answer, but Baker lacked the necessary capital to take this course of action. He therefore made arrangements with the British-owned Atlas Steamship Line, and after becoming its agent at both Boston and Port Antonio was able to utilize any spare capacity for the carriage of his bananas. As this line already provided a service between Jamaica and New York (with the benefit of a £5,000 p.a. subsidy from the colonial government) this arrangement had the effect of helping Baker to widen his markets as well as ensuring that his principal outlet in Boston was catered for more efficiently.[23]

These innovations proved to be very beneficial, but many of Baker's cargoes continued to be carried in the sailing vessels of the Standard Steam Navigation Company. To a large extent this was on the grounds of sentiment, for the principals of the firm were sailing men of long conviction. Economic considerations could not be totally ignored in the long run and so it was agreed that the company should order two steamships. These were both designed by Baker himself and proved to be three-masted sailing ships fitted with auxiliary steam engines, and as their mizzen masts also acted as smokestacks they looked little different from previous vessels. They were, however, considerably larger than any of their predecessors. Thus, while earlier schooners carried a maximum of 2,000 bunches, the *Jesse H. Freeman* (1883) had a capacity of 12,000 bunches and the later (1884) *L. D. Baker* could cope with nearly 20,000 bunches. In addition these vessels were able to maintain regular year-round schedules, so completed many more voyages than contemporary sailing craft. Both 'steamers' proved to be highly practical and *L. D. Baker*, which also had accommodation for ten passengers, was able to undertake eight trips a year with such precision that Lorenzo Baker is said to have reported:

> She kept Andy Preston so busy selling bananas that his pants never got shiny behind, but he wore out a pair of shoes every two weeks.[24]

The satisfactory arrangement which Captain Baker had made for the procurement of fruit in Jamaica and the success of the transport system which he had devised did not, in themselves, guarantee automatic profitability. This was because the banana business was becoming increasingly competitive during the early 1880s and the entire activity was to remain in a state of flux for some time:

> According to Ansell Hart, by the mid 1880s Jamaica's banana export trade had become somewhat chaotic with numerous concerns operating shipping lines between the island and America. The Frank Brothers had transferred their banana business from Panama to Jamaica, Henry Brothers ran a weekly service from Kingston to Baltimore, J. Hart and Company operated one steamer and several sailing ships between Jamaica and Baltimore, Seaverns and Company ran steamers to Boston weekly in the summer and to southern U.S. ports in the winter, Kerr's *Edith Gooden*, *Pomona* and *Vutummes* did a regular trade in fruit, Clark and Company of New Orleans were also in the Jamaica fruit trade with a line of steamers as also were Warner and Merritt of Philadelphia with steam and sail. It was said that in those days there were more sailings weekly out of Port Antonio than there were out of Liverpool![25]

A major consequence of the intense rivalry which this situation engendered was on the American market where, in September 1884, wholesale banana prices dropped from $1.50 to $0.35 per bunch.[26] Although Baker took instant action to remedy this crisis there is no doubt that L. D. Baker and Company would have become bankrupt but for additional support provided by J. H. Freeman. Although this development had the effect of reducing Captain Baker's freedom of action, this was not particularly important as he and Freeman were of one mind in most cases. They did, however, decide upon a general division of responsibilities so that Freeman would look after transportation and marketing while Dow was to concentrate on the production of the fruit in Jamaica.[27] These events were, in fact, only symbolic of the deeper changes that were taking place in the industry and were to be only the first moves in what was to become a rapid process of rationalization.

The second step towards the consolidation of the trade came when the Standard Steam Navigation Company (already largely owned by Baker and Freeman) was merged with L. D. Baker and Company. This was only a minor action that was more designed to tidy up accountancy procedures than to effect real economies. However, a third step which was also taken in 1885 was to be of fundamental importance, for it created an informal partnership which was soon to become known as the Boston Fruit Company. There has been some considerable academic dispute as to whether Lorenzo Dow Baker or Andrew Woodbury Preston was the prime mover in its creation, but it is certain that it came into being at a time of great difficulty and the twelve New Englanders who provided the capital were men who were prepared to take a risk in pursuit of their vision of the future. They were:

Captain Jesse H. Freeman	$1\frac{1}{4}$ shares	$1,875
Captain Lorenzo D. Baker	1 share	1,500
Lamont G. Burnham	1 share	1,500
Thomas Mandell Hart	1 share	1,500
W. F. Robinson	1 share	1,500
O. S. Crowell	1 share	1,500
A. S. Messner	1 share	1,500
Thomas B. Griffiths	1 share	1,500
John F. Crocker and Elric Elridge	1 share	1,500
Andrew W. Preston	$\frac{1}{2}$ share	750
E. E. Locke	$\frac{1}{4}$ share	375
		$15,000

This new partnership was based entirely on mutual respect and a verbal agreement that no dividends would be claimed during the first five years of operations. As the largest shareholder, Jesse Freeman became President of the new 'Boston Fruit Company' and continued to be responsible for all transport arrangements. Andrew Preston then gave up his position with Seaverns and Company to become the manager of the new firm's Boston office and, in effect, to carry on marketing the bananas as he had since 1871. Captain Baker was not given an official role at this stage, but remained in charge of production and loading in Jamaica. Thus although a fresh structure had been adopted it retained many of the strengths of the previous informal system, and with the additional capital that had become available the new firm was well organized to take advantage of any improvements in the trade.

Edward Wathen Fyffe with his two daughters Gertrude
Ida Fyffe and Marthan Ellen Fyffe.

Mrs Wathen Fyffe neé Martha
Wathen-Dunn with her two sons;
Ebenezer Thomas Fyffe & Edward
Wathen Fyffe.

Edward Wathen Fyffe.

Ida Stanton Fyffe (neé Brown) wife of
Edward Wathen Fyffe.

Rev Ebenezer Thomas Fyffe.

Sir Alfred Jones, KCMG.

Arthur Henry Stockley.

Alfred Roger Ackerley.

James Hudson.

Mrs Agnes Hudson.

Andrew Woodbury Preston.

Captain O. M. Lund (centre), the first Commodore of our Fleet, with Mr. A. H. Stockley and Captain Rowe on board s.s. "Manzanares" at Avonmouth in 1911. Captain Lund joined Elders & Fyffes from Forwood Brothers in 1902. He commanded many of our ships and was Master of our first passenger vessel, s.s. "Chagres", when he became Marine Superintendent in 1913. He died while still in the service of the Company in 1920.

R. H. Sanders.   Sir Owen Philipps (later Lord Kylsant).

The partnership was, in fact, to secure excellent financial returns from its very inception. This was partly because of the gradual expansion of the United States market, which rose from 10 million bunches in 1884 to nearly 13 million bunches in 1890.[29] Other significant factors were the failure of a number of potential competitors at a critical time – no fewer than seven banana importers went into liquidation in 1885 – and a hurricane the following year which caused heavy damage to its rivals but left the Boston Fruit Company largely untouched. However, these fortuitous events only served to support the initiatives taken by the partners themselves. These, which included various measures to increase efficiency and the acquisition of four plantations in Jamaica that could produce up to 150,000 bunches per year, were not only important for their own sakes, but also as an indication of their faith in the future of the industry. The gamble, for that is what it was, paid off handsomely so that 150,000 bunches were sold in its first year and almost 330,000 bunches in its second: as a result, the $15,000 stake with which the business began had risen to $200,000 in less than two years.[30] While much of this profit was to be invested in land, the opportunity was taken to purchase the British ship *Marmion*, a steamer of 700 tons. Later renamed *Bowden*, she had a capacity of 20,000 bunches and, although it was regarded as a massive amount at the time, she quickly repaid her $65,000 purchase price.[31]

The following year, 1888, proved to be a 'lean' one but, nevertheless, preparations for further expansion continued to be made. Thus by 1890 two new steamships, *Ethelred* and *Ethelwold* had entered the company's service and, with a speed of $12\frac{1}{2}$ knots, were so superior to the vessels operated by rival concerns that they made a great contribution to overall competitiveness. This was especially important by 1890 for the growing output of company-produced bananas was reaching a point where they could not all be absorbed in the Boston market. With the aid of the new ships the enterprise was able to spread its activities to other ports, and both Baltimore and Philadelphia rapidly came within its sphere of operations.

The rapid progress made by the partnership trading as the Boston Fruit Company led to further changes being undertaken in February 1888. Although retained profits were reaching extremely high levels, it was felt that additional investment would enable even faster expansion to be achieved. Thus Jesse Freeman, who had become 'General Manager' paid in $14,000: Andrew Preston contributed $10,000 and gained the title of 'Assistant General Manager of Sales', while Dow Baker transferred the entire assets of L. D. Baker and Company and was made 'Tropical Manager'.[32] A second, involuntary, change came in January 1890 when Freeman died after a brief illness. This meant that a new head was required and eventually, after considerable controversy, it was Captain Baker who reluctantly replaced his friend as President. While these discussions were still taking place the original five-year 'trial' period of the partnership was coming to an end and it was time to take stock. The accounts, made up to 1 March 1890, then showed that the enterprise had become the most profitable of all banana-selling firms in America and that the assets were now valued at $531,000.[33] The very scale of this achievement then made a partnership inappropriate, so it was decided to formally incorporate the enterprise as the Boston Fruit Company in the State of Massachusetts.[34]

The new corporation came into effect on 20 September 1890 and for the remainder of the 1890s it continued under the guidance of Lorenzo Dow Baker (President and Manager of its Tropical Division) and of Andrew Woodbury Preston, who had become the Managing Director of the Boston Division. As Captain Baker continued to live in Jamaica much of the day-to-day decisions had to be taken by Preston and, in the course of time, he also unilaterally settled many major policy issues as well. Thus it was Preston who may be said to have masterminded the next stage in the consolidation of the industry, his strength arising from his conviction that it was marketing, not production, that was the ultimate key to success at this particular time.

Preston's belief was based on the experience of cut-throat competition which characterized the banana business throughout this decade. Thus although consumption was gradually rising and, in fact, the Boston Fruit Company did well financially, its results were secured against a chaotic background. It is understood that in 1899 no fewer than 114 companies were engaged in the importation of bananas into the United States although only 22 operated on any real scale.[35] Many of the remainder were under-capitalized and quickly disappeared, but as thresholds of entry were low they were just as quickly replaced by other hopefuls. These constant changes gave the industry a degree of instability which was not diminished by an overall lack of structure and organization. The existence of this 'free for all' led to much waste and inefficiency in both shipping and handling, but it was in distribution that it was most apparent. Thus, while there were many gluts (and low prices) in the ports where 95 per cent of the bananas were consumed, there were few satisfactory arrangements to move the fruit to inland destinations where important markets could have been developed.

The Boston Fruit Company was too small to influence these external factors, but it did set up a number of subsidiary firms which helped to widen the geographic range of its markets so that both Baltimore and Philadelphia became even more important outlets for its bananas. The company also acquired a series of new steamships, each of which was more technically advanced than its predecessor. Thus *Barnstable* and *Brookline* were followed by *Beverly* and *Belvidere*, all of which were capable of carrying up to 30,000 bunches of bananas. In 1898 these were in turn surpassed by the even larger 'Admiral' class – four vessels of 2,100 tons with cargo space for 40,000 bunches and accommodation for 53 passengers each.[36] As these vessels were the most sophisticated then employed in the trade they undoubtedly did much to maintain the company's competitive advantage over its rivals.

Both Baker and Preston were always aware of the dangers of a 'blow-down' which would have crippled their operations. Captain Baker was anxious to continue to concentrate on Jamaica and tried to minimize the risk by obtaining supplies from different areas on the island. Preston eventually persuaded him that further steps needed to be taken and urged him to investigate Cuba. Baker did not wish to follow this suggestion but, appreciating the sense of the argument, decided to see if he could discover an alternative source on the island of Dominica. He eventually found an estate of 40,000 acres that was basically suitable, but disease and political difficulties in what was a very primitive area meant that it took six years for production to start and it was clear by then, in 1898, that there were easier ways of growing bananas.[37]

The fundamental change which had occurred in the production of bananas was mainly due to the activities of one man. Minor Cooper Keith's connection with the fruit had begun almost accidentally when he had been assisting his brother, Henry Keith, in the construction of a railway in Costa Rica. This was designed to link the port of Limon on the Atlantic coast to San José, the capital, which lay on the Pacific slope.[38] Unfortunately this proved to be a much longer and more expensive task than had been anticipated, and until it reached the capital there was no possibility of it attracting sufficient quantities of paying freight to make it viable. As a temporary expedient Minor Keith decided to investigate a number of local commodities with a view to developing an export trade along with the partly completed track. When he found that there was nothing which could conceivably provide the necessary volume he accepted the advice of Carl Frank and planted a few bananas on an experimental basis. In the same year, 1872, he made arrangements to test the market by purchasing 200 bunches in Colon and shipping them to New Orleans. The sale produced a good profit so he rapidly extended his planting activities and with the aid of his rail link to Limon was able to establish a very low-cost operation.[39]

The success of this venture was of vital help in enabling the railway to be completed, athough it took nineteen years before it finally reached San José. It also alerted Keith to the profitability which the banana could offer when grown in suitable soils and conditions with low-cost labour and sound communications. Accordingly he decided to develop plantations in other areas and was subsequently responsible for the opening-up of what became major centres of production in Bocas del Toro (now in Panama) and at Santa Marta in Colombia. He also played an important role in the growth of the Nicaraguan industry but his continued interest in the construction of railways prevented him from devoting all of his time to the production of bananas.

By 1898, after an almost continuous residence approaching twenty-seven years in Costa Rica, Keith was in control of three major banana enterprises.[40] These were responsible for the cultivation of the fruit in Central America and Colombia and found their markets in New Orleans and the other Gulf ports. On the other hand the Boston Fruit Company, by then the second leading firm in the trade, obtained its supplies solely from the West Indies and sold its bananas on the Atlantic Coast and in those sections of the northern interior that were reasonably accessible. The activities of these two concerns can thus be seen to be complementary rather than competitive and, given the need for diversity of supply, to say nothing of the potential gains from economies of scale, the logical case for some form of merger was overwhelming.

As both parties to such an amalgamation remained profitable and continued to expand in their respective areas, the possible advantages were never discussed and it was only the failure of Keith's selling agent in New Orleans that was to precipitate the necessary action. When in 1898, Messrs Hoadley and Company went bankrupt Keith lost a great deal of money, probably $1,500,000, and although (with the support of the Government of Costa Rica) he was able to satisfy his creditors in full, he still needed to make new arrangements for the disposal of his fruit.[41] In due course this brought him into contact with Andrew Preston and an agreement was then made for a portion of his bananas to be handled by the Fruit Dispatch Company which was a wholly owned subsidiary of the Boston Fruit Company.[42] This arrangement worked so well that the two principals considered that it would be sensible to investigate further methods by which they might profitably co-operate and these, inevitably, led to the conclusion that a full-scale integration of all their activities would be mutually beneficial.

Formal negotiation to bring this about began between Preston and Keith early in March 1899. They were later joined by a number of bankers and other banana men, and by the twentieth of the month, in spite of the opposition of Captain Baker,[43] agreement had been reached. This resulted in the incorporation of the United Fruit Company, which at that stage was described as a New Jersey corporation with an authorized capital stock (still unsubscribed) of 20 million dollars.[44] The next step was to itemize the assets of the Boston Fruit Company and their net value ($5,105,000) was then exchanged for 51,050 shares in the new corporation. Keith then traded his interests in the Tropical Trading and Transport Company, the Snyder Banana Company and the Colombia Land Company for a total of £3,964,000 in United Fruit Company stock.[45] From the foregoing it will be seen that the Boston firm emerged with the larger of the two shares so it was able to nominate the first president. Andrew Preston was therefore appointed to this position while Minor Keith became the first Vice-President. It should be noted that Captain Baker was made a director but, in fact, made little further contribution to the business he had done so much to promote.

Once the Boston Fruit Company and Keith's assets had been exchanged for shares, the balance of the stock of the United Fruit Company was offered to the general public. However, the initial response was very poor and only $1,650,000 was invested, but by the end of the first year this had risen to a total of $11,230,000 and the future of the company was assured. It then owned 112 miles of railroad and 212,394 acres of land including 61,263 acres which were actually in production, and it is true to say that:

> The organisation of the United Fruit Company marked the end of the era of pioneering, of risks and hardships, easy profits as well as total failures, and the beginning of a new era that converted the highly perishable tropical banana into an important item of world trade.[46]

3

The Canary Islands and the establishment of the Liverpool banana trade

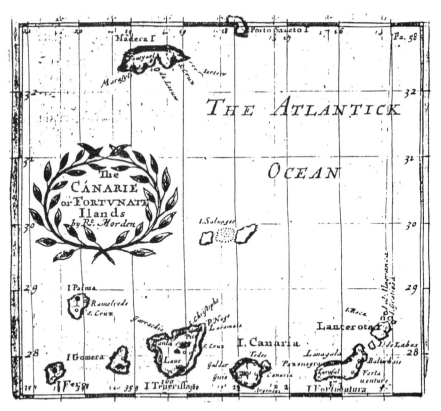

Fig. 3.1   Map of the Canary Islands c. 1748
Source: *The Universal Magazine of Knowledge and Pleasure*, London, April 1748, p. 532.

Prior to the geographic explorations of the European powers in the fourteenth and fifteenth centuries, almost all that was known of the Canary archipelago was that it was situated off the coast of West Africa. They had been given the name of the 'Fortunate Islands' by the Romans, and an accurate record of their position was given by Ptolemy in AD 150.[1] Thereafter they were seldom visited and a landing at Gando Bay in Grand Canary (later Gran Canaria) by the Arabian Ben Farroukh in AD 999 may be regarded as a very rare event.[2] The early Middle Ages were to see an increase in visits, and a number of vessels called in order to secure water or slaves. Until 1402, however, there was no attempt at permanent settlement, but in that year Juan de Béthencourt, a Norman, sold his lands and, after obtaining the patronage of the King of Spain, sailed to the south. On reaching the Canaries he quickly took possession of Lanzarote, and a few years later he returned and successfully occupied Fuerteventura, Gomera and Hierro.

Béthencourt also attempted to land on La Palma but was prevented from doing so by the hostility of the local people. As his forces were so small he was obliged to ignore the larger, more populous, islands of Grand Canary and Tenerife, and it was to be many years before their resistance was finally overcome. Even then success came only in a number of stages with Grand Canary being occupied in 1478, La Palma falling in 1492 and Tenerife being subjugated in 1496. As there was considerable enmity between the individual islands, many Canario warriors were prepared to act as auxiliaries and assisted the Spaniards in pacifying their neighbours. Unfortunately this co-operation was not reciprocated and none of the islands received favourable treatment from their new rulers. Thus, apart from the many individuals who were killed during this very lengthy campaign, many more died from neglect and from the disruption of their traditional way of life. The final factor in their demise was disease, for the Canarios had little resistance to European complaints.[3] Those of the original inhabitants who did survive were therefore relatively few in number and were soon swamped by the hoards of migrants who arrived from the Spanish mainland in search of land. Surprisingly, perhaps, this situation was soon to come to an end and the Canaries settled down to a fresh way of life with a largely European population:

> Within thirty years of the completion of the conquest (in 1496) new immigration was almost at an end, a royal administration had all but replaced the seigneurial, the leading conquistador, Alonso de Lugo, was dead, and the surviving native guanches had been largely assimilated into a colonial society which itself varied greatly from island to island according to geographic position and climate ...[4]

An early priority for the settlers was to discover an export crop that would enable the economy to pay for the imports which would permit the maintenance of what the ruling élite regarded as a civilized standard of living. At first it appeared that sugar would prove to be the entire answer and, with the aid of slave labour, many plantations were established. These proved to be extremely profitable and expanded in size so that at least one plantation, that at Adeje, employed over a thousand negroes.[5] According to Lord Verulam (Francis Bacon) being first in an invention,

> doth sometime cause a wonderful overgrowth of riches, as it was with the first sugar man in the Canaries.[6]

By 1600, however, competition from Brazil and the West Indies was having a significant effect on the price of sugar, so production began to decline. Thereafter the industry only continued at a low level, though it enjoyed occasional periods when increased demand encouraged a brief revival. Fortunately, by then, the Canaries were already developing an alternative export so that by 1650 Tenerife was firmly established as a major wine producer.[7]

George F. Steckley estimated that Tenerife exported an average of 10,037 half-ton pipes in the period 1636 to 1725 and this included an average of 6,859 half-ton pipes of the choice malvasia variety.[8] In the earlier period the wine was exported to a wide variety of markets of which Latin America, Portugal and its possessions and northern Europe were the most important. Gradually, however, the English market emerged as the main outlet, and by 1690 almost two-thirds of the malvasia was sold via London.[9]

This happy state of affairs, which had brought a high level of prosperity to both producer and buyer, was not to last much into the eighteenth century. A longstanding difficulty had been the imbalance of trade between England and the Canaries, for the Islands could not absorb a sufficient quantity of British products. Thus the trade had to be conducted in 'ready money', which was against the mercantilist ideas of many influential politicians, so the business was discouraged by heavy taxes. At the same time the growth in imports of wine from Portugal was encouraged as England was supposed to enjoy a favourable trade balance with that country. A change in the taste for particular wines further enhanced this transition which was virtually completed by the disruption caused by the War of the Spanish Succession.[10]

The difficulties in England could not be compensated for by sales elsewhere but the trade did continue at a moderate level until 1850 when the vines were attacked and virtually exterminated by a fungus known as *oidium tuckeri*.[11] This attack proved to be so severe that the entire stock had to be replaced by other variations of vine. This process, in turn, changed the character – some would suggest the quality – of the wine, and although production and exports resumed they were never again to provide a significant proportion of the islands' revenue.

The decline and temporary cessation of the wine trade did not prove to be as great a loss as might have been expected. This was because of the development of an entirely new export which, for a time, was to make the Canaries so prosperous that all other commercial activities were either neglected or abandoned. The new item was a natural dye-stuff known as cochineal which was produced from the dried bodies of the *Coccus cacti*, an insect which thrived on a cactus which grew freely in the islands. The first shipment of 8 lb. was made in 1831; by 1850 exports had grown to nearly 800,000 lb. and then increased to a peak of over 6 million lb. in 1869. This had a value of £788,993 on the London market which was equal to a revenue of £3.25 for every man, woman and child.[12] By then, however, the signs of decline were already apparent because the invention of aniline dyes in Europe was beginning to force down the price. A steady fall in production followed and exports were down to 5 million lb. in 1874 and to 2,300,000 lb. in 1886.

Of equal importance was the decline in price. At the height of the boom the return for the medium grade of cochineal was 3.25 pesetas per pound, but by the early 1880s it was little more than one peseta per pound. In these circumstances the loans which had been secured to enable the industry to expand could not be serviced and, except in particularly favourable situations, it was not worthwhile to continue with production. Exports were subsequently aided by the discovery of the waterproofing capabilities of cochineal which are not shared by artificial dyes, so it was possible to maintain a small industry on a permanent basis. However, as prices remained low and as only poor returns could be secured from the sale of sugar and wine, the islands lost their state of prosperity and became financially moribund.

The successive loss of competitive advantage in the export of sugar, wine and cochineal led to a search for viable alternatives. One possibility which appeared to offer some promise was tobacco which was first cultivated commercially in 1873. Unfortunately, the quality of the early crop was not good enough to enable it to compete with Cuban products. Thus, although the government attempted to help by purchasing the output in 1876, it found itself incurring heavy losses and refused to repeat its assistance the following year. However, a few planters continued to experiment with the crop and the government were persuaded to re-enter the trade in 1882. The resulting product could not approach the quality of Cuban tobacco, but it did gradually secure a position in the lower end of the market and so made a small contribution to the Islands' employment and revenue.[13]

In spite of the continuation in the export of the three staples – sugar, wine and cochineal – and the growth of tobacco at least as an import substitute, the level of activity remained very low and much hardship was endured by large sections of the population throughout the 1870s and early 1880s. Fortunately, the production of foodstuffs for family consumption provided a basic diet for many people, while some cash crops could be sold for local consumption. In addition, a traditional trade in cereals, potatoes[14] and onions saw a small export of these items, mainly to Cuba, and the victualling of passing ships also offered a tiny outlet for both crops and livestock. None of these agricultural sectors appeared to offer any hope of substantial expansion and the only bright spot was that subsistence farming tended to reduce the quantities of food which had to be imported when export crops monopolized the land.

The non-agricultural industries were in a similar position. Although pumice, sulphur and copper were available there was little effective demand for these items and only a small quantity was extracted. Tobacco processing and sugar-boiling required only a tiny input of labour, while basket-making and the linen and lace trades were minute in character.

Boat-building for local consumption was undertaken, but the failure to develop the fishing industry left this enterprise without a satisfactory market. This omission is the more surprising because the excellence of the fishing and the need for drying facilities were pointed out as early as 1765 by George Glas.[15] Thus, although local fishermen were able to land substantial quantities, the lack of suitable arrangements meant that the catch could only be consumed locally and little was available for export.[16]

It would seem, therefore, that the collapse of the boom in cochineal had left the islands in difficult financial straits. Furthermore, the loss of confidence which then occurred meant that the remaining men of substance were reluctant to undertake any venture with an element of risk. One choice which remained available to the more enterprising citizens was emigration. There had been a long tradition of this in the Canaries, and in the eighteenth century many had settled, with government encouragement, in the Spanish possessions in the New World while in the nineteenth century the main flow had been to Cuba. Hard times at home always promoted further emigration and, in turn, engendered a flow of remittances which could have been used to increase the level of investment in productive activities. Unfortunately the new capital, like the old, was customarily used to purchase land, and there was little inclination or incentive to invest in other projects.

The economic malaise in which the Canaries found itself during the 1870s was all the more frustrating because of the knowledge that the level of world trade had been rising sharply throughout the nineteenth century. There had, of course, been many fluctuations, but the overall trend was consistently upward so that between 1800 and 1913 the value of international commerce rose more than twenty-five-fold. Furthermore, as the following table indicates, most of the expansion, in absolute terms, took place in the later period – just when the economy of the Canaries was faltering:

TABLE 3.1   THE GROWTH OF WORLD TRADE IN THE NINETEENTH CENTURY: ESTIMATED AGGREGATE VALUES, DISTINGUISHING EXPORTS AND IMPORTS IN SELECTED YEARS, 1800–1913 (IN £ MILLION)[17]

	Total trade	Exports f.o.b.*	Imports c.i.f.**
1800	320	150	170
1820	340	155	185
1840	560	260	300
1850	800	370	430
1860	1,450	680	770
1872–73	2,890	1,360	1,530
1895–99	3,900	1,870	2,030
1913	8,360	4,055	4,305

* free on board
** cost, insurance, freight

To make matters worse, Britain, with whom the Canary Islands had usually enjoyed a close commercial relationship, was now dominating world trade in an impressive manner. Details of Britain's trade with the principal nations and areas of the world in the latter part of the nineteenth century are provided in Table 14 in the Appendix to A. W. Kirkaldy's *British Shipping* (David and Charles Reprints, Newton Abbott, 1970). From this it will be seen that trade with Spain (as a whole) rose from just over £6 million in 1858 to £9 million in 1870, to nearly £15 million in 1880 and to over £18 million in 1890. Thus it seems apparent that commerce with Spain was expanding at a rate that was little different from that of Britain's other trading partners. When, however, Britain's trade with the Canaries is examined it will be seen that there was a decline in her imports from £215,781 in 1869 to £163,398 in 1884 and the earlier figure was only just exceeded in 1887. Canary exports declined even more drastically with the total of £845,390 for 1869 followed by an average value of under £300,000 per annum throughout the 1880s.

Between 1840 and 1887 there was a seven-fold expansion in the volume of world trade,[18] but although the Canary Islands were situated at what can best be described as a strategically positioned maritime 'crossroads', both its imports and exports declined in absolute and real terms. The reasons for this failure to expand – or at least keep pace with

Year.	Imports.					Exports.					Remarks.
	England.	France.	Germany.	Spain.	Total.	Cochineal.	Wine.	Spirits.	Tobacco.	Total.	
	£	£	£	£	£	£	£	£	£	£	
1865	179,914	51,004	11,669	47,366	391,492	295,208	11,007	4,630	Wanting	404,055	Woven goods imported, 119,313l., chiefly from England. Silk figures among exports for 12,615l.
1869	215,781	127,959	11,298	162,690	719,544	789,993	5,470	Wanting	,,	845,390	The largest sum realised by the export of cochineal was in this year; price 3s. to 3s. 6d. per lb. in London.
1874	206,714	84,771	8,435	66,000	436,239	429,931	Wanting	,,	,,	566,432	Panic in cochineal; price 1s. 6d. to 2s. per lb. A commission was appointed by the Spanish Government for fomenting the growth of tobacco, but the results were disappointing.
Total					1,797,275					1,815,977	
1884	163,398	38,755	26,923	70,035	335,820	100,844	6,740	5,530	10,380	224,418	Company formed to start Grand Hotel in Orotava.
1885	210,464	59,574	31,590	75,036	419,911	127,028	4,855	6,358	10,454	351,097	About 45,000 bunches of bananas exported. Woven goods imported, 112,215l. The Government agreed to take tobacco of a fixed quality at a fixed price, and much land was planted in consequence.
1886	207,350	70,280	49,115	45,966	447,568	154,456	10,009	10,570	50,937	341,720	About 300 visitors to Orotava. About 50,000 bunches of bananas exported.
1887	224,996	51,675	49,922	48,920	488,310	117,819	49,957	8,027	25,458	248,774	Tomatoes first exported. Bananas, tomatoes, and potatoes exported from Grand Canary to England roughly valued by the Consul at 16,000l. Owing to sale of tobacco monopoly to a company Canary crop largely refused as below sample.
1888	273,449	57,306	56,873	50,875	476,793	97,050	21,126	5,456	21,107	281,180	Export of silk, 608l.; sugar, 8,500l. English church commenced in Orotava. Company formed for building Catalina Hotel in Las Palmas, and other objects.
1889	286,296	48,642	81,024	42,116	517,918	82,923	18,264		32,557	302,175	The Vice-Consul at Orotava speaks hopefully about the increase in export of tomatoes and potatoes. Tobacco largely imported in the raw and exported as cigars.
1890	315,259	70,133	85,954	39,465	591,136	60,940	23,963	9,648	30,064	319,577	Completion of steam tramway in Las Palmas (Belgian material).
Total					3,227,519					2,068,941	

* Values expressed in 1l. sterling at 25 pesetas.

Fig. 3.2 A comparative synopsis of the progress of Trade in the Canary Islands

Source: Foreign Office Miscellaneous Series, no. 246, *Report on the Social and Economic Conditions of the Canary Islands*, p. 35.

that of other areas – are not hard to discover. The successive collapses in the export of sugar, wine and cochineal and the difficulty of finding a substitute was one major problem: the other was the impossibility of attracting passing shipping because of the growth in their scale. Thus, although ever larger numbers of vessels were obliged to voyage within a few miles of the archipelago, the inadequate and dangerous nature of its harbour facilities meant that only very limited numbers chose to stop. The advent and increasing size of iron steamships further emphasized the deficiencies of the existing harbours, and representations were made to the central government as early as 1852. The process of securing funds was extremely slow, but was eventually successful and resulted in the construction of additional new capacity at Puerto de la Luz (adjacent to Las Palmas) and at Santa Cruz de Tenerife.

The completion of the first phase of the opening of Puerto de la Luz in 1884 has been fully described in a centenary publication of great merit.[19] A similar programme was undertaken at Santa Cruz de Tenerife where the extension of the mole commenced in 1885. By 1893 the works at both ports had been virtually finished and they could then offer suitable accommodation to even the largest of contemporary vessels.[20] The combination of these new facilities with the growth in world, particularly British, tonnage was then to issue in a fresh period of activity in the Canary Islands and, indeed, was to mark the beginning of its modern economy.

The first consequences of the improved facilities were on the number of vessels which called in at the two main ports and on the quantity of coal which was supplied as bunkers. As will be seen in Table 3.2, both of these activities increased enormously after the port improvements had been partly completed in 1883.

Although some small coaling facilities had previously been available in the Canaries, the expansion of the two main ports generated much interest among British shipping companies. Of these the Liverpool firm of Elder Dempster and Company[22] was the most directly affected, for its routes to West Africa brought its vessels close to the islands as a matter of course. Word of the work at Puerto de la Luz reached (Sir) Alfred Jones,[23] the senior partner of this line, and he visited the newly extended port in 1884. He had long wished to develop a coaling depot that would enable his ships to re-fuel during the course of their voyages, for the more coal they carried the smaller was the amount of space that was available for paying cargoes. The situation of the Canaries on the direct route from Britain to West Africa made them an ideal location once a harbour was available, so Jones immediately formed the Grand Canary Coaling Company to operate at Puerto de la Luz. The success of this project and that of a similar enterprise – the Tenerife Coaling

TABLE 3.2 NUMBER AND TONNAGE OF STEAM VESSELS ENTERING THE PORTS OF SANTA CRUZ (TENERIFE) AND LAS PALMAS (GRAND CANARY), WITH A STATEMENT OF THE QUANTITY OF COALS SUPPLIED TO THEM.[21]

Tenerife

Year	Coasting trade Number of vessels	Tons	British Number of vessels	Tons	% of British Number of vessels %	Tons %	All Nations Number of vessels	Tons
1884	–	–	195*	263,700*	45	58	429	457,000*
1885	–	–	206	278,560	44	55	465	501,182
1886	–	–	246	317,669	43	51	553	620,229
1887	–	–	250*	395,000*	46	48	542	843,440
1888	51	12,904	310	444,238	47	47	666	948,802
1889	158	41,696	349	549,375	48	49	733	1,118,652
1890	178	40,432	350	575,000	46	48	766	1,204,026

* estimate

Grand Canary

Year	Coasting Trade Number of vessels	Tons	British Number of vessels	Tons	% of British Number of vessels %	Tons %	All Nations Number of vessels	Tons
1884	–	–	160*	264,000*	68	52	238	505,000*
1885	–	–	220	263,000	66	50	336	725,000
1886	–	–	369	600,500*	72	63	506	950,000*
1887	–	–	414	680,000*	63	61	660	1,103,700*
1888	51*	12,904*	539	890,977	59	59	912	1,505,089*
1889	158*	41,696	601	1,360,000*	59	56	1,022	2,432,000*
1890	178*	40,432*	718	1,635,000*	57	56	1,263	2,918,570*

* estimate

Total

Year	Total of both groups Number of vessels	Tons	Coal supplied Tenerife Tons	Grand Canary Tons	Total Tons
1884	667	962,000	28,924	6,700	35,624
1885	801	1,226,382	33,963	18,390	62,353
1886	1,059	1,570,220	38,046	38,827	76,873
1887	1,202	1,938,140	53,277	78,070	126,347
1888	1,080	2,479,699	76,913	130,188	213,101
1889	2,071	3,634,044	101,432	166,341	267,773
1890	2,385	4,203,470	107,519	226,409	333,919

Company based at Santa Cruz – then led Jones to purchase two coal mines in South Wales. Their output was sufficient to cater for the Elder Dempster fleet, but Jones was gradually forced to buy more and more bunker coal on the open market as he found it profitable to supply the vessels of other owners when they called at Las Palmas.

As noted earlier, a direct consequence of the construction of the new extensions (and incidentally of Alfred Jones' visit) was that the number of steamships calling at the Canaries rose sharply and the quantity of coal supplied increased at a dramatic rate. The bunkering, watering and victualling of these vessels provided useful employment, but their true significance for the islands' economy lay in the opportunities they provided for two other separate activities. These were the fruit trade and tourism and, as will be seen, it was the pioneer work of Jones and other British entrepreneurs that was to lay the foundations for the successful development of these two crucial industries.

As noted earlier, *Musa sapientum* and *Musa paradisiaca* arrived in the Canary Islands no later than the fifteenth century and it was from there that they were transported to the New World in 1516.[24] Once established in the archipelago both the banana and the plaintain spread rapidly and provided a valuable addition to the local diet. They were, of course, produced entirely as a subsistence crop as there was no possibility of exporting them to distant markets. Thus for several hundred years while the banana was an everyday commodity throughout the islands and Madeira it remained barely known in Europe. This is made absolutely clear by reference to an article published as late as 1748:

> ... Canary Island (Grand Canary) is exceeding fruitful, and the Soil so fertile that they have two Harvests in one Year, its Commodities are Honey, Wax, Surgar [sic], Oad (?), Wine and Plantains, which bear an Apple like a Cucumber, which when ripe, eats more deliciously than any Comfit. (Pear)[25]

Subsequent visitors to the Canaries and Madeira either commented on the super-abundance of the fruit[26] or found it so commonplace as to be unworthy of notice.[27] In spite of the availability and cheapness of these bananas, few were ever brought to the United Kingdom until the later part of the nineteenth century. Small vessels which called in the Canaries, Madeira or the Azores on their way home to Europe were primarily concerned with other cargoes or wished to replenish their water or provisions. However, it was to be expected that officers and men alike would frequently take local products on board with a view to selling them at a profit when they arrived at their home base. In the circumstances these inevitably included some bananas, and enough of

45

these survived the rigours of an ocean voyage for the fruit to become at least slightly known at the larger British ports. With the introduction of steam and the consequent reduction in the time spent at sea it became easier, though still not certain, to carry these bananas without deterioration. Nevertheless, the official statistics for 1840 in respect of the importation of fruits and vegetables into Great Britain and Ireland still made no mention of this item.[28]

Teneriffe.

Landing of Goods.

Goods are landed from Steamers in Barges - the Barges land at the Pier at Mole - the streets of Santa Cruz are paved with small round stones closely set as at Funchal, and the mode of Conveying goods is similar, one yoke of oxen drawing a wooden sleigh, the wooden sleighs or trucks are about two inches thick, and when we were there, it being rainy and wet, in many places water was above trucks, and the Bales got wet, the goods were hauled from Wharf at Mole to Mess: Bruce Hamilton & Co's store; Captain Parsons pointed this out to Mr. Hamilton who was present.

Fig. 3.3   Abstract of s.s. *Faith*'s log

The failure of s.s. *Faith* to load bananas at either Tenerife or Funchal in Madeira while homeward bound in 1853 confirms that the lack of suitable loading facilities for the larger types of ship was a major factor in retarding the development of an export trade.[29] Consequently any of the fruit which did reach Britain before the 1880s continued to be carried in small sailing vessels, and these only provided tiny quantities on an *ad hoc* basis. By the 1870s a minute business had grown up so that the London market was being irregularly supplied with what was regarded as an expensive luxury. It should be stressed, however, that there was little if any organized trade in bananas at this time – many vessels brought the odd few bunches, but this was mainly due to the initiative of individual seafarers. This situation began to change later in that decade because of the activities of the *Forwood Shipping Line*. This Company had established a route from Madeira to London in 1872 and by the early 'Eighties it was shipping small quantities of bananas to the capital on what was by then a three-weekly service. The limited extent of this trade can, however, be judged by the fact that in 1884 it was authoritatively estimated that total imports into England were no more than 10 thousand bunches.[30]

Abstract of Manifest of Cargo on board S.S. "Faith." 1st Voyage Homewards.

From	Palm Oil	Gold Dust	Gum	Ginger	Camwood	Pepper	Arrowroot	Sundries
Fernando Po	Casks 151	65 ozs						
Cape Coast		1,085	Casks 15					
Sierra Leone	11	554	11	Bags 1,700	Billets 423 Tons 22	Bags 130 Barrels 6 Punchion 1	Boxes 217	Ivory Bales 5 Palm Nuts Bags 80
Bathurst	.		.		.		.	Bees Wax 6 Bales Ivory 5 Bales
Teneriffe	Cochineal 111 Bags wt 150 lbs each	Wine 10 pipes 20 h hds 41 qt casks						
Madeira		76 Boxes Lemons.						

Fig. 3.4 Abstract of s.s. *Faith*'s cargo manifest

Further developments which were to result in the banana business being placed on a proper commercial footing occurred, when, as noted earlier,[31] the first vital stage in the construction of a modern harbour at Puerto de la Luz near Las Palmas was started in 1883.[32] The

47

subsequent visit of (Sir) Alfred Jones and the establishment of a coaling depot there and (after 1885) at Santa Cruz de Tenerife then led to regular calls by Elder Dempster vessels *en route* to Liverpool. As a matter of normal policy their captains were instructed to purchase commodities which could profitably be loaded to fill up any space which remained empty when a ship had left West Africa. It then rapidly became clear that a large market existed in Britain for bananas and tomatoes, but it was also apparent that a whole series of problems would have to be solved before this new trade could really flourish.

One major difficulty was that of distance, for Liverpool lay six days to the north, and during that period the fruit inevitably deteriorated even if it were not to spoil altogether. Small, experimental, shipments then showed that both bananas and tomatoes could be carried on deck without the provision of special facilities. However, this required that the bananas (and to a lesser extent the tomatoes) needed to be picked before they were ripe so that they could mature en route. This skill was eventually acquired, though at some cost, and then a second important problem had to be solved. This occurred because bananas were virtually unknown to the Merseyside retailers and it took much effort to persuade them to handle this exotic and delicate fruit. Indeed the early, experimental, shipments could not be disposed of via the normal channels at all and Alfred Jones had to resort to the expedient of dealing directly with the Liverpool 'barrow boys'. It is reported, in fact, that in the initial stages of the trade the fruit was actually given away with the suggestion that it be sold for what the market could bear.

The use of these tactics quickly established a growing demand for the banana, firstly in Liverpool and then throughout the whole of the north-west region. This convinced Alfred Jones that it would be advisable to establish a branch of Elder Dempster in Grand Canary, and an office at Puerto de la Luz was accordingly opened in 1885. This then became the headquarters for all of the firm's activities in the Canaries but was principally responsible for the selection and loading of both bananas and tomatoes. Jones' success in solving the difficulties of carriage and marketing then led to a further problem, for bananas were mainly grown as a subsistence crop and, in the new circumstances, supply threatened to lag behind the quantities which could be sold. Never a man to leave matters to take their own course, he acted with his customary vigour once he had decided what was required:

> ... the land was lying waste and the people sunk in a apathy of
> despair. Well, observing the prolific character of the soil, I bought up
> what land I could and grew fruit on it. Then, as I knew that that was
> not enough for the trade I could forsee, I went round to the farms and

offered so much for all the fruit they could grow and, where
necessary, made them advances and financed them generally. The
consequence is that land has now (1898) gone up to £1,000 per acre,
the Islands receive a million a year for fruit, and the people are
prosperous and comparatively speaking contented for they more than
pay their way ... [33]

The net effect of Jones' initiative was that the export of bananas from
the Canaries to the UK rose from an estimated total of 10,000 bunches
in 1884 to 45,000 bunches in 1885 and to 50,000 bunches in 1886.[34]
Although no firm statistics are available until 1900 it is certain that
shipment of the fruit rose rapidly and it quickly became a valuable and
extremely cheap addition to the diet of all classes of society that were
within close proximity to the port of entry at Liverpool. Thus Jones'
enterprise paid off handsomely. Although far removed from shipowning,
this was a vital aspect, as he was able to utilize spare capacity on his own
vessels at practically no cost and was able to take advantage of the
improved port facilities at La Luz to load the fruit while his steamers
were taking on coal. With the low level of economic activity then ruling,
Jones was also able to take advantage of both cheap labour and land.
Consequently he did not just content himself with the acquisition of
sites for his bunkering and other shipping interest, but also bought large
areas of land in the Las Palmas area which were subsequently to be
planted with bananas and, at a later date, to be developed for housing
and commercial property.[35]

When Elder Dempster's office in Puerto de la Luz was opened in
1885 the organization of banana exports was just one of its many tasks.
The subsequent growth of this activity – which was to amount to
1,500,000 bunches by 1901 – plus the beginning of the tomato trade in
1887, then made it necessary to create a separate Fruit Department. At
first this operated under the guidance of a Spanish Manager[36] but the
further expansion of the business and the need to understand the market
on Merseyside then led Alfred Jones to look for a suitable expatriate to
take overall charge. His choice was to fall upon A. H. Stockley, the son
of an old acquaintance, and in view of his later importance in the
development of the British banana industry his antecedents and background must now be examined.

The death of Henry Stockley, a leading average adjuster in the
Liverpool firm of Lowndes and Stockley, took place in 1873. By
agreement with the surviving partner, Arthur H. Stockley joined the
business after he had completed his education at Clifton School. After a
five-year apprenticeship he was made office manager and it was
understood that he would become a partner within the following two

49

years. However, young Mr Stockley was not keen on this type of work so on the death of Mr Lowndes he decided to resign and proposed to try his luck in the South African goldfields. This was not to be, for in May 1888, just one week before he was due to depart, he was approached by Alfred Jones. How Jones had heard of his plans is not now clear but as a result of their conversation Stockley agreed to go out to the Canaries on a trial basis, and after a year he was placed in charge of all of Elder Dempster's banana business in the islands.[37]

During his first year in the Canaries, A. H. Stockley was attracted to a Miss Lambert who was spending a winter in Las Palmas with a married sister. Eight months later they celebrated their marriage at her family's church in Nottingham, before returning to set up their first home in Grand Canary.[38] Stockley was then to spend several years building up Elder Dempster's banana business with Liverpool, and during this period the firm made little or no contribution to the London market. By 1892 this situation was changing dramatically, for the availability of increasing quantities of fruit meant that it was now possible for Alfred Jones to consider supplying the capital. The knowledge that a rival concern was already building up a strong position in London then provided an additional argument for action to be taken, so Jones arranged for Stockley to move to Covent Garden. This was to bring him into direct competition with E. W. Fyffe and Company who, by then, were second only to Elder Dempster in the size of their banana imports.

4

The contribution of Edward Wathen Fyffe

Throughout the nineteenth century small quantities of bananas reached the London market via the initiative of individual seafarers. The change from sail to steam which gathered momentum after about 1860 had the effect of shortening voyage times, so that the possibility of carrying the fruit so that it arrived in an edible condition was considerably improved. Thus the general improvement in the efficiency of shipping did gradually result in larger quantities of bananas reaching the capital but until the development of new harbours in the Canaries or Madeira there was little chance of establishing a regular trade. The creation of satisfactory facilities at Puerto de la Luz and at Santa Cruz de Tenerife was then to transform this situation, but as Elder Dempster's main services tended to terminate in Liverpool the supplies to London were not greatly affected. Nevertheless the fact that after 1884 more and more ships were calling at the Canaries[1] did mean that opportunities for acquiring bananas became more frequent. Then, as the example set by Elder Dempster became more widely understood, the practice of carrying small quantities on deck, when space permitted, was adopted by an increasing number of vessels, so that a variety of ports, including London, began to receive the fruit on a much less spasmodic basis.

It is not, unfortunately, possible even to estimate either the scale or regularity of these small deliveries. However, the general background to the business at this time can be gleaned from an examination of the trade press which then included the *Covent Garden Gazette and Market Record, The Horticultural Times* and *The Fruit Grower, Fruiterer, Florist and Market Gardener*. Thus in November 1885 a major biography on Simeon Jacobs – a prominent importer and fruit trader – has no mention of his firm dealing in bananas.[2] Nor is there any mention of the fruit being sold at auction either in this or in the following year. These facts may suggest that bananas were seldom if ever available in Covent Garden during this period, and this view is partly supported by a letter written to the editor of the *Covent Garden Gazette* in which a correspondent refers to bananas by stating that:

> ... the shopmen actually ask 2*d.* each for them, though they are of the very worst kind, only used to feed pigs with in the Indies ...[3]

On the other hand the following paragraph, published on 14 August 1886 in *The Horticultural Times,* shows that the banana was being imported in some quantities and that a rudimentary system of ripening had already been evolved:

> Bananas. – A leading importer uses his cellar for ripening his bananas. The bunches are hung from the ceiling, and after the cellar is closed the air inside becomes so oppressive during the process of ripening, from the heat thrown out by the fruit, that a man coming from the outer air would be scarcely able to breathe therein. The banana is a fruit that has to be carefully handled; for although hard while green, it soon gets soft and rots after the ripening process has set in. No one cares to eat a banana that had become too ripe, for the fruit is black and is not pleasant looking. It presents a slimy appearance, while the properly ripened banana is white and firm, although soft.

An even more informative item appeared in the form of an editorial in the same journal later in 1886.[4] This proclaimed the banana's ease of digestion and its growing popularity and estimated that from 40,000 to 50,000 clusters (or bunches) had been imported into Europe during the previous. year. It thought that Grand Canary had contributed between 25,000 and 30,000 bunches of this total. It then calculated that the average wholesale price may have been about 3*s.* per bunch, but quoted many examples when the price reached 20*s.* or even 30*s.* Clearly there must have been some occasions when there were gluts of over-ripe fruit and it had to be disposed of quickly, but equally there must have been many periods when scarcity drove up the value of whatever bananas were available. Two especially important points emerge from this publication. Firstly it refers to the anticipated increase of imports that will occur when direct communication between Grand Canary and London is established, and secondly it concluded with the hope that 'increased consumption consequent upon a just and equitable reduction in price [will enable] it to be brought not only within the reach of one class, but of all.'[5]

From the foregoing evidence it might reasonably be assumed that the banana still remained a relatively scarce and expensive item at the end of 1886. Clearly it was becoming more available, but could not be provided on any scale until regular direct shipping services from the producing areas came into being. In addition, apart from times of particular plenty, the banana continued to be a luxury fruit that was almost entirely the sole preserve of the wealthy.

It was against this background that Edward Wathen Fyffe was to begin his association with the Canary Islands and the banana. Although this was largely due to a series of accidents and unforseen circumstances, the Fyffe family had been involved in commerce for many generations so Edward was well placed to take advantage when a favourable opportunity presented itself. While there is a tradition that the Fyffes had established a tea-importing business during the reign of James I (1603–1625),[6] the earliest documentary references to the family occur in 1705 when Nathaniel and Henry Fyffe were both merchants in the Scottish city of Perth. The former's 'Account Book', covering the period from 1705 to 1713, which has survived, suggests that they were concerned with a more general trade at that time and the items handled including buttons, calico, candles, hay hemp, indigo, oats, soap and tobacco.[7] In 1715 Colonel John Hay of Cromlix took Perth for the Jacobites and subsequently expelled the magistrates for refusing to recognize 'the Pretender'. He then appointed himself Governor, and amongst those selected to act on a new 'town council' was the merchant, Nathaniel Fyffe.[8] This position was, of course, of short duration but does not appear to have damaged the family's fortunes, for in 1749 a Henry Fyffe (son or grandson of Henry and Sarah Fyffe) became Town Treasurer, and he was to serve as Bailie for several terms between 1751 and 1774 and acted as Dean of Guild from 1774 to 1776.[9]

The reasons which then persuaded at least one member of the Fyffe family to move to London cannot now be ascertained but it may well have been the greater opportunities offered by the capital for an individual interested in business that was the deciding factor. In any event a Henry Fyffe was listed in Andrew's *New London Director* for 1789 as being a 'Grocer and Tea Dealer' with premises at No. 313 High Holborn.[10] (This site, on the corner of Chancery Lane, is now occupied by a branch of Barclay's Bank.) In 1800 the entry was changed to 'Henry and George Fyffe' although the other details remained unaltered.[11] Further changes were reported in 1813 when the firm's name was recorded as 'H. M. and E. Fyffe' with additional premises at 5 New Cavendish Street.[12] In 1824 Henry Minten Fyffe is listed at 313 High Holborn, as a wholesale tea-dealer, while Edward Fyffe and Company are noted as retail tea-dealers at 5 New Cavendish Street.[13] This division in the business was later to be ended so that by 1841 the only entry is for Edward Fyffe and Company, wholesale tea-dealers, of 3 Howford Buildings, Fenchurch Street.[14]

It is understood that Edward Cooper Fyffe handed control of the firm to his son, Ebenezer Wathen Fyffe in 1849. The following year Ebenezer married his cousin, Martha Wathen Dunn, and in due course the couple were blessed by the arrival of two sons. The elder, Ebenezer Thomas Fyffe, was not interested in a career in commerce. Instead, after completing his education at Queen's College, Cambridge, he was ordained, and served as a chaplain in the Royal Navy until 1902. He then took a living at Landcross, near Bideford, which he held until 1921.[15] He died, unmarried, at the age of 73 in 1925.[16]

Edward Wathen Fyffe, the younger of the two brothers, joined what then became known as E. W. Fyffe and Son when in his early twenties and was left as the sole partner when his father died in 1882. At that time the firm was still operating from Howford Buildings, 148½ Fenchurch Street, as wholesale tea-dealers[17] and it was profitable enough to enable him to marry. His choice fell on Ida Stanton Brown, the grand-daughter of Isaac Hillier, a prominent local businessman in Nailsworth, not far from the village of Box in Gloucestershire where Edward had spent most of his childhood. Two children, both girls, were born as a result of this marriage: one in September 1885 and the other in October 1886. The nearness of the two births led to a weakening of their mother's health and she developed a form of tuberculosis. This was regarded as being so serious that her husband was advised to take her to a warm climate to convalesce. The fact that Edward Wathen Fyffe then decided that a long stay in the Canary Islands would be most beneficial for his wife's health was to have a major effect on his subsequent career – it was also to have significant consequences for the British banana industry.

The Fyffe family were to spend most of 1887 and the early part of 1888 in the Canaries, and the climate proved to be so helpful that Ida Fyffe was able to make a full recovery. Little in the way of actual treatment was required so the couple undoubtedly took full advantage of the few social opportunities that were available. They certainly had the time to travel extensively throughout the islands and had the leisure to examine thoroughly both their culture and economy. The existence of so many cheap bananas must have come as a great surprise to the Fyffes, who thought of them as being expensive and rare, and at some stage the business opportunity which they represented must have crossed Edward Fyffe's mind.

The small British colonies in Las Palmas and in Santa Cruz de Tenerife would have made their middle-class visitors very welcome and it is known that the Fyffes became friendly with a number of expatriates as well as with several Anglo-Canario families. It is tempting to postulate that they met Arthur Stockley during their stay but as he did not arrive until May 1888, this appears to have been very unlikely. Nevertheless, Fyffe must have become aware of Elder Dempster's increasing success in shipping bananas to Liverpool and, equally, of the difficulties which other firms had experienced when they had attempted to follow their example. One such case concerned the firm of Peter S. Reid who operated as a general merchant and commission agent at what was then (1888) called Port Orotava. As part of his normal business he imported china from Britain. This arrived in barrels which had to be returned at considerable cost, so Mr Reid hit on the idea of filling them with a return cargo to help defray the freight charges. Unfortunately, as he was in the centre of a banana-growing area, he decided to utilize the fruit for this purpose! Then, after the lid had been firmly fixed back in place, the barrels were taken to the port to await the next available ship. As only a brown sludge arrived back in London this experiment was quickly terminated ...[18]

Problems such as this were, of course, well known to Elder Dempster but as they paid little for their bananas and used spare capacity to ship it at virtually no cost they could afford to accept a relatively high proportion of over-ripe consignments. Fyffe soon appreciated that without these special conditions he would be at a great disadvantage so he decided not to attempt to ship on his own account. Instead he proposed to establish an import agency in London for those potential growers who wished to find an outlet for their surplus products. His lengthy stay in the Canaries had enabled him to make friends with many of the principal families and a number, including the Barkers, Blandys, Leacocks and Wolfsons agreed to back him. The exact nature of their agreement is not known, but it seems certain that Fyffe was to sell whatever was sent to him on a commission basis and that the onus for the provision of saleable fruit lay with the growers.

As a result of these agreements a small consignment of bananas arrived at Fyffe's office, where he conducted his work as a tea importer, in September 1888. The quantity was too tiny to be noted in official statistics but three separate events have enabled this occasion to be accurately recalled. The first of these came in 1922 when *The Banana Budget*[19] asked Mr J. Clifford to make a contribution to its series entitled 'Canary Reminiscences'. This included an account of how the first shipment arrived and was dumped in the courtyard outside their office in Howford Buildings at 148½ Fenchurch Street. Mr Clifford stated that this occurred in September 1888, but as he was by then very elderly and was writing about an event which took place some thirty-four years earlier it might be suggested that his memory may not have been completely accurate.

Fortunately in a later part of his account Mr Clifford mentioned that

'Jack the Ripper' committed a murder outside their warehouse in Mitre Street, Aldgate, during the first week of their occupation. As all of the Ripper's atrocities took place during a period which only ran from 31 August to 9 November 1888, Mr Clifford's recollection of the date is conclusively collaborated.[20] As the only victim who was killed in Mitre Square was Catherine Eddowes (otherwise known as Kate Conway) who died on Sunday 30 September, this suggests that Fyffes moved into their new warehouse on Monday 24 September. Thus it would appear to be highly probable that the original shipment of bananas arrived sometime between 10 and 21 September 1888.

Fig. 4.1   Howford Buildings about 1855

A third stroke of good fortune enables us to visualize the sequence of events still further, for Mr Clifford subsequently acquired a print of Howford Buildings and marked with a cross the point at which the first consignment actually arrived (see Fig. 4.1). His statement is finally confirmed by the *Post Office Directories* which show that in 1888 Messrs E. W. Fyffe, Son and Company acquired premises at 3 Mitre Street and also retained their existing offices at 148½ Fenchurch Street.

The bananas which arrived before Fyffes were ready to receive them proved to be something of an embarrassment. Many were fairly ripe and the 'authorities' quickly ordered their removal. In these circumstances Fyffe contacted a local fruit merchant who took them away and they were subsequently sold in Covent Garden at a price which provided excellent profit. Further shipments soon followed and, with the benefit of experience, the quantities that were spoilt were kept to manageable proportions. Most of the fruit was disposed of by auction at Covent Garden but Fyffe also developed a wholesale business which sold directly to the 'better class' fruiterers in the capital and also began the practice of disposing of inferior stock via the 'barrow-boys'.

Although the premises at Howford Buildings at 148½ Fenchurch Street were retained, and presumably used for Fyffe's ongoing tea business, those at 3 Mitre Street soon proved to be inadequate for the growing throughput of bananas. Accordingly, in 1890, new premises were secured at 124 Long Acre and three years later a further move saw E. W. Fyffe, Son and Company (now described as fruit-growers and importers) firmly established in 9–12 Bow Street, EC. The growing success and prosperity of this enterprise then enabled Mr Fyffe to move from his former home at Stafford House in Hadley near Barnett to Oak Lodge in West Wickham.[21] His progress was, of course, considerably eased by the lack of competition in the London market, for it was not until 1892 that Elder Dempster began to offer any serious threat in the metropolis.

Although Elder Dempster had gained its experience in the carriage of bananas on the Canary to Liverpool route, the company had always been aware of the potential market in the capital. However, as most of its voyages terminated on the Mersey, and as the production of bananas tended to lag behind the growth of demand, there was at first little incentive to widen the range of ports to which it carried the fruit. A few boxes were sent to London as and when space was available, but until the early 1890s these small amounts were conveniently handled by agents. Thereafter, the increasing availability of bananas in both the Canaries and in Madeira led to a rise in the scale of Elder Dempster's imports into London and then to Alfred Jones's decision to open a branch office to deal with these shipments.

Arthur Stockley's task was, therefore, to build up a suitable organization which could cope with the rising quantities then being planned. As a first step he recruited an old friend, Mr A. Roger Ackerley, to assist him.[22] The two young men then proceeded to Covent Garden and attempted to persuade Charles E. Howard that they seriously wished to rent a substantial amount of property.[23] He was eventually convinced, with the aid of the Elder Dempster name, and then arranged for suitable premises at 46 Long Acre, WC, and at 16 James Street, Covent Garden. These were subsequently extended with the addition of further capacity in Neal Street,[24] so that the quantities dealt with by Elder Dempster could be steadily increased. In spite of this progress, which gave Elder Dempster a rising share of the London market, there can be no doubt that in 1895 Fyffes were still, by far, the largest banana importers in the capital (see Fig. 4.2).

E. W. FYFFE, SON & CO., FRUIT GROWERS AND
IMPORTERS,
9, 10, 11, AND 12, Bow Street, W.C.

Any record of the notable industries of the Metropolis would be sadly deficient without reference to the important part taken therein by the importers of fruit and other produce, and in this connection mention must be made of this well-known firm, which, dating back in its foundation for a century, has developed a business which is practically unique, trading under the style and title above designated, and operating as the largest banana merchants in Europe. They own extensive estates at Grand Canary, Teneriffe, and Madeira, where they operate on a very vast scale as growers and shippers of bananas, tomatoes, potatoes, and all the small fruits of these islands, which they export direct to the various European markets. The Bow Street building covers a considerable area, having a frontage of about eighty feet and being six storeys in height, and the whole of the ample accommodation thus afforded is specially constructed for the warehousing of the bananas, which arrive in a green condition, and are rapidly distributed through their medium to all parts of England and Europe, the fruit being matured and ripened in specially warmed cellars and floors. They also have various other depots in the Provinces for storing and distributing their imports. The trade controlled by the firm is simply enormous, amounting almost to a monopoly, and the entire business is conducted upon a thoroughly sound and well-balanced basis that is eminently calculated to secure for future continuance the influential relations so long maintained with all the leading distributors of high-class produce throughout the United Kingdom.

Fig. 4.2   E. W. Fyffe, Son & Company (Advert)

58

Although the above extract from the trade press tends to exaggerate the scope of Fyffe's business and attributes 'ownership' where 'agency' would be more appropriate, it is still clear that his firm had grown at an enormous rate since it began to deal in bananas. Consequently, Edward Fyffe decided it would be of advantage if he could take a partner who would be prepared to share his responsibilities as well as to help widen the basis of the enterprise. After much consideration his choice fell upon James Hudson who, it is thought, had obliged Fyffe by disposing of his first bananas when they had been so inopportunely delivered outside his office in September, 1888.[25] As the senior partner of Hudson Brothers, James was also a valuable contact in that his company operated a string of high-class fruit and grocery stores on a number of sites throughout the central London area:[25]

50 & 52 Ludgate Hill, EC (Head Office).
444 Strand, WC.
64 Fore Street, EC.
9 Islington High Street, W.
1 & 2 Railway Place, EC.
Railway Approach, Cannon Street Terminus, EC.
76 Cannon Street, EC.
17 Pilgrim Street, EC.
45–47 Liverpool Street, EC.
6 Wilton Road, SW.
86 Waterloo Road, SE.
160 New Bond Street, W.
251 Finchley Road, NW.
141 Kensington High Street, W.
156 & 157 Bishopsgate Street (without EC.).
10 Russell Street, Covent Garden

The family tradition was that the long-established firm of Hudson Brothers had operated on a small scale in London for many years prior to 1870. It is then believed that James saw the opportunity presented by the siege of Paris, so that when it was lifted in 1871 he was ready to rush in a trainload of provisions to sell to the starving population at prices which gave him an excellent profit.[26] These gains were then used to strengthen the financial base of the firm so that it was able to expand and acquire the numerous properties detailed above. To what extent this was the whole story cannot now be ascertained, but there is no doubt that by the 1890s Hudson Brothers were regarded as being amongst the leaders in the retail fruit trade. Thus James was in an excellent position to complement Fyffe's role as an importer and distributor and was, equally, able to benefit from such an association. Consequently, it was not difficult for the two men to reach an agreement and thus in 1896 the new partnership of Fyffe, Hudson and Company came into existence.

Messrs Fyffe, Hudson continued to trade from what had been the former premises of E. W. Fyffe at 9–12 Bow Street, but the tea business at $148\frac{1}{2}$ Fenchurch Street was not included in the partnership and operated as an independent entity. The firm of Hudson Brothers also operated as a separate concern, although it remained an important customer for the bananas imported by the new partnership. Thus the stage was set for a further expansion of Edward Fyffe's enterprise or, at the very least, the maintenance of its market share against the growing threat posed by the activities of Stockley and Ackerley. However, the new arrangements had barely had time to settle down when Fyffe received news from the growers' syndicate in the Canary Islands that his services were no longer required.

Whether Edward Fyffe's action in taking James Hudson into partnership sparked off this response is now unclear: perhaps it merely brought the existing situation into sharper focus? It may just have been an inevitable consequence of the growing success of the enterprise and of the desire of the members of the syndicate to maximize their profits. In any event, it certainly posed Fyffe with a very real problem in that he was obliged to decide if he was to continue as a banana importer or whether he should settle with his former suppliers on the best terms he could obtain. Any consideration of remaining in business must have taken into account the likely difficulty in generating a sufficiently high level of regular supplies at competitive prices from the Canaries, and also the probable enhanced competition in the British market. These factors, together with a knowledge of the rising aspirations of Stockley and Ackerley and the strength of their Elder Dempster backers, must then have persuaded Fyffe that he should consider whatever other alternatives were available.

A series of meetings were then held between the members of the syndicate and Edward Fyffe. The 'growers' made it clear that they thought that the time was ripe for a reorganization of the business and that they wished to acquire all of Fyffe Hudson's assets and organization so that they could undertake their own marketing. This, of course, involved the buying out of Fyffe and of James Hudson and although the terms have never been revealed it is obvious that they were so generous that the partners felt it would be foolish to reject them. Once the principle had been accepted, a legal agreement[27] was drawn which summarized these arrangements and this was subsequently encapsulated when the ongoing business was consolidated under the title of Fyffe, Hudson and Company, Limited (see Fig. 4.3).

An Agreement made this 7 day of *Sept* 1897 BETWEEN RICHARD RIDPATH BLANDY, HENRY WOLFSON, JOHN MILBERNE LEACOCK a.. EDWARD CECIL BARKER all of No. 9 Bow Street in the County of London Fruit or Vegetable Growers, Buyers, Importers and Salesmen (hereinafter called " the Vendors ") of the one part and FYFFE, HUDSON AND COMPANY LIMITED (hereinafter called " the Company ") of the other part.

WHEREAS the Vendors have for some time past carried on business in partnership together with others as fruit or vegetable growers, buyers, importers and salesmen at 9 Bow Street aforesaid under the style or firm of " Fyffe, Hudson & Company " at Las Palmas Grand Canary under the style or firm of " Blandy, Barker & Company " at Teneriffe under the style or firm of " The Teneriffe Fruit Company " or " Henry Wolfson " and at Madeira under . style or firm of " The Madeira Fruit Company " or " Leacock & Co."

AND WHEREAS the Vendors have recently acquired the goodwill of the said business which was carried on in partnership between Edward Wathen Fyffe, James John Hudson and the Vendors and the goodwill of any business or businesses carried on between any five, four, three or two of them (all of which businesses are hereinafter referred to as " the old businesses ") and the Vendors have recently caused the Company to be incorporated for the purpose of acquiring the goodwill of the old businesses and of carrying on the same.

AND WHEREAS the nominal Capital of the Company is £94,000 divided into 83,000 Preferred Shares of £1 each and 11,000 Ordinary Shares of £1 each and such Shares have respectively attached thereto such respective rights as are specified in the Company's original Articles of Association.

NOW IT IS HEREBY AGREED as follows :—

1. The Vendors shall sell and the Company shall purchase as from the 1st day of July 1897 all the goodwill of the old businesses and the exclusive right to use the names of Fyffe, Hudson and Company, Blandy Barker & Company, The Teneriffe Fruit Company and The Madeira Fruit Company as part of the assets of the Company and to represent the Company as carrying on the old businesses in succession to the Vendors, And also the benefit of all contracts and engagements connected with the old businesses and pending on the said 1st day of July 1897.

2. The consideration for the said sale shall be the sum of £11,000

Fig. 4.3 Fyffe, Hudson & Co. Ltd. (Formation document)

These arrangements came into effect on 1 July 1897. Thereafter, although the business continued to operate in much the same way from the same premises, it was then under the direct control of the 'growers' and neither Fyffe nor Hudson retained any interest or connection with it. This situation created no difficulty for James Hudson as he had never relinquished his interests in his family firm. Although aged sixty-five he returned to play an active part in this concern and was largely responsible for reorganizing the partnership to form Hudson Brothers London Limited in 1898.[28] He continued to direct the resulting firm for a further six years and only retired in 1904 at the age of 72. When his partnership with Edward Fyffe was dissolved he was living at 'Reigate Lodge' in Reigate, but subsequently built a more prestigious residence named 'Capenor' at Nutfield in the same area.[29] It is tempting to surmise that he used his undoubted gains from his Fyffe Hudson venture for this purpose, but this may be rejected on two counts. In the first place he was very much the 'junior' partner in financial terms, so did not receive a very large pay-out, and secondly he was already quite a wealthy man. Thus, when he died in 1907 his estate was valued at over £152,000.[30] Hudson Brothers London Limited was liquidated in 1910, but a successor, Hudson Brothers (Holdings) Limited owned and operated high-class grocery stores, particularly on the south coast, until it was wound up in 1960.[31]

Edward Fyffe's position was rather different from that of his partner. In 1897 he was still only forty-four years of age so could have anticipated another twenty or so years in business. He still retained his interest in his family's tea company but as this was only operating on a very small scale it did not offer the kind of challenge which might have stimulated him to have remained in London. Instead he decided to sever all his links with commerce, and after winding up the tea business took up permanent residence in a splendid stone house named 'Trullwell' in the Cotswold village of Box near Minchinhampton.

Mr Fyffe was to spend the next thirty-eight years in these delightful surroundings, during which time he took a great interest in the welfare of the village and of the locality. During this period he undertook a number of civic duties, serving on the Minchinhampton Parish Council and helping to raise and administer the funds which enabled Minchinhampton Common to be acquired by the National Trust. A keen golfer, he was a founder member of the Minchinhampton Golf Club and he also pursued other hobbies through the County Archaeological Society and the Cotswold Naturalists Field Club. Having decided to abandon commerce in London, Fyffe was not anxious to become involved at a local level but he did agree to become chairman of Hillier's Bacon Curing Factory in Nailsworth.[32] This firm had been

Charles McCann.

Alexander Baillon at Hoya Grande,
Tenerife, c. 1917.

s.s. Faith of the African Steam Ship Company, c. 1853.

Puerto de la Luz, Grand Canary, c. 1884.

Puerto de la Luz (Las Palmas) Grand Canary, c. 1890.

s.s. Angola of the African Steam Ship Company (Elder Dempster agents) c. 1891.

Elder Dempster's Banana Department, 1899.

Puerto de la Cruz, Tenerife, with Mount Teide in the background, c. 1890.

established by his wife's grandfather and by the early twentieth century had become a substantial business. Nevertheless Fyffe's responsibilities here were quite small and only occupied a small amount of his time. As there is no record of any contact between him and the banana industry after his retirement in 1897 it would appear that this was his only form of employment. He was, therefore, able to live with his wife and growing daughters in precisely the way that appealed to him.

Fyffe's wife died in 1911 but as his daughters remained unmarried he continued to live at 'Trullwell' and his lifestyle was little altered. It is reported that he was the first person in Box to own a motor car and subsequently always possessed a large and expensive one. Apart from employing a full-time chauffeur/gardener, Mr Fyffe also benefited from the services provided by a number of indoor servants and enjoyed a very comfortable type of existence. He died in October 1935, at the age of eighty-two, and was buried in the nearby churchyard at Amberly, alongside his wife and mother. His will later showed that he had left the sum of £38,493. This was a considerable amount for the 1930s and was all the more impressive after such a long period of affluent retirement. Clearly Edward Fyffe's ten-year association with the banana had proved to be highly profitable! Neither of his daughters ever married: Martha Ellen, born 1885, died in 1966 and Gertrude Ida, born in 1886, died in 1946.[33]

5

The adoption of cooling techniques and their impact on the trade

The replacement of the unlimited partnership between Edward Fyffe and James Hudson by Messrs Fyffe, Hudson and Company, Limited, in 1897 had no immediate impact on the British banana market. By then, however, a number of changes were in train that were already beginning to alter the character of the seaborne carriage of food. These were largely to be concerned with the innovations which were to lead to an ability to carry frozen or chilled meat halfway round the world, but this advance in technology was also having an impact on the general fruit trade and was ultimately to have major consequences on the importation of *Musa sapientum*.

Attempts to carry tropical and other fruits to the mass markets in the temperate zones had always been constrained by a series of factors which included the pace of ripening, the distance involved and the speed of the available transport. With the benefit of relatively short voyage times it had been possible to solve this equation so that sailing vessels were able to supply parts of North America with bananas in commercial quantities from the 1870s. The greater mileage between the Canaries and the United Kingdom meant that it was not until the advent of the steamship that the banana could become a regular import into Liverpool and, later, London.

Sailing vessels were, as noted earlier,[1] quick enough to cope with a range of fresh and dried fruits which originated in the western Mediterranean and the Azores. By far the most important part of this business was the trade in citrus fruits, so that by 1854:

> ... sixty million oranges were imported for the London market alone, and some fifteen million lemons. In that year there were 240 schooners in the business; of these seventy supplied the local demands of London. At any time between December and May,

schooners from the Azores and Lisbon could be seen unloading cargoes in the London river, for the season was a short one and oranges were a winter luxury. Besides these specialized cargoes mixed loads of grapes, oranges, lemons and currants were sometimes picked up at Mediterranean ports. There were other fruit trades. The West Indies pineapple trade began about 1842 and rapidly increased so that by 1854 200,000 pineapples were brought yearly into London in schooners. There was a trade in melons, which came from both Spain and Portugal, there was a currant trade from the Greek Islands, which, since the cargo was less perishable, employed larger and slower vessels.[2]

The potential of the British market also attracted the attention of other would-be suppliers. These included a number of South African growers, but their attempts to build up an export business utilizing sailing vessels were not very successful. The establishment of regular steamship services[3] then enabled a trade in dried fruit (especially raisins) and preserves to be developed, but efforts to carry fresh items were to prove to be more difficult. However:

> ... [a] special consignment intended for display at the Indian and Colonial Exhibition which marked Queen Victoria's Golden Jubilee was shipped from Natal in 1887. Among the sub-tropical varieties like limes and bananas there were also peaches and apples. When the display was over, the fruit went to Covent Garden ...[4]

A report on this fruit was subsequently sent to the Governor of Natal and its favourable predictions convinced a number of producers in Cape Colony that something should be done. It was, and in 1888 two shipments of apples were sent to England with the expectation that they would achieve good prices. This was not to be the case:

> Considerable trouble has been taken to procure buyers for this fruit. It proves, however, to be altogether unsuitable for this market. England itself produces a great variety of apples, which are probably the last fruits that should have been sent here. When indigenous apples cannot be obtained, there are always large supplies of the best kinds from America. Under these circumstances I cannot too strongly urge you not to encourage any further exports of this fruit from the Colony to England, as disappointment seems inevitable.[5]

In February 1888 the Society for the Promotion of Agriculture, Horticulture and Colonial Industry promoted an exhibition of fruit in Cape Town. This was regarded as such a success that it was decided to send the entire show to London. By then, of course, the fruit was already mature and by the time it reached the capital the whole consignment was in a very poor state. On the other hand private attempts were more fortunate, perhaps because the individuals concerned took better care! This can be seen by reference to the experience of two passengers who travelled to England in 1888 carrying gifts of grapes. The first of these was the Hon. J. H. Hofmeyer:

> ... who took 7 boxes, each of which contained 16 lb. white hanepoot grapes. They were relatively ripe, but not overripe, and were placed in the cool-chamber of the ship. On arrival after 19 days only 5 per cent of the grapes were rotten. The other passenger wrapped (his) bunches of grapes individually in newspaper, placed then in a basket and simply kept them in an empty cabin. On arrival in England only a few berries were spoilt.[6]

Experiences such as this gave further encouragement to commercial grape producers, and later in 1888 two tons were booked to be carried to London in the coldroom of the s.s. *Moor*. Unfortunately the fruit arrived in Capetown too late to catch this vessel so was shipped on s.s. *Pembroke Castle* which did not have cold storage facilities. The grapes arrived in an inedible condition and the conclusion was reached that it was the lack of suitable cooling arrangements that was at the root of the problem.

TABLE 5.1   IMPORTATION OF FROZEN MUTTON INTO THE UNITED KINGDOM, 1880-93
Carcases

Year	Australia	New Zealand	Falkland Islands	River Plate	Total
1880	400	–	–	–	400
1881	17,275	–	–	–	17,275
1882	57,256	8,839	–	–	66,095
1883	63,733	120,893	–	17,165	201,791
1886	66,960	655,888	30,000	434,699	1,187,547
1890	207,984	1,533,393	10,168	1,196,531	2,948,076
1893	605,692	1,893,604	16,425	1,373,723	3,889,444

Although the precise nature of what was required was not fully understood, South African growers were aware of the tremendous advances which had been made in the carriage of frozen meat and now wished to see this new technology applied to their own products.

Progress had, in fact, been very rapid from 1874 when an experimental shipment of meat was chilled with the aid of natural ice and successfully carried between the United States and Britain.[7] A regular trade began in 1877 when *Frigorifique* utilized mechanical refrigeration to bring a first cargo of meat from Argentina and this example was quickly followed when, in 1880, the first shipment from Australia brought 400 frozen carcases of mutton to London.[8] Thereafter the frozen meat trades were to grow at an impressive rate, so clearly any technical difficulties had been largely overcome (see Tables 5.1 to 5.3.[9]

TABLE 5.2   TOTAL EXPORTS OF FROZEN MEAT FROM NEW ZEALAND, 1882–1911

Year	lbs	Year	lbs
1882	1,707,328	1900	206,621,072
1883	9,853,200	1903	266,408,800
1886	38,758,160	1905	189,356,608
1890	100,934,756	1910	297,269,952
1893	100,262,453	1911	252,063,280
1895	127,018,864		

TABLE 5.3   EXPORT OF FROZEN MUTTON FROM ARGENTINA, 1895–1911

Year	Tons	Year	Tons
1895	41,882	1910	75,102
1900	56,412	1911	85,916
1905	78,351		

Although superficially similar, the carriage of 'live' produce (typified by fruit) and of 'dead' produce (typified by meat) require separate and distinctive forms of treatment during long ocean voyages:

> The carriage of both of these groups have certain things in common, but there are also some wide differences. The major one being that in live cargoes – fruit and vegetables, the living process continues after harvesting and during this retarded ripening process, heat continues to be given off and the produce 'breathes' in oxygen and exhales CO_2 and other gases. With dead cargoes – meat and fish, on the other hand, the main requirement is to prevent the development of micro-organisms which live on the produce ...[10]

From the foregoing it will be appreciated that the fact that meat could be carried successfully did not necessarily mean that it would be automatically possible to transport fruit over long distances. In fact the first consignment of refrigerated fruit and vegetables to arrive in England was reported to have been sold in Covent Garden around 1880.[11] This included both ripe pears and green peas in their pods, and although they had only been imported from the relative closeness of Italy this suggested that the technical problems were not insurmountable.

It was against this background that Sir Donald Currie, Chairman of the Castle Mail Steamship Company, was persuaded to fit a cool chamber into the RMS *Grantully Castle*. A description of this facility, which measured 9 ft × 16 ft × 6 ft with a capacity of 21 tons, has survived from the day in February 1889 when it arrived at the Cape:

> On either side are curious sights – fish of all sizes, shipped cold and hard as stone; fowls, carcases of beef, hams, livers, all looking and feeling as if they were ice, and withal the air is keen and sweet.
> English beef is here as fresh as when first shipped, and huge blocks of ice are numerous enough to give one the ague.[12]

Fifteen tons of grapes were loaded into this chamber but for a number of reasons they failed to arrive in London in good condition. Apart from the basic error in keeping the temperature too low a later investigation suggested that the fruit had been badly packed and that in any event the wrong variety of grape had been chosen for the experiment. Little attention had apparently been given to this latter point and the ordinary Cape muscatel which had been shipped lacked the type of thick skin which was essential to avoid bruising and damage. These were relatively easy matters to put right and both the Union and the Castle steamship lines were subsequently encouraged to install cool-chambers which were specifically designed for the carriage of fruit. This policy then reached a viable conclusion when in February 1892, the *Drummond Castle* arrived in London with fourteen trays (some sources say seventeen boxes) of peaches.[13] As less than 5 per cent of the fruit was damaged and as excellent prices were achieved this was to mark the beginning of what was to become a large and prosperous business.

The wider impact of these developments must now be considered. With the evolution of effective forms of cooling systems and of refrigeration it was clearly possible to carry a wide range of perishable commodities over long distances. The extent to which this could be undertaken on a commercial basis still remained to be seen. The carriage of meat had certainly passed this critical test by about 1890 but the question of the large-scale transport of fruit had still not been fully answered. However, the fact that it had been demonstrated to be technically feasible meant that numerous possibilities were explored. In the course of time these experimental voyages resulted in the emergence of many new sources of overseas fruit and vegetables and thus to the growth of numerous trades in these products. These were ultimately to include the banana.

Elder Dempster's shipment of bananas from the Canaries to Liverpool originally employed no form of cooling except that provided by the forward motion of the vessel. Indeed the entire business was conducted on very simple though practical lines, as the following description confirms:

> ... the fruit is sold green to the packer for prices which now [1898] run to as much as five pesetas a bunch, though not many years ago two and a half pesetas was a good price. Packing costs the shipper as much as the fruit. There is, practically speaking, no wood in the islands, and all timber for crates has to be laboriously carried from Norway.
> Leaves form some of the packing material, but the supply is short; and paper, cotton wadding and straw are all used, all of which have to be imported.
> The crates are made by woman labour entirely. The packer can hire a woman for a peseta or less a day, whilst a man costs him two pesetas fifty. The man has to stop to smoke. The ladies do not indulge in cigarettes during business hours; and, moreover they are handier (queer to relate) with a hammer and French nails; and so they get this job. And after the bunches are packed in their crates, they are loaded on a mule cart, or sometimes on a camel, and taken down to some harbour on the coast, where boats tranship them to the English steamers.
> On the steamer sometimes they are stowed below, where there is no cargo which will heat or spoil them, but as often as not they travel to England stowed on the open deck and go through any weather which may befall in the Bay or elsewhere.[14]

In spite of this rather primitive system, Canary exports of fruit and vegetables rose sharply in the period from 1884 to 1902. Details are not available for the earlier years, but those from 1897 are given in Table 5.4.

Banana shippers in Madeira employed a similar system:

> The usual method of packing is in large rough wooden crates, taking a dozen or more bunches, between each of which straw is placed to keep them firm and to prevent rubbing; another method is in

baskets made of coarse native broom, one bunch being placed in each basket, straw or bracket leaves being placed round to ensure safety in transit ...[16]

TABLE 5.4 CANARY ISLANDS EXPORTS, 1897–1902[15]

	Bananas	Oranges	Potatoes	Tomatoes
1897–1898	660,461	8,456	111,241	399,004
1898–1899	783,418	13,389	155,241	492,075
1899–1900	1,044,630	8,526	110,396	341,136
1900–1901	1,208,596	14,401	169,563	458,119
1901–1902	1,597,616	8,505	224,267	414,859

(The figures refer to cases. A banana case sometimes contains two bunches. Reckoning 100 bananas to a bunch, the last year's export is, roughly, 170,000,000 bananas!)

Unfortunately for the growers in Madeira the similarity with the Canaries was only of a limited nature, for little real effort was made by the government to develop its banana industry:

Of late years the export of this fruit from Madeira to England has been greatly reduced, owing to the inducements afforded to both growers and shippers at the Canary Islands, where native labour is cheaper; free importation of artificial manure is permitted; the shipping companies offer greater facilities for the conveyance of the fruit; and the Customs authorities place no obstacles in the way of the shipper. Therefore Canary-grown bananas can be bought wholesale in England at a lower rate than Madeira fruit, although the voyage is one day longer than from Madeira.[17]

In spite of these disadvantages Madeira was reported to be providing 30,000 bunches of bananas a year in the mid-1890s.[18] These, together with the much larger supplies being received from the Canaries, made up practically all of the bananas then being imported into Britain. At that time the trade had grown to such an extent that although Elder Dempster vessels continued to bring bananas into Liverpool as deck cargo, and other lines filled up any spaces when proceeding to London, a number of more specialized ships were now being employed. These were mainly operated by Messrs Forwood Brothers and by Messrs Donald Currie and Company. In 1897, on the occasion of the maiden voyage of Forwood's *Orotava*, it was stated that the company was now providing a weekly service from the Canaries, and Arthur Stockley claimed that Elder Dempster were receiving 2,000 bunches from each sailing and that:

70

... he did not believe that they had more than one bunch soft out of the 2,000 per boat between October and the present date [February 1897]. The splendid machinery and ventilating apparatus on board was everything to be desired ...[19]

The only other regular supply of bananas to reach the UK in the late 1890s came from Minor Keith's plantations in Costa Rica. These were transported:

> ... from New York to Liverpool in the fastest available Atlantic liners of that time. The bunches, with the end of the stems covered with asphaltum, were packed in dried banana leaves and placed in crates or boxes. One thousand to two thousand bunches were shipped weekly in this manner and the fruit was sold at auction at Covent Garden, London. Some of the fruit arrived in good shape and sold as high as the equivalent of fifteen dollars a bunch, but too often it arrived in spoiled condition. At the end of a three-year period, Keith found that he had lost some $15,000 in the venture and stopped shipments.[20]

By the 1890s it is clear that the carriage of bananas over relatively long distances was possible providing that the speed of the ship and the slickness of the organization kept the time span within the normal ripening cycle of the fruit. The use of 'natural' or 'forced' systems of ventilation on board could not delay this process by a single day but they did help to prevent any artificial acceleration of ripening which would have followed if heat had been allowed to build up. These methods were, of course, much simpler than the refrigeration techniques which were to follow. Even these were not unfortunately foolproof, as will be seen by the case of s.s. *Andes*. This vessel, which was owned by the Atlas Line,[21] carried bananas on the route between Jamaica and New York for the Boston Fruit Company, and in June 1894 it was arranged that a fan ventilation system be fitted to her:

> The fans were fitted in the forward stokehold bulkhead in the fruit deck, one on each side so as to exhaust into the fidley; two more were fitted in the engine room to do the same in the after deck, and special ventilators were fitted both forward and aft as intakes.
>
> Before leaving New York the manager had, special instructions made out for the master's guidance, it being particularly emphasized that we had to carry out these rules whatever happened, and I am sorry to say the result was disastrous to the fruit in the forward deck. After loading in Jamaica and closing down the hatches the fans were started, and before the third day out we noticed the

temperatures were very high and they continued to rise until we arrived in New York, six days from Jamaica. We all knew something had gone wrong, as the smell of cooked bananas was very strong, but there were the orders not to touch anything and not even to open a hatch.[22]

It was later discovered that one of the forward fans had been fitted the wrong way round so had been forcing hot air from the stokehold into the fruit deck. When this had been rectified and more powerful fans installed, the system proved to be extremely efficient.

The example of the successful carriage of meat and the gradual introduction of cooling systems which enabled many varieties of fruit to be carried with greater certainty over longer distances then encouraged other producers to investigate the new options that were becoming available. Amongst these were a number of Jamaican planters and merchants who wished to reduce their almost total dependence upon the North American market. It was already possible to send fruit to England via New York, but as this method was time-consuming the consignments tended to deteriorate before their arrival. In addition this was an expensive route and as the fruit was seldom in prime condition it could not attract high prices. Thus the trade was barely profitable and so could not develop on any real scale. It was against this background that the Jamaica Fruit Importing and Trading Company was formed, with the intention of providing direct sailings between Kingston and London.[23]

The new line began rather inauspiciously when *Port Victor*[24] was obliged to return to Kingston after a fault had developed, '... in the refrigeration of its cold chambers'.[25] It was then necessary for its cargo of oranges and bananas to be removed and sold locally, but after suitable repair a fresh assortment of fruit was taken on board and the vessel sailed for London on 12 December 1896. In the meanwhile a second ship, s.s. *Elderslie*, had been loaded, and reached England on Christmas Eve.[26] Unfortunately its cooling machinery had also broken down and its cargo proved to be unsaleable.[27] However, when *Port Victor* finally arrived on 28 December after a sixteen-day voyage, most of its fruit was found to be in a reasonable condition.

An experimental consignment of tangerines was described as being '... as handsome a sample of that variety as was ever seen in the English markets', while the larger quantities of oranges, each individually wrapped in tissue paper, were also reported to have travelled extremely well. The same was not, however, true for the bananas, for although the cooling arrangements proved to be suitable many of the stems were spoilt by poor packaging:

72

For the bananas, all that is claimed in the way of success for the oranges can be equally said of a large part of the consignment of this more delicate fruit. But we regret to find that, owing to very bad packing, a portion of the bananas have arrived unsaleable. This will, of course, be improved upon on future occasions. Ranging from five to nine hands a bunch, the bulk of these fruits is very large and of fine flavour. A considerable proportion range from 6in. to 6½in. long, and are very broad and full. Here, again, two systems of packing have been tried, the bulk of the 1,600 bunches being packed in crates as usual, but a small number have been 'packed loose'. So far as we could judge from a casual glance, the fruit packed in crates arrived in rather a better condition than that sent loose; and we think it will turn out that the oranges packed in boxes will show an improved condition over those in the barrels.[28]

It is interesting to note the details of the arrangements which were made for cooling the fruit on board *Port Victor*. Its machinery provided:

> ... for 'cool storage' and not for 'refrigeration'. We are informed that the temperature during the voyage averaged from 52 deg. to 53 deg., never going below 50 deg., or exceeding 55 deg.; and the condition of the fruit on arrival proves that it can bear this temperature without deterioration in any way.[29]

The original delay in *Port Victor*'s sailing meant that her cargo was too late to catch the Christmas market. Consequently it was sold at Covent Garden by Messrs Garcia, Jacobs and Company on Wednesday 30 December. The prices achieved at this public auction were quite high, with the exception of the bananas: the relatively poor condition of this fruit caused by the lack of appropriate packing led to only moderate returns being achieved.

The failure of s.s. *Elderslie* and the only partial success of *Port Victor*'s first voyage were not sufficient to deter the Jamaica firm and a second cargo was delivered to London by *Port Victor* in March 1897. It was expected that the experience gained with earlier shipments would have ensured a satisfactory outcome on this occasion. This was not to be the case so far as its bananas were concerned:

> ... The second actual shipment of Jamaican fruit has now arrived, but we regret to record that the consignors in their endeavours no doubt to profit from their previous experience, have gone to the other extreme, and in consequence the fruit has arrived in an almost equally unmarketable condition. With the first shipment the packing of wool

and 'trash' was excessive, in addition to which the requisite
temperature of the cool storage chambers was sadly mis-calculated.
The result was that the bulk of the fruit arrived in a deteriorated state
and the prices realised were consequently low. In the present
consignment the consignors appear to have practically reversed their
programme; and the fruit, or a large portion of it, has arrived in green
condition, loosely packed, in many cases chilled, and in some
instances discoloured, possibly by subsequent forcing.[30]

This view of the state of the bananas was confirmed when they came
to be auctioned. A first lot of 1,000 bunches realized only from 2s. to
4s.9d. a bunch. The following day a further 3,000 bunches were sold;
presumably these were of inferior quality for they only reached an
average of 1s.6d. per bunch.[31] When these results are compared
with those obtained for Canary Island fruit it will be seen that they
were extremely poor. This will be fully appreciated by reference to
typical returns which were achieved during the period that the
Jamaica Fruit Importing and Trading Company was operating. Thus
in December 1895 the following wholesale levels were quoted in the
trade press:

PRICES OF BANANAS PER BUNCH (IN SHILLINGS)[32]

Gold	10–12
Medium	9–10
Green	8– 9
Fine	10–12

Two and a half years later, in July 1898, the levels had changed very
little:

PRICES CURRENT PER BUNCH (IN SHILLINGS)[33]

Coloured	10–12
Fine	9–10
Green	5– 8

Clearly this latest shipment from Jamaica was greatly inferior to that
of average Canary bananas, and many doubts were expressed as to
whether its fruit could ever be really competitive.

In spite of this further disappointment, a third cargo was sent via s.s.
Port Pirie[34] and arrived at the West India Docks, London on 5 May
1897. This shipment then demonstrated that earlier faults had been
completely rectified:

The possibility of the satisfactory consignment of Jamaica fruit to the British markets has at length been conclusively established. Hitherto, the efforts in this direction of the Jamaica Fruit Importing and Trading Company have met with but qualified success. The latest shipment of the Company, however, has, we are pleased to record, realised the highest expectations of all concerned; while it has fully justified our own anticipations that the commendable enterprise displayed by this Company, in the face of apparent failure and defeat would eventually be crowned with success.[35]

The excellent condition of these bananas was then reflected in the results which they achieved. The majority of the 4,000 plus bunches were sold at Covent Garden with prices ranging from 12s. to 6s.6d. and a very satisfactory average of over 9s. per bunch. The balance of the shipment was sent to a number of provincial centres, and good returns were reported from Manchester, Hull and Glasgow.[36]

Strangely enough, although the shipment was a financial success it was not repeated. While there is no satisfactory explanation for this surprising event, some light has been shed upon it by the reminiscences of Arthur Stockley:

In 1896 our [Elder Dempster's] trade had increased very considerably, and it was early in that year that I first met Arthur Farquharson, a Jamaican who has [since] taken such a prominent part in the affairs of Jamaica Producers. He came to my office one day with an introduction from a banker, and informed me that he had come to make arrangements for the sale of Jamaica bananas in England: that some leading merchants and planters in Jamaica had chartered two refrigerator meat ships to carry the fruit to London, that our Canary fruit, since it was of a much smaller variety, would soon be driven off the market, and so on and so forth. His confidence was boundless. The two promised cargoes arrived in London about two months and three months later respectively; the first one was over ripe and had to be dug out of the ship, the second one was frozen hard and uneatable. As the backers of the scheme had only about £30,000 that was the end of the enterprise ...[37]

While Stockley's account is a very general one, written many years later, which appears to have been over-critical of a potential competitor, it does seem to outline the main events. The official returns made by the Jamaica Fruit Importing and Trading Company of London Limited also tend to support this overall picture.[38] It was first registered on 30 July 1896 with a nominal capital of £50,000. Of this, £1,000 was in founders' shares with the balance being made up of 24,500 ordinary shares of £2

75

each. In fact, ordinary shares to a value of only £38,914 were ever issued, with the vast majority of these being taken up by merchants and bankers in London. A small number (650 shares) were acquired by a group of five Jamaicans, led by Charles Gordon Farquharson, described as a merchant of Black River, Jamaica, to whom Arthur Stockley referred earlier. A leading role appears to have been taken by John White, a shipbroker of 23a Great St Helens in London. He was a major shareholder, and the company's first office was located on his own premises. It seems likely that his prime motive was in the provision of the ships for the trade.

The official records do not include any balance sheets or profit and loss accounts so it is impossible to do more than guess at the financial problems which quickly beset the new company. The total loss of *Elderslie*'s cargo, together with the cost of her charter, must have placed an immediate strain on its very limited capital resources. The subsequent problem with *Port Victor*'s first voyage and the poor prices achieved from her second delivery probably meant that the firm was already nearly bankrupt. Why then did it arrange for what proved to be the final voyage to be undertaken by *Port Pirie*? The explanation is that the charter for this vessel had almost certainly been fixed some time in advance and it was calculated that the costs of cancellation were liable to be more than the likely loss on one more cargo of fruit. The fact that the final voyage proved to be successful was, therefore, quite incidental. The promoters were quite happy to use these unexpected profits to reduce their losses but their previous experience had shown the great uncertainty of the business and they were then satisfied to bring the enterprise to an end.

Accordingly no further voyages were undertaken, and at a meeting on 19 December 1898, it was agreed that the company 'be wound up voluntarily'. A liquidator was then appointed and the firm's legal existence came to an end on 13 November 1901.[39]

The failure of this attempt to provide direct sailings from Jamaica and thereby to open up the British market to West Indian fruit could be attributed to two main factors. Firstly, there was an imperfect understanding of the technical requirements, so that insufficient attention was given to packaging and to temperature control. Secondly, the smallness of the company's capital base ensured that it did not have time to learn from its own mistakes. The only way in which it could have succeeded would have been if all of its early cargoes had arrived in good condition and had then secured high prices. Under those circumstances confidence would have risen and, perhaps, more substantial backers would have appeared. In the event this did not happen, so Jamaican fruit was, for the moment, denied direct access to the UK. This state of affairs was then to bring about a whole chain of related consequences which were ultimately to transform the entire British banana industry. Of course, had the Jamaica Fruit Importing and Trading Company been successful, the futures of both Messrs Fyffe, Hudson and Company and of Elders Dempster's fruit department would have been very different indeed!

6

A new outlet for Jamaican bananas

The island of Jamaica, situated in the Caribbean Sea, was first sighted by Christopher Columbus on 4 May 1494.[1] The Spanish began to establish permanent settlements in 1510 but only slow progress was made. This was because alternative colonies on the South American mainland proved to be more attractive in many ways. Thus Jamaica and its neighbours tended to become just stopping points for vessels *en route* to territories which offered the lure of gold and silver. The Spanish possessions in the Caribbean were also made less attractive by the continued activities of primarily English pirates and privateers. Nevertheless, the numbers of Spanish settlers gradually grew and it was during their occupation that the banana was introduced to serve as a subsistence crop.[2]

By the early seventeenth century Britain was beginning to take a serious interest in the West Indies, and Barbados was claimed in 1605. It was not, however, until 1624 that permanent settlement commenced, with the island of St Kitts being the first to be occupied. During the following year Barbados was also settled and both Antigua and Montserrat were secured in 1632. These incursions provided further knowledge of the region and led to a desire to extend British interests. The presence of the Spanish meant, however, that any addition acquisitions could only be secured by force of arms, so progress could only be made by the direct action of the state. The political circumstances for such an enterprise never seemed appropriate until Oliver Cromwell became Lord Protector of England in 1653. He was then advised that the Spanish possessions in the Caribbean were only lightly held and that they could all be captured with very little effort. An expedition was subsequently organized and instructed to secure Hispaniola and Puerto Rico. If all went well it was then hoped that Cuba might also be occupied at a later date.[3]

78

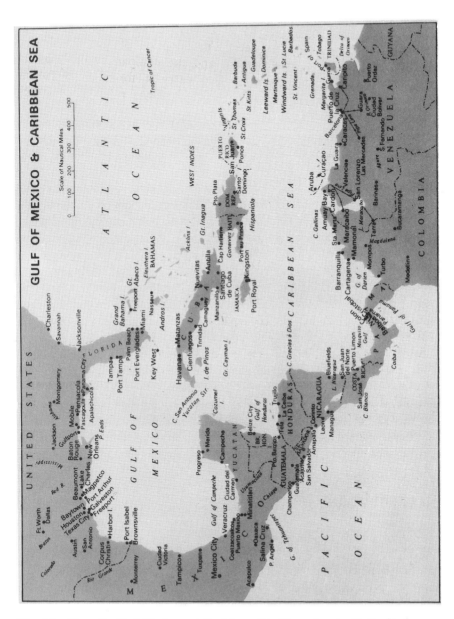

Fig. 6.1   Map of gulf of Mexico and Caribbean Sea (Reproduced with the kind permission of George Philip Limited)

Unfortunately the incompetence of both the military and naval commanders, together with the mutual jealousies that quickly developed, meant that it was not possible to achieve any of these objectives. Fearing to return to England without some alternative prize, the commanders turned their attention to Jamaica which was understood to be lightly defended and, at this time, had a population including whites and slaves of only 3,000.[4] Early in May 1635 a landing was made and the Spanish were obliged to withdraw. They were soon to capitulate, so the invasion marked the end of 165 years of Spanish rule. Their former slaves, however, who became known as the *Maroons*, continued to resist, and it was a further five years before the island was completely in British hands. Even then the *Maroons* were to cause constant trouble for many years to come.[5]

The island acquired as a kind of afterthought proved to measure 144 miles by 50 miles and its 4,200 square miles enjoyed a pleasant climate. Although the lowlands near the coast tend to be warm and humid, the higher ground is extremely mild and equable. At first the British were no more successful than the Spanish in developing Jamaica, but after it had been given a constitution in 1661 and British title had been confirmed by the Treaty of Madrid in 1670 its affairs began to improve. A first step came with the removal of the buccaneers who had made Jamaica their home, and the stage was then set for an era of great prosperity. This lasted throughout the eighteenth century and was based on the export of many crops including sugar, coffee, cocoa, pimento, ginger and indigo. The use of slaves was an essential part of this production, and after they had been emancipated in 1834 major financial difficulties arose. These were made worse by the removal of the differential duty on foreign sugar so that the price to the grower fell by 50 per cent.

These events led to a period of low economic activity and this was a major factor which led to the outbreak of riots in 1865. Although these were rapidly controlled with the aid of martial law, it was not until 1884 when a new constitution was granted that the situation completely returned to normal. In the intervening decades the development of fruit exports, including the beginning of the North American banana trade mentioned earlier,[6] did something to offset the poor performance of the sugar industry.

The banana and the plantain had, of course, played an important role in the economy of Jamaica since they were first introduced by Spanish settlers in the sixteenth century. Both were quickly adopted as subsistence crops by the Europeans and their slaves and from an early date any surplus would be offered for sale at local markets. The type of banana which was grown at that time was an unimproved variety that was undoubtedly very similar to that first introduced by Father Tomas de

Berlanga in 1516.[7] The potential for the export of this particular kind of fruit may well have been extremely limited, even when transport and marketing facilities became available. Fortunately an innovation of the 1800s was to ensure that a much more resilient banana was being widely cultivated when exports to the United States became feasible in the 1870s:

The *Gros Michel* banana originated in the Americas. It was the product of a graft from parent stocks of Old World origin. It was introduced into Jamaica about 1836 by Jean Francois Pouyat, a French botanist and chemist who owned a plantation, 'Belle Air', in St Andrew. On his return from a visit to Martinique, Pouyat planted the rhizomes of this banana on his estate. At first known as the 'Banana-Pouyat', it was later renamed the *'Martinique'* and, still later, the *'Gros Michel'*. It is quite likely that the tens of millions of banana plants now cultivated in Jamaica, Central America, and elsewhere around the Caribbean, came originally from this single plant of M. Pouyat.[8]

As a result of the pioneering work of Captain George Busch and, particularly, of the enterprise of Captan Dow Baker[9] Jamaica's fruit exports to the United States were valued at £124,000 in 1882.[10] In his report for 1883, Daniel Morris, Director of Public Gardens and Plantations in Jamaica, noted the rapid progress being made in the export of bananas:

... This is the most extensive and most valuable fruit interest in the island. The exports for 1883 were 937,951 bunches (sic, 'stems') of the value of £93,795 which is more than six times the number and value of those for 1877 ...
As the bananas are utilized in many cases as nurse-plants for cacao, nutmegs, oranges, Liberian coffee, cinnamon, coconuts, cardamoms and rubber yielding plants, the banana culture is leading to numerous permanent cultivations, which will remain after the bananas have died out. In this respect, it is the means of permanently reclaiming extensive areas which hitherto had been utterly neglected.[11]

The continued decline in the export of sugar, which fell from providing 31.6 per cent in 1875–76 to 15.9 per cent in 1885–86 and to only 11 per cent of the total in 1895–96 increased the pressure to promote other industries.[12] Fruit was, of course, a valuable alternative, and by the mid-1890s bananas alone were providing 20 per cent of all Jamaica's exports.[13] This was almost all being handled by the Boston Fruit Company[14] and, although the trade was steadily growing, there were a number of reasons for disquiet. It was felt that the very strong

81

position occupied by the one, large, producer and buyer enabled it to effectively control the terms of sale.[15] This was undoubtedly true, but the underlying reason for the moderate prices received by Jamaican growers was that better quality bananas were being produced in Central America and in Colombia where costs were extremely low.[16] However, this situation then gave rise to worries that the Boston Fruit Company might decide to concentrate its operations elsewhere. On both counts, therefore, it was widely believed that an additional outlet for the island's fruit would be extremely beneficial.

These fears came to a head during the summer of 1898. It became known at that time that the Boston Fruit Company had purchased large tracts of land in Cuba and it was rumoured that this would soon be used to cultivate large quantities of bananas. As the shipments of the Jamaica Fruit Importing and Trading Company had come to an end and showed no signs of resuming, this seemed to indicate that the future of the Jamaican banana industry was in real danger. This assumption led Bishop Gordon, the Roman Catholic Bishop of Jamaica, to visit London where he was able to discuss the situation with the Colonial Secretary, Joseph Chamberlain. During this meeting he pointed out that as Cuba was twenty-four hours nearer to New York and Boston it was inevitable that Jamaica must suffer. The Bishop therefore asked if Mr Chamberlain would use his good offices to see if it would be possible to develop an alternative market in Britain to cater for the surplus which he thought would quickly emerge.[17]

Although originally a 'free-trader', Joseph Chamberlain had gradually been converted to the ideas of 'constructive imperialism'. This meant that he became convinced of the need for stronger economic links between Britain and her colonies and believed that if the Empire's resources could be fully developed this would be greatly beneficial for the welfare of all its inhabitants.[18] Consequently he was extremely sympathetic to Bishop Gordon's request and, as a first step, turned to his old friend Alfred Jones. Jones was an obvious choice because of his previous experience in the importation of Canary Island bananas, and was also well known to the Colonial Secretary for his work in the development of West Africa.[19] Jones immediately agreed to investigate the matter fully and after further discussions with Mr Chamberlain it was agreed that Mr A. H. Stockley should visit Jamaica and produce a report.

Arthur Stockley travelled to Jamaica in September 1898, and quickly discovered that the Boston Fruit Company did indeed occupy an enormously important position on the island. He also found that Bishop Gordon had greatly exaggerated the dangers of Cuban competition and that it was unlikely that this would have a major impact on Jamaican fruit exports to North America. During his stay, which lasted for over eight weeks, Stockley was able to learn a considerable amount about the Jamaican banana industry and came to the conclusion that there was little surplus fruit to be had during most of the year. Somewhat to his surprise he found that the employees of the Boston firm were only too pleased to help him, and with their co-operation he was able to follow the path of a cargo from beginning to end:

> ... It was an entirely different proposition from the handling of our Canary fruit, where the bananas are half the size and each bunch is carefully packed in a crate. The Jamaican variety is carried loose, and packed in railway trucks on land and in bins tightly piled up on end aboard ship. The Gros Michel variety grown in Jamaica and Central America is a much tougher species than the Cavendish from Canary, and can stand far more rough handling.[20]

On his return to England Arthur Stockley informed Alfred Jones that it would be very difficult to establish a viable trade. In his report he pointed out that such a business would be dramatically different from their existing one with the Canaries: the distance was very much greater and special ships fitted with some form of cooling would have to be provided. In addition there was no way of knowing how the public would react to the new, much larger, variety of banana. The uncertainty of assessing the level of supplies which could be attracted at existing prices was the final factor which then led Mr Stockley to conclude that the venture was too hazardous to be undertaken.

Alfred Jones accepted Stockley's recommendation and it was decided that Elder Dempster's Fruit Department should just continue with their highly profitable importation of Canary Island bananas. This implied that they would forego the potentially larger, but more risky, returns which the shipment of Jamaican fruit would have entailed. At a slightly later stage Jones confirmed to Stockley his view that they had adopted the right course of action (see Fig. 6.2).[21]

Alfred Jones's decision was received with dismay by Joseph Chamberlain who remained convinced that an alternative outlet for Jamaican fruit was essential. He was, therefore, receptive to a proposal made by a Captain Lamont and a Mr Cousins who were partners in the Jamaica Produce Company. This resulted in a contract under which three small steamers were to be built and a fortnightly service to Jamaica operated. The promoters were to be given a subsidy of £20,000 per annum and were to import a minimum of 20,000 stems of bananas each voyage.[22]

Joseph Chamberlain had many reservations about this contract, as he was aware that the partnership did not have a large amount of capital at

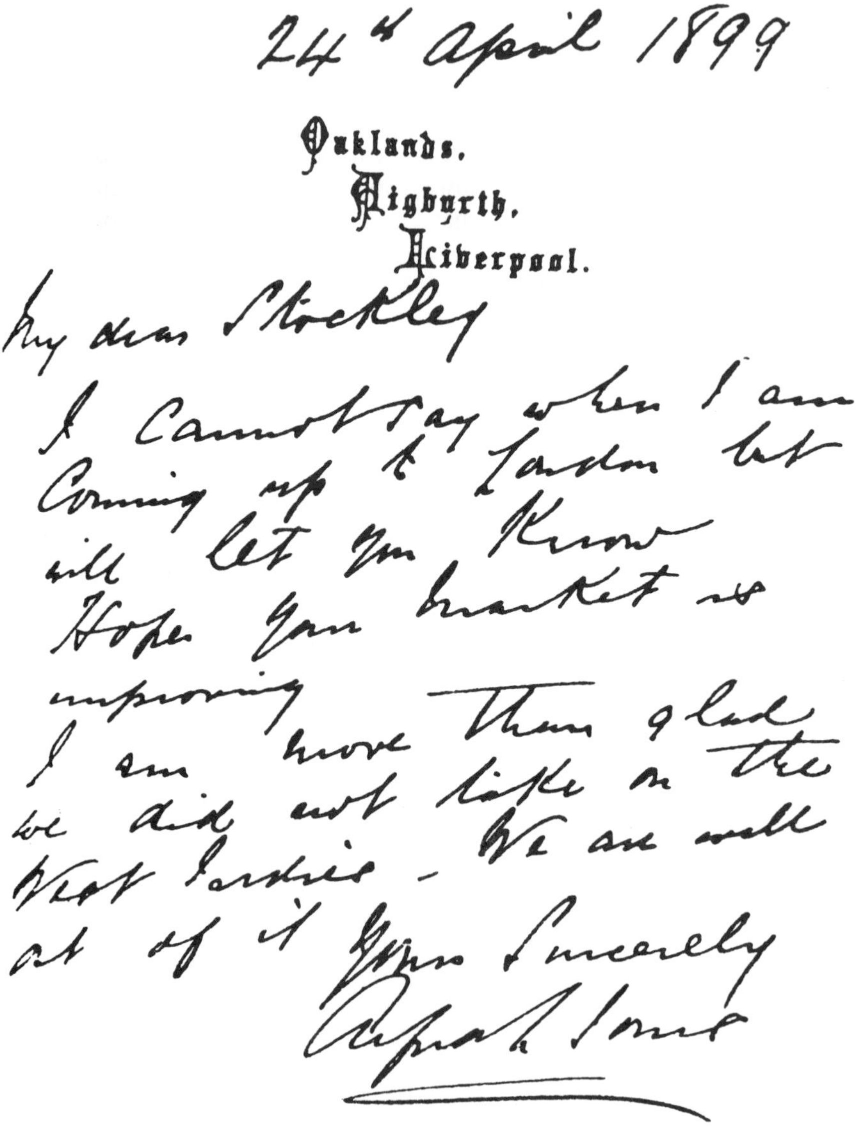

24ᵗʰ April 1899

Oaklands,
Aigburth,
Liverpool.

My dear Stockley

I cannot say when I am
coming up to London but
will let you know
Hope your market is
improving
I am more than glad
we did not take on the
West Indies - We are well
at of it Yours Sincerely
Alfred Jones

Fig. 6.2   Alfred L. Jones letter

their disposal.[23] His premonition was to prove well founded, for although the Jamaica Produce Company ordered the three ships and paid the necessary deposits it was subsequently unable to pay the instalments on them as they became due. This placed the Colonial Secretary in a considerable dilemma, and in the absence of any other alternative he was obliged to approach Alfred Jones for a second time.[24] Accordingly he invited the Elder Dempster chief to his home at

'Highbury' in Birmingham on 26 December 1899 when the following conversation is reported to have taken place:

Chamberlain: Oh, Mr Jones, I want to see if you can help me out of a somewhat disagreeable business. The man I trusted to take on my Jamaica contract has let me down. Now, you have done so much for West Africa and the Empire that I feel sure you will reconsider your decision of a year ago and come to my help. I will see that you shall be met in every possible way as regards the contract, and the only condition which I must make is that you take the two ships now in frame off the builders' hands.

Jones: It is a matter I shall have to think over and consider very carefully; what subsidy were you to pay for the fortnighly service?

Chamberlain: £20,000 per annum.

Jones: I certainly could not think of accepting that amount, and I should say offhand that £60,000 would be the very least the service could be run for; you must remember the great risk that the proposed market for the fruit might not materialise, and in that case the whole thing would mean heavy loss.

Chamberlain: I certainly must ask you to go further into the figures, as £60,000 is far more than I can ask to be granted. I can, however promise you that should this service be started early in 1901, I could then see that your patriotic action was rewarded, and I hope that will be some inducement to you.[25]

The appeal to Jones's patriotism and the suggestion that he would be suitably rewarded then persuaded him to take a fresh look at Chamberlain's proposal. Later events suggest that Jones quickly made up his mind to proceed. A mutually acceptable scheme, based on the earlier negotiations,[26] was then produced so rapidly that it placed the Colonial Secretary in some difficulty:

... Now Mr Jones has returned to the charge and has offered us a contract involving a smaller subsidy (speaking without the book I think it is £40,000 a year but am not certain) which gives us most of what we want although it is less comprehensive than the original contract. Mr Jones insists on an immediate reply failing which the ships attributed to the service will again be diverted. I have asked the Governor of Jamaica to agree to pay half the subsidy. The balance must be found by the Imperial Exchequer and, as I have already said, will be less than the amount (£52,000 p.a.) to which you previously gave your consent.

> I regard some arrangement of this kind as absolutely essential if Jamaica is to be preserved from bankruptcy. I am convinced that the fruit trade is the only salvation for the colony unless we are prepared to countervail the (sugar) bounties. The matter is one of life and death ...[27]

The contract agreed in such haste between Jones and Chamberlain provided for an annual subsidy of £40,000 to be paid for a ten-year period. In return, Jones undertook to establish a new company which was to acquire two of the vessels which had been ordered but not paid for by Captain Lamont's Jamaica Produce Company. These, together with other vessels, were then to be used to provide a fortnightly direct service from Jamaica to the UK, and not less than 20,000 bunches of bananas were to be carried on each voyage. In addition each ship was to have the capacity to carry 100 first-class and 50 second-class passengers. Chamberlain had asked that a freight rate of 2s. a bunch would be charged, but when Jones pointed out that this was the cost of shipping bananas from the Canaries a rate of 2s.6d. was agreed. Jones also found that a proposal return fare of £30 for first-class passengers was too low and this was later settled at £40.

As a result of these arrangements the Imperial Direct West India Mail Service Company came into being almost immediately, although the firm was not to achieve 'limited' status until the following year.[28] From the first it was envisaged as an entirely Elder Dempster subsidiary, and this was confirmed when details of its shareholders were revealed when the company was officially established in December 1901. These showed that Alfred Jones had the largest interest with over 18,000 of the 25,000 shares that were issued, and this was a pattern which was to continue for the whole life of the enterprise.[29] However, although Jones was the prime mover in these events, it was Arthur Stockley who undertook the task of bringing the new firm into operation. He quickly found that this presented a number of problems of which those concerning the 'Lamont' ships were the most pressing. Basically these were too small, and although Stockley was able to have both lengthened by 30 feet the resulting *Port Morant* and *Port Maria* of 2,830 and 2,910 gross tons were never large enough for the trade.

On the credit side both vessels had the virtue of an excellent turn of speed and their 15 knots was quite sufficient to maintain the proposed schedule. Unfortunately it was soon discovered that no provision had been made for cooling their cargoes. Stockley was therefore obliged to break this news to Jones who had not given this matter any previous consideration. Jones:

86

... was no man for details, and was accustomed to taking chances, and his first shock came about March (1900) when I took the manager of J. and E. Hall's of Dartford to see him about the necessary refrigeration plant and fans for the carriage of the bananas. I had been very worried about how we were to get over that difficulty, when I luckily heard that there was at Tilbury one of the White Star ships fitted with a cool-air system for the carriage of apples from Australia. I went over the ship, and found that it embodied the very thing we wanted. I may say that the cool-air plan proved quite successful and since then the United Fruit Company and Elders and Fyffes must have fitted well over a hundred ships with the Hall system.[30]

Although Alfred Jones claimed that he had never been told that it would be necessary to undertake the heavy expense of artificial cooling and had thought that the fruit would be carried under natural ventilation as in the Canary trade, he quickly accepted the situation. Thus both *Port Morant* and *Port Maria* were equipped with Hall's machinery, and when Jones introduced *Port Royal* and *Port Antonio* into the service later in 1901 they too employed the same cooling system.[31] Had Arthur Stockley not been so knowledgeable and so well advised it is possible that some other method of cooling would have been adopted and this might have had disastrous consequences. It should be appreciated that by this time the carriage of both chilled and frozen meat and of many kinds of fruit, utilizing various types of cooling, were all well established, but the shipment of large quantities of bananas over long distances remained to be demonstrated. The experimental nature and dangers of attempts to carry bananas across the Atlantic are well illustrated by the case of the Royal Mail steamer *Para* which left Jacmel in Haiti on 20 November 1901:

... The ship's after hold had been fitted out as an hermetically sealed chamber for the carriage of fruit in accordance with the plan of an American inventor, a Mr. Lawton. Lawton had discovered that fruit breathed and if kept at a fixed temperature in a hold filled with carbon-dioxide gas, it would remain in the same condition for a considerable period of time.[32]

On this particular voyage the hold was partly filled with bananas and *Para* set out for London with Mr Lawton and two of his colleagues on board. For several days all went well but then, just after the first-class passengers had finished their evening meal and had left the saloon, a terrible accident took place:

Mr. Lawton and his engineers were seen to go down with their instruments to test the gas in the chamber and shortly afterwards there was an awful explosion which lifted the ship so far out of the water that that the propeller began to race although the sea at the time was perfectly calm. A hole was blow up through the first-class saloon and poop deck at least twenty feet long and ten feet wide. Not one single bunch of bananas was left in the chamber and, what was more surprising, not one pitched on the ship. The silicate of cotton forming the insulation was blown far and wide, and hung on the masts and shrouds like snow.[33]

Mr Lawton and his two assistants were killed instantly but, miraculously, the passengers and crew of *Para* escaped with only minor cuts and bruises and the vessel itself was able to reach port safely. As by the time of this accident the vessels of the Imperial Direct West India Mail Service Company were already delivering bananas in good condition on a regular basis, so Alfred Jones could, perhaps, be excused for being grateful that Arthur Stockley had secured the help of Messrs J. and E. Hall.

Proof of the efficiency of the Hall system came with the first voyage of *Port Morant*. She sailed from Avonmouth in February 1901 and arrived in Kingston on 1 March. Arthur Stockley was already there, and through his efforts a substantial return cargo was waiting to be loaded. His task had been eased by the fact that it was a low-price month for bananas destined for North America, so all of the growers with whom he had arranged contracts were happy to supply their fruit to *Elder Dempster* at the slightly higher rate which had been previously agreed. As will be seen later,[34] when American prices rose during the summer months it was much more difficult to persuade the producers to fulfil their contracts.[35] However, when the bananas came to be taken on board it was found that 2,000 stems were unsuitable for shipment, and as replacements were not immediately available the cargo was smaller than had originally been planned. Nevertheless:

The *Port Morant* returned to Avonmouth on 18 March, with 18,000 stems of bananas, a quantity of oranges, mangoes and pineapples, 250 puncheons of rum and 160 tons of sugar. Had Alfred Jones been superstitious he might not have viewed the auguries of that arrival with much pleasure, for a bitter north-east gale caused the ship to miss the morning tide, and kept a number of spectators waiting from five-thirty in the morning until docking was effected at four in the afternoon. When at last the ship could be inspected it was seen that she bore many signs of a rough passage and it transpired that one of the crew had suffered a broken leg and that several other officers and men had been injured. Nevertheless a band struck up *Under the British Flag* and, amid a scene of some chaos owing to the uncontrolled presence of spectators, 35 passengers and 14 bags of mail were escorted to the uncompleted passenger terminal nearby. The train pulled away at last to the strains of the National Anthem.[36]

The following morning Arthur Stockley announced that the bananas were in excellent condition after their thirteen-day voyage. As 2,500 of the stems were approaching ripeness they were quickly disposed of locally while the remainder were packed in straw and loaded onto railway wagons for onward transmission. These were not heated so there was considerable fear that the fruit would be damaged by the cold. That this did not happen was no thanks to the railway companies, who lacked confidence that the trade would provide a large and regular item of freight and so failed to supply the type of wagon that was needed. In spite of this difficulty it was later reported that more than forty towns had shared this first cargo, and on all counts it was regarded as a great success.[37]

This first voyage was quickly repeated by *Port Morant* and in April 1901 she was joined on the route by her sister ship *Port Maria*. As both had been lengthened during their construction they were able to cater for the quantities of bananas per voyage laid down by the government contract. It had not, however, been possible to enlarge them sufficiently so as to provide the amount of accommodation which the agreement required. Accordingly the contract was modified so that these two early ships only needed to carry 40 first-class and 15 second-class passengers. This was a temporary measure which would have also covered*Port Royal* and *Port Antonio*, but when they entered the service later in 1901 they were each capable of accommodating the 100 first and 50 second-class passengers called for in the original agreement.[38] Both of these vessels were of 4,450 gross tons so had ample capacity for the 20,000 stems of bananas which were officially required; in addition they had a considerable amount of extra space to cope with other anticipated cargoes.

From the foregoing it is clear that sufficient tonnage had been made available so that a fortnightly service could be maintained. In fact twenty-three round voyages were completed in the period from mid-February to the end of December 1901, and as the bananas were generally delivered in a sound condition it could be rightly assumed that the maritime transport problem had been largely solved. Unfortunately this did not necessarily mean that the way was now open for a massive expansion of imports into Britain and the automatic relief of Jamaica's economic ills. Stockley found that it was increasingly hard to obtain the appropriate quantities of fruit at moderate costs throughout the year, for the grower was inevitably influenced by the level of American prices. At the same time it had become apparent that the marketing of Jamaican bananas required very different treatment than that used to sell the Canary variety. These considerations led Arthur Stockley to the conclusion that the amalgamation movement which had led to the creation of the United Fruit Company in the United States during 1899 should be repeated in the United Kingdom. While appreciating the enormity of this task which would involve a complete reorganization of the British banana industry, Stockley felt it was the only way in which progress could be made. Accordingly, much against the wishes of Sir Alfred Jones,[39] he began the moves that were ultimately to result in the formation of Elders and Fyffes Limited.

7

The formation of Elders and Fyffes, Limited

The decision of Alfred Jones to establish coaling depots at Puerto de la Luz and at Santa Cruz de Tenerife and the chance visit of Edward Wathen Fyffe to the Canaries resulted, as we have seen, in the development of commercial imports of bananas into the UK. In so doing they had transformed the trade from one which was extremely spasmodic and conducted on an entirely *ad hoc* basis to one which increasingly provided regular supplies to, first, Liverpool, and then to the London area.

Alfred Jones's original intention was to fill any empty spaces on his ships when they called for bunkers in the Canary Islands, and the fact that bananas proved to be such a profitable cargo was something of a surprise. As ship-operators, his Elder Dempster lines would naturally have expected to earn a profit on any items that were carried (or at least anticipated that they would make a contribution to the costs of the voyage). In the case of the banana, however, as they were acting as principals and they owned as well as carried the fruit, they undertook all the risks and in turn retained all the profits. The potential of this business quickly became obvious to Jones, but before it could really flourish a number of serious problems had to be overcome.

The initial difficulty of ocean carriage was rapidly solved on the relatively short route from the Canaries to Liverpool by the introduction of steam vessels and by the gradual acquisition of experience in the selection and handling of the fruit. The marketing of the bananas also created early problems, but once the fruit became familiar to local merchants this soon disappeared. Thus the original reliance upon 'barrow-boys' was ended and Elder Dempster then disposed of most of their cargoes by auction. By 1890 six firms of brokers were concerned with this side of the business in Liverpool (Messrs James Adam, Son and Company; J. C. Houghton and Company; Woodall and Company;

L. Connolly and Company; McGeorge and Jardine; and Messrs Edgecome, Rogers and Company).[1] These firms, based in Queen Square in the centre of the city, operated through the Stanley Street saleroom which had been opened in 1878.

The auctions were held three times a week from 10 a.m. to 6 p.m. with each broker being given two forty-minute periods to sell his wares. Samples of the wide range of varieties and types on offer were then displayed, and once a sale was agreed the fruit was collected from either the warehouse or the quayside. (Liverpool did not follow the London rule that all fruit must be moved from the ship into a warehouse before it could be collected.) Any consignments which remained unsold after the close of business would then be obliged to wait for the next auction. If this was impracticable because of the degree of ripeness, then the necessary quantities would be disposed of 'after hours' to the large numbers of small traders, shopkeepers and costermongers who relished such opportunities. As Elder Dempster were quite content at this stage to undertake nothing but the carriage and discharge of their fruit, and exercised little control over quality, substantial amounts of over-ripe – hence, cheap – supplies of bananas were frequently available.

This system ensured that all of the bananas imported into Liverpool were quickly sold with little effort on the part of the shipowners. The banana thus gradually became more and more known on Merseyside, but as demand from the surrounding north-west region steadily increased a further problem tended to emerge. This concerned the supply of the fruit, for although Canary Island exports rose from an estimated 45,000 bunches in 1885 to over 1,500,000 bunches in 1901[2] this was never sufficient to satisfy the potential market. It was partly because of this shortage that Elder Dempster were never tempted to cater for the lucrative London market, even though this would have been technically possible by utilizing rail from Liverpool.

The absence of a major banana importer to service the capital was then to provide Edward Wathen Fyffe with a relatively easy opportunity to fill this particular niche. There were, however, a number of significant differences between the Liverpool and London operations. Unlike Elder Dempster, Fyffe was obliged to rely upon whatever shipping was available to carry his fruit, but the growth in the number of vessels sailing from the Canaries (and Madeira) to London which could carry bananas as deck cargo meant that this was never a serious drawback. A further distinction between the two businesses was that whereas Elder Dempster purchased their fruit from the growers and, later, developed their own plantations, Fyffe merely sold whatever was sent to him by the Canary Islands' syndicate which he represented. As supplies were the key to success in an unsatisfied market Fyffe was able to expand his operations very rapidly, and even Elder Dempster's entry into the London arena in 1892 did little to slow his progress.

Alfred Jones's decision to open a branch of his fruit department in the capital was the result of a number of changing factors. The work of A. H. Stockley had resulted in larger quantities of Canary Island bananas becoming available, and although these could have been absorbed in the 'northern' market the amount of shipping was proving to be a (temporary) limiting aspect. This was because the business had been based on the shipment of the fruit on the decks of Elder Dempster vessels which were already *en route* to Liverpool on their traditional services from West Africa. No special tonnage had been constructed or was contemplated to carry bananas, and the company had not yet adapted any of their existing fleet to cater for the fruit. As the number of vessels employed by Elder Dempster was to rise only at a very slow rate a shortage of deck space gradually evolved, and this situation was only to change with the advent of the more specialized ships which were later provided by such independent operators as the Forwood and Yeoward lines.

In these circumstances the London market, which had always promised great rewards, appeared to be even more attractive and, inspired by Fyffe's example, Elder Dempster decided to follow suit. An increasing quantity of bananas was therefore sent to Covent Garden as shipping space became available, but as these consignments were at first quite small they were easily handled by the company's agents. By 1892, however, the size of this business was such as to require a permanent presence and, as previously noted,[3] Mr Stockley and his friend Mr Ackerley, were then sent to establish a suitable organization. The success of this venture did little to damp down Fyffe's expansion so although Elder Dempster did well there is no doubt that Fyffe's did even better.[4]

Edward Wathen Fyffe's decision to take James Hudson into partnership was an indication of the growing scale of his enterprise. It was, of course, fully justified by the circumstances and Fyffe could not be blamed for the subsequent action of his suppliers when they decided to dispense with his, and his new partner's services. The resulting transformation of Messrs Fyffe, Hudson and Company (which was legally a partnership) to Fyffe, Hudson and Company Limited,[5] with Richard Blandy, Henry Wolfson, John Leacock and Edward Barker (the former 'growers' syndicate) as its major shareholders then significantly altered the structure of the firm, but made no difference to its operations. Thus Elder Dempster and Fyffe Hudson continued to share the London market and both were certainly alarmed, and then relieved, by the activities and subsequent failure of the Jamaica Fruit Importing and

Trading Company.[6] Both were also equally dependent upon the Canary Islands and (to a small extent) Madeira for their supplies of fruit, so the extent of their trade can be estimated by an examination of the statistics in Table 7.1. Unfortunately these details relate to Canary *exports* and, although it is certain that Britain was the Islands' principal market at this time, it is not clear that all of these items were imported into the UK. The values quoted are at the port of shipment, so bear only a small relationship to their impact on the British market.

TABLE 7.1 CANARY ISLANDS' EXPORTS OF PRODUCE IN 1900[7]

Port	Produce	Quantity	Value
Tenerife:	Tomatoes	5,050 tons	£44,864
	Bananas	204,917 bunches	£20,490
La Palma:	Tomatoes	137 tons	
	Bananas	20,000 bunches	
	Onions	2,313 tons	
Las Palmas:	Tomatoes	138,709 boxes	£17,338
	Bananas	929,235 crates	£174,892
	Potatoes	34,039 cases	£5,318
	Oranges	10,700 boxes	£2,340

Of greater significance for the present study are the official British statistics, which include bananas for the first time in the report for 1900.[8] (Prior to this date bananas, currants, gooseberries and strawberries were lumped together with 'fruit, unenumerated, raw'.) This shows that a total of 1,287,442 bunches valued at £548,956 were imported from all sources during this year.

TABLE 7.2 BANANA IMPORTATIONS FOR THE YEAR 1900[9]

From	Bunches	Value (£)
Madeira	41,981	19,283
Canary Islands	1,243,562	528,540
Other countries	544	256
British West Indies	1,337	874
Other British possessions	18	3
Total	1,287,442	548,956

As the vast majority of these bunches would have been handled by either Elder Dempster or Fyffe Hudson, the scale of the banana industry can be judged with reasonable accuracy. The figures demonstrate quite clearly that the importation of bananas had made enormous

In the Canary Islands, camels
were frequently used to carry
bananas to the nearest harbour.

Small boats were used to carry
the crates out to the ocean-going
ships: this scene is at Puerto de
la Cruz, Tenerife.

Foredeck load of banana crates
crossing the Bay of Biscay.

s.s. Appomattox, the first vessel acquired by Elders
& Fyffes.

s.s. Port Morant, of the Imperial Direct Line, carrying the first commercial
cargo of bananas from Jamaica, 1901.

The first Jamaican banana cargo being loaded on board s.s. Port Morant
in Kingston, Jamaica in March 1901. Mr Stockley is third from the left.

The cellar at Neal Street showing hanging banana stems, ex Jamaica, c. 1905.

Canary Island bananas being housed at Bow Street. Note the continuing use of crates to protect this delicate variety of fruit.

Elders & Fyffes' head office in Bow Street, London WC1, c. 1940.

strides since its inception on a commercial basis in the mid-1880s. Equally, however, they show that the business was still in its infancy and that apart from the immediate hinterlands of Liverpool and London the banana remained an exotic item that was only rarely, and expensively, available.

Alfred Jones's rather lighthearted agreement to commence the importation of bananas from Jamaica promised to dramatically change this situation, for it should be appreciated that as no change in Canary shipments was envisaged this fruit would be a large, net, addition to the total. As the contract called for a minimum of 20,000 bunches (stems) to be brought into the country each fortnight, this presupposed that at least an additional half-million 'bunches' per annum would need to be marketed. This was an aspect of the business which had concerned Arthur Stockley from an early stage. Although originally convinced that the importation of bananas from Jamaica was impracticable, once Elder Dempster were committed he threw all his energies into making the enterprise a success. Thus as soon as the arrangements for the carriage of the fruit had been finalized he turned his attention as to how it was to be disposed of in the UK.

Stockley quickly came to the conclusion that what was required was a large, integrated, importing, handling and distributing organization. With this in mind he approached E. C. Barker and Henry Wolfson whom he had known well during his time in the Canary Islands but who were now major shareholders and actively in control of Messrs Fyffe, Hudson and Company, Limited. Both were favourably inclined for they could see that the Jamaican trade offered great rewards if the difficulties of production, carriage and marketing could be overcome. Like Stockley, they also appreciated that this potential could only be achieved if the operation could be organized on a large scale. His proposal that Elder Dempster's fruit business should be merged with their own to form a separate company that would be entirely distinct from Alfred Jones's shipping interest was therefore provisionally accepted. However, as Stockley was due to travel to the West Indies to inaugurate the new service, it was agreed that a final decision would be delayed until his return. Meanwhile it was thought wise to keep these negotiations secret from Jones, for although it was envisaged that an arrangement would be made for him to provide the necessary tonnage it was understood that he would not welcome these suggestions for what amounted to a total reorganization of the British banana industry.

The ease with which Stockley, Barker and Wolfson reached agreement was partly because of their awareness of recent amalgamations in North America. As noted earlier, the joining of the interests of the Boston Fruit Company (itself a merger) with those of Minor Cooper

Keith had resulted in the formation of the United Fruit Company in 1899.[10] An extract from the firm's first annual report published on 31 August 1900 shows the size of the resources which this amalgamation had brought together. It then:

> ... owned 212,394 acres of land in Costa Rica, Cuba, Honduras, Jamaica, San Domingo and Colombia. It had leased lands in Costa Rica and Jamaica to the extent of 23,807 acres, making its total holdings 236,201 acres. Of this area 66,294 were under cultivation of some sort, and 169,907 acres were unimproved. Much of this unimproved land was unfitted for cultivation, and belonged to tracts which had to be purchased intact in order to secure an acreage suitable for bananas or other purposes. All save a small portion of the lands then owned by the United Fruit Company had been acquired by purchase from the Boston Fruit Company and from the interests headed by Minor C. Keith.

The company had 38,463 acres planted to bananas, as is shown in the following table which is of interest as showing the agricultural resources of the enterprise in its initial year of operation:[11]

STATEMENT SHOWING THE LOCATION AND THE ACREAGE OF THE UNITED FRUIT COMPANY'S FRUIT, SUGAR CANE, AND MISCELLANEOUS CULTIVATIONS, AUGUST 31, 1900
Location and acreage

Description	Costa Rica	Cuba	Honduras	Jamaica	San Domingo	Colombia	Total
Fruit:							
Bananas	10,626	5,841	400	5,749	3,300	12,574	38,463
Oranges				315			315
Pineapples				17			17
Sugar Cane		7,803					7,803
Miscellaneous:							
Cocoanuts				1,830		12	1,842
Coffee	46			10		2	58
Cocoa				115		140	255
Rubber	65			79		163	307
Para Grass	2,380					78	2,458
Guinea Grass	3,417						3,417
Vegetables						12	12
Other lands	3,276	3,539	100	4,151	200	81	11,347
Total Acreage	19,810	17,183	500	12,266	3,500	13,035	66,294

United Fruit's first annual report also showed that its tropical investments were conservatively valued at nearly $17 million.[12] These assets enabled it to supply the American market with approximately eleven million bunches of bananas, and a net profit of US $1,831,815 was achieved.[13] This allowed a 10 per cent dividend to be paid at precisely the time that the British amalgamation was being actively considered by Barker and Wolfson. This demonstration of the advantages of scale and of an integrated production and marketing operation must then have played an important part in persuading them and the other shareholders in Fyffe, Hudson and Company that their future lay in the merger proposed by Arthur Stockley. Thus when Stockley returned to the UK on *Port Morant*'s first voyage in March 1901, agreement was quickly finalized and he then had the task of putting the proposal to Alfred Jones.

As anticipated, the head of the Elder Dempster concern was totally opposed to the new arrangement, and it was only after a considerable period of argument and acrimony that he gave the scheme a cautious approval. The reasons for his change of heart are fairly clear. Once he was convinced of Stockley's determination to proceed irrespective of the consequences, Jones was obliged to consider his own position. He was, of course, committed to a ten-year contract to provide a shipping service between UK and Jamaica, and the viability of this venture depended heavily upon the revenue which was to be generated by the carriage of bananas. Had Fyffe, Hudson and Company (with or without Stockley) decided to set up a rival trade, any chance of keeping the Imperial Direct Line solvent would certainly have disappeared. There was also the possibility that if Fyffe, Hudson were not prepared to act, then Stockley, with the aid of his many contacts in the business, might well have established his own firm which would also have had dire financial results for Jones.

Thus in the final analysis it was the fear that an amalgamation in some form or another was almost bound to emerge to challenge his own precarious trade in Jamaican bananas that persuaded Jones to agree to Stockley's suggestions. It should also be appreciated that his principal interest lay in the British–West African shipping trade, and he could not spare the time to develop the fruit business in the way that was required. Accordingly he accepted what he undoubtedly felt was the lesser of the two evils and this then enabled the new company to be quickly brought into being (see Fig. 7.1).[14]

With the establishment of Elders and Fyffes, Limited, it might be thought that Arthur Stockley had achieved all of his objectives. This was not the case. Jones had certainly been out-manoeuvred by Stockley, in that a separate company had been formed against his wishes and this had now acquired all of Elder Dempster's fruit business. However Jones had extracted a high price for his agreement, and with 70,500 shares

FINANCE NOTES.

ELDERS AND FYFFES (LTD.)—This company was registered on May 9, with a capital of £150,000 in £1 shares, to acquire the fruit and vegetable businesses now carried on by Messrs. Elder, Dempster & Co. and by Messrs. Fyffe, Hudson & Co. (Ltd.), to adopt an agreement with A. L. Jones and W. J. Davey (trading as Elder, Dempster & Co.) and Fyffe, Hudson & Co. (Ltd.), and an agreement between the same parties of the first and second parts, H. Wolfson, J. M. Leacock and E. C. Barker of the third part, A. H. Stockley, R. Ackerley and R. Atcherley of the fourth part, and the company of the fifth part, and to carry on the business of fruit and vegetable growers, buyers, importers and salesmen, shipowners and charterers, fruit merchants, jam, preserve, sauce and pickle manufacturers, freight contractors, forwarding agents, &c. The subscribers are Alfred L. Jones, African House, Liverpool, one share ; William J. Davey, African House, Liverpool, one share ; Henry Wolfson, 9, Bow-street, London, W.C., fruit merchant, one share ; John H. Leacock, 9, Bow-street, W.C., fruit merchant, one share ; A. H. Stockley, 46, Long-acre, W.C., fruit merchant, one share ; Edward C. Barker, 9, Bow-street, W.C., fruit merchant, one share ; and Alfred R. Ackerley, 46, Long-acre, W.C., fruit merchant, one share. There will be no initial public issue. The first directors are A. L. Jones, A. H. Stockley, R. Ackerley, R. Atcherley, H. Wolfson, J. H. Leacock, and E. C. Barker. Qualification £2,000.

Fig. 7.1   Elders and Fyffes Ltd. (Finance Notes)

owned nearly half of the equity of the new firm. As his close friend and partner Mr W. J. Davey held a further 23,493 shares, it is quite clear that the Elder Dempster interest was easily able to dominate the business, so Stockley's aim to be free of Jones's interference had not been accomplished.[15]

Sir Alfred Jones (he was made a Knight Commander of the Order of St Michael and St George in 1901) became the first Chairman of Elders and Fyffes but was quite content to leave Arthur Stockley to run the business. The other directors of the new concern were Barker, Wolfson and J. M. Leacock (all former shareholders in Fyffe, Hudson and Company) and they concentrated upon the Canary Island trade in which they were especially experienced. Mr Robert Atcherley, a fruit merchant, and Roger Ackerley completed the board and these had special responsibility on the marketing and distribution side of the enterprise. Far from Jones interfering in the company's arrangements, he seems at first to have been conspicuous by his absence and he did not attend a statutory board meeting until 18 February 1903. Thereafter he was a regular attender, but this was mainly in connection with attempts to reconcile the interests of the 'A' shareholders (Elder Dempster) with those of the 'B' shareholders (Fyffe, Hudson) than with any real intention of taking an active part in the company's affairs.[16]

The strength of Jones's position as Chairman and principal share-holder in Elders and Fyffes was offset, to a large extent, by his dependence upon the firm to provide the cargoes for the fortnightly sailings of the Imperial Direct Line. While the welfare of both concerns was at this time mutually inter-dependent, and Elders and Fyffes required shipping to carry their bananas, it was Jones who was most vulnerable. This was because under the terms of his contract with the government he was obliged to guarantee that his service was maintained irrespective of whether his ships were full or not, whereas Elders and Fyffes' contract included a clause which stated that if no fruit was available then no freight would be paid.[17] In addition, the early months of Elders and Fyffes' existence were characterized by a whole series of difficulties in both Jamaica and Britain. Thus it is quite probable that Jones, who was involved in the detail of organizing the sailings of his new line as well as being concerned with his numerous other commercial activities, was moderately happy to leave these problems in Stockley's capable hands.

Arthur Stockley's headaches began with the need to secure the bananas to load Jones's ships. Although the minimum requirement of 20,000 stems per fortnight was a relatively small quantity, the need to provide it on a regular basis created many strains. The fruit for *Port Morant*'s first voyage was obtained in accordance with the fixed-price contract which had been arranged with a number of local growers, but this was because March was a low-price month for the American market. It was a different story in May and June, for once demand in the United States rose, the price of bananas in Jamaica quickly exceeded those negotiated with Elders and Fyffes. This was not a problem which could be solved by Stockley in the short term. His success in finding fruit to comply with the government contract was achieved by the use of various temporary expedients, but it was a near thing on many occasions! The domination of the Jamaican growers by American banana firms – particularly the United Fruit Company – meant that Elders and Fyffes were in a permanently difficult situation and could never be sure of regular supplies at what would be a commercially viable price for the UK market. This was not fully realized until a later stage, when much larger quantities of bananas were required. The solution which was then adopted was so fundamental that it was to mark a major turning point in the history of the company.

Elders and Fyffes were also to face very serious problems once their Jamaican bananas reached Britain. This was partly because the fruit was of a very different variety than that previously imported, so required very different handling. The *Musa cavendishii* produced in the Canaries was extremely delicate. It was therefore picked when it was just beginning to mature, carefully packed in open crates and then allowed to ripen naturally on the relatively short six-day voyage to the UK.[18] On arrival in Liverpool or London it was ready for sale, so there was no need for either the importers or their customers to provide any special facilities. On the other hnd the bananas grown in Jamaica (and in Central America) were of the *Gros Michel* variety.[19] These were not only much larger than the *Cavendish* but were also much more hardy and could stand far more knocking about and even a certain amount of cold. Thus while Canary bananas were normally covered by some form of packaging, the Jamaican fruit could be shipped 'naked'. The other major difference in the two trades was that of distance, and the voyage from the West Indies usually took between fourteen and seventeen days. Thus although the cargo was loaded in a 'green' condition it was still necessary to provide artificial cooling so that it arrived in a 'hard' state.[20]

Once the bananas were unloaded and removed from the controlled environment of the ship's hold, the ripening process would begin to accelerate. In practice this meant that most of the cargo would not reach its peak condition for a few days and might well remain saleable for up to a week. Consequently it was no longer necessary for the fruit to be sold as quickly as possible in the hinterland of the port and, as the first shipment of *Port Morant* amply demonstrated, a system of national distribution was quite feasible.[21] At first, however, this was achieved in spite of the indifference of the railway companies and of the lack of proper ripening rooms where the bananas could be hung until they were ready for sale. Arthur Stockley was, of course, aware that the full potential of the national market could only be fulfilled if these restraints were to be removed. However, he also appreciated that the cost of providing a fleet of specialized banana wagons and of a national network of ripening facilities could only be justified if a very high throughput could be maintained. As a result he became increasingly convinced that the fortnightly service supplied by the Imperial Direct Line was not sufficient, and he therefore pressed that weekly arrivals should be introduced.[21]

The difficulties of attracting sufficient supplies of bananas of the right quality at reasonable prices, some minor problems with the ocean carriage, and the early attempts to develop the necessary facilities within the UK all cost a great deal of money. Thus by February 1902 Elders and Fyffes were approaching a liquidity crisis and, as Sir Alfred Jones adamantly refused to provide additional capital, the future of the company was very much in jeopardy. Jones's viewpoint is not hard to understand. In spite of the government's subsidy, the Imperial Direct Line was operating at a substantial loss and, having been manoeuvred by Stockley into agreeing to form what was now proving to be an unprofitable separate concern, he was heartily sick of the whole business. Both Wolfson and Barker were also disillusioned with the enterprise, but their friendship with Stockley and Ackerley ensured, for the present at least, that they would continue to maintain their support. In these circumstances the company was only able to operate at a moderate level and it was certain that it could not remain viable unless some new initiative was forthcoming.

The solution to these problems was very obvious to Arthur Stockley. Larger quantities of fruit would be part of the answer and if they could be phased so that the existing (and envisaged) facilities could be more fully utilised a much greater return on capital could be expected. Assuming that some arrangement could be made to ensure regular supplies of bananas throughout the year, this meant that additional shipping services would be the key to survival and ultimate success. But how was this to be brought about if Alfred Jones wished to reduce, rather than extend, his investment in an enterprise in which he had no confidence?

... I suddenly thought of one alternative – to try to form a subsidiary shipping company, to beg or borrow enough, to charter three ships, fit them with Hall's system, and approach the United Fruit Company to come to our assistance as soon as we could start the fresh tonnage to

Jamaica. I wonder how many men I interviewed regarding this scheme? When they heard that our chairman, A. L. Jones, would have nothing to do with it, and that we actually had the foolhardiness to contemplate sending ships out to the West Indies in ballast to load a cargo of bananas home, they smiled and turned me down flat. But luck at the last moment came our way: at that time the shipping trade was dead, and I met a man who knew that the Furness Line had three cargo-ships running to the U.S.A., in connection with some railway business there, which they were anxious to get rid of (and when I remember the condition they were in I don't wonder). These ships were just the right size, and had a fair speed – namely 12 knots. We managed to raise £60,000, and secured the ships – I think it was for £40,000 each of which the greater part was left on mortage ...

The three ships concerned (and a fourth which was acquired later in 1902) were the *Appomattox, Chickahominy, Greenbrier I* and *Oracabessa*. All were of approximately 3,300 to 3,400 gross tons and were about eight or nine years old.[23] A new company, Elders and Fyffes (Shipping), Limited, was set up in April 1902 to own and manage these vessels. A majority of the shares in this firm were held by Elders and Fyffes or its shareholders on a personal basis but, significantly, none were taken up by Alfred Jones.[24] This shipping line remained in existence until 1907, by which time it was a fully owned subsidiary of Elders and Fyffes and was then incorporated within the parent company.

Once these ships had been acquired it was necessary to adapt them from general dry-cargo vessels to specialized banana carriers. The firm of J. and E. Hall, Limited, of Dartford, who had supplied the refrigerating machinery for the Imperial Direct Line, were entrusted with this task and duly installed their CO_2 cooled air system. This had already proved to be extremely successful in the 'Port' vessels and was to continue to be so in the many Elders and Fyffes' vessels in which it was subsequently to be fitted.[25] The system was also to be adopted by the United Fruit Company. However, as the original apparatus was rather bulky and took up to a fifth of the available cargo space, experiments were made in order to reduce this wastage. A chartered vessel, *Venus*, was chosen for this purpose and after a number of disappointments successfully carried a full cargo from Port Limon to New Orleans with less than 2 per cent of 'ripes'. This achievement was followed by the ordering of three new vessels from Messrs Workman Clark of Belfast – all of which were fully refrigerated – and these were then to form the nucleus of the 'Great White Fleet'.[26] By 1908 Hall's system was claimed to be in use in over seventy ships that were either owned or chartered by the United Fruit Company.[27]

102

Having secured the ships with which to provide the kind of service which he felt would solve one major problem, Arthur Stockley set out for Boston in May 1902, hoping to resolve another. Arriving un-announced he found A. W. Preston, President of the United Fruit Company, in a receptive mood and within a week a tentative agreement had been reached. Under this arrangement the UFC was to buy a half-share in Elders and Fyffes and in return was to guarantee to provide full cargoes of bananas as required. Although this provisional plan could not be confirmed until it was approved by Alfred Jones, Preston agreed to assist in the loading of *Chickahominy*. A cargo of 50,000 stems was then placed on board, and after a twelve-day voyage the vessel arrived at Manchester where it had been decided to base the new service.

Arthur Stockley then assumed that these arrangements had placed the company on an entirely new and viable basis. In fact he still had to overcome the opposition of his Chairman, for Alfred Jones

> ... saw the matter in a different light altogether. He took objection to the whole scheme, although it was clear that unless new blood was infused at once, Elders and Fyffes would be completely bankrupt. But A. L. Jones was a shipowner first and foremost, and he did not really worry a rap about Elders and Fyffes troubles, and was quite prepared for a split up. Wolfson and Barker, on the Fyffe side, could go back to their Canary Islands business, and he would make the best of his Jamaican Line for the balance of the ten years; he strongly objected, and had done so from the start of our venture in ships, to Elders and Fyffes owning their own vessels. We wrangled and fought over the matter until I quite expected that Preston would give up the idea. However, after much patience and persuasion on our part, our chairman gave in, and when he died in 1909 his shares in Elders and Fyffes, which were quite valueless in 1902, were worth £450,000 ...[28]

It later transpired that Preston was so amenable at this particular time because the rapid growth of production in Costa Rica meant that the United Fruit Company was, at least temporarily, over-supplied with bananas. Thus the development of a new, albeit small, outlet was a positive benefit: it is also clear that the opportunity to establish an interest in a potentially powerful rival in Jamaica was another considera-tion which undoubtedly influenced Preston's actions. With both sides seeing advantages, and the opposition of Jones finally overcome, it only remained for the details to be settled before, in August 1902, the 'American Agreement' was duly signed. Jones's arguments had, how-ever, had one important consequence. Instead of Preston purchasing 50 per cent of Elders and Fyffes, he was obliged to settle for only 45 per cent. Technically, therefore, the company remained under British control, but in practice the United Fruit Company were in such a strong position that future decisions could only be made with their approval. It was against this background that the British banana market was to expand at a tremendous pace during the next decade.

8

The establishment of a national market

The signing of the 'American Agreement' with the United Fruit Company in August 1902 was to mark the beginning of a new era for Messrs Elders and Fyffes, Limited. For the first time it did not have to worry about the procurement of its fruit in Jamaica, for the arrangement covered the shipments required by the Imperial Direct line as well as those for the vessels operated by Elders and Fyffes (Shipping), Limited. This policy, however advantageous to the company, was severely criticized (and defended) by many in both Jamaica and Britain. This was because the ten-year subsidy of the Imperial Direct Line (half of which was supplied by the colonial government) was granted in order to secure certain objectives. The prime aim was to ensure a fresh outlet for Jamaican bananas (and other fruit) and thus lessen the growers' dependence upon what was regarded as a potentially uncertain market in the United States. A secondary aim, which was not stated but which may have been implied and was certainly assumed by many in the colony, was to help reduce the dominance of the UFC in the Jamaican economy:

... One reason why Jamaica agreed to the Elder Dempster contract was the understanding that besides developing the English fruit trade it would end the monopoly then held by the United Fruit Company. This company, however, which was already exporting millions of bananas to America, and was also to some extent, a competitor for the English trade, was approached with the view of its taking up the loadings of Elder Dempster ships. Under the terms of the contract the contractors were forbidden to 'assign, underlet or dispose of this contract, or any part thereof without the previous written consent in writing of the Crown Agents'. However, according to the *Times* the arrangement was made that the United Fruit Company should do the work at cost, and receive 25% of the profits, and the agreement was soon taken a big step further. The Americans proceeded to swallow the English Company. They purchased half of the capital stock of Messrs. Elders and Fyffes in the usual fashion, and the British firm, we are told, is now to be worked 'as one of the associated companies of the American organisation.' The upshot of this magnificent subsidy policy – a result worth pondering in the era of subsidies upon which we now seem to be entering – was to bring to England poor and indifferent goods in the first place, and in the second, our proteges in whose interests the contract was made, at the mercy of an American trust. The fruit grower in Jamaica, who before this would have had two outlets for his goods – two possible customers for his produce – has now only one, and must therefore take from the American trust such prices as it may care to pay. Surely this was not the intention of the British Government when it entered into the subsidy agreement?[1]

In actual fact the UFC had not acquired control at this stage – merely a strong interest – in Elders and Fyffes. It should also be noted that the criticism that Jamaica was not getting good value for its share of the subsidy ignores the point that the service was still incurring heavy loses:

... For 15 months the business was conducted at a loss. New and specially fitted ships had to be used, and with the outlay upon these steamers, and with coal at that time at double its normal cost, no return was obtained, even with the aid of the £40,000 p.a. from the Government.

Subsequent recompense, however, has afforded ample justification of faith the firm held in the undertaking. Now [December 1902] they are carrying over 60,000 bunches of bananas a fortnight from the Island. To accomplish this volume of business many difficulties had to be overcome. The U.F.C. had a contract with the growers of the Island to take so many million bunches of the fruit per annum. At that time this contract covered 10 million bunches, which was regarded as almost the maximum output. When Elders and Fyffes appeared on the scene they came, in a sense, as competitors with the U.F.C., and had to be content with the surplus bunches over and above the number required by the American firm. This necessitated dealing with all the principal growers of the Island, who thus sold their surplus crop to E. & F. and were thus encouraged to increase their annual output ...[2]

Unfortunately it was not possible to base a large business which required heavy capital investment on such insecure foundations. For the enterprise to succeed constantly high load factors were essential – both for the vessels and for the distribution and ripening facilities in Britain. One way in which this might have been achieved would have required the support of a substantial number of producers:

> ... From the first Sir Alfred's buyers were hampered by the active rivalry of the United Fruit Company, which strained every nerve to divert from the ships of the Direct Line the bananas for the purchase of which Sir Alfred Jones' agents contracted. This they were able to do by the simple expedient of offering higher prices, owing to the loose wordings of the agreements made with the growers, and the absence of any legal protection against proceedings calculated to break the loyalty of producers to the new line ...
>
> ... Sir Alfred Jones complained to me (as Governor) very feelingly of the lack of support and co-operation which he had received from Jamaica planters, who could, he believed, had they been willing, have kept him independent of the United Fruit Company. Banana growers had in fact not yet at that time learnt how to combine and co-operate ... Either they were tempted by firm contracts with the (United Fruit) Company, and thought its security better than that of the Direct Line, or they were afraid to throw in their lot entirely with the latter for fear of being left in the cold should anything happen to it ...[3]

From the foregoing it is clear that the Jamaican growers must share at least part of the blame for Elders and Fyffes being forced into the arms of the United Fruit Company. Had they been better organized and had they been prepared to take a longer view of the situation instead of being solely concerned with short-term benefits, the independence of the British firm might well have been secured. However, the events of 1903, when a hurricane decimated the island and production dropped dramatically, suggests that membership of a larger group has many advantages in this particular industry.

Thus when Jamaican bananas were no longer available it was a relatively easy matter for the UFC to increase its production and purchases of fruit from its other sources of supply. As part of this temporary reorganization virtually every ship of the Imperial Direct Line as well as those operated by Elders and Fyffes were diverted to Costa Rica to be loaded. Without this support Elders and Fyffes may well have been forced into bankruptcy, for it would have been impossible for them to have acquired sufficient fruit on the open market at prices which would have enabled them to remain viable. In the event it was only the Imperial Direct Line which really suffered. It was obliged to maintain its fortnightly service to Jamaica and the costs of deviating to Costa Rica were an additional burden which added at least £40,000 to its existing heavy losses.[4] On balance, therefore, the unlooked-for link with the

UFC may well be seen to have been beneficial to Elders and Fyffes. It was, in any case, highly probable in the long run, for the banana industry works best when it can take advantage of the economies of scale and of a wide diversity of sources. This fact can be easily demonstrated by the gradual emergence of a small number of multi-national fruit corporations which currently (1990) dominate the world banana market.

The security of supply guaranteed by the 'American Agreement' enabled the new service to Manchester to be fully maintained. This northern port had been chosen partly because of its geographic position, but also because of the enthusiasm of the Manchester Ship Canal Company, who were very keen to attract this new banana trade to their city and were happy to provide whatever facilities were required. In addition Manchester enjoyed excellent rail links with the rest of the country, and the Manager of the London and North Western Railway, Sir Frank Ree, was also prepared to give the venture his fullest support. As a result large numbers of properly designed trucks were constructed and the banana trains were always given the necessary high degree of priority. Elders and Fyffes then utilized Manchester to supply all markets to the north of Birmingham, while Avonmouth provided the bananas to all outlets south of Birmingham. At the same time Canary Island fruit continued to be imported into Liverpool and London via its traditional routes and was normally disposed of within the immediate vicinity of these ports.

The development of Manchester thus complemented the existing arrangements at Avonmouth which had also been chosen for its 'splendid geographic position'. Its Dock Committee had also been very helpful to the new trade and had provided an exclusive berth at 'N' Shed. This was situated on the south-west side of a new arm which had been added to the 'old' dock in 1886, and was quite convenient for the requirements of the trade. While the initial arrangements made by the railway companies were less than adequate, these gradually improved as heated wagons were introduced and as the potential of the banana business was increasingly appreciated.

As noted earlier,[5] the original sailings of *Port Morant* and *Port Maria* were quickly supplemented by those of the larger *Port Royal* and *Port Antonio*. These vessels enabled the fortnightly schedule to be maintained without difficulty, and it was not until 1904 that the fleet was to be enlarged with the addition of *Port Kingston*. This was a fine new liner of 7,584 gross tons which had accommodation for 220 passengers, space for 50,000 stems of bananas and a substantial capacity for general cargo. She was, therefore, the biggest British carrier until *Golfito* came into service in 1949.[6] Although it had been intended to build a sister ship to partner *Port Kingston* this was never undertaken. The Imperial Direct

Line was, of course, still losing money, and it is thought that this class of vessel had proved to be too large (and too expensive) for the trade. Accordingly Sir Alfred Jones decided to transfer a ship from another part of the vast fleet and his choice fell upon *Lake Megantic* of 5,167 gross tons. This was an old ship, built in 1884, which had not been included when Jones had sold the business and some of the tonnage of the Canada Shipping Company (the Beaver Line) to the Canadian Pacific Railway Company in 1903.[7] As she had originally been constructed as a chilled-produce carrier for the Australian trade it was an easy task to adapt her for the carriage of bananas. Renamed *Port Henderson* she and *Port Kingston* then replaced *Port Morant* and *Port Maria* which were placed into reserve.

Although both had proved to be successful carriers of fruit there was no possibility of expanding the banana trade and keeping them employed. Jones's concern was to fulfil the terms of the contract with the minimum of loss, and so he was attempting to undertake the fortnightly service with the most efficient tonnage at his disposal. While the larger vessels were certainly more economic than the smaller ones, the demands of the schedule and the need to consider the requirements of passengers and general cargo meant that they were much more expensive than the specialized banana carriers operated by Elders and Fyffes:

> The freight rate by these (Port) boats is far too high and at present works out at £6 3s.0d. per ton compared with £4 3s.0d. per ton by our own boats.[8]

Statistics of this kind ensured that the increasing demand for bananas in the United Kingdom was to be catered for by Elders and Fyffes' own tonnage. As noted earlier,[9] the three original ships obtained from Furness Lines were joined by a fourth from the same company later in 1902. This gave some degree of flexibility which, with ten-year-old, adapted vessels, was highly desirable. Minor breakdowns were frequent and these culminated on Christmas Day 1902, when *Greenbrier* was in Kingston with a full load of bananas but minus her propeller which had dropped off, *Chickahominy* had just put into Queenstown with leaking boilers, and *Appomattox* was arriving at Avonmouth four days late after a mechanical failure.[10] In spite of problems of this type, Elders and Fyffes had no choice but to keep these vessels in service and, albeit with much difficulty and ingenuity, they continued to carry bananas across the Atlantic for a further four years.

At an early stage it became obvious to the directors of Elders and Fyffes that their ex-Furness vessels could only be regarded as a temporary expedient. As the cost of carriage via the Imperial Direct Line was so high this offered no solution to their problem and they shipped only sufficient bananas on its vessels to satisfy the requirements of the government contract and the wishes of their Chairman. With a rising demand for their products, the company was thus faced with the need to both replace its existing tonnage and to expand the size of its fleet. The adoption of such a policy would have been extremely expensive and the company, still in its infancy, lacked the financial resources to carry it forward. In fact the capital base was progressively increased and reached £450,000 in December 1904,[11] but at a time of rapidly increasing growth in its market little could be spared to purchase the new, specialized carriers that were so urgently needed.

Early in 1903 the situation had become so desperate that it was decided that three new vessels must be secured at all costs. As the necessary funds were still not available, Arthur Stockley was obliged to approach a number of shipbuilders to see if some form of deferred payment could be arranged. Fortunately, as this was a period of slack demand, some firms were at first prepared to quote in spite of their potential customer's lack of capital. However Elders and Fyffes

> ... were also greatly handicapped for two other reasons: first and foremost, because our chairman was entirely hostile to the idea, which was bound to create difficulties with any builders we approached, and, secondly, because we were proposing to build an entirely new and then unheard-of type of vessel which would only be of use for one special purpose – namely, banana-carrying. Also everyone concerned with shipping who knew we were not intending to take any outward cargo simply jeered at the idea of such an arrangement being feasible ...[12]

After many rejections Stockley was able to persuade W. Ferguson of Barclay Curle to build one ship, with a small deposit and the balance over ten years. A chance meeting with the head of Swan Hunter's then resulted in arrangements being made for two more ships to be constructed on similar terms. Although G. B. Hunter subsequently attempted to cancel this contract when he heard of the hurricane in Jamaica which had destroyed the plantations, all three vessels were duly completed:

> These came into operation in 1904 and were named *Manistee*, *Matina* and *Miami*, built under the supervision of the then marine superintendent, Captain Bartlett. The first two came from Swan Hunter's yard at Wallsend and the other from Barclay Curle's at Glasgow. With dimensions of 351 ft. by 46 ft. beam on a gross

Mrs K. Reid, an early Glasgow retailer.

Charles McCann's retail shop in Dundalk, c. 1906.

Geo. Jackson & Co. Ltd, Birmingham.

Steam-heated rail truck specially developed for Fyffes.

Unloading bananas into rail trucks at Avonmouth, c. 1904.

A typical delivery vehicle of the early 1920s showing the banana slogan then being used.

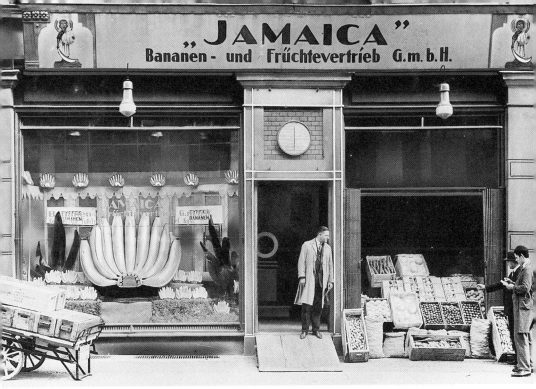

Fyffes' bananas were equally popular on the Continent.

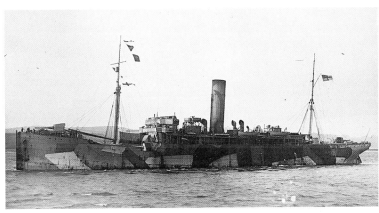

s.s. Changuinola in her special livery during the First World War.

s.s. Ariguani showing damage received during the Second World War.

s.s. Tetela in dry dock showing damage received in September 1941.

Destruction of the company's Head Office in Bow Street on 11 January 1941.

The bombed area around Covent Garden close to Elders & Fyffes premises.

tonnage of 3,760 these were well suited to the trade and had very successful careers.

They became the prototypes for another series of steamers and this policy of building a number of sister ships over an extended period has continued with few exceptions, to the present time. They were fitted with triple-expansion engines giving a service speed of about 13 knots, a good speed for the period. Accommodation for 12 passengers was provided and this addition proved later a worthwhile venture as this traffic increased owing to the prosperity of the islands and opened the way to regular services by 100 passenger ships.[13]

The guaranteed loadings undertaken by the United Fruit Company and the introduction of the three specialized carriers meant that a plentiful and increasing supply of Jamaican and/or Central American bananas could be transported to the United Kingdom. The growth in the size of the fleet, together with the rising volume of cargoes then led to a reorganization at the ports of entry. The fortnightly sailings of the Imperial Direct Line terminated at Avonmouth as before, and this frequency of arrival meant that many expensive facilities stood idle for long periods. Accordingly, from the end of 1903, it was arranged that Elders and Fyffes' vessels would also call at Avonmouth on a fortnightly schedule so that, in effect, there was a weekly flow of bananas through the port. Although the number of sailings by each company was therefore about the same, the tonnage of bananas landed by Elders and Fyffes was much the larger as its ships had the greater capacity. At the other port of entry, Manchester, Elders and Fyffes were responsible for all of the fruit that was imported, and as the newer carriers were concentrated on this route the quantities of bananas landed there were consistently higher than at Avonmouth.[14]

Once the steamer arrived in port every effort was made to unload it as quickly as possible. Although each stem had to be handled separately and needed to be treated with care, some very rapid discharge rates were achieved. One such came when *Chickahominy* arrived into Manchester to inaugurate the new service with 50,700 stems on board:

> This 1,000 ton shipment of bananas was then a record and four hundred stevedores created a further record by unloading it by hand in less than twelve hours.[15]

It was intended to move each stem across the quayside to the waiting railway wagons so that the loaded train could be off to deliver its fruit on a pre-arranged route. A small amount was usually earmarked for local ripening rooms or markets and these would be moved with equal rapidity to their destinations by road transport. In every shipment a proportion, hopefully small, would already be in various degrees of ripeness so could not be distributed in the normal manner. Instead, 'ripes' were sold to local fruiters and barrow-boys for whatever could be obtained, and when the quantities were too large to be absorbed in this way special trainloads were sometimes run to London and sold to the costermongers who had been advised of their imminent arrival at either Euston or Paddington.[16]

The vast bulk of the bananas would, of course, be unloaded from the ship in a hard, green condition. They would then be placed in trucks which in the early days were little more than closed wagons with straw on the floor.[17] Then, as the railway companies came to appreciate the growing value of the business, they supplied more and more sophisticated trucks which were fully insulated and fitted with steam heating. This helped to protect the fruit during the winter months while efficient ventilation was developed to assist in keeping it cool during hot weather. By 1912 over 500 of these sophisticated vans were in service[18] and being used to transport the bananas to a number of strategically chosen principal centres. Some of the loaded trucks were subsequently attached to scheduled passenger trains and redistributed to smaller cities and towns, while others were trans-shipped into road vehicles while still green and moved to local wholesalers and retailers.

At this stage it was necessary for the bananas to be ripened under controlled conditions so that no more than the daily demands of the market would be produced. Originally most of the larger fruit merchants insisted that the bananas delivered to them should be in a saleable state and refused to install their own ripening rooms. This forced the importers to create a network of their own facilities from where they could distribute nearly-ready bunches to both wholesalers and retailers. Once Jamaican bananas were well established, many of the more substantial firms experienced a change of heart and found it more profitable to do their own ripening. Some then found it to be convenient to supply other local retailers when they had a surplus and, over time, many of these grew to become genuine wholesalers. Thus a large number of independent handlers and ripeners were appointed at this time, and some of these were subsequently to maintain their links with Elders and Fyffes for a very long period. These included Messrs Thomas Dowd of Liverpool, George Jackson of Birmingham, Tom King of Nottingham, L. and H. Williams of Glasgow, and Charles McCann of Dundalk who, in 1906, became the first firm to import bananas into Ireland on a regular, large, scale.

This system of distribution was already well advanced as early as November 1901:

NEWS FOR MARKET SALESMEN
BANANAS AT BIRMINGHAM

The development of the Jamaica fruit trade under the auspices of Messrs Elder, Dempster, and Co. has been of a highly satisfactory nature. Last week, on one day, seventeen vans, each containing 25,000 fingers, were required to deliver the fruit to Birmingham alone. They came from the Bristol Dock. The next day 25 vans full of bananas were delivered. A total of 600,000 fingers where thus put upon the Smithfield Market in the two days. The fruit was retailed from 6*d.* to 1*s.* a dozen fingers.

THE JAMAICA BANANA TRADE

At present time four special steamers are engaged in the Jamaica banana traffic. Messrs Elder, Dempster, and Co. run a fortnightly service of steamers between Jamaica and Bristol, and bring to this country on each journey a minimum of 20,000 bunches of bananas. Two more steamers are in course of construction, and before very long the service will be made a weekly one. As a distributing centre Bristol has so far given satisfaction. When a vessel arrives a force of 200 men are engaged in unloading, and within nine hours a full cargo is landed. The railway facilities to the Midlands are good, and consignments leaving Avonmouth in the early morning are placed on the Birmingham market at eight o'clock. Two hours later they are distributed all over the Midlands. The Jamaica fruit trade is as yet practically limited to six or eight large centres, including London, Liverpool, Glasgow, Birmingham, and Nottingham. So far the Midland metropolis has taken its full proportion of the supply. Already the effects of this fruit export are being felt in Jamaica, and steps are being taken to develop other branches of fruit and other vegetable culture.[19]

A month later came the first Christmas when bananas were freely available:

CHRISTMAS BANANA SUPPLIES

Supplies of bananas have been immense. Every day, from early until late, vans loaded with these fruits are to be seen wending their way to Covent Garden especially. The stocks in the warehouses must be phenomenal, for never were such quantities sent into London before. Fifty thousand bunches in a week – and such bunches, too – are nothing out of the way, for as soon as they are delivered they disappear as if by magic. The buyers seem on the wait for the fruit, and many of the loads are sold without being unloaded. True, the London dealers do not dispose of all the supplies to the trade here.

Thousands of bunches go to the country buyers in different parts to order, and the market packers, who particularly make these distributions a special business, know where to send the fruit long before it comes into the market. An original bunch of bananas changes hands wholesale at values which run from 6s. to 12s. a bunch, and the sale of this fruit in quantity is highly lucrative, the demand always being active. At Christmas time, in spite of such huge supplies that come to hand, the buyers have to be on the alert to get all they want, for any mishap or delay to the coming banana boats would mean a mad rush for available fruit on the markets, and that would send up values twenty and even fifty per cent.[20]

This pattern of distribution proved to be extremely successful so that ever-bigger quantities of bananas became available throughout the country on a regular basis. But what was necessary to ensure that all could be disposed of in a satisfactory manner? The original demand around the ports was based on the appeal of a previously exotic and expensive item which had suddenly been placed within the reach of a much wider segment of the population. This widening of the market was supplemented by the necessity to get rid of over-ripe bananas very quickly, so that a new and exceptionally cheap and nutritious supply of food was occasionally placed within the grasp of even the poorest members of the community.

These were the foundations on which the Canary Island bananas gradually gained acceptance within the hinterlands of Liverpool and London docks and they were also adequate for the first imports of the fruit from Jamaica. The growth in the amounts shipped by the Imperial Direct Line and especially in the specialized banana carriers of Elders and Fyffes then meant that a whole fresh market needed to be developed. This situation was early appreciated by Arthur Stockley, and his old friend and fellow director was therefore given the task of popularizing the fruit and thus stimulating national demand. This was to be a job which he was to undertake with great flair and enthusiasm.

Roger Ackerley's first task was to counter the claims of a number of, mainly ex-Army, Anglo-Indians, who wrote to the press stating that the Jamaican banana was really a variety of plantain. As such, they informed the public, it should only be eaten after cooking as a vegetable. The fears which these stories generated were at first supported by a large number of the fruit-dealers in the capital who did not wish to see their lucrative trade in Canary bananas jeopardized by the arrival of the much larger and cheaper fruit from Jamaica.[21] Fortunately, although this belief was to persist for a very long time and is even occasionally met with today, Roger Ackerley's publicity campaign was able to ensure that this incident did not have an adverse effect on sales. Criticism of the banana also came indirectly from those who saw the skin as a major danger to both men and horses, as '... if it falls with the inside next to the pavement, [it] is certainly more treacherous if trodden upon than orange peel'.[22] Ackerley, who believed that there was no such thing as a bad publicity, quickly turned this to the company's advantage. He was

> ... a salesman of rare talents and as such he would never admit that his markets had reached anywhere near saturation point. He believed in the banana as a health-giving food and was determined to educate the public to regard it as an *essential* part of their everyday diet. He arranged banana promotions at carnivals and festivals. He employed lecturers to tour schools to speak of the banana's value in nutrition. He devised banana competitions for magazines. He organised a press campaign that introduced the banana sandwich for picnics and quick luncheons and suggested its inclusion in 'snaps', 'elevenses' and 'dinner pails'.
>
> Much was made of stories of banana diets – like that of the South African farmer who ate four pounds of fruit a day (steeped in sweetened whiskey!) and was active at the age of eighty-nine, or of the shipwrecked seaman who lived exclusively on bananas for over a month, and was rescued in the very best of health, complaining only of the monotony of his diet ...[23]

While Ackerley was always ready to utilize whatever gimmicks or stunts were available he concentrated his campaign to popularize the banana on two of its characteristics. It was, he rightly claimed, an extremely healthy food which had many beneficial aspects; it was also very cheap! As it was easily digested when ripe, it could be strongly recommended for young children, invalids and the elderly. Originally, when many people were poorly fed, its nourishing qualities were highly praised and were a major selling point. Even then, however, its value as a non (or less) fattening food could be usefully stressed in some quarters and, in more affluent times, its role as part of a calorie-controlled diet has become increasingly important.

A small pamphlet providing banana recipes proved to be so popular that it was subsequently expanded and produced each year. Ultimately this suggested over 120 different ways of preparing the fruit. Some of these were extremely sophisticated, but these were counterbalanced by the fact that the vast majority of bananas were eaten between meals or as a dessert in what might best be described as their natural state. Nevertheless Ackerley's campaign was extremely successful and culminated in the gratuitous interjection of 'Have a Banana' into the song 'Let's All Go Down the Strand'. How this originated is still a mystery but there is no doubt it was taken up by the public with great enthusiasm and for many years thereafter the company enjoyed a vast amount of priceless publicity entirely free of charge.

Whether the prime factor in the popularity of the banana was its health-giving qualities (as espoused by Roger Ackerley) or whether it was due to other considerations is difficult to determine. It is certain, however, that the very moderate cost of the fruit was immensely important at the lower ends of the market. In the early days of the Jamaican trade a wholesale price of 9s. per bunch was the average that was achieved.[24] This was also about the average received for Canary bananas in the 1890s. Once Elders and Fyffes began to import fruit from the Caribbean on a large scale these figures began to change quite sharply so that while Canary fruit still remained at about 9s., that from Jamaica fell to an average of perhaps only 6s. As these could be expected to sell for 10s. retail (an average of 135 fingers at just under a penny each), a considerable gross profit could, in theory, be earned. In practice many bananas had to be sold for much lower prices, for they ripened so quickly that on many occasions they had to be disposed of for whatever they would bring.

Thus the average return per banana was often much less than had been hoped but, nevertheless, in spite of the cost of handling and distribution, a satisfactory net profit was usually obtained overall. This meant that even the best quality fruit in prime conditon rarely cost more than a penny, while the market was increasingly widened by the availability of inferior or ripening bananas.

In the real terms the banana was, therefore, extremely cheap, and by 1905 it had become the most popular fruit in the United Kingdom:

PROGRESS OF THE BANANA

The most astonishing development during the year has been in connection with the banana business. The trade at the close of 1905 shows that the banana has now become the most popular fruit handled in the British markets. At one time it was the orange, the apple, or the tomato. Today the banana heads the list easily. Over 5,500,000 cwts. of this fruit were imported during the present year, against 4,350,000 cwts. of oranges, 3,250,000 cwts. of apples, and 1,100,000 cwts. of tomatoes. If only from this fact alone 1905 as far as the import fruit trade is concerned may well be termed a remarkable year. The banana business is only in its infancy. We may soon see the day when 20,000,000 or even 25,000,000 bunches of this fruit will be consumed annually in this country. The three great centres of production are of course the Canaries, Jamaica and Costa Rica. So far the attempt to market the West Indian Claret skinned banana in

Fig. 8.1 'Now then, Mister, Three-a-Penny, wot d'yer mean by knocking the bottom out of the bloomin' market?'
Source: PUNCH, Vol. CXXXIX, 5 October 1910, p. 235.

perfect condition has failed, so that the trade of the year has practically been confined to the favourites from the above named three old trade centres. As far as quality is concerned the Canary fruit heads the list, and is likely to do so for some years to come. Over a quarter of a million bunches of bananas from all sources were stocked for the Christmas sales alone, and they were all sold readily. We paid over £2,000,000 for our banana supply this season.[25]

It should be appreciated that virtually all of these bananas were imported by Elders and Fyffes, and during the following year the company was responsible for handling 4,663,000 bunches and a profit of £95,753 was achieved. By then the firm was operating thirty-eight branches and was employing a staff of over eight hundred.[26] However, not all of this fruit was destined to be consumed within the United Kingdom. As early as 1905 Mr R. H. Sanders, then based at Hull, saw the potential in overseas sales and made a few experimental shipments to Holland and Norway. The enthusiastic response which this aroused then led to a company decision to pursue this activity, and its originator was placed in charge. At first the bananas were transported to Holland in the returnable crates in which a Dutch wholesalers exported his vegetables to Hull. Under the guidance of Mr Sanders suitable clients were subsequently found in a number of European countries and were taught how to handle and sell the fruit. As demand grew, proper arrangements for the packing and carriage of the fruit from this country had to be made and this required the interest and co-operation of many shipping lines. In hot summer months it was necessary for some provision for holds to be kept cool, but at certain times this was not necessary and, during the colder parts of the year, steam heating was required to prevent the bananas from spoiling.

At a later stage, truckloads of fruit arrived at Hull from Manchester (later from Garston) and were marshalled at the railway depot. The bananas were then carefully loaded into 'lift vans' built to Mr Sanders's specification by local carpenters. These vans, which held between 60 and 80 bunches, were slung into the ships to be returned empty in due course. The outward voyages from Hull to Holland, Belgium, Denmark, Norway, Sweden, Germany and France thus provided ever-larger quantities of fruit and, together with the enterprise of Continental handlers, then enabled the banana to find its way as far afield as Baku, Bucharest, Budapest, Moscow, Petrograd, Riga and Warsaw. It was in this way that the business was gradually enlarged until such time as direct shipments to Continental ports became feasible.

The growth in demand outlined above meant that it was necessary to extend the Elders and Fyffes' fleet and a further seven specialized

118

carriers were constructed by Alexander Stephen and Workman Clark of Belfast:

> ... The first *Nicoya*, built in 1905, deserves special mention as she was the first ship constructed for the company by Stephen's and laid the foundation for a very successful association between owner and builder covering 24 ships (to 1967). In length, these seven exceeded the earlier by up to 25 feet though breadth remained similar, the extra space being a welcome addition as trade increased ... With a fleet of 10 ships built for the trade it was possible to dispose of four ex-Furness ships and these were sold out in 1910.[27]

Thus at the end of the first decade of the twentieth century the British banana industry had been firmly established on sound foundations. By then the sources of supply had been well organized in the Canaries, Central America and in Jamaica, and excellent arrangements for the carriage of the fruit to the United Kingdom were fully operational. Facilities to unload the vessels had been developed on a large scale at Avonmouth and Manchester and a sophisticated system of distribution by rail had been carefully evolved.

A series of company and/or privately owned ripening rooms then completed this network so that bananas could be supplied to practically all parts of the United Kingdom in sound condition. Virtually all of this enormous enterprise continued to be organized by Elders and Fyffes who had initiated it in the first place, and by 1909 the firm was in such a strong position that the loss of its principal shareholder had little immediate effect on its fortunes. In the longer term, however, the death of Sir Alfred Jones was to have significant consequences for both the future of the Imperial Direct Line and for the relationship between Elders and Fyffes and the United Fruit Company.

9

A British institution

The period from 1910 to 1929 was to see an enormous growth in the scale of banana imports into the United Kingdom but, in spite of the efforts of a number of potential competitors, Elders and Fyffes remained totally in command of the British market. The company's domination at this time was so marked that the name of 'Fyffes' became synonymous with the banana and it acquired the status of becoming 'a British institution'. However, this is not to suggest that the situation was static, for these two decades were in fact to witness a whole series of changes – the most fundamental of which were to occur right at the beginning of this era. These came about as a direct result of the death of Sir Alfred Jones in December 1909, for within a few days of his decease an option to his entire commerical estate had been secured by Sir Owen Philipps, Chairman of the Royal Mail Group, in partnership with Lord Pirrie, the Chairman of Messrs Harland and Wolff Limited, the Belfast firm of shipbuilders.

As a first step towards taking up their option, Philipps and Pirrie formed Elder Dempster and Company Limited, on 31 March 1910. The new firm then issued 500,000 £1 cumulative preference shares, 400,000 £1 ordinary shares and 10,000 management shares. With the addition of 5 per cent debenture stock of £1,000,000 this gave the new concern a capital of £1,910,000. A formal agreement was then entered into by Philipps and Pirrie with Jones's executor, Mr O. H. Williams, under which the business and goodwill of Elder, Dempster and Company, the Grand Canary Coaling Company, the Tenerife Coaling Company and the Sierre Leone Coaling Company were sold for the sum of £500,000.[1]

In return the new firm received many assets. These included land, cottages, stables, warehouses and offices (including Colonial House, Water Street) in Liverpool, and land and buildings in Bristol. In the

120

island of Grand Canary the property consisted of two hotels, several estates (which included much of the land on which the harbour area of Las Palmas was later constructed), warehouses, stores, stables, offices, a coal depot, a shipbuilding yard and a slipway and jetty. In Tenerife the company acquired a hotel, land, offices, stores, water-tanks and a slipway. In Jamaica it obtained two wharves, besides a large area of urban land and a steam laundry. Land and buildings were also secured at many places in West Africa, sites being situated at Banana Creek, Saltpond, Ilaro, Calabar and Freetown.[2]

The main consideration, however, was the fleet of 109 vessels. At the time of Jones's death these steamships were registered as follows:

	Ships
British and African Steam Navigation Company	36
Elder Dempster Shipping Limited	26
African Steam Ship Company	24
Elder Dempster and Company	15
Imperial Direct West India Mail Service	5
Compagnie Belge Maritime du Congo	3
	109

In addition the new 'Limited' firm received a large number of shares in other companies from the original Elder Dempster company in which Alfred Jones was by then the sole partner. These included 68,995 shares of £1 each, fully paid, and 34,498 shares of £1 each, 5s. paid, plus £15,437 of debenture stock in Elders and Fyffes, Limited, and also 24,896 shares of £10 each, fully paid, and £7,500 debenture stock in the Imperial Direct West India Mail Service Company, Limited.[3] It should be appreciated, however, that all of these assets were mortgaged in one way or another, or were used to secure overdrafts and loans. Hence the low purchase price of Jones's estate. Nevertheless there is no doubt that Philipps and Pirrie obtained a great bargain by acting quickly.

When Arthur Stockley heard of the death of Sir Alfred Jones, he approached the executor and made an offer for his shares in Elders and Fyffes on behalf of Ackerley, Barker, Wolfson and himself. When this was not immediately accepted (Stockley did not know that an option had already been granted) it was decided to wait until an approach could be made to the new owners of the estate who, it was thought, would not be especially interested in these particular shares. Thus, when Stockley learned that Owen Phillips was the principal buyer, he fully expected that Philipps would be in touch with him:

121

However, nothing happened, and in July we heard that Preston, on behalf of the United Fruit Company, had negotiated for the shares and secured them at, I think, nearly the cost of the whole 'caboodle' [i.e. the purchase price of the whole of Jones's estate]. This was a real body-blow to us, but we could do nothing and had to agree to the whole of our shares in Elders and Fyffes being vested in the United Fruit Company. We were given a very fair settlement and an under-taking which has been faithfully carried out, that there should be no American interference in the management of Elders and Fyffes.[4]

When Jones's shares were added to those already held by its nominees, the United Fruit Company possessed a controlling interest in Elders and Fyffes. This position was to be further strengthened in 1913 when an additional 550,000 £1 shares (to make one million altogether) were issued and all were acquired by the American firm. The oppor-tunity was then taken to purchase the balance of the shares from their individual holders – including Stockley and his associates – so that from that date Elders and Fyffes became a completely owned, though autonomous, subsidiary of the UFC.[5]

Although Stockley would have welcomed the chance to have bought Jones's shares in Elders and Fyffes, he was not interested in obtaining his holdings in the Imperial Direct Line. As it was known to be making heavy losses (it had cost Jones over £400,000 by the time of his death) no one else came forward with a bid. Philipps and Pirrie continued, therefore, to run it until the ten-year agreement made with Joseph Chamberlain expired in 1911. There was then a difference of £13,000 per annum between the terms offered for its renewal and those required. Whether the failure to reach a compromise was the fault of the British and Jamaican governments or of the shipping company is not clear; at any rate the service ended in January 1911.[6] Thus the work of the Imperial Direct Line was terminated, although the company was not wound up until 1937.[7] Of the fleet, *Port Morant* and *Port Maria*, which had served as reserves, had already been sold in 1909 and 1910 respectively. The remaining four main-line vessels (*Port Royal, Port Antonio, Port Kingston* and *Port Henderson*) were then disposed of as conveniently as possible.[8] *Jamaica*, of 1,138 gross tons, which had been used as a feeder ship round the island since 1908, was, however, retained in Royal Mail service until 1929.[9]

The net effects of these changes must now be considered. Once the United Fruit Company had acquired control of Elders and Fyffes' shareholdings it was already in a position to dictate all aspects of its operations. In fact the 'gentleman's agreement' that there would be no undue interference in the company's affairs was to be scrupulously observed for many years. Thus only matters of general policy and of common concern were discussed when meetings were held between the UFC and its subsidiary. This was partly because of the excellent relations which Arthur Stockley enjoyed with A. W. Preston, President of UFC at the time of the deal, and subsequently with his successors, Victor M. Cutter, William Newsome and Francis R. Hart. However, this very friendly association, which was to continue when Henry (Hal) Stockley replaced his father as Chief Executive, was based on very sound financial foundations. There can be no doubt that the UFC's investment in Elders and Fyffes proved to be extremely profitable, so that it undoubtedly obtained a high return on its capital.

Details from Elders and Fyffes' General Minute Books show that in the period from 1901 to 1909 dividends varied from 6 per cent in the earlier years to 12 per cent in the later years. However, once the United Fruit Company had secured control, little informtion was at first made available in respect of what now had become internal transfers between UFC and its subsidiary. As Elders and Fyffes' capital base remained at the £1,000,000 to which it had been raised in 1912 it is reasonable to assume that most of its subsequent expansion was financed by retained profits. To some extent, therefore, the UFC seems to have been prepared to have deferred any short-term returns in favour of building up its British interests in anticipation of even larger dividends in the longer term. This policy proved to be extremely successful, so that in 1923 the sum of £3,525,000 (free of tax) was transferred to it from Elders and Fyffes. Thereafter the company's accounts show annual dividends which ranged from £1,250,000 in 1925 to £500,000 in 1924 and 1926, but no payments were to be made during the depressed years of 1932 and 1933.

In addition the growth of the business, which saw imports of bananas into the UK grow from 81,700 tons in 1910 to 193,400 tons in 1929 and to 305,000 in 1938, meant that the value of its investment grew enormously during this period.[10] Furthermore the price at which the UFC supplied its fruit to its subsidiary already included an element of profit, while the expansion of the British market provided a welcome outlet for its ever-growing output.

It would seem that, on balance, Elders and Fyffes also gained from its closer association with the UFC. Although the American firm had guaranteed to provide whatever bananas were required from 1902 onwards, this was at a time when the fruit was plentiful. The particular value of this arrangement was then seen in August 1903, when a serious cyclone destroyed virtually all of the banana plantations in Jamaica. As noted earlier,[11] the UFC were able to offset this calamity by providing supplies from its other sources, especially from those in Costa Rica. It was, fortunately, able to meet all of Elders and Fyffes' requirements because of the abundance of production at that time – the question which never arose was what would have been the UFC's priorities in the event of an overall shortage? Once the UFC actually owned Elders and Fyffes any temptation to favour its other outlets was, of course, limited by purely market considerations, and the British importers were always well served by this arrangement.

The final take-over of Elders and Fyffes in 1913 was marked by an increase in its capital base from £450,000 to £1,000,000. The business was thus able to expand on a broader foundation and, although much future growth was to be financed by retained profits, the additional strength provided by the link with the UFC meant that extra resources could be more easily obtained when they were needed. The benefits of this support were to be felt at a very early stage in the new relationship between the two companies. The ending of the sailings of the Imperial Direct Line naturally reduced the level of imports of bananas into Avonmouth. This, in turn, lowered the efficiency of the facilities at the port which depended upon regular, frequent shipments in order to maintain a viable throughput. The solution was a simple one, but the acquisition of additional company-owned tonnage was only possible because of the financial support provided by the UFC.

The need to replace the capacity lost due to the demise of the Imperial Direct Line, and the continuing growth in the trade, then led to six vessels being added to the fleet in the period from 1911 to 1914. Thus *Manzanares* and *Aracataca* came into service in 1911. Although completed by Stephen's and Workman Clark respectively they were practically sister ships which were very similar, but a little larger and faster, than previous vessels built for the company. These did much to fill the immediate gap which had developed between the demand and supply of bananas, but they did nothing to offset the shortage of passenger accommodation which followed with the withdrawal of the Port ships. Accordingly:

> ... the directors decided on building a larger type of steamer, similar
> to the *Port Kingston,* and carrying 50 and upwards in first-class
> conditions. The decision was greeted with enthusiasm in the West
> Indies as facilities for travel were rather sparse and this trade has
> remained an important consideration in the operation of the West
> Indies service.

The outcome was the appearance, in 1912, of the *Chagres*, the company's first passenger vessel. Built at Linthouse, she was a very smart steamer and became immediately popular with the travelling public. On slightly increased dimensions to the other contemporary vessels, she had an extended midship house with a further two decks above. Passengers were accommodated on the main and promenade decks in excellent cabins for that time, with officers on the boat deck above.

Though a little top heavy in appearance, she was a good sea ship, but her design was altered in the following vessels by placing the bridge at the forward end of the boat deck to secure more favourable lines. She was by no means a large steamer but it must be remembered that dimensions are governed by the ports used and they are limited considerably by some of the smaller entrances in Jamaica such as Port Antonio. For the first time twin screws were provided and the engines gave a speed of 14 knots. In 1913 a further three passenger vessels entered service – the *Bayano, Patuca* and *Patia* – and a passenger service which included, at various times, Barbados, Trinidad, Jamaica, Bermuda, Cristobal and a variety of Central American ports could be maintained, on a fortnightly basis.[12]

With these additions the Elders and Fyffes fleet consisted of sixteen vessels in 1914. This was sufficient to permit satisfactory services to both Avonmouth (which remained the principal passenger terminal) and to Manchester. It was then decided to move from the latter port:

... The increased passage time owing to the traversing of the Manchester Ship Canal made it desirable to obtain a suitable berth nearer the Mersey estuary and application was made to the Mersey Docks and Harbour Board. Unfortunately they were not willing to make a berth available at the time and one was secured eventually at Stalbridge Dock, Garston. This was a good site well served by the railway company and with warehouse and offices alongside the berth. It was opened for operation on January 1, 1912, when all the Manchester port staff were transferred and that office closed.[13]

The importation of bananas into the United Kingdom during the first nine months of 1912 was as follows:[14]

	Bunches
Elders and Fyffes:	
From Costa Rica	2,481,855
Colombia	2,709,137
Jamaica	150,678
Canary Islands	638,552
Other companies:	
From Canary Islands	853,403
	6,833,625

Almost all of Elders and Fyffes' fruit from Costa Rica, Colombia and Jamaica was imported via company-owned tonnage, but that from the Canary Islands was shipped into Britain with the aid of a large range of independent carriers. The most important of these was still Elder Dempster, although its interest in the sale of the bananas had ended when its Fruit Department had been joined with Fyffe Hudson in 1901.[15] As Alfred Jones had then become the principal shareholder in the newly formed Elders and Fyfes, and as he still remained the Senior Partner in Elder Dempster, the continued use of its vessels can be easily understood. The death of Jones removed this informal link, but the shipments were not affected. This was now for purely commercial reasons:

> ... The Elder-Dempster Company's steamers returning from Africa call on an average once a week at Teneriffe [sic] and twice a week at Las Palmas. From Teneriffe [sic] they have carried in a year 300,000 crates, or an average of 5,555 crates per steamer; from Las Palmas 400,000 crates, or an average of 4,300 crates per steamer: total for twelve months, 700,000 crates, to Liverpool. The steamers are not insulated, but the fruit is invariably landed in excellent condition, especially from those steamers having sheltered deck accommodation.[16]

Additional quantities were brought into London by the specialized vessels of the Forwood Line[17] and, after 1900, by Yeoward Brothers into Liverpool.[18] Many other firms also brought small quantities of the fruit into Britain after calling at the Canaries for bunkers. These included the Royal Mail Steam Packet Company (Central America to London), the Pacific Steam Navigation Company (South America to London, Liverpool and Swansea), Shaw, Savill and Albion Company (New Zealand to London), Union Castle Line (South Africa to London and Southampton) and the Nelson Line (River Plate to London and Liverpool). Other companies which carried occasional cargoes of bananas (mainly on deck) into the UK at this time were R. P. Houston, Otton Thoreson, J. T. Rennie & Son, Bullard King, Lamport and Holt, Houlder Brothers, the Harrison Line, G. Thompson, David McIver and the Bucknall Steam Ship Company.[19]

The Royal Mail Steam Packet Company also operated a mail service which connected the West Indies, Barbados and Trinidad with Southampton. On one leg of its route its vessels, which were fitted with refrigerated holds, would carry bananas from Jamaica to New York. These same ships would frequently bring bananas back to Britain on their homeward voyage, but the quantities were comparatively small.[20] This small opposition to the activities of Elders and Fyffes was of no real consequence, but the threat of entry into the British market by the Atlantic Fruit Company was a much more serious matter.

126

This firm had originally been established in Baltimore as the Di Giorgio Importing and Steamship Company. At first it used only one small steamer to import bananas, which it bought on the open market in Jamaica but, following rapid progress, it was reorganized in 1905 as the Atlantic Fruit Company. At this stage the United Fruit Company acquired a controlling interest in the new firm, but these shares were sold to Mr Di Giorgio in 1910. The following year a further reconstruction was undertaken and the firm was renamed the Atlantic Fruit and Steamship (AF & SS) Company. By then it had secured 196,000 acres of land in Nicaragua and 35,000 acres in Cuba, and had obtained 35,000 acres of banana land in Jamaica. Difficulties caused by too rapid an expansion then led to Di Giorgio withdrawing from the company and his interests were then taken over by the Hamburg-American Line. This very large German combine had become extremely interested because of the growing need to carry the output to markets in the United States – a task which was beyond the capacity of the AF & SS Company's own tonnage. An agreement with the Hamburg-American Line had then worked very successfully, so in January 1913 the enterprise was reconstituted as the Atlantic Fruit Company (AFC) with the German shipping firm taking a substantial interest.

By that date the Atlas line (owned by the Hamburg-American Group) was operating eight specialized banana carriers between the West Indies and Central America to New York, so it will be appreciated that the AFC was a major competitor of the UFC. It is not suprising, therefore, that the two groups would clash, and one consequence was that the Hamburg-American Line threatened to establish a weekly banana service to the continent with regular calls at a British port. As part of this plan, two existing ships were scheduled to begin the service and two others were laid down. However, early in 1914, the dispute was resolved, so the Hamburg-American Line did not go ahead with its proposed sailings to the UK. This meant that it then owned two vessels which were surplus to immediate requirements, so one condition of the deal was that Elders and Fyffes would take this tonnage off the Germans' hands.[21] Thus *Emil L. Boas* and *Carl Schurz* were transferred in April 1914, and were then renamed *Motagua* and *Changuinola*. As they had been constructed by Swan Hunter and were, in effect, a less elaborate version of existing vessels, they proved to be a useful addition to the company's fleet.

The Atlantic Fruit Company was not a party to this agreement so in spite of the disapproval of one of their major shareholders they decided to go ahead as planned:

> ... In 1914 the Atlantic Fruit Company negotiated with the
> Manchester Ship Canal Company, who leased them part of a shed for
> the discharge of bananas. The Atlantic Fruit Company chartered two

Dutch steamers, the *Van der Duyn* and the *Van Hogendorp*. These two vessels were 2,200 tons net register. They had two arrivals in Manchester in September 1914, one cargo of 50,000 stems naked bananas, and one cargo of 38,000 stems naked bananas.[22]

As the facilities previously used by Elders and Fyffes had remained unused since their departure for Garston in 1912 this was a very welcome development for the Manchester port authorities. Unfortunately for them, the outbreak of the First World War led to the two vessels being chartered on a permanent basis by the Atlantic Fruit Company and as it chose to use them on other routes the service came to a premature end.

Elders and Fyffes' domination of the British market at the outbreak of the Great War was complemented by its development of its Continental trade. The enormous task of arranging for the reception, distribution and ripening of such large quantities of bananas created a massive administrative burden so, in order to cater for this, new premises were acquired at 31–32 Bow Street, London, in July 1910. The European business, which had originated in Hull,[23] was at first organized from Humberside, but the growing scale of the operation then, also in 1913, led to a transfer of its Continental headquarters to Hamburg. Thus:

> ... the total shipments from England to the Continent for the year ended September 30, 1912, were 1,023,641 bunches. One thousand bunches are sent every week to St. Petersburg, although the import duty into Russia is £11 18s. a ton; 1,200 bunches a week go to Sweden, duty £5 10s. a ton; 2,000 to Norway, duty £1 2s. a ton; 1,000 to Copenhagen, duty 11s. a ton; 8,000 to 9,000 to Germany, some being from the Canary Islands, duty nil; 3,000 to 4,000 to Holland, duty 5 per cent on invoice value, plus 5s. duty on vans; 2,500 West Indian bananas to France, via Liverpool and Dunkirk, duty £2 13s.4d. a ton plus octroi duties, besides some from the Canary Islands.[24]

The way in which imports into Hamburg developed demonstrate the pace at which the continental trade expanded from virtually nothing in 1895:

TABLE 9.1 IMPORTS OF BANANAS INTO HAMBURG (IN DOZENS)[25]

	1895	1905	1906	1908	1909	1912
Canary Islands	130	18,952	29,575	65,444	121,345	10,500,000
Madeira	271	917	264	–	–	–
West Indies and Central America	–	–	590	27,208	34,359	1,895,000
Cameroon	–	–	–	165	82	–
England	–	–	1,370	6,388	11,721	2,980,00
Holland	–	–	75	57	–	–

128

While the majority of West Indies/Central American bananas and a smaller proportion of Canary Island fruit was supplied to Hamburg (and the remainder of Europe) by Elders and Fyffes at this time, it was quickly realized that the potential was tremendous and according to Roger Ackerley:

> The demand on the continent is something we can't pretend to satisfy. In Hamburg alone the trade has grown enormously and there are agents in other parts of the world tumbling over each other in their eagerness to snap up the fruit.[26]

As a result of this increasing pressure Elders and Fyffes made the appropriate plans, and in March 1913 began a regular service to Rotterdam and early in 1914 the company's steamers also began a direct service from the West Indies to Hamburg.

Thus on the outbreak of hostilities in August 1914 Elders and Fyffes was in an extremely strong position on all fronts. In that year it handled more than 90 per cent of the 120,700 tons of bananas that were imported into the UK, besides playing an important role in supplying many European countries. The first effect of the war was to bring the Continental trade to an immediate end, and the *Nicoya*, which was unloading in Hamburg, was seized by the enemy three days before the conflict officially began. The second consequence was upon the fleet, for many vessels were to be requisitioned by the Admiralty and there were to be a large number of losses:

> The extent to which West Indian merchant shipping was dislocated and damaged by the war is well illustrated by the record of Elders & Fyffes Limited. From October, 1914 till after the Armistice five of the Company's ships were requisitioned for employment as armed merchant cruisers and two of them were torpedoed and sunk. Three more were requisitioned to act as armed escorts convoying merchant vessels. Ten were requisitioned at different dates by the Director of Transports or the Ministry of Shipping; among the ten, five were torpedoed and sunk and two others lost. Two ships, while on the Company's own service, were torpedoed and sunk, one of them, the *Zent*, while in ballast, unarmed and without warning, forty-seven men out of a complement of fifty-eight being drowned. Over and above this loss, sixty-seven of the Company's men were killed in action or died on active service on land or sea. When the Armistice came, only one vessel out of the whole fleet was being employed on the Company's own business.[27]

Thus the Elders and Fyffes' fleet which had consisted of sixteen vessels in service, plus the recently acquired *Montagua* and *Changuinola*, but less the *Nicoya* (taken at Hamburg) began the war with seventeen ships. A building programme provided an additional four vessels but as ten were lost by enemy action and a further one was sunk after a collision, only ten plus *Nicoya* survived to sail when peace returned.[28] The reduced capacity of the shipping at the company's disposal was felt all the more because of the effects of the German submarine campaign and the subsequent shortage of shipping led to the Company's service to the Canaries being terminated in December 1916.[29] This meant that whatever bananas were imported had to be transported over the longer routes from the Caribbean, so the remaining tonnage could not be used in its most effective manner. The combination of these two factors then led to a rapid reduction in the cargoes received in Britain:[30]

	Tons
1915	109,200
1916	81,700
1917	29,900
1918	9,800

In spite of this reduction in supplies and the ever-increasing cost of operating their steamers – a typical voyage rose from £3,250 in 1914 to £17,000 in 1919[31] – the company made every effort to hold down its prices. As the sole importer of the fruit at this time, Elders and Fyffes was determined that the public would not be exploited and therefore issued instructions that the maximum retail price should be no more than 2s.6d. a dozen, or 2½d. per individual banana. Thus, in addition to providing many volunteers for active service and the majority of its fleet for government purposes, the company did what it could to assist in resisting inflationary pressures at home.

The ending of hostilities at the end of 1918 then saw Elders and Fyffes, under the dynamic leadership of Arthur Stockley and Roger Ackerley, determined to restore the banana industry to its pre-war position. This was not too difficult on the supply side, for many of the larger Jamaican producers had managed to survive the war moderately well by concentrating upon the American market. Smaller growers had tended to restrict their output by diversifying into other products or by just selling in the open markets for whatever prices could be realized. Once the war was over it was relatively easy to re-establish former links, so that in 1919 Jamaica was able to contribute 37,100 tons of the 65,600 tons which were imported into the UK that year.[32]

As exports from the Canary Islands had almost totally ceased during the First World War, it took some time to reactivate its fruit trade. However, although bananas were difficult to secure in the early post-war

130

period there was no shortage of shipping to get them to market. This was because a wide range of vessels continued to call at Las Palmas and Tenerife for bunkers while on their way back to Britain, and were happy to fill any empty spaces with whatever was available. As a result of this shortage of Canary fruit, and the limited quantities available in Jamaica, Elders and Fyffes attempted to fill the gap by utilizing the resources of the United Fruit Company in Central America. This policy was reasonably successful but was constrained by the lack of suitable specialized vessels. Consequently the company's top priority became the building up of its fleet as quickly as was practical.

As a first step *Nicoya* was reclaimed from the enemy and energetic steps were taken to obtain the release of those vessels which were still under government control. Two ex-German ships, *Pungo* and *Pionier* were then purchased from the Shipping Controller who had seized them as war reparations. *Pungo*, which had sailed as the commerce raider *Moewe* during hostilities, was renamed *Greenbrier II* while *Pionier* was renamed *Miami II* and both were to give excellent service for the ensuing thirteen years. However, the only real solution to the loss of so many fine vessels was to build new ones, and Elders and Fyffes were quick to place their orders with the British firms of Workman Clerk (Belfast), Alex Stephen (Glasgow) and Cammell Laird (Birkenhead). The first, in what was to become a class of nineteen sister ships, was the *Chirripo II* which was delivered in 1920. In the same year *Zent II* also came into service and four other, similar vessels had joined the fleet by 1922.

The addition of these eight ships, plus the return of those requisitioned during the war, meant that sufficient tonnage was then available to cope with the level of imports that was required. In 1922 these amounted to 147,900 tons but as demand increased during the 1920s further vessels became necessary. Thus between then and 1930 an additional nineteen ships were constructed, and as only *Matina II* and *Nicoya II* were sold during this period the fleet increased to comprise thirty-six vessels. While most were designed to operate on routes to the West Indies and Central America, three were built specifically for the Canary Islands trade. These were much smaller than the company's other ships and *Telde*, *Argual* and *Orotova* also differed in that they were fitted with a mechanical ventilation system rather than the customary refrigerating machinery.

This vast fleet was then employed to bring ever-larger quantities of bananas into Britain and Europe – by 1930 imports into the UK alone amounted to over 193,400 tons.[33] By then the Continental business was also on a considerable scale, and Elders and Fyffes and its associated companies were responsible for a very large part of both the British and European trades:

TABLE 9.2 ALL BANANA IMPORTATIONS INTO EUROPE DURING THE YEAR 1930[34]

From	Stems		
	Continent	UK	Total
British West Indies and Central America	13,879,555	12,777,744	26,657,299
Canary Islands	6,264,096	1,091,855	7,355,951
Brazil	124,800	1,428,351	1,553,151
French Guiana	258,607	–	258,607
Guadeloupe and Martinique	138,894	–	138,894
British Mandated countries	67,083	–	67,083
Madeira	3,434	3,268	6,702
Other countries	420	–	420
Total	20,736,889	15,301,218	36,038,107

With the aid of a temporary headquarters set up in Paris, supplies to the Continent had been resumed very quickly once the war was over. At first this trade was conducted entirely on an *ad hoc* basis, but as demand proved to be so buoyant it soon became obvious that more permanent arrangements would be beneficial. A fresh appraisal of the situation indicated that Rotterdam would be the most appropriate place from which to direct the trade, and so Elders and Fyffes established their administration centre at that port city. The further growth of the business then led to the formation of a number of specialized subsidiaries to cater for this expanding market. These included *Elders and Fyffes S.A.* (later renamed La Compagnie des Bananes Société Anonyme) which was set up in December 1922 to act as an independent selling organization in France. This had a capital of 1 million francs and a ripening depot at St Ouen near Paris which was said to be half as long again as the huge Floral Hall at Covent Garden.[35] Similar firms were then established in Holland and Germany: *N.V. Elders and Fyffes Algemeen Agenturen en Handel Maatschappij* (later N.V. Internationale Bananen Maarschappij) being founded in Rotterdam during September 1925 and the *General Trading Agency GmbH* (later the Deutsch–Westindische Bananen Gesellschaft) which was incorporated in November 1926.[36] The rising scale of these operations then led to the introduction of direct sailings, and after 1926 both Rotterdam and Bremerhaven were provided with a weekly service.

The growth of the banana market within the British Isles was at least as impressive as that in Europe during the 1920s. Although by 1930 the Continental business was larger than that of the UK, Elders and Fyffes continued to make home sales their top priority. This was because the company remained responsible for almost all of the bananas that were imported into Britain, whereas it was obliged to share its European trade with a number of competitors. The need to maintain this position led Elders and Fyffes to adopt highly innovative policies, and throughout this decade a series of changes was introduced which helped to make their organization more efficient and cost effective.

The build-up of an extremely modern and well-equipped fleet of specialized banana carriers has already been described. This was then to be complemented by an improved system of distribution which widened the market geographically and also reduced the seasonability of the business. By 1921 this network was based on Elders and Fyffes' seventeen regional branches and a further thirteen which were organized by the associated Fruit Distributing Company.[37]

These branches were strategically placed and with the aid of large numbers of firms which provided their own ripening facilities – and sometimes also supplied other retailers in their neighbourhood – the whole country was covered reasonably well. In a number of areas where gaps in the network still remained, Elders and Fyffes encouraged some of their managers who were already experienced in ripening to establish their own banana ripening depots and the Company were happy to provide the necessary finance for this purpose. A number of these independent handlers developed over time into full-scale fruiterers and many successful businesses today can trace their origins back to this initiative.

The principal method of internal distribution was of course by rail, and by 1921 there were few places of any size which did not have a banana warehouse somewhere in the sidings on the edge of town. At Elders and Fyffes' persuasion, the railway's service was steadily speeded up so that delivery could be guaranteed the day after despatch.[38] Thus even distant cities like Aberdeen – 350 miles north of Garston – could be properly served. As the insulted wagons used for the carriage of bananas were themselves greatly modified over time, the extremes of both winter and summer could be offset and it became rare for fruit to arrive in anything less than perfect condition.

The technical advances made by the motor lorry during the war were now to be utilized for peaceful purposes. Large number of ex-Army vehicles were acquired and fitted for their new task but, in most cases, they were to be employed to support the railway system rather than to replace it. A lack of modern trunk roads meant that rail was clearly the best for carrying the fruit quickly over long distances. However, motor transport soon showed that it could distribute bananas up to a twenty-mile radius from a main-line station far more effectively than by the use of local lines. In the course of time this distance was to be gradually

8   *THE BANANA BUDGET*

ELDERS & FYFFES Ltd.

31 & 32, BOW STREET, LONDON, W.C. 2

Telegrams : " Fyffes, London and Branches "   Telephone : 104. Gerrard (5 Lines)

Branches :

AVONMOUTH DOCK : Nr. Bristol.
Tel. Nos : 27 Avonmouth ; 1413 Bristol.
BIRMINGHAM :
    11 & 12, Edgbaston Street.
    Tel. No. : 1755 Midland.
BRIGHTON :
    23 24, Black Lion Street.
    Tel. No. : 4489 Brighton.
BRISTOL : 25, Welsh Back.
    Tel. Nos. : 4664 and 4665 Bristol.
CARDIFF : 1 & 2, Hope Street.
    Tel. No. : 3733 Cardiff.
CHATHAM :
    Sun Wharf, Medway Street.
    Tel. No. : 336 Chatham.
GARSTON DOCKS : Nr. Liverpool.
    Tel. No. : 333 Garston.
GLASGOW : 39, Bell Street.
    Tel. No. : 2113 Bell.
HULL : 22, Humber Street.
    Tel. Nos. : 5447 and 5448 Central.
LEEDS :
    East Lane, Kirkgate Market.
    Tel. No. : 26320 Leeds.

LIVERPOOL : 40, Victoria Street.
    Tel. No. : 1327 Bank.
MANCHESTER :
    Aldreds Buildings, High Street.
    Tel. No : 4008 City.
NEWCASTLE-ON-TYNE :
    St. Andrew's Street.
    Tel. No. : 1732 Central.
PLYMOUTH :
    Jamaica House, Woolster Street.
    Tel. No. : 276 Plymouth.
PORTSMOUTH :
    1, Pearl Assurance Buildings.
    Tel. No. : 3246 Portsmouth.
SHEFFIELD : 37, Exchange Street.
    Tel. No. : 3773 Central.
SOUTHAMPTON: 80, High Street.
    Tel. No. : 322 Southampton.
ROTTERDAM :
    c/o W. H. Muller and Co.
    P.O.B. 509.
PARIS Agency : 89 91, Rue de la
    Chapelle, St. Ouen (Seine).

LAS PALMAS, TENERIFFE, JAMAICA, COSTA RICA, COLON and SANTA MARTA (Colombia).

FRUIT DISTRIBUTING Co., Ltd.

40, VICTORIA STREET, LIVERPOOL

Telephone : Bank 1329   Telegrams : " Porticorum," Liverpool and Branches

BELFAST : Aberdeen Fruit
    Market, Oxford Street.
    Tel. No. : 932 Belfast.
CARDIFF : 18, New Street.
    Tel. No. : 2329.
GARSTON DOCKS :
    Near Liverpool.
    Tel. No. : 333 Garston.
GLASGOW :
    College Goods Station, High St.
    Tel. Nos. : 2426 and 3056 Bell.
HALIFAX : Market Hall.
    Tel. No. : 1416 Halifax.
HANLEY : 13a, Etruria Road.
    Tel. No. : 457 Hanley.

LEICESTER : Shaftesbury Road.
    Tel. No. : 2895 Leicester.
MERTHYR : Penry Street.
    Tel. No. : 248 Merthyr.
NEWPORT (Mon.) :
    Gloucester Wharf, G.W.R.
    Tel. No. : 3844 Newport.
PONTYPRIDD :
    Ynysyngharad Road.
    Tel. No. : 318 Pontypridd.
ST. HELENS : 73, Tontine Street.
    Tel. No. : 360 St. Helens.
SWANSEA : 10, Nelson Street.
    Tel. No. : 604 Central.
WIGAN : 72, Market Street.
    Tel. No. : 232 Wigan.

Printed for the Proprietors, ELDERS & FYFFES, LTD., 31, BOW STREET, LONDON, W.C. 2, *by* HUDSON & KEARNS, LTD., LONDON, S.E.1.

Fig. 9.1   Branches of Elders and Fyffes Ltd. and the Fruit Distributing Co. Ltd. in 1921

increased, but it was to take many years before the development of a motorway network meant that railways were no longer required to perform any tasks for the industry.

The rapid growth of banana imports after the First World War was also encouraged by the adoption of two technical innovations within the industry. The first of these involved the provision of automatic temperature control for all ripening rooms. Elders and Fyffes themselves supplied the necessary devices at low cost so that the gas could be pre-set at the appropriate level and it was not longer essential to make frequent inspections of the fruit at all times of the day and night. A second development concerned the adoption of the standard 'flat' box in which bananas were to be transported to retail outlets. This had been introduced as early as 1907[39] but it was not until 1920 that it was used universally throughout the trade.[40] The advantage of 'flatting' was that the fruit was unlikely to be damaged in transit and that, as it had been already cut into 'hands' the retailer could see exactly what he was getting. In turn, the hands could more easily be displayed within a shop, and this enabled the customer to make his selection more easily and thus encouraged him to buy.[41]

Another initiative taken by the company at this time was designed to equalize the price of fruit throughout the country. Until 1921 the cost of delivery of green bananas from the ports to the wholesalers was mainly determined by the distance involved. Under these circumstances it was difficult to move towards Elders and Fyffes' objective of a truly national system which could provide bananas at all times of the year at competitive prices. Accordingly a carriage-paid agreement was made under which the cost of the green gruit included all rail charges and was the same per ton to every wholesaler in the country, delivered to his nearest railway station.[42]

These arrangements had only a marginal effect on the cost of bananas in Ireland, for the additional cost of shipping from Great Britain always had to be taken into account. The fruit had first arrived in Belfast in 1893 when James McGahen had brought five crates in from Liverpool as an experiment.[43] Two years later Daniel Devine, amonst others, was importing five or ten crates a week by the overnight Liverpool–Belfast steamer. In the course of time these quantities grew, so that up to 100 crates might be carried by some steamers. A new system was then adopted whereby 'lift vans' capable of holding up to two tons of bananas were introduced. These were also shipped by the scheduled services between the two ports until the further growth of the business persuaded Elders and Fyffes that it would be of advantage to charter a small coaster. Thus from about 1913 to the outbreak of the war the tiny *Roma* was loaded in Garston directly from the main-line vessel and the 'lift vans' were gradually phased out. This system was to be reintroduced once hostilities had come to an end:

> Today we use a little 200-ton coaster called the *Marie*. In appearance she may not be called a pretty thing, but, like some customers we know, she has abundant driving power – and she gets there! The ship is fitted with steam pipes running from the boilers and encircling the hold in order that the bananas may be kept warm during cold weather.
>
> Leaving Garston as a rule in the afternoon the *Marie* crosses to Belfast in about 16 hours.
>
> When she arrives at Belfast there is a fleet of motors and vans, all with specially fitted sides and oil sheets, ready for the discharge. Bananas – and in season, coconuts and oranges – are soon on their way to our Store and customers' rooms. Twenty-four hours after leaving Garston all bananas destined for those towns within a radius of 35 miles from Belfast, are safely housed in the ripening rooms.[44]

This situation in Southern Ireland was rather different. Bananas appear to have been imported on a small scale via the overnight sailing from Liverpool to Dublin during the 1890s. A number of firms became interested in the trade but were apparently content to order on an *ad hoc* basis and no special arrangements were made to provide a company branch in the city. However, the firm founded by Charles McCann, which was already engaged in wholesaling fruit in the Dundalk area in the north east of the country, did take an active role in the business, and in 1906 it was appointed as Elders and Fyffes' first official handlers. For a ten-year period McCann's retained this position, and ripened and distributed the bananas it received via Belfast through-out large parts of the south. The inconvenience of this system, plus the disruption caused by the war and 'the Troubles' then brought this arrangement to an end, although McCann's continued to deal in bananas on a large scale. The establishment of an Independent Irish Free State in 1921 was ultimately to see a new structure evolve for the industry, but in the meanwhile shipments from Liverpool to a number of firms in Dublin ensured that a steady supply of bananas continued without interruption.[45]

The task began in 1904 by Roger Ackerley to popularize the banana was to continue throughout the 1920s. Advertising and promotion remained based on the health-giving qualities of the fruit and its cheapness, and were now stressed through a widely used slogan: 'Bananas – The All-Food Fruit' (see Fig. 9.2).

The campaigns mounted by Ackerley were always backed by expert analysis. That provided by Messrs Atwater and Bryant was followed by a treatise entitled *The Question of Diet and its Relation to Health*, by a

Mr Richard Haynel who was described as a specialist in 'Balneo-Phys. Therapy'. One aspect of this study was concerned with the percentage of indigestible fibre found in various fruits, and the banana, with 0.2 per cent, was clearly much superior to all other varieties which ranged from the grape with 2.0 per cent to the fig with 7.3 per cent.[46] At the same time the value of the banana to the sportsman and athlete was also given considerable prominence with 'Bicycle Riders Engaged in Long Gruelling Races' being paid special attention.[47]

Fig. 9.2 'The All-Food Fruit' (Banana motto)

An 'Analysis of Ripe West Indian Bananas' by Mr. F. W. Richardson, FIC, from the County Analyst's Office, Bradford, was undertaken in 1923. Mr Richardson's conclusions subsequently formed the basis of a series of public lectures and concluded with the statement: 'I shall not fail to recommend bananas as a valuable adjunct to the people's food.'[48]

Roger Ackerley was a great believer in pressing the claims of the banana at cookery and food exhibitions. One, in a long line of such events, was held at the Holland Park Hall, London, in November 1927. Although heavily patronized and attended by the principal *chefs* and *restauraters* of the capital, its prime aim was to stimulate and improve domestic cooking. Consequently many housewives were encouraged to attend, and Elders and Fyffes set out to show a series of inexpensive and easily prepared banana dishes. The company's demonstrator, Mrs Clifford, made the stall of real practical value,

137

and the opportunity was taken to distribute copies of its pamphlet, *Bestway Banana Dishes*.[49]

Successful as Roger Ackerley may have been in promoting the banana, his efforts were far surpassed (as in the campaign of 1904) by the chance emergence of a popular song. 'Yes, We Have no Bananas', based on an authentic remark heard by the composer from a Greek fruitseller, swept the country in 1922. It was sung by Florrie Ford, who auctioned bananas at the end of many performances for the benefit of military hospitals throughout the country. At the other end of the musical spectrum it was played by the combined bands of the Brigade of Guards to an audience of 80,000 people at the Shrewsbury Flower Show. Elders and Fyffes then co-operated with the publishers of the music and no fewer than 10,000 cardboard hands of bananas were sent to music shops and other outlets.[50]

The combination of planned activities and of unlooked-for bonuses thus helped to strengthen Elders and Fyffes' position, and the consumption of bananas went up year by year. As virtually the sole importer, however, the company felt especially vulnerable to public opinion, and was most anxious not to appear to take advantage of its highly favourable situation. Thus the company took it upon itself to ensure that only bananas in perfect condition would be offered for sale. As part of this policy Ackerley issued the following circular in June 1922:[51]

An Appeal and a Warning

I was genuinely astonished, and I may say disgusted, to see on a coster's barrow in Central London *green* hands of West Indian bananas during the recent holiday season.

There is evidently in London at least one handler who cares nothing for our trade, and to him this appeal is addressed. Do not allow any fruit to leave your ripening rooms *until it is ripe*. The warning should hardly be necessary, but there it is.

We, as importers, cannot allow our business to be ruined by such a short-sighted policy, and any offender on being found out will have his account closed.

The message in this circular was then to be pressed home by the constant repetition to the shopkeeper of a second slogan: 'Remember: They Must Be Ripe'.

In addition to insisting that bananas should only be sold when in prime condition, Roger Ackerley also wished to protect the company's reputation by ensuring that the consumer was able to buy his fruit at a reasonable price:[52]

A Timely Hint

We are all prone to use the phrase – 'Law of supply and demand' – in connection with the Banana Trade and ruling prices, but it seems to me there are other points to be considered. If figures in our books were to be analysed it would be found that since January 13th last, when we started selling West India bananas at £30 a ton, the average cost price to our customers has not reached 1s. per dozen. This is a fact which is indisputable. Now that the summer is waning, that spending money is scarcer, and that the retail prices of all foods show a downward tendency, it is up to everyone concerned in the Banana Trade to see that the retail price is kept within reasonable limits.

I claim that we are justified in asking our customers to follow this point up, as the cause of gluts in the fruit trade can often be directly traced to the rooted objection on the part of the retailer to lower his selling price. All of us who have been lucky enough to have a holiday this year have seen West India bananas ticketed at 2s. 6d. and even 3s. 0d. a dozen. This must stop. If it does not, we shall be compelled in sheer self defence to publish some facts in the daily Press to enlighten the public again.

However, we will first of all see what the effect of this appeal will be.

Signed: A. Roger Ackerley

This statement was made even clearer a month later when the following was published *The Banana Budget* during September 1921:[53]

The Question of Retail Profits

The Editor is calling on me again for what he calls a 'message'. This very week the Editor of a very well known London evening paper asked for a 'message' about retail prices of bananas, and when I saw my message in print later on I confess I hardly recognised portions of it. I did and do claim, however, and I trust that all direct banana handlers in the country will support me, that between the price we as importers sell the fruit at and 2s. a dozen to the consumer, there is a very handsome margin of profit for all intermediaries, and I hope all managers will rub this in as occasion arises. There should be no bananas priced at 2s.6d. and even 3s. a dozen, and it is a great pity that the public don't realise this.

Signed: A. Roger Ackerley

The net effect of this policy, and of Elders and Fyffes' ability to enforce it, was that falls in the world price could be passed on to the

139

consumer and the 'penny banana' would once again become a reality in due course. At this level the importers, their wholesalers and the retailers could all make a good living, but only if they operated in a cost-effective manner. The company did not see its function to be as a protector of inefficiency, and its success in establishing a modern structure can be judged by the expansion of the market and the general satisfaction of the public.

The economic environment in which Elders and Fyffes operated was a very uncertain one, and any person able to secure employment with this 'British Institution' regarded himself as extremely fortunate. Although the pay was never particularly high, the jobs at all levels were permanent and secure and there are many examples of individuals spending their entire working lives with the firm. Long-serving employees were then rewarded on their retirement with either lump sums or pensions at a time when such payments were still comparatively rare within most of contemporary industry. Both Stockley and Ackerley encouraged what they called the 'get-together' spirit, and actively supported many company-based sports and social facilities, and a genuine feeling of what would now be termed 'corporate identity' steadily developed.

Proof of this loyalty came in June 1923 when a national dock strike suddenly began. At the time *Coronado* had just arrived at Avonmouth with a full load of bananas which urgently needed to be unloaded. An appeal by Roger Ackerley saw the entire staff or Head Office volunteer to help, and by working twelve hours a day for a week this untrained force managed to discharge the entire vessel. A similar attempt was made to unload *Manistee* at Hull, but this was less successful owing to the lack of support from the police and the staff of the railway company.

In many ways these events were to prove to be a dress rehearsal for the General Strike of 1926. When this began, five full vessels were awaiting discharge at Avonmouth and Garston, so once again there was a call for volunteers and, once again, there was a 100 per cent response:

> The strike began on 3 May and, by some means or another, the entire personnel of the Company managed to get to their places of work. From there the greater proportion were transported to the ports by every available means of transport. Luxurious Rolls-Royce limousines, creaking pre-war lorries, motor-cycles with side-cars and pillions – even pedal-cycles – were used to get the volunteer work force to Avonmouth, Hull and Garston. Once there they succeeded in unloading a total of 100,000 bunches of bananas during the nine days of the strike. Not only was the fruit unloaded but also, in the absence of railway transport, it was loaded on to lorries – both those belonging

Fig. 9.3   First Press Advertisement of the 'Blue Label'

to the Company and others manned and driven by university students – and taken to its various destinations. It was a superbly organized operation carried out with a quiet determination by men who, at times, could hardly stand through lack of sleep and at others were man-handled by pickets. Apart from being a demonstration of the loyalty of its staff this exercise was further evidence of the Company's ability to adapt its entire organization to meet difficult situations whether large or small.[54]

Once the industrial strike of 1926 had been overcome and left behind, Elders and Fyffes were able to resume their upward progress. Thus, in spite of growing levels of unemployment and a deterioration in the world economic situation, by 1929 the company was in a sound financial position. This was, of course, the year of the 'Wall Street Crash' which was to trigger off a long period of depression and was to result in a massive down-turn in world trade. It was against this background that a number of momentous changes were to occur within Elders and Fyffes' field of operations. These began with the onset of direct competition from the Jamaica Banana Producers Association and continued with the dropping of 'Elders' from the brand name and the decision to market all of its bananas under what was to become the famous Fyffes' *Blue Label*. Other moves saw the enterprise converted into a private, limited, company and the termination of the existence of the Fruit Distribution Company. The activities of this wholly owned subsidiary were then subsumed within the parent firm, and subsequently operated under the Fyffes' banner. Finally, in October 1929, came the death of Roger Ackerley and thus the ending of a major era of the banana business in Britain.

Henry ('Hal') Stockley, Chief Executive, 1930 to 1958.

Captain John A. Moore, OBE Joint Managing Director, 1958 to 1961; Managing Director, 1961 to 1963.

H. Jim Stockley, Joint Managing Director, 1958 to 1961.

Captain T. H. Bull, Commodore of the fleet until his retirement in 1958.

Wilfred Moore, Fyffes' General Manager
in the Canaries, 1935 to 1969.

Jack Theed, Company Secretary and
Chief Accountant, 1957 to 1966.

Harry Holt, Fyffes' Sales Promotion and
Publicity Manager, 1948 to 1962.

D. J. Easterbrook gave 49 years' service
to the company before retiring in 1962; his
final appointment was as Cashier at Head
Office.

ss Tilapa arriving at Avonmouth with the first cargo of bananas following the end of the Second World War, December 1945.

Transferring bunches direct from truck to ripening room by means of chain conveyor.

Loading aboard a steamer at a tropical port, c. 1923.

SS Patuca under the banana discharge elevator at Avonmouth, 1923.

Loading wrapped bunches into elevator pockets in holds of ship at Southampton Docks.

10

Enter Jamaica Producers: the British industry in the 1930s

The introduction of the *Gros Michel* banana into Jamaica in 1836 meant that for the first time a fruit which could stand a moderate degree of handling was now available. This was of little consequence when bananas were only grown as subsistence crops or disposed of in local markets, but was of supreme importance when an export trade gradually evolved. This was primarily to North America where the relatively short distances involved meant that small sailing vessels were adequate for this purpose. The economies of scale then saw the emergence of ever-larger firms which could justify an integrated operation utilizing steamships. The Boston Fruit Company was the most important of these and when it amalgamated with the interests of Minor Keith to form the United Fruit Company the resulting corporation was able to dominate much of the Jamaican banana industry.

Other American firms, including the Atlantic Fruit Company (organized by Joseph Di Giorgio) and the Cuyamel Fruit Company (whose principal was Samuel Zemurray), provided a spasmodic degree of competition to the United Fruit Company but all were totally concerned with the supply of United States and Canadian markets. This was primarily due to the technical difficulties of carrying bananas over long distances, and it was generally considered that it would not be practical to deliver the fruit to Europe in a viable manner. This meant that Jamaican bananas had, in effect, only one potential customer for their products. In an attempt to provide an additional outlet a number of Jamaican merchants, led by Charles Farquharson,[1] had helped to establish and operate the Jamaica Fruit Importing and Trading Company of London Limited. However, the failure of its early shipments and the small capital of the firm led to its premature demise, so the island continued to be totally dependent upon the American market and on the United Fruit Company:

The rapid development of the industry in its early stages was due almost entirely to the capital and enterprise, first of Captain Baker's *Boston Fruit Company*, and, after 1899, to the enterprise of the *United Fruit Company*. From 1877 to 1883 about 12,500 tons of bananas a year were exported; by 1896 exports had risen to 67,000 tons; by 1902 the figure stood at 149,000 tons and in 1907 217,000 tons were exported ...[2]

It is clear, therefore, that the Jamaican economy owed much to the investment and enterprise of the United Fruit Company and to the smaller, but vitally important, efforts of what became the Atlantic Fruit Company and after 1931 the Standard Fruit Company. In many ways these American corporations proved to be beneficial, for they 'introduced a great deal of expertise and set a fine example both in respect of wages paid to their employees and the quality of the housing provided for them'.[3]

On the other hand, all of these companies were ultimately responsible to their shareholders and were consequently obliged to make whatever decisions were necessary for them to maximize their return on their capital. Of course they were able to take a long-term view of many activities, but in the final analysis all operated in what they thought was in their own best interest. There were, therefore, numerous issues which caused resentment with the growers, with price, quality and the refusal to buy stems less than those of seven hands being constant bones of contention. There was also the ever-present fear that the American firms would 'abandon' or reduce the scale of their operations in Jamaica if a cheaper source of bananas became available. Developments in Colombia, Costa Rica and Equador were subsequently to demonstrate that the fruit could, indeed, be produced much more efficiently than in Jamaica if the conditions were appropriate but, in the event, the advantage of having a diffused range of options meant that demand for the island's fruit continued at a high level.

It was, however, the fear that Cuba might replace Jamaica as a major source of bananas that led to Bishop Gordon's visit to London in 1898. Although these premonitions were to prove unfounded, they were sufficient to persuade Joseph Chamerlain that an additional outlet for Jamaican fruit must be provided in the United Kingdom.[4] The consequence was the formation of the Imperial Direct West India Mail Service Company and, ultimately, the establishment of Elders and Fyffes, Limited. By solving the technical problems of long-distance carriage these firms certainly widened the range of markets for Jamaican bananas, so that many thousands of extra tons were exported to new customers in Britain and Europe. The loading agreement made by these

144

firms with the UFC subsequently proved to be of great commercial value when Jamaica was badly affected by hurricanes but it meant that the Jamaican growers were still left with only a single buyer for their fruit. As a result there was a feeling within the industry that alternative arrangements would be valuable – either as a back-up or as a replacement to the existing organization. No one was clear what form this new system should adopt, but it was generally agreed that it would involve some form of co-operation.

Banana co-operatives were not a new idea in Jamaica: 'As far back as 1887 David Gideon of Port Antonio promoted and managed the *Jamaica Co-operative Fruit and Trading Company* which prospered for several years.'[5] The next important step came in 1904 when the St Catherine Fruit Trust was formed by a combination of growers. As the UFC refused to deal with a co-operative organization, its fruit was shipped by the Atlantic Fruit Company, then controlled by Joseph Di Giorgio. These arrangements proved to be only transitory for there was a considerable amount of movement within the business. Nevertheless the outbreak of war in 1914 saw the Jamaican banana trade firmly in the grasp of the UFC and the AFC, with many growers sadly disillusioned with the prices they received for their fruit. The shortage of shipping which then developed left the smaller producers with only the local market to fall back on, and even those with firm contracts found that they were badly affected by a rigid selection system.

These circumstances led to further calls for some form of co-operation to protect the interests of the industry, and in 1917 Arthur Farquharson was encouraged to establish the Jamaican Imperial Association. Once the war was over, this body attempted to set up a co-operative to organize banana exports, but it could make little progress because of the opposition of the American fruit corporations. As a result the Jamaica Fruit and Shipping Company began to make independent shipments of bananas to the United States in September 1919. This was made possible with the aid of an arrangement made with the Di Giorgio Fruit Corporation which was now entirely separate from the Atlantic Fruit Company.[6] The 1920s were thus to see the emergence of a degree of competition, so prices to the growers rose to a more acceptable level. Further improvements came in 1924 when the Jamaican Fruit and Shipping Company/Di Giorgio Group introduced a profit-sharing scheme which came into operation when selling prices achieved a pre-determined figure. However, the smaller producers still found that many difficulties remained, and representations were therefore made to the Imperial Economic Committee in London.[7]

This Committee's report for 1925 then recommended:

... the establishment of a Jamaica Co-operative Association and of a Direct Line between Jamaica and Great Britain. A grant of £1,200 a year for a period of two years was made to assist in the formation of a co-operative Association. In the same year negotiations were proceeding with Canada which resulted in the Canada–West Indian Trade Agreement under which the governments of Canada and Jamaica had the control of the allocation of space for the carriage of bananas in the ships of the Canadian National Steamship Line. Propaganda in favour of a Co-operative Association of producers were started on a considerable scale at this time and was given encouragement by the then Governor of Jamaica, Sir Edward Stubbs.[8]

Many suggestions were made as to what form the proposed organization should take, but ultimately a two-tier structure was adopted. The Jamaica Producers Association Limited, then became the parent body responsible for all primary products with the Jamaica Banana Producers Association Limited, acting for this one important item. The significance of the banana in the Jamaican economy at this time can be judged from Table 10.1.

TABLE 10.1   JAMAICAN BANANA EXPORTS, 1910–17[9]

Year	Stems	Value	Percentage of total exports
1910–14 (average)	14,354,860	£1,263,657	49.4
1919	9,673,557	£1,141,480	20.6
1922	12,713,849	£1,787,884	44.2
1927	21,151,881	£2,365,464	49.8

NB Figures supplied by the fruit companies differ slightly from the above (probably due to a difference between in-turn and out-turn figures).

A preliminary, unofficial, visit to England by Mr F. H. Robertson, General Manager of the Jamaica Producers Association in 1926 confirmed that a number of important wholesalers, including T. J. Poupart, Limited, and George Monro and Son would welcome the opportunity to buy direct and thus bypass the Elders and Fyffes' organisation. He also discovered that there would be no practical difficulties in obtaining a berth at London or in arranging for the railway firms to distribute the fruit as required. The major problem which remained was in respect of finance to purchase the necessary ships. It was anticipated that the whole enterprise would cost approximately £1,500,000 and unsuccessful attempts were made to persuade the Secretary of State for the Colonies to authorize the colonial government to guarantee debentures to the value of £1,000,000. However, when a modified scheme which required less capital was put forward it was approved by the Governor in spite of the disapproval of the Colonial Office.[10] Joseph Di Giorgio then agreed to find half of the cost, so that it was only necessary for the Jamaican government to guarantee debentures amounting to £200,000. With this reduced amount it was necessary to cut costs to the minimum, so four old meat-carriers which the Nelson Line was about to scrap were all that could be afforded. Although at 11 knots they were rather slow and were subject to many mechanical failures they proved to be just about adequate for their task and were able to maintain a service until new vessels could be introduced in 1931. As a result of these developments:

> The Jamaica Producers' Association began operations on the 1st of April 1929 and in the nine months to the end of the year shipped 4,020,235 stems of fruit, reckoned as 2,610,000 count bunches grown by 7,694 of its members. In the twelve months of 1932 out of a total of 20,270,000 stems shipped from the Island the Association supplied 6,351,000. This fruit was supplied by 11,628 operative contractors, members of the Association. The Association includes only 20 properties cultivating more than 200 acres of bananas; 78 between 50 and 200 acres; 1,958 between 5 and 50 acres, and 9,572 not exceeding 5 acres.[11]

Needless to say, Elders and Fyffes did all they could to oppose these developments for which they saw no need! As part of this campaign Arthur Stockley gave a major interview to the Jamaican *Gleaner* in 1928 in which he pointed out that if the profits to be made were as great as had been suggested then other competitors would surely have entered the trade. He also referred to the large numbers of bananas which the United Fruit Company (via Elders and Fyffes) were sending to England and asked what would happen to the proposed new firm if a hurricane reduced the quantity of bananas available for export?[12]

In spite of these and other efforts the scheme did, of course, go ahead, and in 1932 the Association was able to pay its members fivepence per 'count bunch' more than the United Fruit Company paid its contractors in Jamaica.[13] This satisfactory situation came to an end in November of that year when a massive hurricane struck the island. As a result the co-operatives' production was reduced by 50 per cent, load factors on its ships fell sharply and the whole enterprise became much less profitable. It was at this point that the UFC made a determined attempt to put the Association out of business by offering higher prices than the co-operative could afford:

The United Fruit Company had no objection to the growers forming a co-operative to sell their bananas to them, but they regarded a co-operative with its own shipping line and its own marketing organisation abroad as a direct competitor, one likely to make serious inroads in the company's business in Jamaica and possibly throughout the world.

An inefficient, amateurish co-operative would not have worried the United Fruit Company but, by 1933, it was quite apparent that the Jamaica Banana Producers Association was neither amateurish nor inefficient and, as a consequence, was forcing the U.F.C. to reduce their customary profit on Jamaican bananas because of the need to match the price for fruit that the co-operative was returning to its members.

Sam Zemurray, President of the U.F.C., regarded this as an intolerable situation, especially as a successful co-operative in Jamaica might well lead growers in other banana-producing countries to follow this example.

The official account of *Jamaica's Banana History* goes on to allege that:

The U.F.C. attacked by raising the price that it paid to its suppliers in Jamaica to a level which was higher than the selling price abroad could support. They could afford to do this for as long as necessary because they bought bananas in many countries and what they lost on Jamaican bananas could be made up on bananas from other sources.

The co-operative, with its meagre resources and its only source of supply being Jamaica, could not follow suit. The higher prices offered by the U.F.C. soon proved to be too tempting to large numbers of the co-operative's members, and so the quantity of fruit available to the co-op steadily declined. This meant that on each voyage the co-operatives' ships carried fewer and fewer bananas and as a consequence the freight cost per ton increased progressively as time went on. By 1935, it was clear that the co-operative could not long survive under these conditions.[14]

This crisis in the affairs of the co-operative called for urgent measures to be taken. As a first step a public meeting was held in Kingston at which over 1,200 people expressed their concern. This then resulted in a petition being sent to the Secretary for the Colonies and, in turn, to the appointment of a three-man commission to investigate the situation. The report of these banana commissioners was submitted to the Governor in May 1936, and this made it clear that the future of the industry was of major significance to the island's economy. It also made a number of recommendations and after a series of negotiations with the

148

United Fruit Company, the Standard Fruit Company (which had taken over the Jamaican interests of the Atlantic Fruit Company in 1931) and with the Jamaica Banana Producers Association, a final agreement was achieved.

This arrangement, which owed much to the generosity and the long-term view adopted by Mr Sam Zemurray, President of the United Fruit Company, provided for the Jamaica Banana Producers Association to be converted into a limited company.[15] Its principal terms were as follows:

1. The Association would cease exporting bananas to the USA and Canada and would confine its marketing operations to the UK and Continental Europe.
2. The Association would limit its exports to the quantity of bananas that March (this amounted to a maximum of about 70,000 tons of bananas per annum, which represented a bit less than 25 per cent of the UK market at the time).
3. The United Fruit Co., the Standard Fruit co., and the Association would, week by week, pay growers the same price per count bunch. (This price to be in accordance with a sliding scale proposed by the United Fruit Co. and accepted by the Jamaica Banana Producers Association Ltd. The price to growers rose as the selling price in the UK rose, and fell as that selling price fell.) The basic selling price was £16 per ton and the minimum price to growers was 2s.3d. per count bunch.
4. In return the United Fruit Co. undertook to buy from the Association at dockside Jamaica, week by week, all bananas it had in excess of the capacity of its ships and to sell to the Association at dockside Jamaica any shortfall in the supply of bananas available to the Association below the capacity of its ships.
5. In the event of the Association's supplies of bananas falling below the capacity of its ships due to hurricane, drought or other natural causes, the United Fruit Co. undertook to supply the shortfall to the Association from other sources.
6. The United Fruit Co. and the Standard Fruit Co. undertook not to import bananas into the UK from any other source so long as Jamaica was able to supply the requirements of that market. In this way the Association was assured of sufficient supplies to fill its ships and supply its customers and was also insured against the loss it would incur if it had delivered to it more bananas than its ships could hold or its marketing company could sell. The advantages to the United Fruit Co. were that:

   (a) The Association was no longer a co-operative (we have already recorded the reasons why the United Fruit Co. regarded a

149

successful co-operative as a threat to its international operations and to its operations in Jamaica).

(b) The size of the Association's operations was limited.
(c) The Association was no longer a competitor in the vast US market nor in the Canadian market.
(d) The United Fruit Co. had earned the goodwill of both the Jamaican and Imperial governments.

As the members of the Association were still permitted to market six-hand stems, smaller growers were able to secure firm contracts and all were to share in any additional returns when prices were high, it will be seen that they lost little (if anything) and gained a great deal from this agreement. The shares in the new, 'limited', company were issued in proportion to the quantity of fruit which had been delivered to the 'co-operative'. Thus the original issue was widely distributed throughout the industry and, although many were subsequently to be sold to non-growers, only those who were normally resident in Jamaica were allowed by law to become shareholders.

The agreement came into force in 1936 and worked well in practice so that the Jamaica Banana Producers Association Limited made steady progress. This can be judged by the fact that its four vessels were able to consistently achieve load factors of over 90 per cent until the outbreak of the Second World War. These ships – *Producer, Planter, Pioneer* and *Progress* – owned by a subsidiary (the Jamaica Banana Producers Steamship Company), had been built by Lithgows, Limited, of Port Glasgow in the early 1930s to replace the original fleet, but prior to the agreement they had never been used to their full capacity. Both the United Fruit Company and the Standard Fruit Company also found the new system to be beneficial, for Jamaica's banana exports reached what was to prove an all-time peak of 361,200 tons in 1937.[16] As 263,200 tons of these were sent to the UK there was also a major impact on the British market.

The growing role of Jamaica Producers was, of course, only one of the significant changes which were to alter the characteristics of the domestic banana industry in the 1930s. The death of Roger Ackerley at the end of 1929 was followed almost immediately by the retirement of Arthur Stockley, and in May 1930 his son 'Hal' Stockley succeeded him as Managing Director. As these events coincided with the 'Wall Street Crash'[17] and the catastrophic decline in world trade which was to follow, it will be seen that Messrs Elders and Fyffes were to face many problems. Athough the tonnage of bananas imported into Britain continued to grow, these had increasingly to be shared with Jamaica Producers and great pressure was exerted to keep prices to the lowest possible levels.

Thus the new managing director was obliged to provide a considerable amount of dynamic leadership. Fortunately 'Hal' Stockley had already spent many years in the banana industry and his vast experience was to play a vital part in overcoming the difficulties which gradually intensified during the early 1930s. He understood from the start that the selling price was the key to survival, both against the additional competition now taking place and the attractions of other fruits and of substitutes such as sweets and chocolate. Consequently, although costs were now very much higher, he insisted that bananas should once again be sold at their pre-war price of one penny each.

To the Retail Trade

Dear Sir,
THE PENNY BANANA
On account of the depressed conditions prevailing generally, we have decided on a very drastic reduction in the price of FYFFES Blue Label bananas to your wholesaler, with a view to stimulating sales and increasing your turnover.

As from Monday next, September 14th, our price to your wholesaler will be such as will permit his selling to you at a figure which will enable you to obtain a fair return at a retail price of ONE PENNY each or less.

We do not want to have to use the Press for price advertising, and we feel sure that with your co-operation the penny FYFFES Blue Label banana will increase sales and consumption enormously.
Yours truely, [sic]
Elders and Fyffes Limited

September 1931

Amongst the other measures which 'Hal' Stockley then instigated to promote efficiency was one which concerned the shipment of bananas and tomatoes from the Canary Islands. In the 1920s three special vessels – *Telde*, *Argual* and *Orotava* – had been built to cater for this trade, but it was now decided that it would be more economical to revert to the traditional system utilizing spare capacity on outside steamers.[18] Of even greater significance was a subsequent decision which removed the direct link between the company and its Continental subsidiaries:

On the 15th April 1932, it was decided that, in view of Continental currency and other restrictions, it was essential that the entire control of the operations of each of these Companies should be vested in the country of registration, in order to provide complete freedom of action both in selling and invoicing. The connection between Elders and Fyffes and Continental Companies is now only insofar that

Elders and Fyffes transport the bananas in their ships to Continental Ports at an agreed freight rate. Elders and Fyffes decide the number of stems to be discharged each week ex their ships on the Continent in consultation and mutual agreement with the General Manager of the Internationale Bananen Maatschappij, Rotterdam. Elders and Fyffes audit the accounts of the Continental Companies for which service they receive a fee. Other than the foregoing the Continental Companies are [now] separate entities and independent (of Elders and Fyffes).[19]

Although these developments undoubtedly helped to make the company more cost effective and it continued to make moderate profits throughout the Depression, they were to be totally overshadowed by political events on the national level. The deepening of the recession after 1929 highlighted Britain's vulnerability to changing economic circumstances which were characterized by a decline in its share of world trade (see Table 10.2).[20]

TABLE 10.2   UNITED KINGDOM'S SHARE OF THE WORLD TRADE, 1913–37

	1913	1929	1937
World trade quantum	100	133	128
UK exports quantum	100	82	72
UK share of world trade	14	11	10

When these statistics are further broken down and analysed it will be seen that trade declined much more than world production (see Table 10.3).[21]

TABLE 10.3   WORLD PRODUCTION AND TRADE, 1929–37

	1929	1932	1937
Foodstuffs:			
World trade	100	89	94
World production	100	100	108
Raw materials:			
World trade	100	82	108
World production	100	74	116
Manufacturers:			
World trade	100	57	87
World production	100	70	120

As British manufactures, its predominant export, were affected more than its imports of food and raw materials, an adverse balance of trade rapidly developed and persisted (see Table 10.4).[22]

152

TABLE 10.4 BRITAIN'S BALANCE OF TRADE, 1929–38

1929	−£259
1930	−£282
1931	−£323
1932	−£217
1933	−£196
1934	−£221
1935	−£185
1936	−£260
1937	−£339
1938	−£284

Losses on this scale had a major impact on the balance of payments, although credits from invisible exports and income from overseas investments helped to keep these deficits to manageable proportions. Nevertheless they were sufficient to lead to a loss of confidence in the pound and this, in turn, led to a serious financial crisis for the United Kingdom. This grew to such a magnitude that the newly formed National Government was obliged to take a number of emergency measures. These included the abandonment of the 'Gold Standard' and of the longstanding policy of 'Free Trade' which had been fundamental to British overseas trade for the best part of a hundred years. The latter was then replaced by a general tariff on virtually all imports. It did, however, provide for the possibility of exemption, and the Ottawa Agreement signed in 1932 arranged for a number of preferential duties to be applied to many Empire (or Commonwealth) products. Amongst these was a remission of £2 10s.0d. a ton in favour of bananas.

As Jamaica was the only important banana exporter within the Empire at that time – supplying 38.1 per cent of the British market in 1930 – it became the principal beneficiary of this new policy. Severe hurricanes in November 1932 and in October 1933 at first prevented the rate of expansion that had been expected but by 1937 Jamaica was satisfying 86.8 per cent of Britain's requirements.[23] In the interim Elders and Fyffes were obliged to import a considerable number of stems from Central America. As the full cost of the tax had to be paid on this fruit, the company became responsible for the sum of £333,439 in the year ending 31 December 1933.[24] Other smaller sums also had to be paid in later years whenever there was a shortfall in 'Empire' bananas but, as this tax also had to be borne by Jamaica Producers and any other potential importers, the company was not at a competitive disadvantage in this respect.

The increasing importance of Jamaican bananas, plus the growing competition from Jamaica Producers, and other companies ensured that

153

Elders and Fyffes' operations were all conducted as efficiently as possible. However Hal Stockley appreciated that the level of sales was the critical factor that would determine success or failure, so in addition to providing the 'penny' banana he also undertook a series of massive sales campaigns. These utilized the Fyffes' 'Blue Label' – one of the earliest, successful attempts at branding – to give its fruit a distinctive character, and every aspect of its publicity made full use of this emblem. Thus every hand of bananas was marked with a stick-on Blue Label tag, and as the company was importing over 12,000,000 stems a year in the early 1930s the placing of these items on each hand was a major task, especially as each label had to be individually wetted and fixed into position. The device was also employed on all of the company's vehicles, railway trucks, posters and advertisements, and played an important role in its early films. Its impact was, in fact, so great that the public continued to regard all bananas as 'Fyffes' Blue Label' long after other bananas, particularly those of Jamaica Producers, had become available.

In the early years of the 1930s Elders and Fyffes' share of the British Market had gradually declined. The result of Stockley's policies was that this process of erosion came to an end, and after the United Fruit Company's agreement with Jamaica Producers in 1936, Elders and Fyffes' proportion was stabilized at just over 75 per cent of a much larger market. While this represented a decrease from the near monopoly held in the 1920s, the reduction in percentage terms was more than offset by the overall increase in the quantities of bananas that were imported. This can be easily seen from the statistics, which show that while 195,800 tons arrived in the UK in 1930, this figure had risen to 305,000 in 1938.[25] As noted earlier, the vast majority of this fruit came from Jamaica – encouraged by the preference – and was 'topped up' as necessary with bananas from Central America. However, it should be understood that throughout the inter-war period bananas continued to be supplied from the company's original source in the Canary Islands.

The amalgamation of Messrs Fyffe Hudson and Company with the Fruit Department of the Elder Dempster Shipping Line in 1901[26] had brought together and combined their individual interests in the Canary Islands. Thereafter a viable business was developed which, although it was overshadowed by Elders and Fyffes' enterprise in the Caribbean, provided a useful contribution to the company's revenue. This was provided by tomatoes as well as bananas for, from the inception of the trade, it was found to be convenient to grow these two products in association with one another. The scale of these operations made it essential that they conformed with the provisions of Spanish law, so in June 1908 they were transferred to a new company – Fyffes Limited – which was specially established for this purpose.[27] This was a wholly

154

owned subsidiary of Elders and Fyffes, Limited, with an authorized capital of £500,000 (£425,000 issued) in which both Mr E. C. Barker and Henry Wolfson took a special responsibility.[28]

Henry Wolfson, who in 1887 had been the first to export tomatoes to England,[29] was appointed as the General Manager of the new concern, but he died after a brief illness in October 1909. This had the effect of placing E. C. Barker in charge of Canary affairs – a position he was to hold until his retirement in 1912. Thereafter no member of Elders and Fyffes' main board of directors maintained this special link with the islands and its authority was then exercised by a series of general managers. These were normally based at the company's offices at Santa Cruz de Tenerife, and in the period up to the outbreak of the Second World War were successively R. H. Rush, Eric Bisset and Wilfred Moore. Fyffes Limited owned three large farms in the south of Tenerife near the town of Adeje. These were Hoya Grande and Los Olivos (where bananas and tomatoes were grown) and Los Altos (which was situated high in the mountainous area and which collected rain water to be piped down to irrigate the working areas). A 'Southern' office was maintained at Hoya Grande to organize these activities, and A. F. Baillon, Thomas Maxted and Cyril Deniel were in turn estate managers on this site.[30]

As noted earlier,[31] the export of Canary bananas to the UK in the first nine months of 1912 amounted to 1,511,955 bunches (stems) of which Elders and Fyffes were responsible for 638,552 bunches. These were substantial amounts even though they were dwarfed by the more than 5 million bunches brought in from the West Indies and Caribbean in that year. The outbreak of the First World War then brought the Canary trade to an end – partly because of the collusion between the Spanish authorities and the Germans but also because of the desperate shortage of shipping. Banana and tomato production was consequently reduced, but some barley and maize was grown on the company's farms and sold in local markets. Before the war came to an end A. F. Baillon was given the task of renting as many farms as possible in the fertile Orotarva Valley. This he did at what were to prove very advantageous prices so that Fyffes were well placed to expand production once hostilities were terminated in November 1918.

The subsequent growth in Canary exports of both bananas and tomatoes then led to the opening of a branch of the company in Barcelona during October 1923.[32] This was followed by a similar offshoot at Marseilles which was designed to handle Canary fruit in France and Germany.[33] However, the vast majority of the two items continued to be brought to Britain, and it was for this reason that three specialized vessels were ordered for this trade in 1926.[34] The problems which beset Elders and Fyffes after 1929 then led to a decision to dispense with these ships, and the company then reverted to the use of space on external steamers as it was available.[35] This was partly owing to the cheapness of Central American fruit and the relative ease with which it could be handled, but it was also because of the difficulty of obtaining full cargoes in the Canaries and the adverse effects of Britain leaving the Gold Standard.[36].

The adoption of 'Imperial Preference' at the Ottawa Conference, plus the availability of cheaper Brazilian fruit, then further weakened the competitiveness of Canary bananas in the British market. As a result, and also because of the political unrest,[37] which marked the early 1930s in the Canary Islands, it was decided to reduce the company's commitments in the archipelago. Estates in the outlying islands of Gomera and La Palma were therefore sold or their leases returned, while those which had been rented in the Orotarva Valley in Tenerife were relinquished as quickly as possible.[38] This then left Fyffes with its administrative centre and warehouses in Santa Cruz de Tenerife, its three farms in the south and an office in Las Palmas on the island of Grand Canary. Thereafter the company continued to export bananas and tomatoes, which it produced on its own estates, and supplemented these in accordance with market conditions by puchasing whatever was required from local growers.

The increasing political tension in Spain in the mid-1930s was reflected in the Canaries by further tension and industrial strife. At that time General Franco was 'Captain General' of the islands, and was based at Santa Cruz de Tenerife. The delicate nature of Spanish political life tended to limit the range of individuals with whom Franco could associate, but he appears to have found some degree of companionship in the ranks of 'neutral' expatriates. Wilfred Moore, as Fyffes' General Manager, was of sufficient rank to be acceptable in this respect, and a friendship developed between the 'Captain General' and both Mr and Mrs Moore. Indeed Franco was alleged to have played a round of golf with Mrs Moore on the very afternoon before he slipped away to join his troops in North Africa. This, it was thought, was designed to deceive the Republican authorities into believing that the General was engaged in his normal social activities.[39]

Franco's departure was to signal the start of the Spanish Civil War. His followers in the Canaries were quickly able to obtain control of the entire archipelago, but in the confusion Fyffes' operations were seriously affected. This was partly due to the reduction in the number of ships which called for cargo, but also because of the requisitioning of many of the company's properties. In many areas Fyffes' warehouses were, apart from churches, the only really substantial buildings, and in the immediate aftermath of the revolution these were used to house many Republican prisoners. As these were officially referred to as 'Prison Militar Fyffes' it may be thought that the company was in some way involved. This was not the case – the Nationalists merely seized what was to hand and used the warehouses as temporary holding areas until they could screen the many individuals who had been denounced to them as 'troublemakers'.[40]

As the turmoil generated by the beginning of the civil war gradually subsided, Fyffes' buildings were steadily returned to them. The wider difficulties could not be so easily resolved. The continued lack of shipping that was prepared to call into what had become a 'war zone' meant that exports to the United Kingdom came to a virtual end. Another problem which also arose concerned the trade with the Spanish mainland. By the mid-1930s the Spanish market was absorbing 600 or 700 tons of bananas a week. These were carried from the Canaries in the vesels of the Trans-Mediterranean Company into Cadiz or Barcelona, and were then distributed by rail so that the whole of Spain was covered.[41] This substantial business also came to a halt once Franco's forces had landed from North Africa, so Fyffes had lost their second most important market as well as their first.

The loss of these sources of revenue inevitably led to the company making heavy losses, and these were compounded by the fact that new regulations meant that they were forbidden to sack any employees and had to continue to pay the wages of any men who were mobilized for the armed services. Some relief was obtained when the Military Government set up a body to market all Canary bananas, and shipments then recommenced to those areas of Spain which came under the Nationalists' control. As these were insufficient to cope with the supplies available, Fyffes reduced their output of bananas and turned over part of Hoya Grande to the production of wheat and barley for local consumption. Some attempt was also made to produce tobacco, but this was of poor quality and its 'Bicycle' brand was only saleable when imported cigars were not available.[42] The export of tomatoes was also greatly reduced at this time, but, as these were produced on a 'share-cropping' basis, Fyffes only lost their proportion of any potential profits. In order to help their employees, permission was given to continue planting the crop, but the resulting tomatoes were then either consumed by the growers and their families or sold locally to defray the cost of fertilizers and other expenses.

These temporary expedients did little more than alleviate Fyffes' near desperate position and it was against this harsh background that an even more sinister threat appeared. This was one of expropriation, for it was

157

an avowed policy of the Nationalist Party to reduce the extent of foreign control of the economy. Although Franco regarded this as a popular and desirable objective, he was aware of the difficulties which it could bring, and was frequently persuaded to exempt particular companies because of 'extenuating circumstances'. In the case of Fyffes Limited he was, of course, aware of the importance of the firm to the well-being of the Canaries and did not wish to damage its long-term prospects. After a period of uncertainty it became known that a compromise could be arranged which only required that the Fyffes name should be replaced. The necessary action was then taken by the company and was subsequently minuted as follows:

> Turning to the Canary Islands side of the business, which had virtually disappeared owing to the continuance of the Civil War in Spain, your Directors decided in March 1937 that, in order to avoid the gradual extinction of all our assets in the Canary Islands, the Lands, Houses, Buildings and Reservoirs should be sold as quickly as possible, and that the Subsidiary Company of Fyffes Limited, should go into Voluntary Liquidation.
>
> As it was considered an inopportune moment to dispose of the Hoya Estate the Company accepted as tenant Mr. Wilfred Moore, the late Resident Director of Fyffes Limited in the Canary Islands, and we are selling Tomatoes raised on the Hoya Estate and other fruit from various shippers on a Commission basis which it is hoped will result in satisfactory profits.[43]

It should be noted that the Hoya Estate included both Los Olivos and Los Altos as well as Hoya Grande. The arrangement left Wilfred Moore with great autonomy, and although it was envisaged as a temporary measure, the outbreak of the Second World War meant that his role as 'tenant' had to be continued. It was, in fact, not until 1963 that any significant change was made in this situation.

Although the Spanish Civil War had such a dramatic impact on the Canary banana industry, its original market was already being seriously undermined by Britain's adoption of 'Imperial Preference'. The other consequence of this policy was for producers, real or potential, who would benefit from the lower rate of duty. Jamaica was, of course, the only major exporter within the Commonwealth and her proportion of UK sales rose very rapidly. Unfortunately visits by hurricanes and disease, together with a number of industrial disputes,[44] made these supplies uncertain from time to time, so Elders and Fyffes were obliged periodically to obtain considerable amounts of their fruit from the United Fruit Company's plantations in Central America. As these imports were subject to the full rate of duty, the company was naturally

MV Zent sails past the Royal Liver Building on her way out from Garston.

The scene outside platform 11 at Waterloo Station, showing the special notice board in position over the barrier.

Tom Beardsley, General Manager of the Canary Islands from 1969 to 1973 is seen here handing over some bananas and a banana rootstock to Mr Arnold Eiloart and the crew of the *Small World* balloon, which subsequently made a successful flight from Tenerife to Barbados.

MV Revantazon loading bananas at Tiko Wharf, Cameroons, c. 1953.

Fyffes pionneered the *Cushioncraft*, forerunner of the *Hovercraft*, for use in the Cameroons.

Mr A. Maclaurin, our General Manager in the British Cameroons, hands over the signed agreement to Dr the Hon E. M. L. Endeley.

Lightering bananas to ship at Santa Isabel, Fernando Po.

The West Indies cricket team during a visit to New Malden in 1950. Standing (l. to r.)
J. Theed, C. S. Spiller, C. B. Williams, R. F. Edwards, O. J. Insole, L. R. Pierre,
H. T. Bartlett, R. E. Marshall, J. Skelton, R. J. Christiani, G. H. G. Doggart, B. Castor,
A. F. Rae, S. C. Griffith, G. E. Gomez, G. O. Allen, C. L. Walcott, E. R. T. Holmes,
J. M. Kidne.

General view of the new Coventry Store showing railway trucks alongside. Photo by H. C.
Woods (Northampton Branch).

interested in the possibility of developing alternative sources of 'Empire' bananas to supplement those from the West Indies.

This was part of an ongoing policy, for Elders and Fyffes had always been aware of the advantages inherent in a diverse range of sources. In accordance with this desire, and of the company's need to be aware of its competitors' activities, A. F. Baillon was sent on a mission to West Africa in 1914. His task was to investigate the progress being made by the German African Fruit Company which had planted a considerable area of bananas at Tiko in the then German colony of the Cameroons. This firm had begun the export of dried bananas in 1913 by utilizing the services provided by the Woermann Line of Hamburg and had ordered two new vessels with which it was intended to commence the carriage of 'green' bananas to Germany in the autumn of 1914. The outbreak of the First World War removed this possibility and the two ships, *Pungo* and *Pionier*, were requisitioned for government service as soon as they were completed. (Both were, in fact, to be acquired by Elders and Fyffes when hostilities came to an end.) Having completed his mission at Tiko and having also investigated the potential of Fernando Po, Mr. Baillon was fortunate to be able to leave the Cameroons before war was declared and then produced a detailed report which was, no doubt, of great value to his directors.[45]

The German forces in the Cameroons were quickly defeated, and in 1916 the occupied territory was divided between Britain and France. In 1922 it was agreed that this division should become permanent, with the two countries administrating their areas under mandate from the League of Nations. For reasons which are now not clear neither the United Fruit Company nor Elders and Fyffes decided to bid for the banana plantations when they came onto the market in 1924. They were, therefore, repurchased by their former owners and, with their aid, banana exports to Germany were resumed and rose from 281 tonnes in 1928 to 17,404 tonnes in 1932.[46]

As noted earlier,[47] La Compagnie des Bananes Société Anonyme had been set up by Elders and Fyffes to act as an independent selling organization for it in France. At first its fruit was brought in mainly from Central America, but in 1932 the French government closed its market to non-franc-zone bananas. At that time J. G. Batten was the President of the Company and it was he who conceived the idea of producing bananas in the French Cameroons to meet this changed situation. With the approval of Hal Stockley he then obtained a lease of suitable land from a Lebanese, H. Nassif, who had just cleared the site of timber. Douglas Gent was subsequently seconded to start the operation and, with the aid of A. 'Sandy' MacLaurin, production began in 1936.[48]

The success of this venture, which enabled the French Cameroons to make significant contributions to the French market, did not encourage a similar development in the British mandated territory. A close watch was, however, kept upon the situation, so that on the outbreak of the Second World War they were immediately able to take over the estates abandoned by the German planters. This then enabled Elders and Fyffes to begin the importation of Cameroon bananas, and the first cargo arrived in Britain on 9 November 1939. This was quickly followed by a further seven, so that by the end of the financial year a total of 11,188 tons had arrived.[49] The Company's *General Minute Book* then records the formal acquisition of the lease of the German properties at Likomba and Tiko – these were later to provide the basis of post-war imports from the Cameroons:

> In the month of October 1939 your Directors purchased from the Chase National Bank of New York at a cost of £81,209–13–5, Promissory Notes held by the Bank in connection with an advance made to a client who had secured the purchase of the majority of shares in the *Guatemala Plantagens Gesellshaft.*[50]

The net effect of these developments in the 1930s was that the import of Jamaican bananas was encouraged and supplemented by Central American fruit, while supplies from the Canaries came to a halt and were only partly replaced by cargoes from the British Cameroons. As the decade had seen a substantial increase in the tonnage received in the UK, Elders and Fyffes found it necessary to expand the number of ports utilized by their ships. Thus although Avonmouth and Garston remained their principal points of entry, Southampton became increasingly important, especially after the company had been allocated a special berth in 1934.[51] Earlier, in 1931, Swansea – which offered special bunkering facilities – had been made the terminal port for that part of the Elders and Fyffes' fleet which operated on its continental routes.[52]

The fleet, which had reached a peak of thirty-six vessels in 1930,[53] was to experience rather more fluctuating fortunes during the 1930s. A direct consequence of the depression and of the need for economy was seen in the decision to end the sailings of the three vessels which had been constructed specialy for the Canary Islands' trade. Another aspect of the recession was on the Continental business, where currency restrictions in Germany and quotas in France reduced the need for tonnage on this route.[54] Of even greater immediate significance was the effect of particularly bad weather in Jamaica, and following hurricanes in November 1932 and October 1933 it was necessary to lay up two-thirds of the fleet.[55] The net effect of all of these difficulties was that the fleet

160

had become too large for the company's needs and it was progressively reduced during the 1930s so that by 1940 it consisted of only twenty-one vessels.

This was not, however, the whole story. Elders and Fyffes' close links with the United Fruit Company meant that a number of exchanges and transfers were made between their two fleets. As a result of a further merger between the UFC and the Cuyamel Fruit Company of Honduras in 1931, three of the latter's vessels were transferred to Fyffes. These were *Aztec, Maya* (renamed *Mazatec*) and *Toltec* and were used on the Honduras to Rotterdam and Bremerhaven service. Following the Nazi regime's refusal to pay for imports in foreign currency the demand for tonnage on these routes was reduced. At about the same time the United Fruit Company wished to employ these three vessels on their new service between the West Coast of Central America as their capacity and speed made them particularly suitable. They were therefore transferred to the small Danish firm of P. A. Jensen but when Denmark was invaded by the Germans they were transferred to one of UFC's Honduran subsidaries.[56]

The changing circumstances outlined above obviated the need for new tonnage, and no new vessels were ordered during the decade. This brought to an end Elders and Fyffes' long connection with Cammell Laird and Company who had constructed so many ships for the firm during the 1920s. This relationship began when Mr R. S. Johnson was made a director of the Birkenhead shipbuilders after moving from Belfast in 1920. The high regard in which he was held can be seen from the following message from the President of the United Fruit Company:

> *Preson cables*: We consider Johnsons knowledge of ship construction for our requirements an important factor and would practically insure our placing orders wherever he may have proper direction.[57]

Johnson, who became Managing Director of Cammell Lairds in 1922, became very friendly with A. H. Stockley, and their co-operation was strengthened when the United Fruit Company purchased US $500,000 of the shipbuilders' shares.[58] Stockley subsequently became a part-time director of Cammell Lairds and this association, plus Johnson's special knowledge of the requirements of the banana trade, then ensured a steady flow of orders until the onset of the depression in 1929.[59]

The growing tonnage handled by Elders and Fyffes in the 1930s and the need to adopt the most cost-effective systems saw a gradual change in the method of distribution. This began in 1933 when the following decision was recorded:

161

With a view to extending the business more directly amongst retailers (as distinct from wholesale handlers) the Company have embarked on a policy of opening *Store Branches* in certain large towns, from which the fruit is delivered by motor lorry to the retailers in the town and surrounding districts. Within the year now under review new Branches have beeen established in the following places:

Blackburn	Oldham,
Bournemouth,	Portsmouth,
Eastbourne,	Stockport,
Kingston-on-Thames	Swindon,
Motherwell,	Somers Town (London N.W.1),

and further Stores will be opened during 1934.[60]

This policy was, in fact, to be continued during the remainder of the decade, so that by the beginning of the Second World War the company was operating 55 branches and supplied 750 independent handlers. Although rail was still utilized to move the bananas from their port of arrival to the principal depots there had been a steady increase in the role of road transport, and at the end of 1939 Elders and Fyffes had 141 motor lorries in service plus two in reserve.[61] This vast network employed a staff of 2,690 British subjects in October 1935, in addition to 1,569 Spaniards who worked for the firm in the Canaries and in Spain.[62] In 1939 its shore staff in the UK amounted to about 1,650, but by the December of that year 282 were already serving in the armed services.[63]

The company quickly adopted the practice of subsidizing those employees who joined His Majesty's Forces by making up their pay to their peacetime salary. This was a continuation of the care which Elders and Fyffes had always taken of their employees: one of the reasons why so many of their staff spent their entire working lives with the firm. While the attractions of a secure job at a time of uncertain employment was certainly a factor in many individuals deciding to spend their entire career with Fyffes it is equally clear that the directors went out of their way to encourage the feeling that all were part of a family.

One way in which this attitude was strengthened involved the provision of retirement pensions for all members of the permanent staff earning less than £2,000 per annum. While many *ad hoc* arrangements had existed from the establishment of the company in 1901, these were placed on a more formal basis when Elders and Fyffes Staff Provident Fund was set up in 1922.[64] This was intended to provide for payments on retirement and also to create a Special Benefit Account. The scheme was financed by a small deduction from each individual's salary or wages – the basic rate varying from **2m** to 5 per cent depending upon their particular activity within the business, with marine staff paying the maximum amount. The company contributed up to an additional 10 per cent, and each year the surplus of income over expenditure was invested in authorized Trustee Securities (Government or Local Authority Stocks). At the same time the interest received on these holdings was added to the capital and re-invested as necessary.

On retirement an individual would be given a lump sum which was based on the amount of contributions he had made. Thus years of service and level of remuneration were automatically taken into account. It was intended that this payment should be invested to provide an ongoing pension but, as it was appreciated that in many cases it would be insufficient for even a moderate standard of living, the directors were usually prepared to top up the amount by the granting of an additional year's pay. This was not guaranteed and members of staff would not know what they would receive until the very last moment; as this extra sum might otherwise be regarded as income, it was not actually paid until after retirement had commenced.

The Staff Provident Fund was rightly regarded as being extremely advanced and progressive for its time, but it did possess a number of weaknesses. One of these concerned the provision for dependents after 'death in service'. The only entitlement was a lump sum which was made up by the deceased member's balances together with the whole of the company's contribution. If this was not enough to provide an adequate income the widow could apply to the Special Benefit Fund but would only be successful if almost destitute. Home-ownership would almost certainly debar any such application; the company might be persuaded to make an *ex gratia* payment of a year's salary, but this was subject to many constraints and there was no actual entitlement.[65]

Another way in which the company attempted to encourage an *esprit de corps* within its staff involved the provision of a sports ground at New Malden in Surrey. Although this was of particular interest to employees living in the London area, every member of Elders and Fyffes – ashore or afloat – and of the Fruit Distribution Company was also automatically given honorary status in Fyffes' Sports Club.[66] In spite of the fact that the pavilion was still being constructed, the ground was opened for the 1922 season and provided the venue for many fierce-fought tussles between the London cricket team and those from the provinces. In the following year J. A. Armstrong's XI, which included a number of Fyffes players, was opposed by an eleven brought together by H. D. Swann who was a member of the MCC. This included many England and county players, and the fixture proved to be such a success that it was to be repeated annually thereafter.[67] These games always included a strong nucleus of Fyffes' employees, with J. N. Crawford (of Surrey and England) and S. T. Theed usually prominent in the scoring. After 1928 many West Indian players were included in Swann's XI[68] and, in appreciation of the company's generous assistance with their travel arrangements, a private match was played between the tourists and a Fyffes' team at the conclusion of each tour.[69]

It should not be forgotten, however, that the New Malden ground complemented similar facilities at Avonmouth and Liverpool. These then provided the basis for many inter-area competitions in tennis, bowls and football, in addition to those in cricket, and there was always a social side to these activities. The spirit engendered in this way then appears to have helped to produce the type of dedicted individual who was always prepared to place his company's interests before his own convenience. The presence of so many employees with this attitude, the sound financial foundations of the firm and the discreet support of the United Fruit Company had thus enabled Elders and Fyffes to weather the many difficulties which had arisen during the 1930s. It was now to face the challenge set by the declaration of the Second World War.

11

The Second World War and its aftermath

The outbreak of hostilities on 3 September 1939 meant that Elders and Fyffes immediately faced a number of major problems. The most pressing of these concerned the fleet, for the German Navy at once began to wage unrestricted attacks upon the merchant ships of the Allied powers. As the twenty-one specialized banana carriers owned by the company continued to operate in their normal trades they were consequently at great risk. This was reflected at the Ordinary General Meeting held in respect of the year ending on 31 December 1939, when the 'abnormal conditions' were referred to:

> It is, however, a source of satisfaction to your Directors to be able to report that although navigation became very difficult and voyages were in some cases prolonged, they were all safely performed and the cargoes were discharged and distributed with remarkable promptitude.[1]

The disruption and delays caused by the beginning of the war, plus the effects of a hurricane in Jamaica, reduced the throughput of West Indian fruit handled by the company in 1939, and at 160,003 tons it was 17,893 tons less than in the previous year. However, this deficit was partly reduced by bananas sold on commission for the Standard Fruit and Steamship Company for these rose by 1,310 tons to 36,654 tons.[2] As most of the remaining shortfall was filled by the new shipments from the Cameroons, it will be appreciated that 1939 was a near-normal trading year in many respects. Thus all of its internal distribution and marketing facilities continued to be fully employed, and in the absence of enemy bombing the only real difficulty was that provided by the increasing numbers of staff who were 'called-up' or who volunteered for the armed services.

The period of what became known as the 'phoney war' came to an abrupt end as far as Elders and Fyffes was concerned when *Chagres II* was mined off the Mersey Light vessel in February 1940. By then two of the five A Class passenger vessels – *Bayano II* and *Camito* – had already been requisitioned, and *Carare* was to be sunk in the Bristol Channel during May 1940 when on her last commercial voyage before being handed over. The other two passenger/cargo liners – *Ariguani* and *Cavina* – were then transferred for war service and both, plus *Bayano II*, were to survive to operate again under peacetime conditions. Unfortunately *Camito*, which had become an armed boarding vessel, was torpedoed and lost in May 1941.[3]

In addition to *Chagres II* and *Carare*, a further six company vessels were to be lost during 1940. These were *Samala I* in September, *Sulaco I* and *Matina II* in October, and *Casanare*, *Mopan* and *Aractaca II* in November. Thereafter the rate of sinkings declined, so that only *Camito* was sunk during 1941. Two vessels, *Cristales* and *Nicoya II* were torpedoed in 1942 – strangely enough both being hit on 12 May – while the final casualty *Tucurinca* was lost in March 1943.[4]

The loss of so many vessels and the requisitioning of others quickly led to a considerable reduction in Elders and Fyffes' ability to import bananas into Britain. This situation was exacerbated by the sinking of three of the four ships owned by the Jamaican Banana Producers Association[5] and so a shortge of specialized banana carriers rapidly became apparent. On the supply side of the equation the severe hurricane which damaged up to 90 per cent of the Jamaican crop at the beginning of 1939 was almost immediately followed by a serious outbreak of Panama disease.[6] As a result of these two factors Jamaican exports to the UK fell substantially and, although they were partly made up from other sources, total imports into Britain fell from a total of 288,000 tons in 1939 to 193,000 tons in 1940.[7]

By the autumn of 1940 over 450 members of Elders and Fyffes' staff had left its employ to undertake military service of one kind or another. The remaining 1,200 shore-based employees were then coping with the reduced throughput as best they could and, in spite of the blackout, rationing, shortages and increasingly of bombing attacks, were ensuring that the available supplies of fruit were distributed on an equitable basis throughout the country. It was against this background that on 9 November 1940 the Ministry of Food – without any prior consultation – decided upon a total prohibition of banana imports.[8] Lord Woolton, the Minister concerned, claimed that it was better to have a good supply of one fruit rather than a poor supply of several.[9] Had the fruit selected been the banana, the company may have taken a different view, but as it was the orange which was chosen Elders and Fyffes quickly mounted a vigorous campaign of opposition! This was pursued with even greater strength when the Government:

... responded by mounting a high-pressure campaign which decried the food value of fruit in general and of the banana in particular. Through radio talks, articles and advertisements in the press, government-paid speakers informed the public that there was 'nothing important in either oranges or bananas that cannot be got from vegetables'.[10]

Statements of this kind went far beyond arguing the case that in wartime many sacrifices had to be made, and that for purely logistical, financial or other (undisclosed) reasons it was beneficial to concentrate upon importing oranges rather than other fruits. To suggest, however, that the banana contained little, if anything, that was of value to the human diet was another matter entirely. Thus

> ... although [the company] was more than willing to make sacrifices in the time of the nation's struggle for survival it was not prepared to stand by and say nothing while the reputation of the banana was destroyed. After all, it had taken the Company years to educate the British public into appreciating the 'all food fruit'. If the ban had to be, it had to be, but said the Company 'let's have the truth even from the Government'.[11]

Elders and Fyffes were supported by many eminent doctors and scientists who upheld their claims in respect of the food value of the banana, but in the end the ban was duly enforced. The nation was then totally dependent upon imported oranges, particularly in the form of concentrated juice, and on the domestic production of such indigenous fruits as apples, pears and plums. As this orange juice was easier to handle than bananas, and as it could be carried in a wide variety of vessels, the decision to import this rather than fresh or refrigerated fruits can be understood. It could also be argued that the specialized vessels operated by the company were better employed in bringing refrigerated cargoes of meat, eggs and bacon from Halifax and New York – as a number were – instead of maintaining their existing trade. However, it is likely that the specific embargo on the banana was caused by purely practical considerations.

In the first year of the war most of Elders and Fyffes' vessels were able to sail independently, for their relatively high speed was considered to be a useful defence against German attacks. Following the capture of Norway and the fall of France the wider range of bases and airfields which became available to the Germans enabled the submarine campaign, aided by aerial reconnaissance, to reach a new intensity. The growing losses sustained by the company's fleet in the autumn of 1940 meant that independent voyages were no longer safe. Most of Britain's

167

merchant ships were by then being grouped together in convoys, but this solution was not really appropriate for banana carriers. The level of technology at the time had been developed to cope with voyage times of approximately twenty-one days, but escorted convoys tended to be slow and were subject to many delays and diversions. Thus it was the fear that cargoes of bananas might overheat and be ruined that was one of the major factors which lay behind the ban. Although military necessity may have prevented this from being stated at the time, the denigration of the banana – and to some extent of all fruit – was surely unnecessary and undesirable!

The ban itself, however desirable in the national interest, was to have serious consequences in many different places. Its impact was particularly important in Jamaica:

> The U.S.A. had not yet entered the war and the *United Fruit Company* was able to continue the marketing of bananas from Central and South America in the U.S.A. and Canada. To provide employment for banana growers and to keep a nucleus of the industry in existence, the British government undertook to buy, although it could not carry away, all the bananas produced in the island up to a maximum of 12,000,000 stems per annum. The price agreed upon was 3s. per count bunch which seemed adequate at the time in view of the fact that the average price received by the growers in 1938 had been 3s. per count bunch and in 1939 3s.10d. But conditions were changing. In spite of efforts by government to control it, the cost of living index began to rise and an increase in the basic wages paid by government led to a general increase in the wage level throughout the island. Additional costs resulted from leaf spot disease which, having made its appearance a few years previously, was now becoming more difficult and costly to control ... [12]

As the Government was not prepared to increase the price it paid to the growers their operations gradually became unprofitable and cultivation fell, so that by 1944 it amounted to only one-third of the pre-war acreage. Thus the number of stems either exported or purchased under the government's subsistence scheme steadily declined so that the 23,699,000 stems of 1938 were reduced to only 4,000,000 stems in 1944.[13] While the government price to growers was increased to 3s.6d. in that latter year, this was not sufficient to stop the fall in output as the cost of production was then running at 4s. per count bunch. A further disturbing development was that the 1936 agreement with the United Fruit Company was cancelled and there was much apprehension as to what the future might bring. The establishment of a 'Banana Committee' and then an 'All Island Banana Growers Association' reflected these fears and were designed to give the growers some say in the way that their industry was to be run after the war was over.

The situation in the Cameroons was similar to that in Jamaica. The ban on banana imports brought the recently established trade with the UK to an end and the Cameroons' industry was then faced with the same problems which had developed in the West Indies. The British government offered the same solution, and compensation at £5 per ton was paid on 50,000 tons each year for bananas which had to be destroyed because they could not be shipped.[14] An increasing proportion of the plantations were gradually turned over to the production of food crops and by 1945 around 50 per cent were being utilized for the growing of leguminous plants.[15] A basis for post-war expansion was therefore preserved.

The ongoing disruption which followed the ending of the Spanish Civil War meant that no bananas and only a small quantity of tomatoes were being sent from the Canaries to Britain when hostilities commenced in September 1939. The subsequent shortage of shipping space then prevented any resumption of these previous large trades, and imports from the islands did not recommence until after the Second World War was over. In the meanwhile some quantities of bananas and tomatoes were produced by Wilfred Moore for local consumption or for export to Spain[16] and Hoya Grande and Los Olivos also continued to grow wheat, barley, maize and tobacco on the balance of their land. This was mainly used to feed their employees and was only sold on local markets when there was a surplus.[17] It is clear, therefore, that while the British government's embargo on the importation of bananas had serious consequences for both Jamaica and the Cameroons, it had virtually no impact on the Canary Islands.

The other potential sufferer from the ban was the company itself, for with a large staff and extensive storage and distribution facilities it suddenly found itself deprived of its *raison d'etre*. Arrangements were, however, quickly made with the Ministry of Food so that all of its store branches and other premises were utilized as emergency food stores, buffer stock depots and distribution centres. Those vehicles that were not required to assist in this task were then hired out on a contract basis and used to perform officially approved journeys for other firms. The Shipping Department was also extremely busy, for it continued to be responsible for that part of the fleet which was not requisitioned for naval purposes and, in addition, it was asked to manage a number of other vessels for the Ministry of War Transport. These included four ex-Finnish steamers: *Brita Thorden, Esther Thorden, Rosenborg* and *Yildum*, and four new vessels: *Empire Abbey, Empire Balfour, Empire Lady*, and the American-built *Samstrule*.[18] It should be noted that the company also managed m.v. *Salzburg* which was renamed *Empire Mole* but this did not commence until September 1945. In addition the Shipping Department continued to manage *Eros* and *Erin*, two *United Fruit* vessels owned by the Morant Steam Ship Company.

This wide range of activities then ensured that Elders and Fyffes' reduced number of employees were kept fully occupied for the remainder of the war. Thus, in addition to making a useful contribution to the war effort, the company was able to obtain a reasonable return on its employed capital. These results were, of course, achieved against a background of heavy losses to the fleet and a rising level of casualties amongst those employees who had joined the armed services. Those engaged on the home front were also at great risk, and

> ... on 11 January 1941, Fyffes' London headquarters received a direct hit during a German bombing raid on London. Thirteen members of the staff who were on fire-watching at the time were killed outright together with nine members of the public who, having just left Drury Lane Theatre, had asked and been granted permission to use the firm's air raid shelter.[19]

The damage at Bow Street was so substantial that Elders and Fyffes were obliged to abandon the building which had served as its administrative centre since 1910. Alternative office accommodation was quickly found in Bush House, Aldwych, and although this was in a deplorable condition with no water, heating or even glass in its windows it provided a temporary base in which the company could continue to operate and could begin to reconstruct its business records. This was a massive task, but with the aid of its customers and suppliers a duplicate set of accounts and correspondence was gradually built up. The building was slowly made more habitable, but in December 1941 Elders and Fyffes were advised that it was required for the use of the civil service and it was obliged to seek other premises. These were found at Astor House, also in Aldwych, and at Hay Hill and these were then to be occupied until it was possible to move to a more permanent home at 15 Stratton Street, Piccadilly, in March 1947. By a strange chance this proved to be next door to the former home of Sir Alfred Jones.[20]

Elders and Fyffes' premises at Eastbourne and Bournemouth were also to be badly damaged by enemy action,[21] but the real cost to the company was the loss of so many of its employees:

> Of the 612 members of Fyffes serving with the armed forces, fifty-four were killed, many wounded and twelve taken prisoner. Fifty ship's officers lost their lives together with a great many men of the Merchant Navy serving on Fyffes' ships. In addition to the thirteen

lives that were lost as a result of the destruction of the Bow Street premises, six other Fyffes staff were killed in enemy air-raids – five in London and one in Bristol.[22]

Throughout the wartime period Elders and Fyffes continued to acquire further businesses with a view to strengthening their distribution network when their normal trade was resumed. Mindful of the rapid development of aircraft, and looking forward to their potential in peacetime, the company altered its Memorandum of Association so that it could operate all forms of 'Aerial Transport'.[23] It also made repeated attempts to have the ban on the banana lifted, but these were totally unsuccessful so that even the importation of dried bananas was not approved:

Application to import Banana Powder was refused in February 1942 on the grounds that compared with other products it was wasteful of shipping space.[24]

Thus, when hostilities came to an end in the summer of 1945, it should be appreciated that it was necessary for the company to resume its traditional trade from absolute scratch. Indeed every aspect of their potential activities was faced with enormous difficulties. On the supply side the growing areas in Jamaica, the Canaries and the Cameroons were in varying degrees of disarray; most of the fleet had been sunk and the remainder were still requisitioned; the internal transport system was very fully stretched and the entire handling, ripening and distributing network was still totally devoted to other purposes. In addition, the sudden ending of the 'Lend-Lease' arrangements with the United States had placed great pressure on the British balance of payments and it remained to be seen when permission would be given for imports of many items, including bananas, would be given.

There were, however, a number of favourable factors which helped to offset these problems. The closure of the Continental and British markets in 1939 and 1940 meant that the United States became responsible for 80 per cent of the world trade in bananas. This constant demand in North America ensured that while Jamaican output declined, that of both Honduras and Ecuador steadily increased. The latter made particularly rapid progress, for it possessed many economic advantages over other regions. On the other hand it was on the wrong side of South America for its principal customers and this disadvantage meant that for it to remain competitive it was seldom able to levy export duties on its fruit. The growth of its exports were, of course, greatly restricted once the USA entered the war, but when it was over Ecuador was in an excellent position to supply North America with large quantities of high-quality (though poor appearance) bananas at very moderate prices. In these circumstances there appeared to be little scope for Jamaica to obtain a share in this market, so once again it looked to Britain to provide an outlet for its fruit.

The new Labour Government in London proved to be very sympathetic to Jamaican approaches, for it was naturally anxious to widen the diet of the war-weary British public as soon as possible. The acute shortage of 'hard currency' made it essential that as many items as practical should be acquired from non-dollar sources, and Jamaican fruit fell precisely into this category. Accordingly, almost as soon as the war was over, a contract was signed under which the British government agreed to buy all Jamaican bananas of exportable quality. This agreement provided for the introduction of a new system under which the importers would act as 'selling agents' on behalf of the Ministry of Food. These developments were then reflected in Elders and Fyffes' *General Minute Book*, as follows:

> The ban on the import of Bananas into this Country imposed by the Ministry of Food in November 1940, has been partially lifted for on 18th September 1945 the Ministry of Food announced that importations of small quantities of Jamaican Bananas would be permitted early in 1946 and, as opportunity offered, the supplies from Jamaica would be supplemented by Bananas from other sources.
>
> Until such time as supplies became normal, distribution will be under the direction of the Ministry of Food, and your Company in conjunction with the Jamaica Producers Marketing Co. Ltd. were appointed 'Selling Agents' in the proportion of 80 per cent ourselves and 20 per cent Jamaica Producers Association at a remuneration of £3–5–0d. per ton on quantities sold, subject to review at the end of 6 months.
>
> In view of the above the Ministry of War Transport permitted the s.s. *Tilapa* and s.s. *Tetela* to be re-conditioned for the carriage of Bananas and Citrus Fruit in August/September of 1945.[25]

The result of these arrangements was that in December 1945 s.s. *Tilapa* docked in Avonmouth with ten million bananas on board, and a new generation of Britons had their first taste of the 'fruit of the wise men'. This cargo was distributed by an *ad hoc* combination of rail and road transport and was assisted by the gradual release of Elders and Fyffes' requisitioned premises: by the end of 1945 the company was administering 135 buffer depots as compared with 177 at the close of 1944.[26]

The first post-war voyage of *Tilapa* was soon followed by many others, and 102,000 tons of bananas were marketed in Britain during 1946.

172

However, for a variety of reasons which will now be examined, it was not until 1955 that the pre-war level of 305,000 tons was again achieved. At first a prime cause was a shortage of suitable shipping, for the release of *Tilapa* and *Tetela* still left a further five vessels being retained for government service. However even when *Ariguani, Bayano II* and *Cavina II* were de-requisitioned in March 1946 the last two were not immediately employed in the Company's service and were at first placed on time charter with Cunard. Thus it is apparent at this very early stage that it was the shortage of bananas (and dollars) that were the limiting factors rather than the availability of tonnage. *Ariguani* therefore re-started the passenger service on her own in May 1946 and then operated on a monthly schedule until she was joined on this route by *Bayano II* in 1947 – this became a fortnightly schedule when *Cavina II* became available in 1948.[27] The remaining B class vessels (*Corrales* and *Tortugero II*) also rejoined the fleet, but even with all its remaining vessels restored to commercial use wartime losses meant that the company lacked the necessary capacity to service the trade adequately.

In accordance with government regulations it had only been possible to order one new vessel while the war was still in progress.[28] Although *Matina III* was completed in time to join the fleet in 1946, a considerable shortfall in tonnage remained, so Elders and Fyffes were forced to adopt a number of urgent expedients. These resulted in the acquisition of *Chirripo II* which was transferred from the United Fruit Company, and the purchase of *Erin* (which was renamed *Manistee III*) from the Morant Steam Ship Company. In addition, four vessels were obtained from the Ministry of War Transport. These were *Pelikan, Pontos* and *Panther* which had formerly been operated by F. Laeisz and Company which were renamed *Pacuare II, Nicoya III* and *Reventazon III*; the fourth ship was the former *Viator*, built for C. H. Sorenson and Sons of Norway and renamed *Angelburg* when sold to the Fruchtreederei Harald Schuldt and Company, KG. It was subsequently taken as a war prize and after being secured by Elders and Fyffes was re-registered as *Zent III*.[29]

The acquisition of these seven vessels, plus the seven which had survived the Second World War, then proved to be sufficient to cope with the available trade, and it was not until 1949, when *Golfito* was constructed by Alexander Stephen and Company, that the fleet was further strengthened. The failure of supplies to expand as rapidly as had been expected was largely due to difficulties in Jamaica. This can be clearly seen from the statistics, which show that the proportion of bananas imported into Britain from the island fell from 76.4 per cent in 1938 (the last full year before the war) to only 48 per cent of a much smaller total in 1946.[30] These problems were partly caused by the wartime disruption which reduced output to a very low level, but a number of hurricanes and a severe outbreak of leaf spot disease also played their part. The net effect of these drawbacks was that production recovered very slowly and, hindered by further storms in 1950 and 1951, exports were virtually the same in 1952 as they had been in 1946.[31]

This shortage of Jamaican bananas was the principal problem which faced Hal Stockley when he replaced Sir Samuel H. Wilson as Chairman of Elders and Fyffes in May 1946. He had, of course, been Managing Director of the firm since the retirement of his father, A. H. Stockley, in 1930, but this concentration of authority in a single person now gave the company the ability to respond even more quickly to changing circumstances. His first task was to persuade the government to agree to approve his plans to import fruit from both the Cameroons and the Canaries. The success of his campaign meant that from 1946 the wartime embargo and Ministry of Food restrictions on the banana was totally lifted and Elders and Fyffes were then able to bring in the fruit from a wider range of non-dollar sources.

As the British Trustee territory of the Southern Cameroons benefited from the Empire Preference of £2 10s.0d. per ton which had been introduced in 1932,[32] it was obviously in the company's interest to attempt to build up supplies from that quarter:

> With hot sunshine, rich deep volcanic soil and an average rainfall of 140 inches a year, a substantial part of the coastal area of the Cameroons is ideal for the cultivation of bananas. When Fyffes returned to the Cameroon territory most of the old German plantations had been absorbed by the recently formed Cameroons Development Corporation and it was together with that association that the Company set about rebuilding the Cameroon banana industry. By 1948 with the industry once more thriving, Fyffes established their own stake in the area by taking a long lease on the 16,000 acre Likomba estate of which, at that time, 9,000 acres were planted with Gros Michel bananas.[33]

During the war there had been no possibility of exporting green bananas from the Cameroons, and many of its plantations had been given over to the growing of food for local consumption. Some bananas continued to be planted and small quantities were dried in an abortive attempt to maintain some overseas trade. The technique was to remove the skin and then to heat the whole banana in a home-made oven fired by wood. The resulting product was dark brown in colour and quite soft. The occupation of France and the refusal of the UK authorities to accept this form of fruit prevented any exports to Europe during the period of hostilities, but once it was over it proved to be quite popular. In

France it was then eaten as a dessert, but in Britain it only found a market in its powdered format. Elders and Fyffes were responsible, under licence, for the whole of the dried banana output of the British Cameroons and it produced good profits. However, as this did not fit comfortably with the remainder of its business it appointed the Mapleton Nut Food Company Limited to act on its behalf in the UK.[34]

One fob (free on board) shipment of Cameroon bananas was received during March 1946, but a serious storm prevented this from being immediately repeated.[35] Negotiations with the British government then made the company the sole shippers and selling agents for all British Cameroon bananas except those from the Likomba Plantations. At the same time Elders and Fyffes undertook to advise the Cameroon Development Corporation (CDC) on all aspects of banana cultivation and on the development of its estate.[36] When imports of green bananas resumed in 1947 it was under these new arrangements, so that the company distributed and sold all of the Cameroon's bananas on account of the CDC and the Custodian of Enemy Property (Nigeria) – the rate of remuneration being 5 per cent per ton on gross sales.[37] Production of the company's own bananas began in 1948, but although it made good progress it was constantly hindered by storms and bad weather. Thus in 1950 a blow-down caused the loss of 2,336,000 plants and in 1952 a further 2 million were again destroyed.[38]

The difficulties experienced in the Cameroons as well as in Jamaica then encouraged Hal Stockley to re-examine the situation in the Canaries. As noted earlier,[39] Mr Wilfred Moore had been appointed as the company's 'tenant' in order to satisfy the needs of the Spanish authorities, and he had remained in charge of its affairs throughout the Second World War. During this period the island's output of bananas had slowly recovered, with most of the crop being sent to the Spanish mainland and the balance being consumed locally. Once the war was over and the British ban on imports was withdrawn, the opportunity of resuming shipments to the UK was grasped and production rose by a further third between 1945 and 1952.[40] Under the guidance of Wilfred Moore, Hoya Grande and Los Olivos were gradually replanted with bananas and tomatoes, and contributed to the growing output. They were not, however, exported in their own name at this time, but formed part of the system organized by the officially recognized CREPE (Confederacion Regional de la Exportacion del Platano).

Britain's share of these banana exports steadily increased during the late 1940s and early 1950s, and in 1952, when production reached over 219 million net kilos, over 118 million were sent to foreign markets – principally those in the UK. All of this fruit was handled by Elders and Fyffes on behalf of the Ministry of Food at the customary remuneration of £3 5s.0d. per ton. As Wilfred Moore's position continued to be advantageous to the company, it was decided to liquidate its subsidiary in the Canaries and Fyffes Limited was legally wound up in November 1946.[41] In order to protect the 'Fyffes' name and trade mark it was then thought necessary to establish a new firm to prevent others from acquiring these rights. Consequently a new Fyffes Limited was duly registered in the UK early in 1948.[42] This precaution was to prove valuable when further reconstructions were undertaken in the 1960s and 70s.

The gradual recovery of production in Jamaica, the Cameroons and in the Canaries enabled imports to rise from the 102,000 tons in 1946 to 167,000 tons in 1952. As this figure was little more than half the pre-war peak, it would be right to assume that the available supply was much less than the potential demand. There had, in fact, been a considerable increase in the acreage devoted to bananas in Central and South America, but Britain's chronic shortage of American dollars meant that this source of fruit was not available to the British market. This was not a constraint which affected the Continental trade, so as soon as the necessary tonnage was available the direct service between the Caribbean and Rotterdam was restarted. This began in May 1946 utilizing chartered vessels but these were gradually replaced after June 1947 as Company tonnage became available – the cargoes being entirely made up of 'dollar bananas', which were largely provided by the United Fruit Company. Passenger services to the UK which had commenced in May 1946 were also gradually extended: '... so that on the seventy-eight voyages completed by Fyffes Line ships in 1947, 4,746 passengers were carried in addition to 117,688 tons of cargo.'[43]

Elders and Fyffes' business had been built up on the principle that it would employ specialized carriers which would transport its bananas so efficiently that the operation would still be viable even though return voyages were made in ballast. Nevertheless every effort was made to carry items needed by the company, such as machinery and fertilizers, in its vessels, but prior to 1939 there is no evidence to suggest that it ever loaded cargo for third parties on a commercial scale. It had been suggested that this arrangement was part of an unofficial understanding which A. H. Stockley reached with Sir Owen Phillipps of the Royal Mail Group and others.[44] The basis of this was that while Elders and Fyffes did not become common carriers other lines would not enter the banana business! While this would appear to be the kind of agreement which was quite usual in the first half of the twentieth century, there is no documentary evidence to give it credence. In any event, the company's prime consideration was the carriage of its fruit and, with the need for precise scheduling, anything more than small parcels of cargo may have been more trouble than it was worth.

It would seem, therefore, that throughout the inter-war period little in the way of outward cargo was carried on the Caribbean route. A typical example (provided by Captain K. Leslie from the manifest of s.s. *Ariguani* in 1931) shows the type and scale of items that were shipped:

13 bales of periodicals	–	private
1 motor car	–	private
5 packages earthernware	–	United Fruit Company,
2 packages cottons		Kingston
1 bale blankets	–	United Fruit Company,
500 bales paper sacks		Santa Marta

During the same period oranges, grapefruit and coffee were carried on the homeward voyage when space was available and, after the Second World War, (when shipments were still under the control of the Ministry of Food) orange and lime juice and oranges were carried from Trinidad and Jamaica.

The post-war development of plantations in the Cameroons then resulted in the growth of a steady outward trade in items for Likomba and for the Cameroons Development Corporation. These included general and medical supplies, building materials, cars and spares of all types.[45] Quantities were usually of the order of 100/200 tons but on at least one occasion *Reventazon* shipped 1,200 tons plus a launch. Apart from bananas the return voyage sometimes included small amounts of cocoa and rubber – the latter being carried on deck. Until 1963 outward cargoes to the Caribbean remained at low, pre-war, levels but then the increasing cost of ship operations led to attempts being made to load on a commercial basis. Unfortunately it proved to be difficult at this time to attract the kinds of paying commodities that were required and the effort was only moderately successful.[46]

The items carried in Elders and Fyffes' vessels were usually organised by the Company's own Stores and Export Department. This was not, however, its principal function for it had been originally established to purchase British and European commodities that were required by the United Fruit Company. It had then evolved to become a separate accounting unit and dealt with large quantities of cocoa via the London Produce Market. Over the years it handled considerable quantities of wood and packaging that were needed for the carriage of Canary bananas and exported much copper sulphate which was an essential ingredient in the Bordeaux spray used to control disease. Fertilizer, machinery, whisky and fish were other important exports. These were usually carried via the regular liner services organised by independent operators and not in the Comapny's own tonnage. Cargoes for United

Fruit were normally trans-shipped at New York and then moved on to their ultimate destination with the aid of its own vessels.[47] These activities played a valuable part in raising Elders and Fyffes' profitability and in doing so made a helpful contribution to alleviating Britain's shortage of hard currency.[48]

Throughout the late 1940s and early 1950s Elders and Fyffes continued to manage a number of depots and other premises for the Ministry of Food. Some of these were the company's own stores, while the remainder were the property of a number of different firms. Thus in December 1945 as many as 121 depots, including 30 of their own, were being supervised, but by the end of the following year these numbers had declined to 75 and 22 respectively.[49] Thereafter the company's role in this activity slowly declined, but it was not until 1954 that it came to a final end.[50]

The gradual release of the company's stores and other facilities was only the beginning of the return to normality. Many premises had been badly damaged and all required complete renovation. At a time of considerable shortages and controls on raw materials this was difficult to achieve and had to be phased over a long period. Nevertheless Elders and Fyffes' operations moved towards a peacetime basis and, in spite of the continuing shortage of bananas, the firm made every effort to reinforce its name in the eyes of the public. Thus a series of advertising campaigns which utilized the 'Blue Label' were launched, and employed every aspect offered by the modern media. This publicity appears to have fallen upon very receptive ears, and the unsatisfied demand for the banana grew to new heights. It was against this background that, in 1951, the newly elected Conservative Government decided to rearrange the system which had controlled the import of the fruit since the ending of the Second World War.

The arrangements made by the then Labour Government with the Jamaican banana industry in 1945 were motivated by a number of important factors. Apart from the need for a non-dollar source of fruit, the most significant of these was the sense of commitment felt towards the people of Jamaica. As the island urgently needed an outlet for its primary product, agreement was quickly reached so that the UK was contracted to purchase all bananas of exportable quality. The UK government was therefore in overall control of the business but relied upon others to undertake the actual transactions. Thus the Jamaica Banana Producers Association, the United Fruit Company and the Standard Fruit Company were appointed as its buying agents and they operated from the stations they had used prior to the war. These, in turn, were managed by commission agents who proved to be extremely cautious in grading the bananas they accepted, for fear that they might be rejected at the port. This was a matter of great contention which was not to be finally resolved until 1959.[51]

The arrangements for the shipment of the bananas were delegated to Elders and Fyffes and to the Jamaican Banana Producers Steamship Company, and Fyffes and Jamaica Producers were then responsible for the marketing of the fruit in the UK. As noted earlier,[52] this was originally to be divided 80 per cent:20 per cent but it was quickly revised so that after six months it was fixed at $77\frac{1}{2}$ per cent to the company and $22\frac{1}{2}$ per cent to Jamaica Producers. It should be noted, however, that whereas Jamaica Producers were to secure all their share from Jamaica, Elders and Fyffes were at liberty to include bananas from the Cameroons within their percentages.[53] The financial details of these activities were finalized at an annual meeting at which the cost price of the fruit and the level of freight rates would be negotiated. In addition the two shippers received a 5 per cent commission on the first 60,000 tons and $2\frac{1}{2}$ per cent on any cargoes above this figure.[54]

The system proved to be a little inflexible but worked reasonably well, particularly in the immediate post-war years. It may then have played a part in the malaise which appears to have overtaken the industry in Jamaica, but a series of 'blow-downs' and the continuing spread of Panama disease were equally significant. Indeed, but for the very energetic way that the All Islands Banana Growers Association acted to have the *Gros Michel* variety replaced by the immune *Lacatan* there would have been no bananas at all to market. When these were subsequently attacked by 'leaf spot' and their roots damaged by nematodes, these diseases were also fought with a great degree of conviction and the plantations were kept in being. Unfortunately a steady transformation of the Jamaican social and economic structure prevented these very positive actions from being translated into larger volumes becoming available for export. This in turn was to lead to two highly significant events.

The first of these came in 1949 when the ongoing shortage of non-dollar bananas and the consequent gap in the market encouraged Paddy Foley and George Band to buy a plantation and commence the growing of the fruit on Dominica in the Windward Islands.[55] Although not important until much later, this development was ultimately to result in a 'third force' being able to establish itself within the British market. The second important consequence was concerned with the system of bulk buying and of government control of the industry. The latter began to be dismantled in April 1951 when an amendment to the Banana Order ended all restrictions on retail sales.[56] This was followed by a decision taken by the British government with effect from 29 December 1952 under which:

... the marketing of bananas in the United Kingdom was returned to free enterprise and all restrictions in connection with price control, distribution etc. were removed. From that date the Company has been working on the agreement made with the Cameroons Development Corporation in 1948, and has also been selling for its own account the bananas grown on the Likomba Plantations ...[57]

These changes did not immediately affect the position of Jamaican bananas which continued to be sold for the account of the Ministry of Food. However, this situation was ended in March 1953, and from that date Elders and Fyffes transported and marketed their proportion of the island's fruit for the account of the Jamaica Banana Board.[58] This body had been established as a statutory banana co-operative and included representatives of the Jamaican government, the industry and the United Fruit Company. (By this time the Standard Fruit Company had ended its operations on the island.) The Jamaica Banana Board (JBB) was then authorized to take complete control of the industry and, under the guidance of Mr R. F. Williams, subsequently arranged for Jamaica Producers and the UFC to purchase, transport and market their fruit in Britain.[59] Thus on both sides of the Atlantic a new, more flexible, structure had emerged; it remained to be seen how effective it would prove to be in the future.

12

The development of the Windward Islands and its consequences

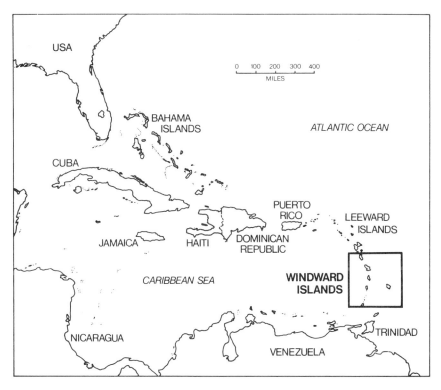

Fig. 12.1   Map of the Caribbean Sea (Reproduced with the kind permission of Geest Industries.)

The ending of restrictions upon the importation of bananas into the UK in 1952 and 1953 was followed by an upsurge in the total quantities which reached the British market. As this was part of a trend which had seen tonnages rise from 138,100 in 1950 to 167,700 in 1952 and to

263,500 in 1953, it will be seen that deregulation was only one factor in this expansion. However, it is equally clear that it was of major significance, for it undoubtedly stimulated exports from Jamaica and these rose from 87,500 tons in 1949 to 138,100 tons in 1953. (The intervening years were affected by hurricanes so cannot be regarded as relevant.) During the remainder of the decade, imports rose still further with tonnages of 308,800 being recorded in 1955 and 333,000 arriving in 1959. As Jamaican exports continued at their previous level (146,100 tons in 1955 and 138,800 tons in 1959)[1] the balance was secured from a wide range of sources with the Cameroons, the Canaries, Brazil, Ghana and Fernando Po all making varying contributions.

The vast majority of these bananas were transported and handled by either Elders and Fyffes or Jamaican Producers in accordance with their previously agreed proportions. Until June 1955 individual licences were required to import the fruit from areas other than Jamaica and the British Cameroons. Elders and Fyffes used these to obtain bananas from Fernando Po, the French Cameroons and the Canaries and also utilized those licences granted to their customers to bring in further quantities from Grand Canary and Tenerife. Thereafter the individual licence system was ended and imports of non-dollar bananas were allowed under an 'Open General Licence'; one effect of this was that from then onwards all Canary fruit was purchased for the company's own account.[2] It should also be remembered that the British market continued to be distorted by the import duty of £2 10s. which had been levied on all non-Commonwealth bananas in 1932; this distortion was further strengthened when the duty was increased to £7 10s. per ton in 1956.[3] While this system mitigated against all bananas outside the Commonwealth, those from 'dollar' sources also required the issue of special dollar licences. These were normally only issued when the demand for bananas could not be met by sterling fruit.[4]

The relaxation of government control meant that there were no longer any serious official constraints for new entrants to the industry to overcome. What remained were the very high financial barriers which needed to be dealt with if an efficient distribution, ripening and handling system was to be established to market their fruit. As the economies of scale dictated that any attempt to break into the UK market would have to be on at least a regional basis, it seemed certain that the position of the two main importers would remain unchallenged. While there had been many instances of small firms bringing in bananas over the years, these had really only been taking advantage of temporary periods when the demand was particularly buoyant and could not be entirely satisfied by the existing companies. One firm which decided to exploit the existence of such a 'gap' in the market was Band and Sons of Liverpool

182

and, unlike the usual experience, its enterprise was to have a major and lasting impact on the entire industry.

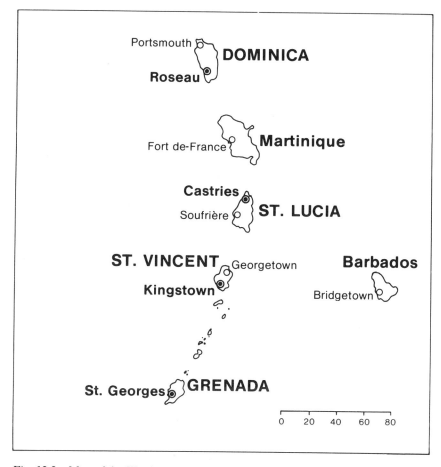

Fig. 12.2   Map of the Windward Islands (Reproduced with the kind permission of Geest Industries.)

Band and Sons' source of bananas lay in Dominica in the Windward Islands. This fruit had long been used as a subsistence crop in the area but the dominant position of sugar prevented it from being cultivated for export on any scale. Competition from other more suitable regions gradually reduced the viability of the sugar industry, so more attention was then given to the banana. An early attempt to promote its export was made by an American firm, the Swift Banana Company, in 1925. This failed because of an outbreak of Panama disease in St Lucia where the firm had acquired land. The lack of a suitable outlet then led to a Dominican merchant trying to establish a direct link with Liverpool during 1931. When this also failed, a United Fruit subsidiary, the Canadian Banana Company, commenced buying bananas from both Dominica and St Lucia. As part of this arrangement a number of banana-growing associations were set up to act as intermediaries, and with their aid the disease-prone Gros Michel bananas normally grown in the Windwards were replaced by the more resistant Lacatan variety.

Thus from the early 1930s the Windwards had a viable product and the beginnings of an appropriate export structure. Thereafter a steady trade was developed with Canada, and regular sailings were made to Montreal until the wartime shortage of tonnage brought the business to an end in 1942.[5] The British government then agreed to purchase any surplus bananas in the same way as it did in Jamaica and the Cameroons, even though it was not possible to ship them away from the islands. This arrangement ended with the return of peace, and as the Canadian trade was not resumed the availability of the fruit – at a time of shortage in the UK – attracted the attention of Geoffrey Band in Liverpool and of his associate Paddy Foley in Dublin.[6]

In 1948, therefore, Messrs Foley and Band acquired land in Dominica, and during the following year they set up Antilles Products Limited (APL) to negotiate with the island's growers. As a result of the discussions a fifteen-year agreement was completed under which the new company was to buy all bananas that were offered to it that were of 'export quality'. This arrangement commenced in 1950 at a time when the fruit was still in limited supply in the UK, so it seemed certain that whatever quantities were obtained could be disposed of at a good price. The only real difficulty was that concerned with shipment, for APL was in no position to provide its own vessels and, in any case, the smallness of the initial trade would have meant that it would have been impossible to have secured whole cargoes. The solution was to join forces with the other 'independent' producers in the Caribbean, so Foley and Band:

> ... approached the Jamaica Banana Producers Association for assistance with shipping and marketing, and for a time the Producers' ships called at Dominica to load bananas on their way to the U.K. It was a difficult operation for it meant that the round voyage now took about a day and a half longer, thereby reducing the time available for loading and discharging general cargo from the U.K. for Jamaica, which was a very important source of revenue. Because of this the calls at Dominica were discontinued. Instead, the Association helped Foley and Band to obtain ships on charter.[7]

The vessels concerned were two 16.5-knot refrigerated ships which were obtained from the A.B. Atlantrafic Line of Sweden. As these proved to be more expensive than the previous arrangements, and as they could only provide a monthly service, it became increasingly difficult for Antilles Products to remain viable. By 1952 the firm was in serious financial trouble, so Foley and Band were obliged to look for a potential buyer for their ailing business. Fortunately for them, these events took place just as the Geest family were seeking to broaden the base of their existing horticultural and nursery activities, so it was not long before the two parties were investigating the possibilities of a co-partnership or outright sale.

John and Leonard van Geest had arrived in Britain from Holland in 1930 to promote exports for their father's market-gardening enterprise. Their efforts proved to be so successful that in 1935 they established Geest Horticultural Products Limited. The new firm then acquired land near Spalding in Lincolnshire so that it could not only sell the produce and bulbs provided via their family connection but also grow many of the items which they found were in demand. Progress thereafter was rapid and the company quickly developed its own distribution network.[8] Wartime constraints were turned to the company's advantage and it continued to expand. Thus when hostilities came to an end in 1945 it was able to build on very sound foundations and found an ever-growing market for its imports of Dutch tomatoes, lettuce, potatoes, cabbages, beans and cucumbers. At first this valuable business was limited by shortages of space on the regular lines which sailed from Holland to Kings Lynn and Harwich, but this problem was then overcome by the creation of the firm's own cross-channel service. This utilized chartered vessels in its early days, but in the course of time these were totally replaced by company-owned and operated tonnage.[9]

By 1950 Geest's corporate turnover had risen to over four million pounds a year, but far from being satisfied John van Geest was carefully looking at ways in which he could expand his commercial activities still further. As a conservative businessman he knew it would be wise to diversify into areas which were related to his principal trades, so although he pursued a number of enquiries these were eventually reduced to just two serious possibilities. One obvious move was for Geest Industries to strengthen its distribution network, and the acquisition of suitable companies to bring this about was minutely considered. The other direction which promised great rewards lay in the widening of the range of items which Geest could market alongside its existing business. Amongst the latter was the banana, but while John van Geest was aware of its potential he also knew that under the existing system it would be virtually impossible for his firm to gain entry into this industry. It was therefore with considerable interest that he learned of the relaxation of government control in 1952,[10] for he appreciated that the continuing limitation of supplies provided an excellent opportunity for anyone who could help to fill the gap!

As a first step he commissioned a survey of potential sources and then, after due consideration, he made up his mind to visit the Windward Islands. The result of this decision was quite remarkable for, as his trip was undertaken at precisely the time that Foley and Band were getting into difficulties, it was to lead directly to a massive restructuring of the British banana industry:

> 'I got to know Antilles Products very well', he recalls, 'and took a 30 per cent interest in the business. Finally they came to an agreement that we should take over their company, so that we were completely free to develop the banana business. After negotiations in the summer of 1954 with Dominica, St. Lucia, St. Vincent and Grenada, I signed contracts with all four islands agreeing to ship and market whatever bananas of marketable quality they could grow for ten years.[11]

The scale of the operation acquired by Geest Industries can be judged from the figures in Table 12.1.

TABLE 12.1 WINDWARD ISLAND'S BANANA EXPORTS[12]

Island	No. of stems exported		
	1952	1953	1954
Grenada	–	39,089	103,301 (11 months only)
St Lucia	56,002	142,904	300,000 (estimate)
St Vincent	–	–	36,000 (approximate)
Dominica	838,035	1,141,344	1,324,354

If the number of stems is divided by 74.6 an approximate number of tons can be calculated. This suggests that in the period from 1952 to 1954 annual exports were running at between 11,000 tons to 23,000 tons. The measures taken by Geest to promote production then led to exports increasing four-fold to 8 million stems in 1959 and to 10 million stems in 1960.[13] These rapidly rising quantities were originally carried in specially chartered vessels, but by 1960 the volume of trade was such that two new ships were ordered and these were to be supplemented by two more in 1964 and a further two in 1966.[14]

The ripening and handling of Geest's early imports of bananas was greatly assisted by the presence of its existing distribution network. Although relatively small and designed to cater for other products it was fairly easy to adapt. This was particularly true after the purchase of Dan Wuille and Company, Limited, of Covent Garden, in 1954, because this firm had considerable experience as banana ripeners and salesmen.[15] As it then had a turnover of 6 million pounds a year and possessed ten branches, it was a major acquisition and was therefore able to provide firm foundations for future expansion.

The gradual but irregular increase in the size of the British market which reached a peak of 363,000 tons in 1962 meant that the rise of Windward Islands' banana exports could be readily accommodated. The continuing increase of Geest imports was such, however, that it became obvious that before very long supply would well exceed projected demand. Before this could occur, events in the British Cameroons were to transform the situation, for what had become an important producer was to quickly disappear from the UK banana business. This difficulty arose when the Trustees of the United Nations decided to hold a referendum to enable the inhabitants of North and South Cameroon to decide between becoming part of Nigeria or joining with the French Cameroon. The ballot resulted in the North joining with Nigeria and the South amalgamating with the French territory to form an independent state. As a result their banana exports to Britain became subject to the preference duty which by then had risen to £7 10s. (£7.50) a ton.[16]

As the addition of this amount raised the price of Cameroon bananas to uneconomical levels, Elders and Fyffes were reluctantly obliged to discontinue their shipments of the fruit to the UK. Although the company then made every effort to find an alternate outlet in Italy for these bananas it proved to be impossible to establish a viable business, and after making heavy losses for three years the venture was abandoned. This had a terrible impact on its employees and upon members of the associated banana co-operatives, and it is likely that at least 7,000 wage-earners were affected. From the company's point of view the situation was equally deplorable, for within the three years from 1961 to 1964 it was to entirely lose shipments of bananas which had previously been running at about 82,000 tons a year.[17]

The increase in duties in 1956 made imports from the Canaries more and more uneconomic and although they were to be held at their previous levels until 1965 they could not be expanded, and then suffered such a dramatic fall that they virtually disappeared from the British market.[18] The duties also helped to eliminate Brazilian and Fernando Po bananas from the UK and, as Ghana and other potential producers within the Commonwealth seemed unable to guarantee the kind of sustained quantities which were required, Elders and Fyffes' plans to fill this unexpected gap were almost entirely based on Jamaica. The island responded very well and its exports to Britain rose from the 145,800 tons of 1962 to 174,400 tons in 1964.[19] By then, however, the Windwards were able to supply most of the balance that was needed to satisfy the British consumer, so that when Jamaican production continued to rise for a further two years this resulted in a vast degree of over-supply.

The gap created by the loss of imports from the Cameroons which could not be immediately offset by fruit from Jamaica, or Elders and Fyffes' other sources, presented Geest with a marvellous opportunity to consolidate its position in the UK. Backed by plentiful supplies from the Windward Islands, it was then able to become a major importer of bananas while Elders and Fyffes' market share was to decline steadily. The continuing growth of the Windwards' production meant that when Jamaican output rose to replace that lost in the Cameroons there was no place for it, and the subsequent struggle between Geest and Elders and Fyffes led to low prices and an increasingly small return on capital.

As may well be imagined, Elders and Fyffes became increasingly worried about the expansion of Geest Industries within the British banana market. The latter's acquisition of Antilles Products and of Dan Wuille and Company had raised a few eyebrows within Elders and Fyffes, but when these deals were finalized in 1954 there was little indication that Geest would either wish or be able to develop the banana side of their business on any real scale. In some respects the company might even have welcomed an additional firm into the industry for, with the ending of government restrictions, it was useful to be able to demonstrate that the freeing of the market included freedom of entry for new competitors.[20] Of course the subsequent growth of imports from the Windwards rapidly changed this attitude, but there was still little real apprehension within Elders and Fyffes' management. This was because it was generally felt that the Windwards would not be able to sustain, let alone expand, its output for any length of time.

Although Elders and Fyffes had investigated Dominica as an alternative source of supply in 1902 before joining with the United Fruit Company,[21] neither it nor the UFC had arranged for any recent form of scientific investigation.[22] However the UFC did have considerable previous experience of the Windwards through the activities of the Swift Banana Company and the Canadian Banana Company.[23] This suggested that the islands had no special advantages and that, judged by Central and South American standards, their potential yields would be distinctly moderate. In this respect the Windwards were in the same position as the Canaries and the Cameroons, but the UFC also believed that the islands suffered from two further disadvantages. Firstly it was thought that ongoing production would only be possible with the aid of large quantities of expensive fertilizers, and this has in fact proved to be the case.[24] Secondly it was felt that, as its production was divided between four separate areas, the collection and shipment of its fruit was bound to be more costly than in a single integrated region. While these conclusions have much to commend them they were not particularly relevant for production destined for the United Kingdom. The question which should have been asked, and apparently was never posed, was not whether Windward bananas could compete with those from Equador or Honduras but if they would be viable when compared with those obtained from other Commonwealth sources!

The reality was that competition was quickly to develop between Jamaican and Windward bananas, and according to the official account in *Jamaica's Banana Industry* the latter did possess two initial advantages:

> ... First, they are much closer to the U.K. than is Jamaica. This made a four-week turn around possible for the ships carrying their bananas as against a five-week turn around for ships of the same speed carrying Jamaican fruit. The Windwards thus enjoyed a freight rate which was nearly 20% less than that enjoyed by Jamaica. Secondly, Geest Industries who transported and marketed Windward Island bananas, had the right of selection of the bananas they shipped while in Jamaica selection rested with the Banana Board, which was subject to political pressure from the All Island Banana Growers Association and the elected members of government. ... The result was that lower standards prevailed in Jamaica and so, in general, Jamaica fruit was of inferior quality compared with that from the Windward Islands ...[25]

The basis of Geest's success was its recognition of the gap which had developed in the supply of bananas to the UK market. A number of potential sources had, therefore, been investigated and, if the Windwards had been developed by Elders and Fyffes, Geest may have sought to have built up imports from elsewhere.[26] As a broadly based firm which could afford to make large investments and which was prepared to wait for a return on its capital, it was able to take a long view.[27] In the event the agreement with the Windwards proved to be part of a well-thought-out market strategy. Its system of selection worked well, and as production increased the need to accumulate cargoes from a number of collecting points on the four Islands became of less and less significance. Thus Geest took full advantage of the breathing-space which the shortfall of Commonwealth bananas provided to establish a highly efficient operation which was well able to hold its own when Jamaican fruit became more plentiful. As a result the management of Elders and Fyffes were faced with a serious challenge by opponents who had many factors in their favour. The way in which its directors reacted to this situation will now be examined.

From May 1946 'Hal' Stockley had been both Chairman and Chief

Executive of Elders and Fyffes. It was therefore under his guidance that the company rebuilt its business in the post-war world, and one measure of his success can be judged by reference to the annual dividends which it paid to the United Fruit Company. This in the period from 1946 to 1953 these had gradually risen from £200,000 to £1,000,000. Geest's entry into the banana industry, together with the shortfall of fruit from Elders and Fyffes' traditional suppliers, then resulted in a lower, though still excellent, return of £800,000 being paid in 1954, but no further transfers were to be made for many years. On Hal Stockley's retirement in 1958 he was replaced as Chairman by Sir John Huggins (a former Governor of Jamaica) and, at the same time, Captain John A. Moore and Hal's son, H. Jim Stockley, were appointed as joint Managing Directors. Although Hal Stockely was to remain as a director until the following year, it was, therefore, this changing management that was to face the challenge posed by the growing level of shipments from the Windward Islands.

Unfortunately the new controllers of Elders and Fyffes thought purely in terms of restoring it to its former dominant position in the British banana market and, at first, they failed to appreciate that the situation had permanently changed. Thus they devoted their energies to building up production in Jamaica and to obtaining other bananas from wherever they could be secured from within the Commonwealth. This was, in practice, a continuation of the policies adopted by Hal Stockley, and there does not appear to have been any major attempt to examine or rethink the company's overall strategy. However, the ongoing reduction in profits and the consequent failure to pay any dividends to its parent corporation did help to concentrate efforts in this direction, and after April 1961 when Captain Moore became the sole Managing Director, there is some evidence of a new approach. Regrettably this change in emphasis had not gone very far when Captain Moore was obliged to resign because of ill health, and it was therefore to be left to others to press ahead with the necessary alterations in policy.

The perceived need for a dynamic change in Elders and Fyffes' corporate strategy then led to Admiral William G. Cooper being appointed as Moore's replacement as Chief Executive. A former administrator in the US Navy, and more recently in charge of United Fruit's operations at Rotterdam, it was Cooper (who also became Chairman of the firm in 1965) who was to begin to implement the ideas which had collectively emerged during the period since the retirement of Hal Stockley. This analysis, which was rapidly accepted by Cooper, suggested that three courses of action were essential and should be vigorously pursued. The first of these recognized that the company was overstaffed and that it must reduce the number of its employees; the

A typical Fyffes banana ripening and distribution branch in the 1950s.

Geo. Monro Produce Ltd in King Street, Old Covent Garden Market.

A larger-type delivery vehicle of the post-war era.

Fyffes' post-war Head Office in Stratton Street, Piccadilly.

Fyffes Group headquarters at York Gate, London.

John A. Taylor, Managing Director, 1966 to 1969.

Admiral William G. Cooper, USN, Managing Director, 1963 to 1965.

Mr A. J. Ellis with Captain G. L. Foster (on his left) and Mr F. A. Hall (on his right).

The Chairman (Mr H. J. Stockley) presides over the meeting of the Junior Board on 10th May, 1950. Pictured with him, reading left to right, are A. B. Rush, F. E. Darter, N. T. Ridge, C. S. Spiller, J. M. Jennings and G. G. Oliver.

Sir John Huggins (Chairman) and J. N. Frank and J. Theed (Directors of Elders & Fyffes) in conversation with T. E. Sunderland, President of the United Fruit Company in 1963.

Pictured at a meeting of the full Board of Directors held at 15, Stratton Street on 24th June, 1960 are (reading clockwise, l. to r.) Mr J. Theed (Secretary), Mr R. Valls, Mr H. J. Stockley, Captain J. A. Moore, Mr G. P. Gardner, Jr, Vice-Admiral W. G. Cooper (Guest), Sir John Huggins (Chairman), Mr T. E. Sunderland, Mr B. S. Caws, Mr L. B. Stoddart and Mr H. E. Godfrey.

second saw the necessity to speed up the modernisation of its banana business, while the third considered that it was vital that the firm diversified into fresh, but associated, areas.

In the early post-war years when bananas were in short supply and when all that were imported could be sold at a good price, Elders and Fyffes' priority was to ensure that every stem reached its customers with the minimum of delay and in the best possible condition. With profits running consistently at over £1 million a year[28] the emphasis on throughput rather than on economy was then fully justified but, inevitably, a degree of overmanning gradually developed. The onset of competition from Geest and the subsequent reduction in returns then led to a more careful examination of the company's labour requirements, but although this resulted in a limitation on recruitment its paternalistic attitude prevented the kind of 'shake-out' that was really required. The ending of imports from the Cameroons in the early 1960s brought this matter to a head, for much of Elders and Fyffes' UK organization had been created to cater for these bananas. In these circumstances it was decided to arrange for a fundamental reappraisal of the company's entire marketing and distribution structure and McKinsey and Company, Inc., an international firm of management consultants, was appointed to undertake this task.

When the consultants produced their report in 1964 they made a series of recommendations which were designed to lead to a more efficient, centralized, administration. These were quite fundamental changes in the company's structure, and included the amalgamation of some related departments and the establishment of a new system of 'Budgetary controls'. The latter, which was placed under the supervision of Mr A. J. Ellis,[29] was instigated so that all items of expenditure and receipt could be more effectively monitored, which would enable a monthly financial estimate to be produced. The need for such a drastic reorganization of the company naturally reflected adversely upon a number of the older members of the Board of Directors. As a result, and following a letter received from the United Fruit Company in November 1964, the Chairman (Sir John Huggins), and three Directors (H. E. Godfrey, L. B. Stoddart and R. Valls) offered their resignations.[30]

It was, therefore, under the guidance of a greatly altered Board of Directors that Elders and Fyffes were to face the future. Admiral Cooper remained as Chief Executive, and in May 1965 also became Chairman of the company. The remaining directors were J. N. Frank and J. Theed and they had recently been joined by J. A. Taylor who had replaced H. Jim Stockley after he had resigned in May 1964. This left three vacancies and these were soon to be filled by the appointment of R. G. Hurrell, Captain G. L. Foster and L. V. Layton.

It became steadily more apparent that an even greater restructuring of operations would have to be put in hand if the changing conditions in the market-place, including the switch from stems to tropical packed cartons and the loss of the Cameroon supply source, were to be properly and efficiently met. As a starting point, John Taylor led a small team to Jamaica in August 1964 for a thorough review of the contractual relations between Fyffes and the Jamaica Banana Board. Six months later, in his capacity as Chief Executive Officer, John Taylor was to implement the outstanding recommendations of the McKinsey Report and that led to a large number of redundancies to reduce over-staffing. He also gave impetus to the part of the Report that agreed that the policy of modernization which had already commenced should be continued and that the possibility of broadening the base of its activities should be further investigated. One aspect of these suggestions was concerned with the streamlining of its banana store branches:

> ... as it was realised that with the every-increasing costs of distribution it was no longer possible to have a large number of small branches trying to deliver bananas to every retail outlet in the country irrespective of size. Between 1962 and 1972 twenty-seven of the old store branches were closed and ten large new ones built or acquired ...[31]

This increase in the scale of the company's premises was then to facilitate two other major innovations in the 1960s. These were the introduction of tropical packed cartons as distinct from stems for the carriage of bananas and the ability to cope with a wider range of products:

> ... Up to the late fifties bananas were exported from producing countries 'on the stem'; new varieties were being developed which although more resistant to disease and yielding heavier crops were delicate and therefore more subject to damage and bruising than the existing commerical varieties. The answer to this problem was to cut the hands off the stalk and pack them in cardboard containers in the tropics. The advantages are obvious, the useless stalk is left behind, the carton protects the bananas from handling damage, cartons can be palletised and modern mechanical handling equipment used. Less space was taken up in ship, banana ripening room, etc. a revolutionary change which Fyffes immediately took advantage of and the first shipments of tropical packed bananas arrived in the ripening rooms in 1961. The change to this method released much warehouse and lorry space for the widening of the product range to cover other fresh fruits and vegetables. The bananas arrived in the branch already in a non-returnable container and it took less than half the space of the (traditional) wooden box and was much lighter in weight. More

efficient refrigeration, however, was necessary, and this was installed during the modernisation and rebuilding of branches which was going on at this time.[32]

By 1966 the efficiency of 'boxing' had been clearly demonstrated, and Elders and Fyffes had arranged for all of their bananas to be transported in this way. However, although this had many advantages it also created many other problems. The use of cartons meant that quality selection was transferred from the UK warehouse to the tropics, so packing stations had to be constructed and fresh skills and disciplines had to be developed in the growing areas, and some of these found it difficult to adapt to the changed conditions. The fact that the hands were detached from the stem in the tropics gave fungi an opportunity to attack the fruit, so careful scientific control had to be exercised. In addition, the greater stowage possible with boxes as against stems imposed higher stresses both on board ship and in ripening rooms. The new system also required that more sophisticated ripening methods were used and made it essential that cargoes arrived in a regular sequence. Much effort was therefore made to secure the appropriate agreements with the producers so that the extremes of excess and shortage could be avoided. This was partly due to the need to keep ripening and distribution facilities fully utilized, but also because of the determination never to return to the situation of July 1963 when,

> ... it had been physically impossible to handle the quantities coming forward and 916 tons of diothene wrapped bananas from West Cameroon were dumped at sea from s.s. *Chuscal*.[33]

The adoption of these new methods of importing bananas to the UK then stimulated further developments within the British market. The moves towards fewer, much larger, depots that were sited for strategic access and bulk distribution fitted in well with the massive changes which were occurring in the wholesale and retail trades. The growth of scale tended, however, to mean that it was more difficult to maintain the kind of personal touch on which Elders and Fyffes prided itself; it also meant that a different system of market intelligence and response was required. These problems were to be largely solved when an advanced computer was installed in 1968, for this enabled Head Office to learn rapidly of market fluctuations and act accordingly. Its physical ability to satisfy its customers was then enhanced by a further move from rail to road transport. The latter had proved to be much more flexible than that which could be provided by the railway and the fitting of VHF radios to some of its motor lorries meant that an even more responsive delivery service could be maintained.

By the late 1960s, therefore, the company's reliance on rail was steadily diminishing, and it was mainly being employed for the carriage of large quantities of bananas where there were considerable distances from the port of entry to the firm's distribution depot. Surprisingly, although there was a doubling in turnover in this period, this was catered for by a reduced number of vehicles, which fell from 316 to 244 units.[34] This was partly due to an increase in their average size, but was mainly because of the improved efficiency of its road transport which had been generated by a more effective control of its operations.

The changing pattern of supply, in particular the ending of imports from the Cameroons, inevitably led to a need to reassess the company's need for ships and docking facilities. In 1961 Elders and Fyffes were still using Avonmouth, where their first vessels had arrived from the West Indies some fifty years earlier; Garston, which had replaced Manchester in 1912, was also in full operation, and Southampton, which had become increasingly important in the late 1930s, had recently re-equipped Berth 25 with what was reputed to be the most modern and efficient banana-discharging machinery in the world.[35] In addition, the company had been actively investigating the Clydeside port of Greenock and a number of experimental discharges had been arranged with a view to making this its principal landing point for bananas destined for the Scottish market.[36]

This situation was to change quite remarkably over the course of the next few years. The collapse of the West African business which had required between four and six ships a month meant that suddenly there was insufficient throughput to justify the expense of three full port organizations. Rising costs at this time were demanding that Elders and Fyffes should operate bigger ships in order to take advantage of their economies of scale but these, in turn, required larger (and more expensive) berths. Consequently it became necessary to concentrate the company's investments at a single point, so, far from wishing to develop additional facilities at Greenock, it was soon having to decide which *one* of its existing ports should be retained. For a variety of reasons, but mainly because of its lack of tidal problems and the recent modernization of its appropriate berth, Southampton was then selected. This was followed by the firm's withdrawal from Garston in mid-1965 and by its final sailing from Avonmouth in February 1967.

The changes in the sources of supply, plus the level of tonnages that were imported, also affected the size and composition of the company's fleet. The seven vessels which survived the Second World War had been joined by seven others during 1946.[37] During the following decade five ships – *Golfito, Camito II, Changuinola II, Chirripo III* and *Chicanoa* – were constructed by Alexander Stephen and Company, and three second-hand vessels – *Sulaco III*, *Sinaloa* and *Samala III* – were acquired from a United Fruit subsidiary, the United Mail Steam Ship Company. During the same period nine vessels were disposed of – *Chirripo II*, *Bayano II*, *Ariguani*, *Cavina II*, *Tortuguero II*, *Tilapa*, *Tetela*, *Pacuare II* and *Nicoya III* – so in 1960 Elders and Fyffes were still operating a fleet of thirteen vessels.

The relative stability of trade which had kept these ships fully employed up to this time was then to give way to much more uncertain conditions. This situation was then to be reflected in the size and organization of the fleet. Thus of the thirteen vessels which it had operated in 1960, eight were to be disposed of by 1969 – *Corrales*, *Manistee*, *Reventazon III*, *Zent III*, *Matina II*, *Sulaco II*, *Sinoloa* and *Samala III* – and as these were replaced by only one new ship – *Chuscal* – and by three elderly vessels – *Pacuare III*, *Rio Cobre* and *Roatan* – the company's fleet was reduced to only nine units. This, however, is only part of a much more complicated picture, for in 1959 the United Fruit Company had established a wholly owned subsidiary in Bermuda to provide a legal home for some of its tonnage.[38] The Surrey Shipping Company subsequently owned between four and eight ships which during the 1960s were managed and manned by Elders and Fyffes. However, as this tonnage was usually employed on United States domestic routes it made little contribution to the UK market and any shortfall in capacity was to be increasingly filled by chartered vessels.[39]

Elders and Fyffes' success in ending its overstaffing and in modernizing many aspects of its banana business went a long way towards restoring the company's fortunes. However, by the mid-1960s it was widely accepted that this alone would not be sufficient to guarantee it a profitable future. The obvious way forward was to widen its product range to include items that would sit comfortably alongside the banana. For many years the company had, in fact, imported tomatoes from the Canary Islands and oranges from Jamaica, but what was now felt to be desirable was to move towards the marketing of a complete range of fresh fruit, vegetables and flowers. This view was, of course, totally alien to the very strong convictions which had traditionally been held within Elders and Fyffes, so although the Board of Directors gradually accepted that this was necessary it found it difficult to take the first decisive step.

During its long history Elders and Fyffes had acquired many individual firms, but this was always with a view to strengthening its banana trade in one way or another. Thus, even when businesses were secured that already dealt with a wide number of products, these were invariably sold off and only the essential ripening or distribution facilities were retained. A typical example of this policy took place in 1954 after the purchase of William Hinton and Sons in Nottingham. This firm was operating a full range of general produce, but although this was quite profitable the new manager was instructed to deal only in bananas. Alan Hall, the man placed in charge, then attempted to persuade his superiors to allow the business to continue to run for at least an experimental period, but the only concession he obtained was in respect of Canary tomatoes.[40]

It was against this background that Mr Len Jackson, Chairman of George Jackson and Company Limited,[41] approached Elders and Fyffes and offered to sell them his shares. The founder of this firm, George Jackson, and his partner Frank Priest, had built up this enterprise from tiny beginnings in 1882 so that by the 1950s it was the second largest general produce dealer in the Midlands. Based primarily at Birmingham it had taken over two local firms, Bousfield Brothers and A. Randall's – and had established branches at Burton, Derby and Wolverhampton. It was, of course, a major banana-handler and was probably the largest dealer in Guernsey tomatoes in the country. As Jackson's had been one of Elders and Fyffes' original ripeners which had taken part of *Port Morant*'s first cargo in 1901, and as the two firms had remained on good terms ever since, Len Jackson's request was given especially sympathetic consideration.

Negotiations began early in 1963 at precisely the time that Elders and Fyffes were actively considering the need to diversify into the general produce business. This fortunate coincidence did much to smooth progress, but once the company had agreed that such a move was desirable it then decided that it must acquire the whole of Jackson's share capital.[42] Thus further discussions needed to be held with the other principal shareholders, and so it was not possible to finalize the deal until April 1964 when the entire enterprise was purchased for £880,000.[43] Mr John Priest, son of Frank Priest, remained as Managing Director of the firm so, in addition to gaining entry to a vast new spectrum of the fruit and produce trade, Elders and Fyffes had gained access to a great deal of experience which was to prove invaluable in the future.

While these protracted arrangements were in progress but had not yet been finalized, Elders and Fyffes had also acquired their direct handlers, Thompson and Company (Parkway) Limited of Sheffield. This firm had run into financial difficulties, so in order to retain what was really a very important outlet, which had the benefit of being an 'Outspan' panellist, Fyffes decided to pay off its creditors and take it over:

> Mr. Frank explained that the most important feature of this acquisition was that Elders and Fyffes Limited would obtain a foothold in the Sheffield Market which was vital to the development of plans for the expansion of the Company's business in that district of Yorkshire.[44]

During 1963 and 1964 when the negotiations for both George Jackson and Thompson's were at their height, Elders and Fyffes finally came to the conclusion that it must make a major effort to establish a strong presence in the fresh fruit and general produce trades. Discussions then took place with Francis Welcome Nicholls, Chairman of the Francis Nicholls Group, with the intention of purchasing his family firm. By the 1960s this long-established enterprise had grown so that it was the largest in Birmingham, had ten branches in many parts of the Midlands and also owned R. E. Jenkinson Limited which operated in Covent Garden.[45] However, as Mr Nicholls was unwell and as his only son had died, he was prepared to enter into discussions and it is understood that he came close to agreement with Mr J. Theed who acted on behalf of Elders and Fyffes.[46]

Unfortunately it did not prove to be possible to bring these negotiations to a favourable conclusion. It is unlikely that this was because of financial considerations, for Elders and Fyffes are thought to have offered 13s. per share and they were eventually to be sold for 13s. 6d. It is possible that what Mr Nicholls really wanted was a major ongoing role within a new combined organisation, with him, perhaps, in charge of its developing non-banana sector. Had Mr Theed been more receptive to such, maybe unspoken, ideas and had he been able to obtain authority to have offered a directorship the outcome might have been different. As Mr Theed tended to have rather an austere and unbending character and was not enjoying good health at that time, a real meeting of minds never occurred and the proposed sale did not therefore materialise.

The failure of these negotiations were to have particularly serious consequences for Elders and Fyffes, for in August 1964 Francis Nicholls' entire share capital of 2,533,922 ordinary 5s. shares were sold to Geest Industries at 13s. 6d. per share.[47] The speed with which this transaction was completed so soon after the ending of abortive discussions with Mr Theed may suggest that Mr Nicholls was never really intending to sell to the company but was merely fixing a price! He was, it appears, close friends with Leonard van Geest[48] and was subsequently to work with him for a ten-year period before retiring in 1974. While this speculation cannot now be proved, what is certain is that the acquisition of Francis Nicholls was an important step forward for Geest. As the largest single banana-handler in the business, it provided an extensive range of additional outlets for the Windward fruit that was now being imported in ever-larger quantities, and it also strengthened Geest's already substantial position in fresh fruit, produce and flowers.

Elders and Fyffes' disappointment obliged it to devise new tactics to achieve its aims. Having failed to acquire this one large firm, it then attempted to secure the same objectives by purchasing a number of smaller concerns. As these were added to the foundations provided by Jackson's, the company gradually lessened its dependence upon the banana, but the continuing growth of Geest in many sectors of the business ensured that Elders and Fyffes was always on the look-out for further opportunities to expand. One obvious choice which was high on Fyffes' list of potential acquisitions was George Monro Limited, but it had always been understood that this firm was positively not for sale. However Fyffes' purchase of George Jackson had given it a half share in A. Brown and Son (Produce) Limited (a Liverpool firm which specialized in South African fruit and which also provided an outlet for the apples, pears, plums and strawberries which were grown on Jackson's farms). As Monro owned the other half of this business, John Priest and Kenneth Monro met on a regular basis, and at one of these meetings it emerged that a sale of the family company was in fact a possibility. Accordingly John Priest was able to discuss a possible deal on a friendly basis, but although he may be said to have started the ball rolling the formal negotiations were to be finalized by others.

On the Elders and Fyffes' side the final negotiations were to be undertaken by John A. Taylor who, in September 1966, had succeeded Admiral Cooper both as Chairman and as Chief Executive, and by A. J. Ellis who had been promoted to Chief Accountant also in 1966. John Priest had originally expressed some doubts about the strength of Monro's management but when Charles Penny (a former director of Francis Nicholls) and Douglas Clithero had been recruited he was happy to withdraw his objections and strongly recommended that the proposed deal be finalized. With both parties seeing advantages in the transaction it was not then difficult to reach an amicable agreement and this was completed in September 1968.[48]

This was an amalgamation of tremendous importance for George Monro Limited was:

> ... a firm which had celebrated its centenary in 1962 and which operated on a scale as widespread as that of Fyffes. George Monro dealt not only on fruit, vegetables and flowers but in a wide range of horticultural sundries. In addition it owned its own transport company and a coach works. It had extensive premises in Covent Garden, as well as branches and depots in Manchester, Liverpool, Spalding, Cheltenham, Waltham Cross, Great Totham, Brentford, Aylesford, Canterbury, Southampton, Chichester, Penzance and the Scilly Islands. It also operated in Jersey and Guernsey dealing in potatoes, tomatoes and flowers.[50]

Even though the acquisition of George Montro Limited was so substantial, it was not to mark the end of Elders and Fyffes' policy of expansion into general produce. Thus within a very short time negotiations were commenced with another large produce company:

> This was Cowlings, a Leed-based concern that had grown from the wholesale fruit and vegetable business of Frederick Cowling, a dealer who, through his family, claimed connections with the fruit industry going back to 1840. In 1955 the sons of Frederick combined their various individually owned wholesale and retail businesses to form Cowling Ltd. At this point they were wholesaling in fruit, flowers, poultry and vegetables and retailing in traditional greengrocery and poultry shops. They were also leaders in the 'barbecued' chicken retail business, having been to America especially to study the process. The wholesale outlets were in Leeds, Bradford and Wakefield while the retail shops were spread over a large area of the then West Riding of Yorkshire.[51]

While these discussions with Cowling Limited were being brought to a successful conclusion, arrangements to purchase the Covent Garden produce firm of A. Coisy Limited and A. Renaudon and Son Limited, based in the Potteries, were also reaching an advanced stage. Thus by 1 May 1969 Elders and Fyffes controlled a large number of companies whose primary interests were not in bananas. In addition to the three mentioned above these then included:

> A. Brown and Son (Produce) Limited
> Caribbean Steamship Agency Limited
> George Jackson and Company Limited
> G. E. Leatherland Limited
> George Monro (Produce) Limited
> George Monro (Manchester) Limited
> Monro (Horticultural Sundries) Limited
> Monro (Flowers) Limited
> Monro Transport Limited
> Wilfred Moore Limited
> Percy Sercombe Limited
> Thompson and Company (Parkway) Limited
> J. Ward and Sons Limited.[52]

The net effect of these developments was that Elders and Fyffes had been transformed from a single-product concern to one that was very much wider-based. The extent of this change can be seen from a single statistic:

> In 1962 bananas represented 93 per cent of total store branch turnover of about £7,000,000. Ten years later this had fallen to about 55% of [a] £15,500,00 turnover.[53]

Recognition of the altering character of the business came at the beginning of May 1969, when its name was changed to Fyffes Group Limited. In a sense this was to indicate that while one chapter in its long history had ended, another one was about to start. This feeling was to be given added strength by the fact that at precisely the same time as this proposal came into effect Mr A. John Ellis was to replace Mr John A. Taylor as the Managing Director and Chief Executive of the enterprise.

13

The emergence of the modern industry

Although the new Managing Director and Chief Executive of the Fyffes' Group was appointed at the remarkably early age of thirty-six, he was already highly experienced and well versed in the affairs of the enterprise. Arther John Ellis had been born in London and attended Chingford Schools, South-West Essex Technical College and the City of London College, qualifying both as an accountant and chartered secretary. Joining the company in his early twenties in 1953, he spent his early years in the headquarters' Finance and Administration Departments of Elders and Fyffes and subsequently made rapid progress within its hierarchy. Thus in 1963 he became the company's Assistant Accountant and then, after playing a leading role in the establishment of a new system of 'Budgetary Controls' and the early development of data processing, was promoted to Chief Accountant in 1966. Mr Ellis's special skills were further recognized during the following year when he joined the Board as Financial Director and thereafter he worked in close association with John A. Taylor during a period of basic reconstruction and diversification.

This collaboration was, however, to be short-lived, as in May 1969 Mr Taylor's appointment as Regional Director of International Operations for the United Fruit Company meant that he was relocated to Boston, Massachusetts. Thus the entire responsibility for the running of the Group rested in the hands of John Ellis, and it was he alone who reported to the main Board of the United Fruit Company via Mr Page B. Pratt who was Vice-President of its International Operations Division. As Mr Ellis was to remain as Managing Director and Chief Executive throughout the 1970s and 80s it will be appreciated that the survival and well-being of the enterprise during this period and up to the present time has lain very largely in his hands.

The situation inherited by the new Managing Director in 1969 had, of course, been building up for some time. The growth of Geest, based upon plentiful supplies of bananas from the Windwards, had been assisted by a shortfall in the quantities provided by Fyffes' traditional sources. The measures taken during the early 1960s had resulted in an effective reorganization of the company's structure so that its banana business operated more efficiently:[1] the decision to develop a major interest in the general fruit trades had been steadily implemented, and temporary measures to obtain bananas from additional outlets had enabled a reasonable level of supplies to be maintained. At the same time, efforts to encourage production in Jamaica had led to a gradual rise in its exports and those shipped to the UK rose from 138,000 tonnes in 1963 to 182,000 tonnes in 1966.[2]

Unfortunately by the time that Jamaican cargoes were able to fill the gap created by the loss of imports from the British Cameroons, the shortfall had already been offset by the additional quantities brought in by Geest from the Windwards. The British market quickly moved, therefore, from a situation of shortage to one of glut, and a battle of quantities between Jamaica and the Windwards then followed.[3] As an over-supplied market inevitably produces low prices and poor profits for all concerned, this situation was no more satisfactory than the previous one and so further remedial action became an absolute necessity.

The concern caused by a prolonged period of weak prices due to excessive supply then led, in 1966, to a series of meetings between delegations from Jamaica and the Windward Islands. These were followed by discussions between the producers and the three principal importers. A subsequent agreement between Jamaica and the Windwards to split the UK market on a 52 per cent and 48 per cent basis was later accepted by Fyffes, Geest and the Jamaican Producers Marketing Company although they were not parties in this arrangement. An essential ingredient of what became known as the Winban Agreement was that whilst this arrangement remained in force:

> Fyffes and Geest undertook not to ship in bananas from other sources unless, between them, the Caribbean countries could not fill the British market.[4]

This arrangement was designed, therefore, to secure a more adequate return for the Caribbean producers but it also had the effect of preventing the importers from developing a second Commonwealth producer to replace the British Cameroons.[5] It was then facilitated by a fall-back system of weekly fruit exchanges so that an even flow of bananas could be maintained to each importer. While this was a sensible measure the overall restrictions on free competition were accepted somewhat reluctantly on a trial basis by Fyffes, although they recognized that without such access to Britain severe damage could be inflicted on the economies concerned. The extent of their dependence on the banana can be judged by the fact that in Jamaica it provided employment for 80,000 workers and accounted for 7 per cent of its exports; it also ensured work for 75,000 individuals and was responsible for 70 per cent of the Windwards' export earnings.[6]

In spite of the Winban Agreement Jamaican banana exports to the UK steadily declined from the high point achieved in 1966, and by 1969 they were down by more than 33,000 tonnes to 149,000 tonnes. Exports from the Windwards also proved to be disappointing and although 1969 was an exceptionally large year their overall trend was to be downward until after 1980. As these two producers were unsuccessfully attempting to sustain the whole of the UK market without competition from other sources, the inevitable consequence was that British consumption of bananas tended to stagnate and then fall:

TABLE13.1 BRITISH CONSUMPTION OF BANANAS PER HEAD

Year	Total imports	Population	Consumption
1961	323,000 tons*	52.9m	13.7 lbs/capita
1963	324,000	53.7	13.5
1967	321,000	55.3	13.0
1968	314,000	55.4	12.7
1969	320,000	55.7	12.9
1970	300,000	56.0	11.9

* boxed

As Fyffes had through its informal acceptance of the Winban Agreement become dependent upon Jamaica for virtually all of its fruit, it became increasingly concerned about the diminishing quantities that were being shipped, and also had an ongoing worry about the quality of the bananas it was receiving now that tropically packed cartons had replaced stems. To some extent these problems were caused by poor weather, droughts and hurricanes but, as the Jamaican government acknowledged, they were also due to the way in which its banana production was organized. This was an old industry which included a high proportion of smallholdings and its progress had been hindered by a lack of concentrated investment and by a fear that modernization would inevitably raise unemployment on an island where it was already substantial.[7]

Fyffes' apprehension as to the wisdom of relying solely upon Jamaica was brought to a head in 1969 when the shortage of bananas led the Group to undertake a complete reassessment of the island's future potential. As this indicated that there was little likelihood of sustained improvement in either the short or medium term, Fyffes notified the Jamaican Banana Board that it could no longer be bound by what had become known as the 'principle of exclusivity'. Although this decision was immediately criticized in many quarters, it was fortunate that Fyffes took this action. Its judgement was, in fact, to be quickly vindicated by events, for Jamaican banana exports to Britain, its only market, continued to decline as had been forecast and reached a low point of only 17,100 tonnes in 1981.[8]

Attempts to resolve the differences between Fyffes and the Jamaica Banana Board were held in London during February 1970. At these meetings it was made clear that Fyffes were not prepared to surrender their right to import bananas from other sources and that they could not allow the Jamaica Banana Board to interfere with its pricing and marketing policy. These considerations made it impossible for the Group to agree to the suggestions made by the Board, and as the latter, in turn, found that it could not agree to Fyffes' proposals in respect of pricing and quality, the discussions ended without agreement.[9]

This failure created considerable alarm in the Caribbean and in official circles in London. It was then raised by the Jamaican Prime Minister with the British Prime Minister at the Commonwealth meeting then being held in Singapore, and in view of the seriousness of the dispute it was decided to ask a senior figure to act as a conciliator between the two parties. The unanimous choice was Lord Denning, Master of the Rolls, for in addition to his unchallenged reputation for impartiality he had recently undertaken a similar task for the Fijian sugar industry. All parties quickly agreed to his appointment and Lord Denning then acted with his customary vigour and quickly impressed all those engaged in the proceedings by the speed with which he grasped a detailed understanding of the way in which the industry worked.[10] Both parties were asked to submit papers explaining their point of view, and then Lord Denning chaired a number of meetings in Jamaica and the UK which were designed to find a mutually acceptable solution.

One suggestion which was put forward by the Jamaican Banana Board, and which received considerable attention, was the proposal that a central, fully representative, banana management committee should be set up to regulate all aspects of the industry. Although superficially attractive, Fyffes felt that it was undesirable for a number of reasons. In particular they believed that as it would be made up of interested parties it would result in a perpetuation of the existing system. By eliminating any prospect of outside competition it would, in their view, restrict the structure of the trade so that the UK consumer might then be offered only moderate quality fruit in variable quantities at prices which were higher than were warranted by international standards. This situation would then tend to accelerate the decline in per capita consumption which was already taking place and this, in turn, would affect the entire profitability of the trade. While such a system might provide some temporary relief for Winban producers it could hardly be beneficial to them in the longer-term.

As Lord Denning appreciated that this proposal would only be workable with the wholehearted support of all the parties he went on to examine a number of other possibilities. When it became clear that none of these were acceptable to both parties he came to the conclusion that it was an entirely commercial matter that could best be left to market forces to prevail within the framework of the existing protection that was already being given to Commonwealth producers. As a result the *ad hoc* arrangements which had operated since the beginning of 1970 were allowed to continue. Under these expedients, Fyffes had undertaken to purchase all the bananas of suitable quality that were offered to it by the Jamaican Banana Board at a fair market price. It further offered to provide experts to assist the Board to improve the structure of its industry and to try to raise the quantity and quality of its output. In addition the Group confirmed that it would only import non-Caribbean bananas when a shortfall developed. In practice this meant that about 20 per cent of the market was being regularly supplied from other sources at this time.

An agreement was later reached between the parties and this included an understanding that the Jamacian Banana Board were to continue to load a proportion of its fruit in Fyffes' ships, were to attempt to increase its output and to at least maintain its existing quality. Thus a *modus operandi* had been achieved and, although it may be thought to have been more in keeping with Fyffes' wishes than with the Board's aspirations, the changes in the supply situation quickly made any such judgement quite irrelevant. This was because of the continuing decline in both Jamaican and Windward exports, which meant that the British market could only be maintained with the aid of non-Caribbean fruit. Thus Jamaica's fears that its bananas might be replaced by those from cheaper sources was never put to the test, and the Board was obliged to devote its energies to the task of solving its internal production and quality difficulties.

From the foregoing it is abundantly clear that Fyffes' reluctance to become totally dependent upon Jamaican bananas was well founded. It had never, in fact, been its policy to rely upon a single source, for it was well aware of the dangers of droughts, 'blow-downs' and outbreaks of disease which it knew could decimate a crop very rapidly. Accordingly it had always attempted to ensure that its suppliers were well spread geographically, and until the introduction of 'Imperial Preference' it had obtained its fruit from a number of areas in Central America as well as from the Canaries and Jamaica. After 1932 the latter's share had certainly increased dramatically, but the company continued to import bananas from the Canaries, and later from the Cameroons, when they were available. Jamaica continued to be Fyffes' major source after the Second World War, but shipments from the Canaries and, increasingly, from the British Cameroons ensured a wide range of suppliers, even though it was not practical to import very much from 'dollar' producers.

The loss of Cameroon bananas during the early 1960s and the steady decline in imports from the Canaries then meant that Fyffes were, in practice, heavily dependent upon Jamaica. Considerable efforts were then made to encourage a rise in the island's output and quality, but other alternatives were also actively examined. Thus as early as 1964 investigations had already been undertaken in British Guiana, British Honduras and Trinidad, and it had been agreed that their prospects for future development should be further evaluated. This was followed by an agreement which was reached in 1965 with the government of British Guiana which it was hoped would lead to the establishment of a viable banana business.[11] The fact that it subsequently proved to be impossible to find a sufficiently large tract of suitable land in a convenient location ensured that this particular venture could not proceed. As a result further investigations were undertaken in neighbouring Dutch Guiana (now renamed Suriname) and were continued in British Honduras (now the independent state of Belize), and both quickly provided evidence that with suitable investment they could supply large quantities of bananas on a long-term commercial basis.[12]

As Chief Accountant and then Financial Director, John Ellis had a considerable experience of the difficulties caused by a total reliance on one source of supply. The problems posed by low quality and decreasing quantities which were a fact of life in the late 1960s made him well aware of the need to develop alternative sources so as to protect Fyffes' share of the British market. His close association with John Taylor meant that he was also privy to the possible courses of action that were being actively considered, but when he was appointed Chief Executive in May 1969 no final decisions had yet been made. It so happened that these problems were reaching crisis proportions at precisely this time, and it soon became clear to John Ellis and his senior colleagues that unless determined and positive steps were quickly taken his company might eventually lose its position as a major banana importer. Action to end the 1966 agreement with the Jamaican Banana Board then followed and measures were taken to promote supplies from Suriname. An invitation from the Belize government through its Prime Minister, George Price, was also readily accepted, so that the early 1970s were to see the gradual development of supplies from both of these new production areas. In the mean while short-term arrangements were made to obtain fruit from the Ivory Coast, and these proved to be so successful that Fyffes were able to plug the gap in their shipments at least on a temporary basis.

It was against this background that the fall in the quantities received from Jamaica and (to a lesser extent) the Windward Islands took place. By 1971 this had become so serious that it had changed the nature of the debate between Fyffes and the Jamaican Banana Board. Far from attempting to restrict the volume of Caribbean bananas, the principal importers found that there was a growing shortfall between what was thought to be the market potential and the quantities that were being supplied. As a result, rising amounts of non-Caribbean fruit were imported, but as the governments of Jamaica and the Windwards believed that this situation was only a temporary phenomenon they still wished to protect the future interest of their banana industries. Thus while recognizing that they could not provide sufficient bananas in the short run, they were anxious to ensure that when their output recovered that they would once again be granted a privileged position in the UK.

Although the British government did not feel it was desirable to give any cast-iron guarantees in this respect, it did recognize the great concern that was felt in the Caribbean. It was also unhappy about the possible consequences of unrestricted access to the UK market so, while its licensing system effectively controlled the volume of 'dollar' bananas being imported, it came to the conclusion that it would be valuable to create a body with a wide remit which would be able to monitor the ongoing situation as it evolved. Thus in 1973 it set up the Banana Advisory Committee, which was composed of representatives of the Ministry of Agriculture, Fisheries and Food, the three major importers (Fyffes, Geest and Jamaican Producers) and the Jamaican and Windward Islands trade organizations (JAMCO and WINBAN). Its terms of reference were as follows:

1. To provide a forum for exchange of statistics and information, including volume and quality on the U.K. banana market.
2. To consider the state of the banana industries in the Caribbean Commonwealth.
3. To study the long term future of the industry.[13]

It should also be noted that:

The committee usually meets monthly and is chaired by the Ministry of Agriculture, Fisheries and Food. It is purely advisory. One of its functions is to give advice on the likely availability of bananas and thus

207

on the quantities of dollar imports required. It has no role to play in setting prices.[14]

The Banana Advisory Committee has continued in this form to the present time (1990), and has therefore played an important role in the stability of the UK market for nearly two decades. While it has no specific legal authority to control imports – apart from 'dollar' bananas – it has had little difficulty in persuading all of the contributing parties to work together where the interests of the Commonwealth Caribbean are affected. This, however, has always been arranged without detriment to full and free competition in the market place, particularly in the sales and distribution of the ripened product. This has been possible because it has accurately reflected the policy advocated by successive governments, irrespective of their political hue: i.e., that the needs and interests of the British consumer should be balanced against the desire to protect the welfare of the Commonwealth producers in the Caribbean. In practice this voluntary system seems to have worked well, so that the level of imports has been largely kept in line with the requirements of the market and so the needs of the consumer have been reasonably well satisfied. At the same time a flexible proportion of the trade has continued to be available to Caribbean growers and all of their fruit of suitable quality can be sold in Britain. Thus the recovery of Windward Island production enabled it to send 229,800 tonnes to the UK in 1988; sadly, Jamaican output is still very low, but a limited recovery has taken place and, but for the ravages of Hurricane 'David', 45,000 tonnes would have been shipped to Britain during the same year. (The actual figure turned out to be only 29,000 tonnes.)

It should be stressed that while the existence of the Banana Advisory Committee helped to protect Commonwealth suppliers and attempted to balance their interests against those of the British consumer, this in no way inhibited competition between the importers within the UK. Thus the rivalry between Fyffes, Geest and Jamaica Producers has continued at a very high level and this has ensured that all three have been obliged to seek continually for the most cost-effective methods of operation so as to offer their customers the best possible service. Nevertheless, although market share is of prime importance to each of these three firms, they do recognize that it is in everybody's interest to see that the appropriate quantities of bananas are brought into the country and that shortfalls are offset by the purchase of 'dollar' fruit. There is also a degree of co-operation in the levelling out of fluctuations from various sources so that they can maintain an even flow through their ripening and handling facilities. However, their greatest co-operation lies in the area of publicity, for in the final analysis the entire business depends upon the volume of sales which can be generated.

After a limited degree of liaison in the late 1950s, Fyffes, Geest and Jamaica Producers joined together to organize their first generic, promotional campaign in 1958. A second followed in 1961 and this produced the highly effective slogan, 'Unzip a banana'. This, in turn, was subsequently succeeded by other mutually advantageous publicity events, and these culminated in a new national generic campaign which began in 1984. This was organized by the Banana Promotion Group which had been set up to act on behalf of the importers and was intended to run on a permanent basis. Its impact was considerably increased by the fortuitous development of a BBC programme which featured 'Bananaman' – a noble cartoon character who obtained his courage and strength from eating bananas. The Group subsequently utilized this personality as its main focus and 'Bananaman's' visits to schools and retail stores have proved to be extemely popular. The campaign has stressed the role of the banana as a part of healthy eating and has employed many posters, 'give-aways', radio commercials and, more recently, television advertisements to deliver its message. Much useful publicity was obtained by sponsoring the Raleigh Banana Professional Cycling team, especially as this has been accompanied by support for a number of 'fun rides' in which the public were able to take part. These, and many other activities, have undoubtedly played a significant role in making the banana, in spite of the competition of an increasing range of exotic fruits, more popular than ever before. The net effect has been that British consumption of bananas rose from a total of 303,000 tonnes in 1983 to 378,000 tonnes in 1988,[15] and exceeded 400,000 tonnes in 1989.

During the same year, 1973, that the Banana Advisory Committee was established, the enlargement of the European Economic Community to include the UK and Eire also made for changes in the banana industry. For the British government the main political problem in this area was to ensure the continued protection of its former and existing colonies while also maintaining harmony with other protected suppliers. It therefore entered into discussions with its new partners and by 1975 the enlarged EEC had signed a wide-ranging treaty with forty-six states which had formerly enjoyed special relationships with its members. This Lomé convention was, in fact, a successor to previous agreements signed at Arusha and Yaounde by the original member states, and included provision for bananas in a protocol which promised that previous advantages would be retained both for former dependencies and for those still to receive their independence. The initial convention was for five years and was then replaced by Lomé II and this, in turn, has been subsequently overtaken by further renewals.

The signing of the Lomé convention in February 1975 marked, therefore, the beginning of a system which has continued to operate until the present time. Under its provisions there was a progressive adjustment of all existing duties so that Britain's Commonwealth Preference of £7.50 per ton was gradually replaced by the EEC's common external tariff of 20 per cent *ad valorem*. As this did not apply to the forty-fix ACP (Africa, Caribbean and Pacific) developing countries or to the dependencies of member states, all of Britain's existing suppliers were granted free access. In addition it confirmed that Suriname – a former Dutch colony – would also qualify for the same treatment, and that Britain could henceforth import from the Cameroons and the Ivory Coast without penalty. The new arrangements also permitted Britain's suppliers to export to the other EEC states on a duty-free basis but, in practice, existing shipping and distributive linkages have in most cases led to trade patterns remaining largely undisturbed. The Third World open-market producers of 'dollar' fruit were, of course, subject to the protective tariff but, as it was feared that this would be insufficient to offset the Latin American cost-advantage, Britain was permitted, with the approval of Brussels, to retain a quantitive restriction on bananas from this region.[16]

The change from a system of Commonwealth Preference to the EEC's common external tariff made no significant difference to the pattern of Britain's banana imports. This is not to suggest that alterations were not to take place, but these were only to represent a continuation of trends which were already taking place. Thus in 1972 the market relied very heavily upon Jamaica and the Windward Islands for the bulk of its supplies and this was also true in 1988. As both of these Caribbean producers were still able to enjoy free access to the UK it is clear that the ongoing decline of Jamaican output and the expansion of Windward exports were due to a range of other factors.

The decline of the combined Caribbean production that was exported to Britain from a peak of 332,000 metric tonnes in 1966 to 275,000 metric tonnes in 1970 created a shortfall which had to be covered from other sources. In these circumstances Fyffes' initiatives in promoting supplies from elsewhere became absolutely vital. Thus, in spite of the fact that they were at first subject to a penalty of £7.50 per ton, a contract was entered into with the Ivory Coast so that 20,000 metric tonnes were secured in 1970. This figure had risen to 30,000 metric tonnes by 1972 but, paradoxically, once Britain was a member of the EEC and produce of a former French colony could be imported on a duty-free basis, quantities gradually declined and were ended in 1978. This was in part due to the failure to replace the French advisers who had done so much to promote an efficient operation, but many other local factors were undoubtedly involved. The only thing which is certain is that the rise and decline of Ivory Coast bananas imported into the UK was not seriously influenced by either the presence or absence of tariff barriers.

While these imports from the Ivory Coast were crucial in enabling Fyffes to offset the immediate shortfall from Jamaica, it was also hoped that they might provide a permanent addition to the company's range of sources. At the same time John Ellis's initiative in seeking to develop supplies from elsewhere was continued and, although arrangements with Suriname were at an early stage, a small number of bananas were received from there in 1970. Then, after an exclusive agreement was signed in the following year, shipments rose rapidly and 20,000 metric tonnes were sent to the UK in 1972. Further arrangements, which were finalized after the UK had joined the EEC, then saw quantities rise to 32,500 metric tonnes in 1975. These bananas were then able to enter Britain on a duty-free basis and this helped Fyffes to enter into a long-term commitment with Surland NV (the government agency responsible for Suriname's banana industry). In spite of these favourable conditions in Britain, production difficulties meant that an average of only 25,000 metric tonnes were available during the late 1970s, but the 1980s have seen Suriname exports stabilize at about 34,000 metric tonnes per year.

The other initiative undertaken by John Ellis soon after he became Chief Executive in 1969 was concerned with Belize. As the former colony of British Honduras, this still had rights of free entry into the UK market. However, even with this considerable advantage and the security of a long-term arrangement with Fyffes, internal problems made progress very slow and it was not until 1975 that a token 500 metric tonnes was received in Britain. Thereafter Belize's exports increased at a steady pace so that 14,000 metric tonnes were shipped in 1980. A plan to expand production to 60,000 metric tonnes was approved in 1982, but output actually fell and exports only amounted to 9,000 metric tonnes in 1985. This decline convinced the Belize government that it should adopt a new approach and the industry was then privatized. This enabled a fresh working relationship to be negotiated with Fyffes and the resulting partnership was able to raise production to such an extent that 19,000 metric tonnes were exported in 1987 and 26,500 metric tonnes in 1988. It is estimated that its shipments will exceed those of Suriname during 1989.

The difficulties experienced in Jamaica and the resulting gap should have provided an opportunity for the Canary Islands to expand its exports to the UK but this did not prove to be the case. The Canaries had supplied the British market with an average of 23,000 metric tonnes in the years 1956 to 1960, but thereafter quantities had gradually fallen and amounted to only 2,000 metric tonnes in 1969. Apart from a limited spurt in 1970 and 1971 when Fyffes were particularly short of bananas, this decline then continued and no fruit has been received from the Islands since 1975. The explanation for this failure to remain in its traditional trade lies in a number of local factors which had led to a rise in its costs and to a continuing dependence upon the drawf Cavendish variety. As will be seen later, these considerations then obliged the industry to concentrate its attention on to the Spanish market, and it played no further role in supplying the UK.

The situation in the Cameroons was rather different from that in the Canaries. A major supplier to the British market in the 1950s, it could not cope when Commonwealth Preference was imposed in 1961, and its exports to the UK steadily fell away. The signing of the first Lomé convention then placed the Cameroons in a more favourable position, and 19,000 metric tonnes were shipped to Britain in each of the three years from 1976 to 1978. Thereafter the trade dried up and was terminated in 1982. This was unfortunate, for it would have been greatly to Fyffes' advantage to have once again had a major producer in this geographic area (having lost the Ivory Coast) and thus spread the risk of potential shortfalls elsewhere. Fyffes were, of course, well aware of this need, and considerable efforts were made to see if this trade could be re-established on a viable basis. These indicated that a very high level of investment would be necessary to bring Cameroon exports up to a standard of quality which was acceptable in Britain's supermarket chains and, after considerable investigation and discussion, it was decided at that time that local conditions did not justify such a vast expenditure. However, Compagnie des Bananes, an associated company of Fyffes, continued to operate in the area, but its objective was to supply the French, and not the British market.

It would seem, therefore, that imports from the Ivory Coast, the Canaries and the Cameroons were in practice only temporary expedients that were useful while longer-term sources were developed. This is not to suggest that any of these producers indicated would not have been given more encouragement if they had been able to promise consistently equal quality with that anticipated from Suriname or Belize. In addition it should always be kept in mind that the greater quality and, on an annual basis, lower real cost of 'dollar' bananas meant that they were able to carry a 20 per cent duty and still remain competitive. Consequently the tariff would not have been sufficient to have kept it out of the British market and this could only be achieved by the imposition of a quota arrangement. As noted earlier, this was operated and monitored in the overall interest of the industry and the consumer by the Banana

Advisory Committee and in the course of time it was recognized that the public good was best served by a more liberal interpretation of its objectives. Thus, over a period, the tiny quantities of 'dollar' bananas imported in the 1960s were enlarged by the Government to provide substantial amounts when shortages threatened. The Committee was, however, equally quick to make recommendations to restrict the importation of this fruit when adequate supplies were available from the Caribbean or EEC/Lomé sources.

From the foregoing it should be quite clear that the situation which had existed in the British banana industry in the immediate post-war years had been fundamentally altered by the mid-1970s. Fyffes' dominant position had been greatly weakened during this period by a shortage of supplies from Jamaica, so they had found it difficult to respond to the challenge posed by the intervention of the Windwards. As a result Fyffes' share of the market had fallen steadily from 56 per cent in 1955 to 38 per cent when John Ellis took charge in 1969. Britain's accession to the EEC and the establishment of the Banana Advisory Committee then injected two fresh ingredients into the trade but did not, in fact, lead to the further deterioration which might have been anticipated. While this was not known in 1974, it was appreciated that the continued protection given to the Caribbean producers who enjoyed close links to the three principal importers might give rise to the feeling that monopoly profits were being earned at the expense of the consumer.

A consequence of this belief was that the Secretary of State for Prices and Consumer Protection and the Minister of Agriculture, Fisheries and Food asked the Price Commission to investigate the distributive margin on bananas. However, it quickly became apparent to the investigators that such an inquiry would be too narrow to be of any real value:

> The provision of bananas to the U.K. market is mainly an integrated chain of supply from the growers in the country of origin through to U.K. retailers, and thus a description of the course of prices and margins within the U.K. needs to be related to structure within the banana supplying trade. Consequently this report, *inter alia*, describes at some length this integrated operation, from growers in the Caribbean area to U.K. consumers against the general world background of the trade.[17]

When the report was published in June 1975 its main findings were that:

> Jamaica and the Windward Islands enjoy a protected position in the U.K. banana market which is dominated by three importers: Fyffes, Geest and Jamaican Producers;

> ... there is adequate competition in the U.K. between the three major importers and their forward selling prices to other wholesalers and retailers are sufficiently competitive;

> ... gross margins in banana distribution are not out of line with margins on other fruit and vegetables, taking into account both the cost of handling and ripening of bananas and their relatively short life and higher wastage:[18]

These extremely favourable comments demonstrate that the British consumer was being charged a fair and reasonable price for his bananas and that the dominant firms in the trade were not taking any undue advantage of the structure of the industry. In this respect it should be noted that the large scale of their operations was essential if they were to supply the market at an economic price. The banana business has always been the preserve of a few large companies because of the need for an integrated infrastructure in dedicated ships, ripening facilities and distribution networks which called for very significant levels of investment when compared with the needs of other imported fresh fruits. Furthermore the structure of the British industry follows what is the common pattern for banana-handling throughout the Western world and Japan.

However, although the Report was generally favourable it did note that there was some limited dissatisfaction with the quality of the fruit that was being imported – this being a reference to the standard that had been set by the growing quantities of 'dollar' bananas. It also commented on the fact that per capita consumption was falling by suggesting:

> ... there seems to be scope and certainly the need for a more vigorous marketing policy on the part of the producers, importers and all those involved in the distribution chain including retailers.[19]

While Fyffes naturally welcomed the Report's conclusions on prices and competition it felt that the criticism of quality in some quarters was counter-productive. The company and other participants in the industry knew full well that it would be virtually impossible to bring all of its bananas up to 'Dollar' standards without a total restructuring of the Commonwealth Caribbean industry. In the meanwhile it was not a free agent and the obligation to purchase all quantities of 'export quality' bananas was a fact which had to be accepted in the interests of the many Commonwealth producers who relied upon the British market.[20]

In 1975, when the Report appeared, Fyffes' market share had slightly recovered and then stood at around 40 per cent of the market. This was a strong indication that the remedial action undertaken by the Group since 1969 had stablized what had become a very critical area for the enterprise. However, as the total imports during 1975 amounted to only 300,000 metric tonnes – nearly 38,000 metric tonnes less than in 1969 – there can be no doubt that Fyffes (and the other importers) still faced a considerable challenge if the potential of their business was to be fully achieved. It was with this objective in mind that the Group was to put great effort into further attempts to rationalize and modernize its activities so that it would not only maintain (or hopefully improve) its market share but would also ensure that British consumption rose to equal that of comparable developed countries.

14

The ending of Fyffes' first century

The speed with which Fyffes could modernize and rationalize their banana business so that it could achieve its full potential was necessarily dependent upon the availability of appropriate amounts of capital. As the firm had been a wholly owned subsidiary of the United Fruit Company since 1913 this was in practice the concern of its parent company, and traditionally any requests for investment funds had been sympathetically received in Boston. In 1968, however, Mr Eli Black of the AMK Corporation had acquired 10 per cent of UFC shares and by 1970 had organized a complete take-over which he subsequently executed by reversing his own interests into the United Fruit Company and changing the name to the United Brands Corporation. As Mr Black, who became Chairman, President and Chief Executive of the new concern quickly found, the creation of a giant company with sales of US $3.5 billion p.a. did not guarantee success:

> By merging a cash-rich company with a capital-hungry company, he had hoped to create one strong company but instead created a weak one.[1]

One important consequence of these financial manoeuvres was that the United Fruit Company found itself within a United Brands Corporation which was handicapped with heavy debts stemming from the amalgamation. For these to be serviced, a series of steady annual profits were essential, but these could not be achieved because of climatic disasters in the Central American producing areas and because many of the producing countries had introduced export taxes on their bananas. Another serious blow came when the general level of international interest rates was raised, for this inevitably increased the burden of repayment. United Brands then chose to meet its deficit by obtaining additional loans and so made the long-term situation even worse. In

216

these circumstances it may well be imagined that requests for significant investment funds by Fyffes, or other subsidiaries for that matter, were rarely given the consideration that they deserved.

Neither did Eli Black's sudden death[2] in February 1975 bring these financial constraints to any early end, for it was followed by a long period of uncertainty within UB including constant changes of management and poor financial results.[3] From this time onwards UB and its subsidiaries operated a common treasury, and the case for any proposed investment had to be argued at the centre. It was generally felt that Fyffes' requests always received a fair hearing, but in a situation where the parent firm was only just being restored to an even keel it was rarely possible to fund every desirable project to its full extent; indeed, any significant expenditure was generally held back to the point that what had steadily become a cash-starved business was being actively disinvested.

As John Ellis's appointment as Chief Executive of Fyffes coincided with Eli Black's acquisition of the United Fruit Company all of his early decisions had to be undertaken in an atmosphere of extreme financial stringency. Thus his attempts to develop new sources of supply and to modernize his company's facilities could not always be implemented on the scale and with the speed that he would have wished. At the same time Fyffes' principal competitor, Geest Industries, was growing at a tremendous pace, so that its turnover of £4 million in 1950 had risen to £116.8 million by 1974 and was to reach £421.1 million in 1986.[4] Although these statistics refer to the whole of Geest's activities, it is clear that a throughput of this size was well able to generate the funds necessary to satisfy its banana operations.

It is against these financial constraints that Fyffes' progress over the past two decades should be judged. On the supply side it could well be argued that the decline in Jamaican production was due to the island's internal problems, and its failure to support its banana industry was not caused by a lack of external investment.[5] Fyffes' initiative in promoting permanent new sources of supply in Belize and Suriname did take much longer to come on stream than had been planned, but the balance of evidence suggests that this was not solely due to a lack of capital but to a whole range of other political, legal and social constraints as well.[6]

As noted earlier,[7] Canary exports to Britain had declined to only tiny amounts by 1965. This long-standing supplier had been badly disturbed by the Spanish Civil War, and although it resumed shipments in the mid-1940s it found it difficult to compete with other producers in the UK market. One major factor was its liability to Commonwealth Preference; another was its reluctance to adapt to changing conditions. Thus it continued to grow *Musa cavendishii* bananas long after the

Western markets required other varieties. As all exports were controlled by the Comision Regional Del Platano, which would only allow the production of dwarf Cavendish, Fyffes and all of the other independent producers were obliged to grow only this type of banana. The United Fruit Company did, in fact, offer to supply Valerie or Grand Nain rootstocks on a large scale in order to revitalize the industry. This was refused by the CREPE, probably because of fear of introducing disease, for the archipelago was well aware of the difficulties which had beset other producers. Whatever its justification this decision meant that the islands remained totally dependent upon a fruit which was less and less in demand due to its relatively short shelf life, the ease with which it bruised and its lack of homogeneity with bananas from other sources. In addition, changes in shipping patterns and the development of tourism, which raised wage-levels, both helped to make the fruit too expensive by international standards[8] but no remedial action was undertaken. This was essentially because of the existence of a guaranteed market in the peninsular and so, while imports into the UK and elsewhere in Europe terminated in 1977, production continued at a high level with virtually all exports being shipped to mainland Spain.

The gradual loss of its links with the UK banana business naturally affected Fyffes' remaining facilities in the archipelago. Following the reconstruction in the mid-1930s, these consisted of two farms (Hoya Grande and Los Olivos) which were connected with a water supply from Los Altos in the mountains above Adeje. In addition the company maintained a number of offices, of which the most important was in Santa Cruz de Tenerife, from where its bananas were normally shipped overseas. The production of bananas at the two farms was usually supplemented by that of tomatoes which were grown on a 'share-cropping' basis by the wives and families of the company's employees. Following changes in Spanish legislation which obliged Fyffes and other producers to alter their method of payment this system gradually came to an end. The company then undertook tomato-growing on its own account and in some years this activity generated a bigger tonnage than its output of bananas. In addition, from time to time, other crops were produced, including flowers, bellpeppers and sweetcorn, and these formed part of a small trade which was catered for by air transport. All of these activities were under the control of Wilfred Moore Limited which had replaced the previous 'partnership' of the same name in 1962. Because of illness, Wilfred Moore was replaced as General Manager by Thomas O. Beardsley in 1969 and the firm was renamed Fyffes (Canary Islands) Limited in 1971.

Mr Beardsley retired in 1973 and was succeeded by John Colville, and it was under his direction that Fyffes was to end its long association with the islands. A steady increase in the differential between the price of Canary bananas and those of other producers led to a concentration upon the Spanish market where Fyffes had no special interest. In any event all such exports were organized by the Comision Regional Del Platano on a quota basis, so there was little scope for an expatriate firm to make a distinctive contribution. The rising cost of labour was a further adverse factor which mitigated against a continuation of the business, while at the same time increasing land values made a sale a more attractive proposition. In 1968 twelve acres of Los Olivos known as 'La Caleta' had already been disposed of, but as this land was not under cultivation this was not of great importance. However the selling of Hoya Grande in 1980 effectively halved Fyffes' commitment in the islands and this process was completed when Los Olivos was sold in 1987. It should perhaps be stressed that these disposals were not caused by a lack of capital and that many alternatives were considered – some of which would have involved substantial investments – before the final decision was taken. On the other hand the sale of Hoya Grande in particular must have made a small but useful contribution to the depleted funds of United Brands.

One area in which the creation of United Brands was to have especially important consequences was concerned with maritime affairs. As noted above, Fyffes' fleet in 1969 consisted of nine vessels and was supported by a further variable number which were operated by the Surrey Shipping Company Limited.[9] Many of these ships were either elderly or unsuited for their tasks, so at the instigation of UB a reconstruction programme was commenced in 1969. After the quadrupling of oil prices in the early 1970s it was decided to accelerate this scheme, and as a result all of Fyffes' existing fleet had been disposed of by 1975 and all the vessels of the Surrey Shipping Company had been sold three years later.[10] Sadly, with the sale of *Golfito* and *Camito II*, Fyffes' passenger service to Jamaica, which had commenced in 1904, then came to a final end. (The service which began in 1901 had been operated by the vessels of the Imperial Direct West Indies Mail Service Company and not by Elders and Fyffes.) While the decision to terminate the passenger service was reached, with regret, the post-war development of ever-cheaper air fares had meant that the demand for sea passages had gradually declined and so the company had no real choice in the matter.

The sale of so many vessels was then to be progressively compensated for by a new class of fuel-efficient motor ships which were constructed by Kawasaki Heavy Industries in Japan. These began with *Matina IV* in 1969 and she was to be followed by a further seven sister ships before the series was completed in 1973. To facilitate the introduction of the

'M' class, four more elderly vessels were employed during the early 1970s, but this was only a temporary expedient and by 1975 *Patia III*, *Patuca II*, *Pecos* and *Ronde* had all been sold. These were then to be partly replaced by two 1964-built motor ships, *Darien* and *Davao*. These were purchased to complement the M vessels and were to complete much good work before both were sold to a Greek owner for further trading in 1981. Two additional, very specialized, vessels joined the fleet in 1972. These were *Barranca II* and *Bayano II* which were constructed for the Company by Hijos de J. Barreras SA in Vigo, Spain. They were each designed to carry 93 forty-foot fully refrigerated containers on the Cortes–US Gulf run and proved to be so successful that they are widely regarded as being amongst the more significant pioneers of refrigerated container ships for banana transport.[11]

This reconstruction of the fleet was then followed in July 1981 by a decision to consolidate all of United Brands' fleet operations including Empressa Hond. de Vapores under the operating management of the Fyffes Line. Under this arrangement UB's Corporate Transportation Department in New York was to undertake responsibility for scheduling, while Fyffes' marine office in Southampton was to arrange for the necessary administrative and logistical support. They were thus jointly to organize an efficient, world-wide, transportation delivery system which, including chartered tonnage, frequently had to deal with up to sixty refrigerated vessels.

After an average service of approximately thirteen years all of the M class were disposed of in 1983 and 1984. The refrigerated containerships *Barranca II* and *Bayano III* were subsequently sold in the following year and this left only *Almirante*, a motor ship acquired in 1979 as the only Fyffes vessel in service. The balance of the company's bananas were then carried on either chartered tonnage or in the vessels operated by other importers. However *Almirante*, which was permanently employed on the Suriname–UK route, was joined by *Nickerie* and *Jarikaba* on the same service in 1985 and 1986 respectively. These were new ships which had been constructed to Fyffes and UB designs by the Hayashikane Shipping and Engineering Company at Nagasaki for Hisafuku Kisen KK and placed on bare-boat charter to Fyffes/UB Two similar, but larger, vessels are currently being completed by the same builder and will join the fleet in 1990. Thus it will be seen that a limited amount of capital had always been found for the provision of this key element in the banana trade. However, it is possible that the rationalization of the United Brands' fleets which was undertaken in 1981 may have had the effect of reducing the total amount of capital which needed to be invested in its shipping services.

As previously indicated,[12] the company's withdrawal from Avonmouth

220

in February 1967 left Southampton as Fyffes' only UK terminal. Although an excellent choice from a physical point of view and with many natural and commercial advantages, these were soon to be outweighed by a series of industrial disputes which closed the port on many occasions. In addition the preference given to passenger vessels and the changes which this induced in the character of the labour force led to Fyffes' interests not being fully satisfied. Accordingly temporary arrangements, which tended to become long-lasting, were than made for the discharge of cargoes at Newhaven and Sheerness. Subsequently Portsmouth was made the terminal for the Suriname trade. Shipments from Belize are treated in a different way. Specialized forty-foot 'Conair' containers are carried by barge from Big Creek in Belize to either Santa Tomas in Guatemala or Cortes in Honduras. They are then shipped to Felixstowe on a fortnightly service provided by a consortium which includes T. and J. Harrison and Company of Liverpool.[13]

In recent years these two dedicated routes have been supplemented by a wide range of alternative arrangements which have varied in scale and usage in accordance with the level of demand and the sources of supply. Most Jamaican bananas are usually imported into Newport, South Wales, via the vessels operated or chartered by a recently formed Jamaican shipping company, and Fyffes take a proportion of these through weekly arrangements with JAMCO, which controls the importing of Jamaica's bananas (and other agricultural items) into the UK. At times of glut in the Windwards and shortages elsewhere, supplies may also be secured from the Windward Islands through Geest whose ships discharge at Barry, also in South Wales. When large quantities of bananas from other producers – including 'dollar' fruit – are consigned to Fyffes these will probably be unloaded at Sheerness; smaller amounts will usually be landed with the remainder of the cargo at the appropriate Continental port and will then be moved to Britain by roll-on/roll-off vehicles. Other part-cargoes of mainly 'dollar' fruit are regularly landed in Eire and are then transported to a variety of British ports with the aid of road vehicles and the cross-Channel services.

Fyffes' decision to concentrate its landings at Southampton was undertaken at a time when it was still utilizing the rail network to distribute a substantial proportion of its green bananas. For many years motor vehicles had been employed for local deliveries, and by the 1960s these were also being used for quite long journeys where only moderate quantities were required. As the road system was steadily improved and the motorways developed, the greater flexibility of the lorry became more and more apparent and many routes were slowly converted from rail. Another relevant factor was that the move from steam to diesel on the railways meant that steam heating of vans was not so easily arranged. Thus by 1968 all of Salisbury and Portsmouth's fruit was being sent by road and there is no doubt that this method of carriage was gradually gaining favour. A major strike by shunters at Southampton in 1969 greatly accelerated this trend because for eight months the railway could not operate.[14] When the dispute was settled, the company only moved its long-distance deliveries back on to rail, and road transport was progressively extended.

There was some use of 'Freight Liner Services' to the North of England and Scotland during the early 1970s but these proved to be unsuitable for the company's changing pattern of distribution. Consequently even more reliance was placed on the very efficient types of motor vehicle then coming into service. This process reached its inevitable conclusion early in 1979 when it was stated that:

> Factors on both sides now indicate the termination in the near future of rail services which, in recent years, have been drastically reduced in favour of road transport for the distribution of green bananas. At present there are only seventeen banana vans in service, and with no commitment being given to us, British Rail are naturally unable to provide any replacements, but offer a service of standard non-insulated traffic in line with their general freight services. The limited number of Distribution Centres with rail facilities, together with somewhat erratic vessel scheduling, and use of outside ports of discharge preclude us from consigning by rail now that British Rail freight services are restricted to 5-day working.[15]

The change from rail to road transport was accompanied by a steady move from smaller to larger branches and depots. This was, of course, part of a process which had been gathering momentum since the early 1960s[16] when the increasing demands of the growing supermarket sector had obliged the company to take a critical look at all of its commercial activities. At first this policy was primarily designed to take advantage of the economies of scale in its banana operations but, with the growth of multi-sourcing of the fruit in response to the specific demands of many important customers, larger premises were clearly very cost-effective in some localities. One major milestone in this programme was reached when a large new ripening and distribution centre was opened at Borehamwood in 1980 to replace two older facilities.[17] Owing to cash constraints this was arranged on a leasehold basis so the capital requirements for this development could be considerably reduced.

At this time Fyffes were distributing their range of bananas, fruits and vegetables from premises on thirty-five separate sites. A plan to

A. John Ellis, CBE, present Chairman and
Managing Director of Fyffes Group Ltd.

A Board Meeting of the United Fruit Company was held in London on the 24th June 1963. At the restaurant are D. A. Philp, R. W. Berry (Vice-President. Transportation), H. C. Cornuelle (Executive Vice-President, UFCo), F. A. Hall, A. J. Wadland (Rotterdam), J. L. Christmas (Caribbean Steamship Agency), Captain G. I. Foster, R. G. Hurrell, J. H. Sturley (Paris), F. E. Darter, L. G. Gasparotto (Milan), P. H. Farrell (The Hague), A. J. Ellis, J. A. Taylor (Chairman and Chief Executive Officer), J. de Clercq (Antwerp), A. P. Hedges (The Hague), J. C. D. Jones, Page B. Pratt (Vice-President & General Manager International Operations, UFCo), Captain H. Q. Murray (The Hague).

David Philip OBE.

Mr John Colville (Manager) and the staff of Fyffes
(Canary Islands) Ltd, taken during a visit by
Mr A. J. Ellis and Mr J. Priest in 1987.

Norman Ridge.

Tommy Tomkins.

Fyffes' traditional 'flat' box,
used for the carriage of bananas.

Wrapping bunches of bananas
in Diothene in the Cameroons.

Original tropical
packed cartons being
unloaded.

Original tropical packed cartons
showing interior.

The modern system of
packaging and transporting
bananas.

Neil V. McCann, Chairman and Chief Executive of FII Fyffes plc.

progressively modernize and, in some cases, to consolidate these depots had been agreed with its parent company but there was a clear understanding that implementation might be retarded by a shortage of funds from time to time. Progress was therefore very limited and, although new ripening facilities were installed at premises in Belfast, Bristol, Exeter, Manchester Market, Newhaven, Pontypridd, Sheffield, Stoke-on-Trent, Sunbury-on-Thames and Swansea, this was a long way short of what had been anticipated. Some of these centres were also extended to cater for a wider range of Fyffes' products but others were to remain solely concerned with bananas. By then, 1985, the firm's structure had been reorganized so that what had become thirty-two locations were regrouped under five Regional Directors: Scotland, Northern, Midlands, Southern and London.

Further developments were to follow with substantial investments at Newbridge in Midlothian and at Blaby in Leicester, where purpose-built depots were constructed. The latter was opened in the spring of 1988, almost 100 years after Mr Fyffe had imported his first tiny cargo of the then exotic banana. This meant that at the time of its centenary the Group was distributing from thirty-two strategically placed locations throughout the UK – twenty-four of which contain some of the most modern banana ripening facilities in Europe. With the addition of two more large centres which were then under construction at Chandlers Ford, near Southampton, and at Wakefield in Yorkshire, Fyffes now have a ripening capacity of over 120,000 tons per year.[18]

By 1972 Fyffes' traditional dependence upon the banana for virtually all of its throughput had greatly changed. In that year the Group's policy of increasing its produce lines meant that the banana contributed only 55 per cent of turnover. In the period between then and 1988 this trend continued so that by the mid-1980s the split between the banana and general produce was usually on a 50:50 basis. With the banana sector growing more slowly than that of Fyffes' other interests this change in emphasis has been maintained in recent times, so that at the end of the firm's one hundredth year the sale of bananas was slightly less than that of its general produce. The growing importance of the non-banana sector of the business was partly due to the purchase of new outlets and companies, but these were offset to a limited extent by the disposal of firms which had joined the Group as part of large acquisitions and which, like Fyffes Monro Horticultural Sundries, did not form a logical fit with Fyffes' principal activities. As a consequence much of the expansion which occurred in the 1980s was generated by internal expansion. A typical example of this kind of development was planned at Liverpool during the final days of Fyffes' first 100 years. This has since

223

Fyffes Group
Distribution1989

Fig. 14.1   Fyffes Group Distribution, 1989

224

resulted in the Group acquiring the premises of Yeoward Brothers which were adjacent to its existing sales location in the wholesale market and so its sale 'pitches' have been increased by 66 per cent from three to five units.

While there are many ways in which the progress of an enterprise can be judged to have taken advantage of the opportunities available to it, conventional financial reports of a wholly owned subsidiary are frequently difficult to interpret. As the Fyffes Group Limited (and its predecessor, Messrs Elder and Fyffe Limited) were totally owned by the United Fruit Company or United Brands for virtually the whole of their existence the integrated nature of the Corporation's accounting systems which were based on a common treasury meant that little information, particularly for the later years, was available on a 'stand alone' basis. However the public record at Companies House, London, shows that Fyffes Group returns for the last three years of its first century were as follows:

TABLE 14.1   FYFFES GROUP LTD: PUBLISHED ACCOUNTS,1986–88, IN £000S[20]

	Oct. 31 1986	Oct. 31 1987	Oct. 31 1988
	£000's	£000's	£000's
Profit before tax	6,663	7.285	9,061

These excellent results were not, of course, achieved overnight and were, in fact, a reflection of the inherent strength of the Group which had been built up over many years. While much of the responsibility for this situation must necessarily go to Fyffes' management team the whole of the staff must also take a substantial part of the credit for overcoming the enormous difficulties which beset the firm during the 1960s and 1970s. Their loyalty and support was, however, to be put to a further test in a different way when it was recognized that the key to survival lay in a reduction in numbers and a rise in productivity.

The size of Fyffes' staff, including the crews of its vessels, had reached a peak in 1929 when 2,682 men and women were employed. In 1976 the total was almost as great, with 2,368, but by 1985, when sea-going personnel and the staff of the horticultural supplies subsidiary were no longer included, the number had shrunk to 1,560. This decline was then to continue so that in 1986 the staff was down to approximately 1,100 and by 1988 was little more than 900.[21]. Although part of these recent reductions may be attributed to the ending of the company's business in the Canary Islands, it was mainly due to the more efficient employment of personnel throughout the enterprise. Thus when it is appreciated that turnover, as indicated above, had risen from £136.2 million in 1986 to £158.5 million in 1988 it will be seen that at least one aspect of productivity had risen to a considerable extent.

The willing co-operation of the workforce has been a long-standing characteristic of Fyffes' industrial relations since its very early days and had been well demonstrated during successive dock strikes as well as at the time of the General Strike.[22] The Company had, in fact, quickly gained a reputation as a 'good' employer but this was based on the *ad hoc* policies adopted by Messrs Stockley and Ackerley rather than on any specific arrangements. Thus while their paternalistic belief that they should look after the welfare of their employees ensured that lump sums and retirement pensions were paid these were not placed on a formal basis until 1922.[23] The establishment of Elders and Fyffes Staff Provident Fund in that year was very advanced for its time and proved to possess many of the benefits which were subsequently to be found in modern pension funds.[24] However, many of its provisions were discretionary and the only legal entitlement was a lump sum which represented the balances paid in by the member, plus the whole of the company's contributions.

It is fortunate, therefore, that the Fund was administered in a sympathetic manner, for it was totally inadequate if a member died before he had the opportunity to build up a reasonable sum in his account. Special arrangements were included to provide for this in 'indigent circumstances' but as these made it likely that the dependants of the feckless were far more likely to receive benefit than the families of those who were careful and thrifty, they were regarded by many as a somewhat mixed blessing. It should also be noted that special provisions were made for the marine staff under this scheme so that their terms and conditions were comparable with those provided for other merchant marine officers by their National Federation.

The changing expectations of the post-war era then saw the Fund replaced by two, separate, pension and life assurance schemes in 1960. These were designed to cater for those earning above or below £2,000 per year, and after they were modified in 1966 they guaranteed a fair and equitable pension related to an individual's service and salary with the company. A new, even more comprehensive, arrangement was introduced in 1974 when the Fyffes Group Pension Scheme, which was open to all permanent employees, came into operation.[25] This was subsequently to be updated so that in 1987 additional provision was made to cope with inflation on a continuing basis.[26]

Another indication of the concern felt by the Group for the welfare of its workforce came with the establishment of Elders and Fyffes Pensioners Association in 1962. This was set up by Mr Harry Holt, the company's publicity manager, and was announced in *Fyffes' Staff Budget* (vol. XV, no. 5) as follows:

As one who is due to retire late this year, it has been my pleasure to carry out the work, entrusted to me by Captain J. A. Moore and Mr. H. J. Stockley, of setting up the Elders & Fyffes Pensioners Association, a labour of love in which I would gratefully acknowledge the assistance of Mr. S. W. Johnson of our Secretary's Department.

Our Directors felt the need to maintain and strengthen contacts with all former employees of the Company who are now living in retirement, and essentially to give each of them the feeling of still belonging to the Fyffes family. In my preliminary work I have been greatly encouraged by the enthusiasm and willingness to help, shown by those I have approached to act as voluntary Visitors in calling upon their fellow pensioners at their homes in a spirit of friendship.

The Association came into being on 29th June when Captain J. A. Moore and Mr. H. J. Stockley sent out a letter, personally addressed to each of our 147 pensioners (6 women and 141 men), giving them preliminary details of the scheme, and expressing the wish that they would welcome the idea of joining the Association. The response has been heartening and has established the fact that the sense of loyalty and the desire to band together are as strong as ever amongst those who have served the Company so faithfully and well in former days.

A little news about locations chosen for retirement may be interesting. Naturally, just over half of our pensioners are living in the three centres of Bristol (21), Liverpool and district (34) and London and Home Counties (26), but choice is bounded by Dundee in the North, Belfast, Holyhead, Bude and Liskeard in the West, the Channel Islands in the South, and by Sunderland, Clacton-on-Sea and St. Margaret's Bay in the East. From this it will be seen that there is a fair amount of territory to be covered by the 24 pensioners who have so readily agreed to call on others, and the British Isles has been split up into workable sections to render their task as simple as possible.

Our oldest pensioner is Mr. Sam Bulley, formerly of Birmingham Branch and now living in Bude, who was 88 in February, and he is closely followed by Mr. Tom Jones, formerly of Accountant's Department and now living in Croydon, who will be 88 in September. We have 48 pensioners up to 69 years of age, 75 in the 70/79 age group and 24 who will be over 80 this year.

227

Those who have undertaken to make calls are being briefed in regard to their adoption of a friendly approach to their fellow pensioners, and let it be stressed that there is no intention on their part to pry into what any individual may regard as his or her own privacy. From calls already made it is clear their visits are welcome, and soon we shall have the satisfaction of knowing all our pensioners so much better and, on request, be in a position to offer suggestions in regard to those problems that are apt to arise with advancing years.

Since then this monitoring system under which each of the company's pensioners has been regularly visited by one of his younger colleagues has worked extremely well. Any difficulties which were discovered by the 'visitors' were then reported to a volunteer organizer who was appointed and supported by Fyffes from the ranks of its retired employees. This was a task which was undertaken for many years by Mr Joe Lees, but at the age of eighty-one he decided that the time had come for him to lay down his burden, and in January 1989 he was succeeded by Mr A. L. (Andy) Anderson. These activities were also supplemented and strengthened by a series of annual luncheon meetings which were sponsored by Fyffes in each area so that, in practice, the welfare of each pensioner could be effectively taken an interest in and checked in two distinct ways.

From the time of its establishment the directors of the enterprise had seen great merit in fostering a feeling of *esprit de corps* amongst their employees. Apart from the welfare and pension provisions, which were always ahead of contemporary industries, this was mainly promoted via a range of sporting and social activities which cut across all differences of status and areas of expertise. In the 1920s and 30s these programmes resulted in a series of formal occasions which were mainly based on Fyffes' sports grounds at New Malden, Avonmouth and Liverpool.[27] The facilities were, of course, also extensively used on a regular basis by many members of staff – some of whom appear to have organized their non-working lives almost entirely around these centres.

The changed conditions of the post-war world gradually led to the evolution of a different type of society in which there was a smaller demand for these kinds of extra-mural activities. In the course of time, therefore, the facilities were disposed of and those arrangements which continued were undertaken in a much more informal manner. Nevertheless, Fyffes were still anxious to support any initiatives that were proposed by individual members of staff, although it no longer thought that it should play a major role in organizing them. Thus the annual regional cricket matches are still played with their customary enthusiasm, and several golfing events are completed each year. The latter are, of course, highly appropriate for it should not be forgotten that Edward Wathen Fyffe, the founder of the business, spent a large proportion of his long years of retirement in establishing and supporting the Minchinhampton Golf Club near Stroud.[28]

In these circumstances it will be appreciated that there was a less than usual need or enthusiasm for trade union membership. The rapport which has traditionally existed between all sections of the firm has resulted in an exceptionally high degree of co-operation being achieved, and it is fully accepted that the progress of the business and the welfare of the workforce are inextricably intertwined. While Fyffes have never entered into national agreements with trade unions, the firm has always been quite prepared to join in local or regional arrangements. The favourable state of industrial relations within the Group, together with the difficulties which are always inherent within a widely dispersed enterprise, has meant, however, that so far few individuals have chosen to exercise their rights in this way.

Recent changes in its ownership have only served to confirm Fyffes' view of its commercial role and of its methods of operating. The first of these came in 1984 when control of United Brands moved to the United States financier, Carl H. Lidner. Mr Lidner had acquired 20.5 per cent of United Brand's outstanding shares after the death of Eli Black in 1975 but was content to leave the management to Max Fisher and subsequently to Paul and Seymour Milstein who, with their associates, had also been significant share holders since 1975.[29] Mr Lidner had then built up his stake in the company and, in the course of time, decided that he could achieve better financial results if he took personal control. Accordingly, he came to an amicable agreement with the Milsteins and their associates to purchase their holdings and was then left in complete command with 55.9 per cent of the share issue.[30] He then took a long dispassionate look at all of the activities which it undertook before commencing to rationalize its whole structure. By this time Fyffes were not only cash hungry but as they were no longer an integral part of United Brands' business, there were less compelling reasons for priority of investment in this area. Further evidence that Fyffes were no longer a fit with the remainder of the organization was provided by the extent of its diversification into fresh produce distribution which had no synergy with *United Brand's* core activities. Thus at the beginning of 1986, during a period when the dollar was weak compared with sterling and other European currencies, Mr Lidner decided that the time was right for a change and let it be known that he was prepared to sell his British subsidiary.

A willing buyer was quickly discovered in *Fruit Importers of Ireland* which by the time of the transaction had become FII Plc. This concern had previously shown a considerable amount of interest in such an acquisition but, even so, it proved to be difficult to reach agreement and much hard negotiating was required before its Directors were able to announce that:

> ... conditional contracts have been exchanged for the acquisition of Fyffes Group Limited, a wholly-owned subsidiary of United Brands, of the U.S.A. – for a total consideration of £26.5 million.[31]

The buyers, FII Plc., are a well established group which achieved net profits before tax, of over £4 million in 1985. Like many other large firms, it has a number of diverse roots, but in this particular case its development can be easily traced by following the enterprise of one, significant, family.

As early as 1904, the firm founded by Charles McCann, was already engaged in wholesaling fruit in the Dundalk area. The vigour of this small firm can be seen from its policy of diversification which, in 1906, resulted in it being the first company to import bananas on any scale into Ireland. The result was a period of steady growth which continued throughout the inter-war years and by the 1950s it was firmly established as one of the leading firms in the Republic of Ireland.

The changing pattern of retailing and wholesaling in the Irish domestic market, plus the differing forms of organization that were being adopted by overseas suppliers, then dictated that those firms which wished to survive in this new environment would have to restructure their operations so as to take advantage of the economies of scale. Thus in 1956 United Fruit Importers Limited was formed by a number of prominent wholesalers in Dublin, and two years later Torney Brothers and McCann Limited whose managing director was Neil V. McCann of Dundalk was established by wholesalers whose interests covered the whole of Ireland. It soon became apparent that it would make good commercial sense for these two companies to amalgamate and, when this was accomplished during 1968, the resulting merger led to the emergence of a new entity: the Fruit Importers of Ireland Limited, in which expanded organisation Neil V. McCann became the Chief Executive.

The new Group then quickly consolidated its position by purchasing Connolly Shaw (Ireland) Limited and over the years has pursued a policy of acquiring other firms when the circumstances seemed appropriate. Thus Southern Fruit Suppliers of Waterford were taken over in 1971, Sheil and Byrne Limited of Dublin was acquired in 1972 and these were then followed by further expansion in Kilkenny and Tralee.

Charles McCann Limited of Dundalk, the successor of the old family business, was merged in Fruit Importers of Ireland Group in 1980 as part of the preparation for a UFM unlisted stock market 'listing' on the Irish Stock Exchange. At that stage Development Capital Corporation Limited took a 25 per cent holding in the new FII Limited which took over the assets and undertaking of Fruit Importers of Ireland Limited and Neil V. McCann became Chairman and Chief Executive of this new public company. During the 1980s the Group made further acquisitions of fruit and associated companies both in the Republic of Ireland and in Northern Ireland. Banana Importers of Ireland Limited, a subsidiary formed in 1965, has continued to play a large role in the company's Irish activities.[32]

As Elders and Fyffes had appointed Charles McCann and Company as its first official handlers for Southern Ireland in 1906, the two firms had enjoyed a close and happy commercial relationship for many years. There were also a number of similarities in their respective operations, for while Fyffes had gradually moved away from its original dependence upon the banana the Irish company was expanding this side of its business and had become important direct importers of this fruit into Ireland. These originated in South or Central America so were 'dollar' bananas of high quality which arrived in Cork on a weekly shipment.[33] It was therefore considered that the market share of both enterprises would be enhanced through the enlarged Group's purchasing power and economies of scale.[34] A further underpinning of the foundations of what then became the holding company, FII – Fyffes plc., was provided by the undertaking given by United Brands that it intended to remain a substantial shareholder in the medium term and that it would contribute two members to the holding company's Board of Directors.

The change in ownership was not intended to make major alterations to Fyffes' business activities which, under the guidance of Mr John Ellis, were recognized as being highly efficient and innovative when the shortage of funds for investment was taken into account. However, the acquiring Irish company's strong balance sheet did enable additional capital to become more readily available for desirable projects and, as its Directors took a strong personal interest, the speed of the decision-making process was greatly accelerated. Mr Ellis's long association with Fyffes and his extensive experience with the fruit trade, which had been an important factor in his being awarded a CBE in 1986, made his continued presence extremely desirable. Consequently it came as no surprise when, after the merger had been completed, his position as Chief Executive was immediately confirmed.

Although only two full trading years remained between these events and the completion of Fyffes' centenary, the financial results so far achieved have suggested that there has been considerable merit in the amalgamation. Thus, as indicated earlier annual profits have increased considerably and future prospects look extremely promising. At the time of the take-over Mr Neil McCann, the Chief Executive of FII, stated that:

> ... as a result of the proposed transaction the enlarged group will be poised to become one of the major fruit and distribution companies in Europe.[35]

The expansion already achieved in the UK and in Ireland has resulted in the construction of a strong base from which these goals can be reached in the future. It is, therefore, as a broadly based business that Fyffes have completed their first century. Nevertheless the banana remains the Group's most important single interest, and although its market share has fluctuated somewhat over the past decade the Company is, in fact, handling larger and larger quantities because of both a rising population and a steadily increasing per capita consumption which is being greatly aided by the current move towards a more healthy diet.

As the following statistics indicate, British consumption of bananas did rise considerably after 1983, but they also show that it still lagged far behind that of virtually all other European states. It should be noted, however, that this is a tendency which it shares with all other varieties of fresh fruit but not with fresh vegetables:

TABLE 14.2 WESTERN EUROPE – PER CAPITA CONSUMPTION OF BANANAS

	1977	1978	1980	1981	1982	1983	1984	1985	1986	1987	1988 (prelim.)
EEC	7.3	7.8	7.2	7.2	7.1	6.7	6.9	7.0	7.4	7.8	8.3
Belgium-Luxembourg	8.9	9.1	7.9	7.7	7.2	6.5	6.4	7.5	7.5	9.2	7.8
Denmark	6.4	7.3	5.0	4.9	4.8	4.6	5.1	6.2	6.8	6.6	6.7
France	9.4	9.4	8.3	8.6	8.6	8.1	8.1	7.7	8.2	8.0	8.2
Germany, Fed. Rep.	9.4	9.9	8.6	8.4	8.1	7.4	8.9	9.6	10.4	11.0	12.1
Greece	–	2.2	–	–	–	–	–	–	–	–	0.3
Ireland	7.2	7.0	7.1	6.2	6.2	5.8	6.6	6.1	6.8	6.4	5.1
Italy	5.4	6.2	5.3	5.4	5.8	5.4	5.4	5.4	5.9	6.3	6.6
Netherlands	8.1	8.8	7.6	7.3	6.7	6.3	6.4	7.2	7.5	8.1	8.6
Portugal	4.4	2.3	3.2	3.1	3.0	3.3	3.1	3.1	3.1	6.4	7.6
Spain	9.0	10.2	10.9	10.9	10.5	10.5	9.6	9.5	9.2	9.3	9.2
United Kingdom	5.3	5.5	5.8	5.9	5.7	5.4	5.5	5.7	6.0	6.3	6.8

Note: The figure for Ireland may be misleading because a proportion of its imports are susbsequently exported
Source: Eurofruit, 1.1989, p. 19.

232

These figures suggest that, although considerable progress has been made in recent years, many further opportunities still remain for future expansion. These represent part of the challenge which the Group and its rivals will no doubt have to face during its second century in business. However, in spite of the growing competition from a wide variety of alternative fresh fruits and substitutes, Fyffes are convinced that the convenience and fair value of the banana will ensure its continued and permanent place in the British market. All concerned with the enterprise are equally sure that Fyffes will be there to help provide it during its next hundred years in business.

Postscript

A look ahead to the future

As the UK and Irish banana markets operate within a global environment which is created by an integrated matrix of climatic, economic, political and social forces, any assessment of their future prospects and trends must necessarily take all of these factors into account. This has, of course, always been the case, so that at about the time that Fyffes were beginning to develop the British market, the same forces were helping to create the United Fruit Company to serve North America. Two further developments were then to see Fyffes widen its market to include many parts of Europe, and as it had by then become a wholly-owned subsidiary of United Fruit this meant that it was acting as a surrogate for this American Corporation.

This in turn was a reflection of the great strength of the United Fruit Company (now United Brands) for it and two other American-owned Corporations (Standard Fruit and Del Monte) had become responsible for a significant proportion of the world's banana business. The economic rationale for the emergence of these companies and for their subsequent development lay in the delicate nature and character of the banana which demanded a fully integrated operation from producer to the point of retail sale for it to be marketed at a price that was competitive with other fruits. These requirements, plus the need to take advantage of the many benefits provided by the economies of scale, meant that the banana industry has been traditionally dominated by large concerns which can afford the necessary investment and also accept the very heavy losses which can occur when things go wrong.

Although originally created by an amlagamation between Britain's two largest banana importers precisely by these very forces, Elders and Fyffes subsequently proved to be too small to be able to maintain a viable existence and for seventy-three years was a wholly-owned subsidiary of the largest of the banana multinational corporations.

234

The acquisition of what had become the Fyffes Group in 1986 by dynamic new owners meant that a new, independent policy could henceforth be adopted and the availability of fresh capital has already resulted in a considerable strengthening of its financial base. This, in turn, has enabled a number of initiatives to be undertaken or accelerated and the combined weight of the FII-Fyffes enterprise suggests that it is now in a strong position to take an even fuller part in all future developments.

Fyffes' re-emergence as a major, independent operator in the banana trade could not have taken place at a better time, for it has occurred just when Europe's drive to become a single market is rapidly approaching fruition. When this is achieved it will inevitably change the historic commercial relationship which individual member states have built up over the years through political linkages with their former colonies and dependencies. As bananas have been subjected to various types of trade preference for many decades any fundamental alteration in the system will provide considerable opportunities for those companies which are adaptable and able to evolve the appropriate type of policies for the new situation. Fyffes' dynamic management team are no doubt well placed to accept this forthcoming challenge so that in addition to seeking to maintain its traditional business they will pursue any opportunities for growth and may also attempt to develop additional outlets in Europe.

When United Brands decided to sell its British subsidiary in 1986 the sale did not include its remaining Canary Island assets and these were subsequently sold to separate buyers. The sale also ended the relationship under which Fyffes had played a vital role in the organization of the United Brands' fleet so that after the transaction had been finalised the only remaining link was via a 20 per cent interest which had been retained on a temporary basis by the American firm. As this holding was disposed of during 1989 this left FII-Fyffes (and incidentally United Brands) entirely free to pursue whatever activities were considered to be in the best interest of their investors and staff.

Fyffes' initiatives in Belize and Suriname have already made considerable progress and it seems probably that their combined output will do much to supplement the Company's traditional supplies from Jamaica. The ongoing role of the Commonwealth Caribbean producers is, however, more difficult to predict as it will partly depend on the decisions of the European Economic Community and the provisions of the latest Lomé convention. It will also be influenced by developments which take place in Jamaica and the Windwards' banana industries but Fyffes remain committed to supporting the long-standing efforts which have been made to encourage and advise its traditional suppliers.

The recent financial results of FII-Fyffes plc suggest that the combined group now has the necessary strength to be able to support its

British operating company in whatever proves to be the appropriate manner. Thus, almost irrespective of the changes which are likely to be introduced by forthcoming events in the EEC and in its producing areas Fyffes are certain to remain as a major banana importer and distributor in the UK. The Group may also find that fresh opportunities develop within the European Community and, perhaps even in Eastern Europe. At the same time the added balance provided by its general fresh fruit and produce business will further consolidate its overall position and under the guidance of a strong management team gives every indication that it will make further, steady progress during its second century.

The extent of these developments will, of course, be conditional upon the continued enthusiasm and dedication of the staff as well as the maintenance of sympathetic links with those responsible for the growing of bananas in the tropics. In the words of John Ellis, Fyffes' Chief Executive, 'We are as good as the people in the Group, bearing in mind we are handling agricultural crops and, therefore, it is vitally important that we have people that can create empathy with the producers and clearly demonstrate that we understand fully their problems and can help them realise their opportunities.'

Notes

Introduction: The Banana – its geographic, botanic and historic background

1 William Fawcett, *The Banana: its Cultivation, Distribution and Commercial Uses*, 2nd ed (1921), pp. 15–16.
2 P. K. Reynolds, *The Banana, Its History, Cultivation and Place among Staple Foods* (1927) pp. 4–5.
3 C. M. Wilson, *Empire in Green and Gold* (1947) pp. 290–1.
4 Ibid., p. 23.
5 F. U. Adams, *Conquest of the Tropics* (1914) p. 28.
6 Reynolds, *The Banana*, pp. 12–13.
7 Wilson, *Empire in Green and Gold*, p. 13.
8 Reynolds, *The Banana*, p. 11.
9 P. K. Reynolds, 'Earliest Evidence of Banana Culture', in a supplement to the *Journal of the American Oriental Society*, no. 12 (Dec. 1951), p. 4.
10 E. W. Perry, 'Tertiary of Colombia', *American Journal of Science*, series 5, vol. 10 (1925), pp. 530–7.
11 This statement is erroneously contradicted by F. U. Adams, *Conquest of the Tropics*, p. 30.
12 Reynolds, 'Earliest Evidence of Banana Culture', p. 18.
13 Ibid., p. 6.
14 Ibid., plates 2, 3 and 4.
15 Theophrastus, *Enquiry into Plants*, trans. by Sir Arthur Hart, 2 vols (1916), vol. 1, intro., pp. xix–xx.
16 Pliny the Elder, *Historia Naturalis*, Lib. xii, cap. 12 (6): *The Natural History of Pliny*, trans. by J. Bostock and H. Riley, 5 vols (1855–57), vol. 3, p. 110.
17 Reynolds, *Earliest Evidence of Banana Culture*, p. 19.
18 Ibid., p. 18.
19 N. W. Simmonds, *The Evolution of the Banana* (1962), pp. 144–5.
20 Reynolds, *The Banana*, p. 25.
21 Gonzales Fernandes de Oviedo y Valdes, *Historia general y natural de las Indias, Islas y Tierra Firme del Mar Oceano*, 4 vols, (1851–55), vol. 1, pp. 290–3.
22 Reynolds, 'Earliest Evidence of Banana Culture'.
23 Bernabe P. Cobo, *Historia del Nuero Mundo*.
24 Reynolds, *The Banana*, pp. 34–7.
25 Wilson, *The Empire in Green and Gold*, p. 17.

26 Adams, *Conquest of the Tropics*, p. 28.
27 Ibid., p. 29.

Chapter 1: The origins of the international fruit trade and the impact of changing maritime technology

1 Peter Mathias, *The First Industrial Nation*, (1969).
2 *Encyclopaedia Britannica*, 11th ed (1910–11), vol. 11 pp. 260–5.
3 Ralph Davis, *The Rise of the English Shipping Industry* (1972), p. 184.
4 Ibid., pp. 228–9.
5 Thomas Leyland, *Letterbook* (1786–88). This is located in the Local History Department of Liverpool City Library.
6 Vicente Abad, *Historia de la Naranja* Comite de la Exportacion de Frutos Citricos, Valencia (1984).
7 House of Commons, *Parliamentary Papers*, 1839 (229) XLVI, 9.
8 'The Fruit Trade of Liverpool', *The Liverpool Courier*, 20 February 1890, p. 4.
9 'The Fruit Trade of the Past Century', *The Fruit Grower, Fruiterer, Florist and Market Gardener*, 3 January 1901, pp. 1–3.
10 *Encyclopaedia Britannica*, 11th ed, vol. 11, p. 261.
11 Ibid., p. 262.
12 *Gaceta Agricola del Ministerio de Fomento*, Tomo X, Madrid (1879), p. 251, 252.
13 Joaquim Nadal Farreras, *Comercio Exterior y Subdesarrollo: Espana Y Gran Bretanade 1772–1914*, Institudo de Estudios Fiscales, Madrid (1978), pp. 335–6.
14 R. S. Best, 'The Day of the Sailing "Fruiter"', *Sea Breezes*, May 1972.
15 P. N. Davies, 'The Development of the Liner Trades', in *Ships and Shipbuilding in the North Atlantic Region*, Memorial University of Newfoundland (1978), p. 177.
16 K. T. Rowland, *Steam at Sea, A History of Steam Navigation* (1970), p. 55.
17 E. C. Smith, *A Short History of Naval and Marine Engineering* (1937), p. 174.
18 G. S. Graham, 'The Ascendancy of the Sailing Ship, 1850–1885', *Economic History Review* 2nd series, vol. 9, no. 1 (Aug. 1956), p. 76 fn. 3.
19 M. F. Maury, *The Physical Geography of the Sea*, 6th edn (1856).
20 A. W. Kirkaldy, *British Shipping* (1970), p. 330.
21 Mathias, *The First Industrial Nation*, p. 106.
22 C. E. Fayle, *A Short History of the World's Shipping Industry* (1927), p. 241.
23 L. Isserlis, 'Tramp Shipping, Cargo and Freights', *Journal of the Royal Statistical Society*, vol. 101 (1938), part 1, table 8, p. 122.
24 D. North, 'Ocean Freight Rates and Economic Development, 1750–1913', *Journal of Economic History*, vol. 18, no. 4 (Dec. 1958), p. 542.
25 M. G. Mulhall, *Dictionary of Statistics*, 4th edn (1898), p. 130.
26 A. G. Kenwood and A. L. Lougheed, *The Growth of the International Economy, 1820–1960* p. 103.

Chapter 2: The early development of the American banana market

1 P. K. Reynolds, *The Banana: Its History, Cultivation and Place among Staple Foods* (1927), p. 33.
2 Baron Erland Nordenskiöld, 'Deductions Suggested by the Geographical Distribution of Some Post-Columbian Words used by the Indians of S. America', *Comparative Ethnographical Studies*, 5, Göteborg (1922), p. 242–6.

3 Reynolds, *The Banana*, p. 34.
4 C. M. Wilson, *Empire in Green and Gold* (1947), p. 24.
5 F. U. Adams, *Conquest of the Tropics* (1914), p. 35.
6 Wilson, *Empire in Green and Gold*, p. 25.
7 Ibid., p. 26.
8 Ibid., p. 26.
9 Adams, *Conquest of the Tropics*, p. 35.
10 Wilson, *Empire in Green and Gold*, p. 27.
11 At this stage the terms 'bunch' and 'stem' appear to have been interchangeable.
12 D. W. Rodriques, *History of the arrival of the banana in Jamaica ...* , quoted in C. V. Black (ed.), *Jamaica's Banana Industry*, published by the Jamaica Banana Producers Association, Kinston, Jamaica (1984), p. 7.
13 Adams, *Conquest of the Tropics*, pp. 38–9.
14 Wilson, *Empire in Green and Gold*, p. 20.
15 Reynolds, *The Banana*, p. 44.
16 Wilson, *Empire in Green and Gold*, pp. 22–3.
17 S. May and G. Plaza, *The United Fruit Company in Latin America* (1958), p. 7.
18 Wilson, *Empire in Green and Gold*, p. 23.
19 R. Bartlett, *Lorenzo Dow Baker: Yankee Entrepreneur in the Caribbean Fruit Trade* (1987), p. 6.
20 Reynolds, *The Banana*, p. 45.
21 Wilson, *Empire in Green and Gold*, p. 27.
22 Ibid., p. 29.
23 Bartlett, *Lorenzo Dow Baker*, p. 9.
24 Quoted in Wilson, *Empire in Green and Gold*, p. 34.
25 Rodriques, *History of the Arrival of the Banana in Jamaica*, p. 12. (Note that the Frank Brothers had moved their operation from Panama because the construction of the canal had raised the cost of labour.)
26 Quoted in Bartlett, *Lorenzo Dow Baker*, p. 11.
27 Ibid., p. 12.
28 Wilson, *Empire in Green and Gold*, p. 71.
29 Ibid., p. 83.
30 Ibid., p. 77.
31 Reynolds, *The Banana*, p. 48.
32 Bartlett, *Lorenzo Dow Baker*, p. 12.
33 Wilson, *Empire in Green and Gold*, p. 80.
34 Reynolds, *The Banana*, p. 48.
35 Adams, *Conquest of the Tropics*, pp. 70–2.
36 Reynolds, *The Banana*, p. 49.
37 Wilson, *Empire in Green and Gold*, pp. 80–90.
38 Adams, *Conquest of the Tropics*, p. 55.
39 W. Stewart, *Keith and Costa Rica* (1964), p. 146–8.
40 Ibid., p. 149.
41 Ibid., pp. 155–6.
42 Adams, *Conquest of the Tropics*, p. 83.
43 Bartlett, *Lorenzo Dow Baker*, p. 16.
44 Wilson, *Empire in Green and Gold*, p. 107.
45 Ibid., p. 108.
46 May and Plaza, *The United Fruit Company in Latin America*, p. 7.

Chapter 3: The Canary Islands and the establishment of the Liverpool banana trade

1   A. Samler Brown, *Madeira, Canary Islands and Azores* (1922), p. G9.
2   Ibid., p. G11.
3   Ibid., p. G15.
4   Norman Ball, Review of: 'The Canary Islands after the Conquest', *Economic History Review* 2nd series, vol. 36, no. 1 (Feb. 1983), pp. 164–5.
5   Charles Edwards, *Rides and Studies in the Canary Islands* (1888), p. 50.
6   Foreign Office Miscellaneous Series, no. 246, *Spain: Report on the Social and Economic Conditions of the Canary Islands* (1892), p. 4.
7   George F. Stecley, 'The Wine Economy of Tenerife in the Seventeenth Century: Anglo-Spanish Partnership in a Luxury Trade', *Economic History Review*, 2nd series, vol. 33, no. 3 (Aug. 1980), p. 337.
8   Ibid, p. 339.
9   Ibid., p. 343.
10 Ibid., p. 348.
11 *Report on the Social and Economic Conditions of the Canary Islands*, p. 5.
12 Ibid., p. 6.
13 Olivia M. Stone, *Tenerife and its Six Satellites*, (*The Canaries Past and Present*), 2 vols. (1887), pp. 364–5.
14 Ibid., p. 262.
15 George Glas, *History of the Canary Islands* (1764).
16 Samler Brown, *Madeira, Canary Islands and Azores*, pp. D33–6.
17 Albert H. Imlah, *Economic Elements in the Pax Britannica*,
18 See Chapter 1, Table 1.6, p. 20.
19 Aguayro, *Primer Centenario del Puerto de la Luz*, Caja Insular de Ahorros, year 12, no. 146, March–April 1983, Las Palmas. Of special reference is the excellent work of Fernando Martin Galan and Francisco Quintana Navarro.
20 Samler Brown, *Madeira, Canary Islands and Azores*, (1894 edn), p. 199.
21 *Report of the Social and Economic Conditions of the Canary Islands*, p. 10.
22 P. N. Davies, *The Trade Makers. Elder Dempster in West Africa, 1852–1972* (1973, re-issued 1980).
23 P. N. Davies, *Sir Alfred Lewis Jones, Shipping Entrepreneur Par Excellence* (1978).
24 See Introduction, p. 8.
25 *The Universal Magazine of Knowledge and Pleasure*, London, April 1748, p. 532.
26 W. R. Wilde, *Narrative of a Voyage to Madeira, Tenerife and along the Shores of the Mediterranean*, (1884), p. 63.
27 C. Piazzi Smith, *Tenerife. An Astronomer's Experiment or Specialities of a residence above the clouds*, (1858).
28 See Chapter 1, Table 1.1, p. 17.
29 See Chapter 1, p. 34.
30 P. K. Reynolds, *The Banana, Its History, Cultivation and Place among Staple Foods* (1927), p. 55.
31 See p. 43.
32 Stone, *Tenerife and its Six Satellites*, vol. 2, p. 2.
33 'A Napoleon of Commerce', interview given by A. L. Jones to the magazine *Great Thoughts*, 18 June 1898.
34 See Fig. 3.2, p. 42.
35 Pavillard MSS: Copies of the records of Elder Dempster (Grand Canary) Ltd., of which the Pavillard Family were the principals, are held by the author.

36 Interview with Mr Luis Ley, former manager of Elder Dempster's Fruit Department in the Canary Islands. *The Fruit Trade News*, 9 November 1901, p. 101.
37 A. H. Stockley, 'Consciousness of Effort, printed privately for the author by W. H. Smith & Son (1937), pp. 23–4.
38 Ibid., pp. 179–80.

Chapter 4: The contribution of Edward Wathen Fyffe

1 See Chapter 3, Table 3.2, p. 44.
2 *Covent Garden Gazette and Market Record*, 28 November 1885, p. 45.
3 Ibid., 8 May 1886, p. 225.
4 *The Horticultural Times*, 6 November 1886, p. 297.
5 Ibid.
6 'Death of Mr. Edward W. Fyffe', *The Stroud Journal*, 25 October 1935.
7 Archives held at the Sandeman Library, Perth, (B59–22–60 and B59–26–10/11).
8 Letter from P. G. Vasey, Sandeman Library, 1 September 1982.
9 Letter from P. G. Vasey, Sandeman Library, 23 August 1982.
10 See also *The Universal British Directory of Trade, Commerce and Manufacture* (1791).
11 *Kent's Directory* (1800).
12 *Kent's Directory* (1813).
13 *Pigot's Directory* (1824) and Robson's *London Commercial Directory* (1824).
14 Robson's *London Commercial Directory* (1841).
15 Crockford's *Clerical Directory* (1925), p. 551.
16 *Stroud News*, 21 August 1925.
17 *Post Office London Directory* (1881).
18 Author's interview with Peter Reid's grandson, Noel Reid, in Tenerife during 1980.
19 *The Banana Budget*, was a weekly bulletin issued by Elders and Fyffes Ltd of 31–32 Bow Street, London, WC2.
20 Tom Cullen, *Autumn of Terror: The Crimes and Times of Jack the Ripper* (1973).
21 Kelly's *Post Office London Directories* for the relevant years.
22 J. R. Ackerley, *My Father and Myself* (1968); Diana Petre, *The Secret Orchard of Roger Ackerley* (1975).
23 A. H. Stockley, *Consciousness of Effort*, printed privately for the author by W. H. Smith & Son (1937), p. 165.
24 Kelly's *Post Office London Directories* for the relevant years.
25 Formation documents of Hudson Brothers (London) Limited, 11 November 1898 (Public Record Office, Kew: box 8214, ref. 59505).
26 Author's interview with John Anthony Hudson, grandson of James Hudson, at Chislehurst, Kent, 12 August 1981.
27 This agreement forms part of the papers of Messrs Fyffe Hudson and Company, Limited, which are held at the Public Record Office, Kew (reference: 53906. BT31, box 7562).
28 Hudson Brothers London, Limited, papers at the Public Record Office, Kew (reference: 59505, box 8214).
29 *Surrey Mirror and County Post*, 9 April and 12 April 1907.
30 Probate of his Will granted 28 May 1907.
31 Interview with John Anthony Hudson, see Note 26.
32 'Death of Mr E. W. Fyffe', *The Stroud Journal*, 25 October 1935.
33 See Fyffe's family tree in the Appendix, Table 1.

Chapter 5: The adoption of cooling techniques and their impact on the trade

1   See Chapter 1, p. 15.
2   Basil Greenhill, *The Merchant Schooner*, (1988), p. 16.
3   Marischal Murray, *Union Castle Chronicle (1853–1953)* (1953).
4   Siegfried Stander, *Tree of Life. The story of Cape fruit* (1983), p. 7.
5   Ibid., p. 7.
6   Ibid., p. 8.
7   R. A. Peters, *Refrigerated Shipping*, Wakefield Lecture presented at the University of Southampton, February 1982, p. 1.
8   A. W. Kirkaldy, *British Shipping: Its History, Organization and Importance* (1914), p. 114.
9   Ibid., Appendix III, p. 581.
10 Peters, *Refrigerated Shipping*, p. 2.
11 'The Fruit Trade of the Past Century', *The Fruit-Grower, Fruiterer, Florist and Market Gardener*, 3 January 1901.
12 Stander, *Tree of Life*, p. 9.
13 Ibid., p. 10.
14 Cutcliffe Hyne, *Banana Farming in the Canary Islands* (1898).
15 Osbert Ward, *The Vale of Orotava* (1903), p. 79.
16 *The Fruit-Grower, Fruiterer, Florist and Market Gardener*, 2 December 1896, p. 363.
17 Ibid.
18 Samler Brown, *Madeira, Canary Islands and Azores*, (1894 edn) p. 237.
19 *The Fruit-Grower, Fruiterer, Florist and Market Gardener*, 25 February 1897, p. 115.
20 P. K. Reynolds, *The Banana, Its History, Cultivation and Place among Staple Foods* (1927), p. 56.
21 See Chapter 2, p. 28.
22 *The Banana Budget*, 22 February 1922, pp. 6–7.
23 As the Jamaica Fruit Importing and Trading Company of London, Limited, was liquidated in 1901, its official file is now held at the Public Record Office, Kew, with the records of other dissolved companies (see BT. 31–6961, registration number 49018).
24 s.s. *Port Victor*, 1,828 net tons, was owned by the Anglo-Australian S.N. Co., (William Milburn & Co., Managers). See *Lloyd's Register of Shipping*, 1897–8, P. 505.
25 *The Fruit-Grower, Fruiterer, Florist and Market Gardener*, 23 December 1896, p. 408.
26 s.s. *Elderslie*, 1,801 net tons, was owned by the Elderslie s.s. Co. Ltd, (Turnbull, Martin & Co., Managers). See *Lloyds Register of Shipping*, 1897–8, E.204.
27 *The Fruit-Grower, Fruiterer, Florist and Market Gardener*, 30 December 1896, p. 427.
28 Ibid.
29 Ibid.
30 *The Fruit-Grower, Fruiterer, Florist and Market Gardener*, 18 March 1897, pp. 170–1.
31 Ibid., p. 171.
32 *The Greengrocer, Fruiterer and Market Gardener*, 18 December 1895, p. 38.
33 *The Fruit-Grower, Fruiterer, Florist and Market Gardener*, 7 July 1898, p. 7.
34 ss. *Port Pirie*, 1,929 net tons, was owned by the Anglo-Australian SN Co., (William Milburn & Co., Managers). See *Lloyds's Register of Shipping*, 1897–8, P. 503.
35 *The Fruit-Grower, Fruiterer, Florist and Market Gardener*, 13 May 1897.
36 Ibid.
37 A. H. Stockley, *Consciousness of Effort*, printed privately for the author by W. H. Smith & Son (1937), pp. 24–5.

38 Company file held at the Public Record Office (BT31–6961: 49018).
39 Ibid.

Chapter 6: A new outlet for Jamaican bananas

1   W. J. Gardner, *A History of Jamaica* (1971), p. 2.
2   S. J. and E. F. Hurwitz, *Jamaica: A Historical Portrait* (1971), p. 164.
3   Ibid., p. 11.
4   *Encyclopaedia Britannica*, 11th edn (1911), vol. 15, p. 134.
5   Ibid.
6   See Chapter 2, p. 25.
7   See Introduction, p. 8.
8   C. M. Wilson, *Empire in Green and Gold* (1947), pp. 14–15.
9   See Chapter 2, p. 26.
10 A. H. Stockley, *Consciousness of Effort*, published privately by W. H. Smith (1937), p. 14.
11 Quoted in C. V. Black (ed.), *Jamaica's Banana Industry* (1984), p. 8.
12 *The Fruit-Grower, Fruiterer, Florist and Market Gardener*, 18 March 1897, p. 171.
13 S. B. Saul, 'The Economic Significance of "Constructive Imperialism"', *Journal of Economic History*, vol. 17, no. 2 (June 1957), p. 180.
14 See Chapter 2, p. 30.
15 Saul, 'The Economic Significance of "Constructive Imperialism"', p. 180.
16 Wilson, *Empire in Green and Gold*, p. 104.
17 Stockley, *Consciousness of Effort*, p. 26.
18 Saul, 'The Economic Significance of "Constructive Imperialism"', pp. 173–5.
19 P. N. Davies, *The Trade Makers: Elder Dempster in West Africa, 1852–1972* (1973, reissued 1980).
20 Stockley, *Consciousness of Effort*, p. 28.
21 Ibid., reproduced opposite p. 30.
22 Ibid., p. 31.
23 *Joseph Chamberlain MSS.*, held at the Heslop Room at the University of Birmingham Library. Letter from Chamberlain to Sir Michael Hicks Beach, dated 11 January 1900 (JC. 14/3/69).
24 Ibid.
25 Stockley, *Consciousness of Effort*, pp. 32–3.
26 *Chamberlain MSS.* Letters from Jones to Chamberlain dated 28 December 1898 (JC. 14/3/47) and Jones to Lord Ampthill, dated 3 January 1899 (JC. 14/3/49).
27 *Chamberlain MSS.* Chamberlain to Sir Michael Hicks Beach dated 11 January 1900 (JC. 14/3/69).
28 Details of the capital structure are provided in Table 2 in the Appendix.
29 Details of the shareholdings are provided in Table 2 in the Appendix.
30 Stockley, *Consciousness of Effort*, p. 34.
31 For full details of Hall's system of cooling, see *Bananas and Refrigeration*, a paper produced by H. J. Ward for the International Congress of the Refrigerating Industries which was reproduced in the *Fruit, Flower and Vegetable Trades' Journal*, 17 October 1908, p. 255.
32 T. A. Bushell, *Royal Mail: A Centenary History of the Royal Mail Line, 1839–1939* (1939), pp. 145–6.
33 Ibid., p. 146.
34 See Chapter 7, pp. 99–100.
35 Stockley, *Consciousness of Effort*, p. 56.

36 R. M. Parsons, *The Banana Trade at the Port of Bristol* (1982), p. 10.
37 Ibid.
38 Ibid., p. 13.
39 Alfred Lewis Jones was made a Knight Commander of St Michael and St George in 1901.

Chapter 7: The formation of Elders and Fyffes, Limited

1   *The Liverpool Courier*, 6 February 1890, p. 4.
2   See Chapter 3, p. 49.
3   See Chapter 4, p. 58.
4   See Chapter 4, p. 58.
5   See Chapter 4, p. 60.
6   See Chapter 5, pp. 72–6.
7   *The Fruit-Grower, Fruiterer, Florist and Market Gardener*, 13 June 1901, p. 380.
8   Ibid., 10 January 1901, p. 21.
9   A. H. Stockley, *Consciousness of Effort*, printed privately for the author by W. H. Smith & Son (1937), p. 249.
10 See Chapter 2, pp. 34–5.
11 F. U. Adams, *Conquest of the Tropics* (1914), p. 91.
12 Ibid., p. 98.
13 Ibid., p. 101.
14 *The Fruit-Grower, Fruiterer, Florist and Market Gardener*, 16 May 1901, p. 316.
15 Full details of these shareholdings are provided in the Appendix, Table 3.
16 Details of these discussions are to be found in Elders and Fyffes Limited's *General Minute Book*, No. 1.
17 Stockley, *Consciousness of Effort*, pp. 56–7.
18 See Chapter 5, p. 69.
19 See Chapter 6, p. 81.
20 See Chapter 6, p. 86.
21 Stockley, *Consciousness of Effort*, p. 60.
22 Ibid., pp. 62–3.
23 See Appendix, Table 8.
24 See Appendix, Table 4.
25 H. J. Ward, 'Bananas and Refrigeration' *Fruit, Flower and Vegetable Trades Journal*, 17 October 1908, pp. 255–7.
26 C. M. Wilson, *Empire in Green and Gold*, (1947), pp. 138–42.
27 Ward, 'Bananas and Refrigeration', p. 257.
28 Stockley, *Consciousness of Effort*, pp. 65–6.

Chapter 8: The establishment of a national market

1   'Curious Story of the Jamaica Banana Trade', *Manchester City News*, 13 December 1902.
2   Ibid.
3   Lord Olivier, *Jamaica: The Blessed Island* pp. 383–6.
4   Patrick Beaver, *Yes! We Have Some: The Story of Fyffes* (1976), p. 43.
5   See Chapter 6, p. 89.
6   R. M. Parsons, *The White Ships: The Banana Trade at the Port of Bristol* (1982), p. 17.
7   P. N. Davies, *The Trade Makers: Elder Dempster in West Africa, 1852–1972* (1973), pp. 129 and 407.

8   Elders and Fyffes, Limited, *General Minute Book* no. 1, p. 77 (Directors' Report for the year ending 31 August 1907).
9   See Chapter 7, p. 102.
10 A. H. Stockley, *Consciousness of Effort*, printed privately for the author by W. H. Smith & Son (1937), p. 71.
11 See Appendix, Table 3.
12 Stockley, *Consciousness of Effort*, p. 79.
13 Capt. K. J. Leslie, 'Banana Fleet', *Sea Breezes*, 41 (1967), 255, pp. 176–7.
14 Parsons, *The White Ships*, p. 17.
15 Beaver, *Yes! We Have Some*, p. 44.
16 Ibid., p. 45.
17 A. Roger Ackerley's speech as reported in *The Banana Budget*, vol. 5, no. 19, 2 December 1925, p. ii.
18 W. Fawcett, *The Banana: Its Cultivation, Distribution and Commercial Uses* (1913), p. 174.
19 *The Fruit Trade News*, 23 November 1901, p. 142.
20 *The Fruit Trade News*, 21 December 1901, p. 211.
21 Stockley, *Consciousness of Effort*, p. 59.
22 *The Fruit-Grower, Fruiterer, Florist and Market Gardener*, 11 April 1901, p. 233.
23 Beaver, *Yes! We Have Some*, pp. 49–50.
24 See Chapter 5, p. 74.
25 *The Fruit Trade Mail*, 6 January 1906, p. 9.
26 Beaver, *Yes! We Have Some*, p. 48.
27 Leslie, 'Banana Fleet' p. 177.

Chapter 9: A British institution

1   P. N. Davies, *The Trade Makers: Elder Dempster in West Africa, 1852–1972* (1973), p. 172.
2   Ibid., p. 173.
3   Ibid., p. 455.
4   A. H. Stockley, *Consciousness of Effort*, printed privately for the author by W. H. Smith & Son (1937), pp. 116–117.
5   See Appendix, Table 3.3.
6   'The West Indian Mail Service', *The Times*, January 1911.
7   See file 72110, dissolved at the Public Record Office, Kew.
8   R. M. Parsons, *The White Ships: The Banana Trade of the Port of Bristol* (1982), p. 28.
9   Ibid., p. 29.
10 See Appendix, Table 5.
11 See Chapter 8, p. 107.
12 Leslie, 'Banana Fleet', *Sea Breezes*, 41 (1967), 255, pp. 178–9.
13 Ibid., p. 180.
14 W. Fawcett, *The Banana: Its Cultivation, Distribution and Commercial Uses* (1913), p. 161.
15 See Chapter 7, p. 98.
16 Fawcett, *The Banana*, p. 163.
17 See Chapter 5, p. 70.
18 C. J. M. Carter, '75-Year Link with the Canaries', *Sea Breezes*, May 1969, pp. 325–33.
19 Fawcett, *The Banana*, pp. 161–4.
20 Ibid., p. 161; C. V. Black (ed.) *Jamaica's Banana Industry* (1984), p. 13.

21 Stockley, *Consciousness of Effort*, p. 124.
22 Note on banana importations into Manchester by Mr di Georgio of the Atlantic Fruit Company, quoted in Stockley, *Consciousness of Effort*, p. 125.
23 See Chapter 8, p. 118.
24 Fawcett, *The Banana*, p. 164.
25 Quoted in Ibid., p. 165.
26 Patrick Beaver, *Yes! We Have Some: The Story of Fyffes* (1976), p. 51.
27 Sir Charles Lucas, *The Empire at War*, (quoted in Beaver, *Yes! We Have Some*, p. 58).
28 See Appendix, Table 8.
29 Stockley, *Consciousness of Effort*, p. 127.
30 See Appendix, Table 5.
31 Beaver, *Yes! We Have Some*, p. 59.
32 See Appendix, Table 5.
33 See Appendix, Table 5.
34 Stockley, *Consciousness of Effort*, p. 249.
35 Beaver, *Yes! We Have Some*, p. 63.
36 Stockley, *Consciousness of Effort*, pp. 244–5.
37 Details of Fruit Distributing Company Limited, see file 75160, dissolved, at the Public Record Office, Kew.
38 *The Banana Budget*, vol. 1, no. 16, 16 November 1921, p. 8.
39 *The Banana Budget*, vol. 1, no. 33, 15 March 1922, p. 3.
40 Ibid., vol. 1, no. 31, 1 March 1922, p. 5.
41 Ibid., vol. 1, no. 19, 7 December 1921, p. 3.
42 Beaver, *Yes! We Have Some*, p. 63.
43 *The Banana Budget*, vol. 1, no. 38, 19 April 1922, pp. 4–8.
44 Ibid.
45 Ibid.
46 *The Banana Budget*, vol. 6, no. 1, 4 August 1926, pp. 2–3.
47 Ibid., vol. 6 no. 51, 20 July 1927, pp. 596–7.
48 Ibid., vol. 3, no. 21, 19 December 1923, pp. 172–3.
49 Ibid., vol. 7, no. 21, 21 December 1927, pp. 245–8.
50 Beaver, *Yes! We Have Some*, pp. 64–5.
51 Ibid., p. 64.
52 *The Banana Budget*, vol. 1, no. 5, 31 August 1921, p. 3.
53 Ibid., vol. 1, no. 8, 21 September 1921, p. 1.
54 Beaver, *Yes! We Have Some*, pp. 67–8.

Chapter 10: Enter Jamaica Producers: The British industry in the 1930s

1 See Chapter 5, p. 75; also A. H. Stockley, *Consciousness of Effort*, published privately for the author by W. H. Smith (1937), p. 229.
2 C. V. Black (ed.), *Jamaica's Banana Industry* (1984), p. 71.
3 Ibid., p. 71.
4 See Chapter 6, p. 82.
5 Black, *Jamaica's Banana Industry*, p. 16.
6 Lord Olivier, *Jamaica: The Blessed Island* p. 389.
7 Black, *Jamaica's Banana Industry*, p. 17.
8 Ibid., p. 18. See also F. Hanington and P. A. Kelly, *The Lady Boats: The Life and Times of Canada's West Indies Merchant Fleet*.
9 Black, *Jamaica's Banana Industry*, p. 19.
10 Ibid., p. 43.

11 Lord Olivier, *Jamaica: The Blessed Island*, pp. 395–6.
12 Stockley, *Consciousness of Effort*, pp. 135–7.
13 Lord Olivier, *Jamaica: The Blessed Island*, p. 396.
14 Black, *Jamaica's Banana Industry*, p. 77.
15 Ibid., pp. 84–5.
16 See Appendix, Table 5.
17 J. K. Galbraith, *The Great Crash, 1929* (Revised 1975).
18 Elders and Fyffes, Limited, *General Minute Book*, vol. 2, p. 71, (year ending 2 January 1932).
19 Stockley, *Consciousness of Effort*, pp. 245–6.
20 A. Lewis, *Economic Survey, 1919–1939* (1949), p. 79.
21 Ibid., p. 58.
22 H. W. Richardson, *Economic Recovery in Britain, 1932–1939* (1967), p. 48.
23 See Appendix, Table 5.
24 Elders and Fyffes, Limited, *General Minute Book*, vol. 2, p. 80.
25 See Appendix, Table 5.
26 See Chapter 7, p. 98.
27 Elders and Fyffes, Limited, *General Minute Book*, vol. 1 (year ending 30 June 1908), pp. 103–4.
28 Stockley, *Consciousness of Effort*, p. 244.
29 A Cioranescu, *The History of Santa Cruz de Tenerife*, vol. 4 (1803–1977), Historia 48 (1979), Santa Cruz, pp. 14–15.
30 A. F. Baillon's 'Memoirs' (unpublished), which were completed in 1955, provide an excellent account of the early days of the business at Hoya Grande.
31 See Chapter 9, p. 125.
32 Elders and Fyffes, Limited, *General Minute Book*, vol. 2, p. 16.
33 Ibid., p. 23.
34 Ibid., p. 42.
35 See above, p. 151.
36 Elders and Fyffes, Limited, *General Minute Book*, vol. 2, p. 72.
37 Baillon, 'Memoirs', p. 171.
38 Ibid.
39 Author's interviews with Mrs D. C. Moore in Santa Cruz during December 1978.
40 Author's interviews with many ex-Fyffes' employees in the Canary Islands, including Snr Pepe Escavil who was foreman at Hoya Grande for thirty years and who began working for the company in 1925. A tape of this and other interviews made in January 1980 is held by the author.
41 Author's interview with Mr M. R. Blairsey in Santa Cruz de Tenerife on 5 April 1982.
42 Ibid.
43 Elders and Fyffes, Limited, *General Minute Book*, vol. 2, p. 107.
44 Patrick Beaver, *Yes! We Have Some: The Story of Fyffes* (1976), p. 73.
45 Baillon, 'Memoirs', pp. 96–108.
46 Barbara J. Heinzen, 'The United Brands Company in Cameroon', PhD thesis submitted to the School of Oriental and African Studies, University of London, Appendix A.
47 See Chapter 9, p. 132.
48 Author's interviews with J. G. Batten and A. MacLaurin during 1981 and 1982.
49 Elders and Fyffes, Limited, *General Minute Book*, vol. 2, pp. 120–1.
50 Ibid., p. 123.
51 Ibid., p. 82.
52 Ibid., p. 73.

53   See Chapter 9, p. 131.

54   Elders and Fyffes, Limited, *General Minute Book*, vol. 2, pp. 88–9.

55   Ibid., p. 81.

56   R. M. Parsons, 'Elders and Fyffes', *Ships Monthly*, April 1988, p. 23.

57   Telegram from Mr Robert Clark, Chairman of Elders and Fyffes to A. H. Stockley, quoting cable from A. W. Preston, 21 April 1920.

58   Cable from Preston to Stockley dated 15 April 1920. (This is part of a large collection of correspondence on this subject in the author's possession.)

59   Stockley, *Consciousness of Effort*, pp. 81–3 and pp. 210–12.

60   Elders and Fyffes, Limited, *General Minute Book*, vol. 2, p. 83.

61   Ibid., p. 123.

62   Stockley, *Consciousness of Effort*, pp. 247–8.

63   Elders and Fyffes, Limited, *General Minute Book*, vol. 2, p. 124.

64   Ibid., p. 13.

65   The author is especially indebted to Mr S. W. F. Johnson and to Mr A. Knight for their assistance with this section.

66   *The Banana Budget*, vol. 1, 24 May 1922, p. 8.

67   Ibid., vol. 2, 5 September 1923, p. 44.

68   Ibid., Vol. 8, 26 September 1928, p. 105.

69   Beaver, *Yes! We Have Some*, p. 66.

Chapter 11: The Second World War and its aftermath

1   Elders and Fyffes, Limited, *General Minute Book*, vol. 2, p. 120.

2   Ibid., p. 121.

3   R. M. Parsons, *The White Ships* (1982), pp. 47–8.

4   Captain H. J. Chubb, 'Elders and Fyffes Fleet List', *Marine News*, August 1960, pp. 5–6.

5   C. V. Black, (ed.) *Jamaica's Banana Industry* (1984), p. 88.

6   Ibid.

7   See Appendix, Table 5.

8   Elders and Fyffes Limited, *General Minute Book*, vol. 2, p. 128.

9   P. Beaver, *Yes! We Have Some: The Story of Fyffes* (1976), p. 75.

10   Ibid., p. 76. This refers to a statement made by Lord Horder which was quoted by Mrs Ingillson in a 'Kitchen Front' broadcast on 7 May 1941.

11   Ibid.

12   Black, *Jamaica's Banana Industry*, pp. 88–9.

13   Ibid. (The 1944 statistics were distorted by the hurricane which occurred in August of that year – the figure otherwise has been estimated to have been 7,000,000 stems.)

14   Author's interview with Mr J. G. Batten in April 1981.

15   Author's interview with Mr A. 'Sandy' Maclaurin in September 1982.

16   See Appendix, Table 6.

17   Author's interview with Mr G. Walker in February 1982.

18   Captain K. Leslie, 'Banana Fleet', *Sea Breezes*, vol. 41, no. 255, March 1967, p. 195.

19   Beaver, *Yes! We Have Some*, pp. 79–80.

20   Ibid., p. 80.

21   Elders and Fyffes Limited, *General Minute Book*, vol. 2, p. 145.

22   Beaver, *Yes! We Have Some*, p. 80.

23   Elders and Fyffes, Limited, *General Minute Book*, vol. 2, p. 146.

24 Ibid., p. 140.
25. Ibid., p. 154.
26 Ibid., p. 156.
27 Parsons, *The White Ships*, p. 49.
28 Elders and Fyffes, *General Minute Book*, vol. 2, p. 155.
29 Chubb, 'Elders and Fyffes Fleet List', pp. 7–8.
30 See Appendix, Table 5.
31 Ibid.
32 See Chapter 10, p. 153.
33 Beaver, *Yes! We Have Some*, p. 85.
34 Elders and Fyffes, Limited, *General Minute Book*, vol. 2, p. 156.
35 Ibid., p. 160.
36 Ibid., p. 163.
37 Ibid., p. 168.
38 Beaver, *Yes! We Have Some*, p. 86.
39 See Chapter 10, p. 158.
40 See Appendix, Table 6.
41 Elders and Fyffes, Limited, *General Minute Book*, vol. 2, p. 164.
42 Ibid., p. 171 and p. 176.
43 Beaver, *Yes! We Have Some*, p. 87.
44 Author's interviews with Captain K. Leslie in February 1986 and August 1988.
45 Elders and Fyffes, Limited, *General Minute Book*, vol. 2, p. 164.
46 Ibid., p. 171.
47 Ibid., p. 187.
48 Elders and Fyffes, Limited, *General Minute Book*, vol. 3, p. 13.
49 Elders and Fyffes, Limited, *General Minute Book*, vol. 2, p. 165.
50 Ibid., pp. 199–200.
51 Black, *Jamaica's Banana Industry*, pp. 90–1.
52 See above, p. 172.
53 Black, *Jamaica's Banana Industry*, p. 91.
54 Ibid.
55 Ibid., p. 94.
56 Elders and Fyffes, Limited, *General Minute Book*, vol. 2, p. 186.
57 Ibid., p. 191.
58 Ibid., p. 195.
59 Black, *Jamaica's Banana Industry*, p. 92.

Chapter 12: The development of the Windward Islands and its consequences

1 See Appendix, Table 5.
2 Elders and Fyffes, Limited, *General Minute Book*, no. 2, p. 203.
3 Ibid., p. 207.
4 R. Thomson, (*et al.*), *Greengold* (1987), p. 29.
5 Ibid., pp. 29–30.
6 Ernest G. Foley was a former employee of Elders and Fyffes and had been its Accountant in Santa Cruz and later at Las Palmas. He left in 1938 and then took over the Tropical Fruit Company of Dublin from George Ackerley in January 1939.
7 C. V. Black, (ed.) *Jamaica's Banana Industry* (1984), p. 94.
8 Thomson, *Greengold*, p. 27.
9 Roy Stemman, *Geest: 1935–1985* (1986), pp. 183–6.

10 See Chapter 11, p. 180.
11 Stemman, *Geest: 1935–1985*, p. 14.
12 Ibid., p. 53.
13 Ibid.
14 Ibid., p. 191.
15 Ibid., p. 126.
16 Patrick Beaver, *Yes! We Have Some: The Story of Fyffes* (1976), pp. 88–9.
17 Ibid., p. 89.
18 See Appendix, Table 6.
19 See Appendix, Table 5.
20 Author's interview with Mr F. Darter, former Secretary of Elders and Fyffes, in April 1982.
21 Author's discussions with Captain K. J. Leslie, September 1989.
22 Author's interview with Mr A. J. Ellis, Chief Executive of the Fyffes Group, August 1989.
23 See above, pp. 183–4.
24 Author's discussions with Captain K. J. Leslie, September 1989.
25 Black, *Jamaica's Banana Industry*, p. 95.
26 Author's interview with Mr R. J. Hilborne, Executive Director of Geest Industries, in February 1989.
27 Ibid.
28 'Making bananas fighting fit', *The Times*, 30 April 1967.
29 Author's interview with Mr F. Darter, April 1982.
30 Elders and Fyffes Limited, Minutes of Directors' Meeting held on 10 November 1964, vol. 15, p. 341.
31 Beaver, *Yes! We Have Some*, p. 97.
32 Ibid., pp. 98–9.
33 Elders and Fyffes, Limited, Minutes of Directors' Meeting held 26 July 1963, vol. 15, p. 277.
34 Beaver, *Yes! We Have Some*, p. 99.
35 'Fyffes Ports', *Fruit Trades Journal* 22 July 1961, p. 39.
36 Ibid., p. 27.
37 See above, Chapter 11, p. 173.
38 Elders and Fyffes Limited, Minutes of Directors' Meeting held 15 July 1959, vol. 15, p. 106.
39 Beaver, *Yes! We Have Some*, p. 124.
40 Author's interview with Mr F. A. Hall in June 1989.
41 'A Famous Name Throughout the Midlands', *Fruit Trades Journal*, 30 October 1954.
42 Author's interview with Mr John Priest, September 1989.
43 Elders and Fyffes Limited, Minutes of Directors' Meeting held 14 April 1964, vol. 15, p. 316.
44 Ibid., Minutes of Directors' Meeting held 10 December 1963, vol 15, p. 297.
45 Stemman, *Geest: 1935–1985*, p. 130.
46 Author's interview with Mr A. J. Ellis, Chief Executive of the Fyffes Group, August 1989.
47 Stemman, *Geest: 1935–85*, p. 132.
48 Ibid., p. 131.
49 Author's interview with Mr A. C. Penny in June 1983.
50 Beaver, *Yes! We Have Some*, p. 95.
51 Ibid., p. 96.

52 Ibid., p. 99.
53 Ibid., p. 98.

Chapter 13: The emergence of the modern industry

1 *Fyffes Staff Budget*, 'Company Reorganisation', vol. XVIII, no. 3, May 1965, pp. 25–6.
2 See Appendix, Table 7.
3 'Personal message from John A. Taylor', *Fyffes Staff Budget*, vol. XIX, no. 10, December 1966, pp. 130–1.
4 Hansard, 26 February 1971, p. 1186.
5 D. A. Philp, *The Winban Agreement*, 8 January 1971.
6 Hansard, 26 February 1971, pp. 1185–6.
7 Philp, *The Winban Agreement*.
8 See Appendix, Table 7.
9 Minutes of Meetings held from 18 to 23 February 1970 between the Jamaica Banana Board and the Fyffes Group Limited.
10 C. V. Black, (ed.) *Jamaica's Banana Industry* (1984), p. 97.
11 Elders and Fyffes, Limited, Minutes of Directors' Meeting held 19 February 1964, vol. 15, p. 309, see also 'A Message for the New Year from Admiral W. G. Cooper', *Fyffes Staff Budget*, vol. XVIII, no. 11, January 1966, pp. 149–50.
12 House of Commons, Foreign Affairs Committee, (Session 1981–2) *Caribbean and Central America, Belize*, HMSO, London, 1982, pp. 215–6.
13 Price Commission, Report no. 4, *Prices and Distribution of Bananas*, London, HMSO (1975), p. 15.
14 Ibid.
15 See Appendix, Table 7.
16 Price Commission Report, p. 7.
17 Price Commission Report, p. 1.
18 Press Release issued by Price Commission: *Prices and Distribution of Bananas*, 12 June 1975.
19 Ibid.
20 Price Commission Report, p. 36.

Chapter 14: The Ending of Fyffes' first century

1 Forbes, (US Magazine), 18 February 1980, p. 104.
2 Thomas McCann, *'An American Company'*, Henry Scammel (ed.), *The Tragedy of United Fruit* (1977).
3 Fyffes Group Limited, Minutes of Board Meeting held 31 January 1978.
4 R. Thomas (*et al.*) *Greengold*, (1987), p. 43.
5 C. V. Black, *Jamaica's Banana Industry* (1984), pp. 102–6.
6 Discussions with Mr D. Philp, September 1989.
7 See Chapter 12, p. 187.
8 Discussions with Mr D. Philp, September 1989.
9 See Chapter 12, p. 195.
10 See Appendix, Table 8.
11 Interview with Mr Russell Peters, *Fyffes Group News*, no. 87, January 1982, pp. 4–5.
12 See Chapter 12, p. 194.
13 Discussion with Mr B. Dawson, of T. and J. Harrison and Company, October 1989. See also: *Fruit of the Wisemen, A.C.T. News*, Summer 1989, pp. 6–7.

14 Discussion with Mr Eric Thomas, formerly at Southampton, in October 1989.

15 Fyffes Group News, An End of an Era, no. 75, Jan/Feb/March 1979, p. 2.

16 See Chapter 12, p. 192.

17 Fyffes open Europes Top Banana and Distribution Centre at Borehamwood, Fyffes Group News, no. 80, April 1980, p. 3.

18 Chandlers Ford – An investment for the future, Fyffes Group News no. 114, Jan/Feb 1989, p. 3.

19 'Fyffes Expand in Liverpool', no. 114, Fyffes Group News, Jan/Feb 1989, p. 3.

20 Extel Financial Limited, London, FR–FZ 29, April 1989.

21 Details supplied by Mr C. Dury of the Fyffes Group.

22 See Chapter 9, p. 140.

23 See Chapter 9, p. 140.

24 See Chapter 10, p. 162.

25 The author is indebted to Mr S. W. F. Johnson and Mr W. H. Knight for their assistance with this topic.

26 'Improvements to the Pension Scheme', Fyffes Group News, no. 108, 1st Quarter 1987, p. 1.

27 See Chapter 10, pp. 163–4.

28 See Chapter 4, p. 62.

29 Fortune, (US Magazine), July 1976, p. 145.

30 Mark Casson *et al.*, *Multinationals and World Trade*, (R. A. Read, The Banana Industry: Oligopoly and Barriers to Entry), London, Allen & Unwin, p. 340.

31 The Merger, Fyffes Group News, no. 106, April/June 1986, p. 1.

32 Ibid.

33 Ibid., p. 3.

34 B.M.P. Business, Press Announcement, 1 May 1986.

35 Ibid., p. 1.

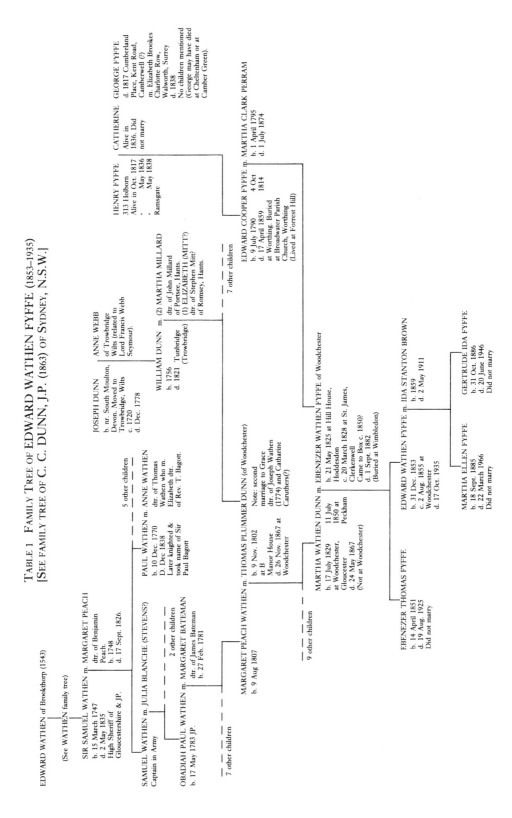

TABLE 2.1 IMPERIAL DIRECT WEST INDIA MAIL SERVICE CO. LTD

Formed:	9.12.1901
Capital:	50,000 share @ 10 = £500,000
Agreement:	31.12.1901. Between A. L. Jones and W. J. Davey, and the new company. This provided for the sale to the company of the U/M ships valued at £475,000 plus £25,000 for goodwill:

Port Royal	*Port Antonio*	*Port Maria*
Port Morat	*Montrose*	*Garth Castle*
Delta		

In return Jones received £250,000 in cash and 25,000 shares @ £10 each – a total of £500,000

Mortgages:	14.1.02. 1st Mortgage of £250,000 4½% debentures. (Trustees: Sir Edward Laurence, Charles McArthur, J. S. Harwood-Rowe)
	16.3.04. Addition of *Port Kingston*
	1937 – Wound up

TABLE 2.2 IMPERIAL DIRECT WEST INDIA MAIL SERVICE CO. LTD. SHARE DISTRIBUTION

	1901	1902	1903	1904	1905	1906	1907	1908	1909	1910	1911
A. L. Jones*	18,672	18,672	18,672	8,672	8,672	8,672	8,672	8,672	8,472	–	–
W. J. Davey*	6,224	6,224	6,224	6,224	1,224	1,224	1,224	1,224	1,224	–	–
H. R. Dixon*	100	100	100	100	100	.100	100	100	100	100	100
Sir W. H. Wills	1	1	1	1	1	1†	1	1	1	1	1
A. Elder	1	1	1	1	1	1	1	1	1	1	1
P. Napier Miles	1	1	1	1	1	1	1	1	1	1	1
John Dempster	1	1	1	1	1	1	1	1	1	1	1
British & African Steam Nav. Co.	–	–	–	10,000	10,000	10,000	10,000	10,000	10,000	10,000	–
E. D. Shipping Ltd	–	–	–	5,000	5,000	5,000	5,000	5,000	5,000	5,000	–
John Craig	–	–	–	–	–	–	–	–	100	100	100
H. W. Davey	–	–	–	–	–	–	–	–	100	–	–
O. H. Williams	–	–	–	–	–	–	–	–	–	100	100
Elder Dempster & Co. Ltd	–	–	–	–	–	–	–	–	–	9,696	24,596
											100
											(Others)
TOTALS:	25,000									25,000	25,000

* Directors. † Became Lord Winterstoke.

Source: File 72110, dissolved at Companies House, London.

255

TABLE 3.1   ELDERS AND FYFFES LTD

Formed:	9.5.1901			
Directors:	A. L. Jones	Ship Owner	H. Wolfson	Fruit Mcht.
	A. H. Stockley	Fruit Mcht.	J. M. Leacock	Fruit Mcht.
	A. R. Ackerley	Fruit Mcht.	E. C. Barker	Fruit Mcht.
	R. Atcherley	Fruit Mcht.		

Registered
Office: 9/12 Bow Street, London.

Capital: £150,000 in 150,000 shares of £1 nominal, divided into 'A', 'B' and 'C' shares. £160,000 in Debenture Stock issued 10.6.1901.

Trustees: Owen Harrison Williams, Alfred Lloyd Barrell.

The Company took over the business in certain spheres of Messrs Elder Dempster & Co. & of Messrs Fyffe, Hudson & Co. Ltd. Alfred Jones was to be Chairman as long as he remained a Director but neither he nor W. J. Davey were to be paid for services as Chairman or Director.

Satisfaction of Debentures
£20,475 repaid on 30.6.02
 10,000 repaid on 16.9.02
 10,000 repaid on 1.7.03
 10,000 repaid on 30.6.04
 10,000 repaid on 30.6.05
 10,000 repaid on 30.6.06
 10,000 repaid on 30.6.07
 10,000 repaid on 30.6.08

Increase of Capital
10.2.03 + 122,460 =   272,460 total
16.2.04 + 77,540 =   350,000
23.12.04 + 100,000 =   450,000
30.8.13 + 550,000 = 1,000,000

Mortgages on Ships
12. 5.04. Mortgage of £50,000 to Barclay & Co. Satisfied on 11.2.05
13. 2.05. Mortgage of 75,000 to Barclay & Co. Satisfied on 30.9.05
 2.10.05. Mortgage of 75,000 to Barclay & Co. Satisfied on 23.8.06
(Also borrowing on the S.S. *Miami*, S.S. *Matina*, SS. *Manistee*)

TABLE 3.2 ELDERS AND FYFFES LIMITED SHARE DISTRIBUTION

Year	1901	1901	1902	1903	1903	1905	1905	1908	1908	1909	1909
A. L. Jones	70,500	70,505	70,505	55,449	–	83,254	1	55,503	27,752	20,000	27,752
W. J. Davey	23,493	23,495	23,495	13,479	–	20,237	1	13	6,752	13	6,746
A. H. Stockley	2,000	2,000	2,000	5,998	4,000	9,006	6,006	10,008	5,004	10,008	5,004
A. H. Ackerley	2,000	2,000	2,000	2,998	1,000	4,501	1,502	4,004	2,001	4,002	2,001
R. Atcherley	2,000	2,000	2,000	1,998	–	2,999	1	2,000	1,000	2,000	1,000
'A' Shares	99,993	100,000	100,000								
H. Wolfson	2,000	2,000	2,607	–	21,644	1	32,497	21,665	10,833	21,665	10,833
J. W. Leacock	2,000	2,000	2,607	–	21,644	1	32,496	21,665	10,832	21,665	10,832
E. C. Barker	2,000	2,000	2,606	–	21,643	1	32,496	21,665	10,832	21,665	10,832
Wolfson, Leacock, Barker	42,180	42,180	42,180	–	–	–	–	–	–	–	–
L. Wolfson	1,820	1,820	–	–	–	–	–	–	–	–	–
'B' Shares	50,000	50,000	50,000								
A. L. Jones	4	A. Preston		16,900	12,100	31,509	31,100	67,229	37,500	67,229	37,500
W. J. Davey	1	J. Jones		12,520	11,700	22,520	19,700	–	–	–	–
A. H. Stockley	1	B. Parmer		11,350	10,300	21,350	14,300	25,150	10,500	25,150	10,500
A. R. Ackerley	1	M. Keith		9,500	9,116	20,600	19,784	18,616	–	18,606	–
		C. Hubbard		8,600	8,000	9,500	9,116	22,384	18,000	22,384	18,000
SUBSCRIBERS:	7	F. Hart		6,521	6,000	14,521	11,000	16,521	9,000	16,521	9,000
				145,313	127,147	240,000	210,000				
				272,460		450,000					
R. Clark								100	–	100	–
Williams & Ross								13,479	–	13,479	–
Robertson & Hughes (Bankers)								–	–	35,503	–
								300,000	150,000	300,000	150,000
								450,000		450,000	

TABLE 3.3   ELDERS & FYFFES LTD

Name	1910 Fully Paid	1910 Partly Paid
'A' Shares		
A. L. Jones	–	–
W. J. Davey	–	–
A. H. Stockley	10,008	4,904
A. R. Ackerley	4,002	2,001
R. Atcherley	2,000	1,000
'B' Shares		
H. Wolfson	21,665	10,833
J. W. Leacock	21,665	10,832
E. C. Barker	21,665	10,832
Wolfson, Leacock & Barker	–	–
L. Wolfson	–	–
A. Preston	67,229	37,500
J. Jones	–	–
B. Parmer	25,150	10,500
M. Keith	18,616	–
C. Hubbard	22,384	18,000
F. Hart	16,521	9,000
R. Clark	100	–
Robertson & Hughes (Bankers)	–	–
R. Miller	–	100
Sir P. Bates	–	–
Elder Dempster & Co. Ltd	68,995	34,498
	300,000	150,000
	450,000	

NOTES:

18.12.1907: Agreement made with the United Fruit Co. of New Jersey re bananas.

4.10.1913: New shares issue of £550,000 in £1 shares taken up by the United Fruit Company.

Dec. 1913: This return shows that Elder Dempster's had sold their 68,995 fully paid & 34,498 partly paid shares to A. Preston.

Source: File 70123, live at Companies House, London.

TABLE 4.1 ELDER AND FYFFES (SHIPPING) LIMITED

Formed:	18.4.1902
Capital:	100,000 £1 shares = £100,000 nominal
Agreements:	1. Elders and Fyffes Ltd. agree to hire three steamers from the new firm
	2. Elders and Fyffes agree to give the new firm the option of providing any new steamers they may require, but have certain rights if new shares are issued
	3. W. A. Angone & Co. are appointed Managers. W. A. St Aubyn Angone, who is a promoter, and one of the first Directors of the Company shall be entitled to enter into an agreement with Elders and Fyffes in the terms of the draft already prepared whereby he is appointed sole Maritime Insurance Broker to Elders and Fyffes upon the terms therein mentioned
Directors:	W. A. St. Aubyn Angone Insurance Broker
	John William Didsdale Underwriter
	Arthur Henry Stockley Fruit Merchant
	Edward Cecil Barker Fruit Merchant
11.11.1902:	3 ships mortgaged for £12,500
28. 5.1907:	Company wound up

TABLE 4.2 ELDERS AND FYFFES (SHIPPING) LTD DISTRIBUTION OF SHARES

Name	Address	1902	1906	
		'A' Shares	'A' Shares	
W. A. A. Angove	9 Gracechurch Street	13,300	34,900	held by Elder & Fyffes
H. W. Richards	9 Gracechurch Street	4,000	100	held by all others
A. T. Richards	9 Gracechurch Street	2,000		
B. H. Hodgson	9 Gracechurch Street	4,000	35,000	
A. W. Symes	Borneo, Pangbourne	1,000		
J. W. Ridsdale	9 Gracechurch Street	500		
T. L. Maycock	9 Gracechurch Street	200		
		25,000		
		'B' Shares	'B' Shares	
Elder & Fyffes		12,000	46,900	held by Elder & Fyffes
			100	held by all others
		37,000	47,000	
		'C' Shares	'C' Shares	
H. Wolfson	9 Bow Street	5,000	17,798	held by Elder & Fyffes
J. W. Leacock	9 Bow Street	5,000	202	held by all others
E. C. Barker	9 Bow Street	5,000		
Mrs E. Hinshaw	Brickhampton Hall, Parshaw	1,000	18,000	
H. Donald	331 Holloway Road, N.	1,000		
A. H. Stockley	9 Bow Street	1,000		
		55,000		
			Elders & Fyffes Ltd held 99,598 out of 100,000 shares	
			Taken over in 1907	

'A', 'B' and 'C' are all ordinary shares and have similar rights for dividend & capital.

Source: File 73475, dissolved at Public Record Office, London.

TABLE 5 JAMAICA'S BANANA EXPORTS 1900 TO 1982 IN LONG TONS
EXPORTS TO UK AND TOTAL UK IMPORTS 1910 TO 1982 IN LONG TONS

Year	Export Tons '000	Hurricanes	To UK Tons '000	Total UK Imports Tons '000	Jamaican Bananas As % of UK Imports
1900	95.7				
1901	140.3				
1902	195.9				
1903	132.4	August, 1903			
1904	90.8	June, 1904			
1905	195.0				
1906	210.8				
1907	196.7				
1908	181.9				
1909	219.5				
1910	189.2		11.6	81.7	14.2
1911	218.7		8.4	90.0	9.3
1912	180.6	November, 1912	0.9	93.6	1.0
1913	150.0		6.7	101.0	6.6
1914	217.9		15.6	120.7	12.9
1915	92.1	August, 1915 September, 1915	6.1	109.2	5.6
1916	46.7	August, 1916 October, 1916	2.7	81.7	3.3
1917	32.0	September, 1917	7.5	29.9	25.1
1918	42.9		4.4	9.8	44.9
1919	120.2		37.1	65.6	56.6
1920	121.3		29.3	108.0	27.1
1921	133.4		18.6	127.4	14.6
1922	163.9		24.2	147.9	16.4
1923	166.8		37.5	158.9	23.6
1924	150.1		22.9	151.6	15.1*
1925	201.0		32.2	161.3	20.0
1926	241.5		48.0	181.6	26.4
1927	282.5		26.4	170.2	15.5
1928	229.6		38.0	168.4	22.6
1929	295.1		54.4	193.4	28.1
1930	331.9		74.6	195.8	38.1
1931	299.1		98.7	211.3	46.7
1932	271.9	November, 1932	93.4	229.5	40.7
1933	141.6	October, 1933	88.9	213.5	41.6
1934	214.2		138.3	228.8	60.4
1935	271.6		210.9	269.1	78.4
1936	254.8		196.4	277.2	70.9
1937	361.2		263.2	303.4	86.8
1938	351.7		233.0	305.0	76.4
1939	251.6	November, 1939	195.0	288.0	67.7
1940	91.8		66.0	193.0	34.2

261

TABLE 5 continued

Year					
1941	200.9	∅	–	–	–
1942	138.4	∅	–	–	–
1943	120.9	∅	–	–	–
1944	61.7	∅ August, 1944	–	–	–
1945	29.6	∅	1.0	1.0	100
1946	74.4		49.0	102.0	48.0
1947	77.9		62.0	105.0	59.0
1948	80.4		67.0	148.0	45.3
1949	87.5		72.7	152.9	47.5
1950	77.4	October, 1950	68.7	138.1	49.7
1951	49.6	August, 1951	40.6	163.7	24.8
1952	59.9		58.5	167.7	34.9
1953	138.1		138.1	263.5	52.4
1954	156.0		158.0	289.4	54.6
1955	146.1		146.1	308.8	47.3
1956	150.3		150.3	315.7	47.6
1957	152.4		149.0	313.8	47.5
1958	130.2		130.2	306.7	42.5
1959	138.8		138.8	333.3	41.6
1960	138.1		138.1	319.0	43.2
1961	140.8		140.8	358.3	39.3
1962	146.2		145.8	363.5	40.1
1963	152.5		152.0	349.8	43.5
1964	174.4		174.4	342.6	50.9
1965	199.6		189.0	353.2	53.5
1966	204.7		200.3	331.0	60.5
1967	191.4		187.7	322.2	58.3
1968	153.2		153.2	318.8	48.1
1969	149.2		149.2	329.1	45.3
1970	133.1		133.1	306.9	43.4
1971	125.9		125.9	315.6	39.9
1972	127.0		127.0	289.3	43.9
1973	107.7		107.7	287.3	37.5
1974	71.3		71.3	278.1	25.6
1975	70.2		70.2	279.4	25.1
1976	78.0		78.0	295.6	26.4
1977	78.8		78.8	304.5	25.9
1978	76.6		76.6	300.6	25.5
1979	67.7		67.7	288.0	23.5
1980	33.6	August, 1980	33.6	303.6	11.1
1981	16.8		16.8	319.2	5.3
1982	22.2		22.2	304.1	7.3

NOTES: (1) Exports from Jamaica and Imports into U.K. when recorded only in stems have been converted to tons at 74.6 stems per ton.

* After 1923 imports into Southern Ireland not included.

∅ Purchased by U.K. government but not exported from Jamaica.

Table 5 Source: Clinton V. Black (ed.), *Jamaica's Banana Industry* Jamaican Banana Producers Association, Kingston, Jamaica, 1984, pp. 107–09.

TABLE 6   CANARY ISLAND BANANA PRODUCTION AND EXPORTS: 1938–1986

Date	Peninsula	Extranjero	C. Local	Industria	Production
1938	45,352,628	59,060,236	7,000,000	–	111,412,864
1939	66,999,322	32,827,724	7,500,000	–	107,327,046
1940	110,614,195	5,777,980	11,000,000	–	127,392,175
1941	112,897,134	594,860	15,600,000	–	129,091,994
1942	100,146,265	2,389,664	39,881.357	–	142,417,286
1943	95,844,466	3,949,518	35,844,038	–	135,638,022
1944	112,341,955	2,499,885	31,767,339	–	146,609,179
1945	116,033,556	8,982,240	32,764,970	–	157,780,766
1946	76,435,667	56,105,486	22,286,030	–	154,827,183
1947	105,555,853	34,089,079	25,834,712	–	165,479,644
1948	117,013,228	48,918,681	18,425,710	–	184,357,619
1949	109,436,630	38,262,690	18,617,857	–	166,317,177
1950	98,413,759	51,408,281	21,983,754	–	171,805,794
1951	91,025,656	91,540,608	18,829,671	–	201,395,935
1952	84,995,798	118,590,233	16,293,311	–	219,879,342
1953	86,651,036	113,985,824	17,345,665	–	217,982,525
1954	87,059,292	105,048,365	17,241,389	–	209,349,046
1955	126,024,126	130,890,578	25,583,046	–	282,497,750
1956	156,608,442	111,366,718	28,003,433	–	295,978,593
1957	159,245,657	97,550,684	21,947,581	–	278,743,922
1958	151,179,234	85,045,173	13,140,749	–	249,365,156
1959	168,370,344	96,908,088	15,452,055	–	280,730,487
1960	181,302,782	86,686,802	20,851,548	–	288,841,132
1961	196,508,462	104,550,150	31,400,796	–	332,459,408
1962	181,965,560	123,240,489	21,627,877	–	326,833,926
1963	196,210,811	105,304,460	23,983,448	–	325,498,719
1964	226,699,450	121,419,822	35,360,826	–	383,480,098
1965	244,506,695	104,324,636	24,820,721	–	373,652,052
1966	302,297,984	91,885,899	40,990,023	–	435,173,906
1967	314,326,197	52,443,988	27,352,834	–	394,123,019
1968	304,916,667	44,259,019	43,047,318	–	392,223,004
1969	369,211,924	34,987,263	37,146,477	–	441,345,664
1970	347,854,047	38,632,878	33,952,315	–	420,439,240
1971	361,266,318	34,370,944	20,838,470	–	416,475,732
1972	316,811,988	15,619,056	27,333,788	–	359,764,832
1973	375,186,756	5,696,292	69,561,493	–	450,444,541
1974	362,205,596	5,777,028	30,834,930	–	398,817,554
1975	331,224,213	4,539,900	20,390,830	–	356,154,943
1976	292,977,282	3,593,364	19,964,714	–	316,535,360
1977	355,679,028	–	21,190,856	–	376,869,884
1978	367,343,112	2,888,040	23,802,499	–	394,033,651
1979	364,092,360	–	34,567,381	–	398,659,741
1980	405,427,428	–	73,836,446	–	479,263,874
1981	409,657,669	1,819,956	76,832,507	–	488,310,132
1982	396,251,040	135,504	44,845,706	257,004	441,489,254
1983	399,837,342	1,053,396	51,665,016	733,896	453,289,650

263

TABLE 6 continued

1984	366,706,836	1,684,464	57,844,158	–	426,235,458
1985	362,978,304	408,756	86,413,969	–	449,801,029
1986	356,462,172	4,791,880	108,693,194	–	469,947,246
Total	11,068,152,266	2,285,906,581	1,571,492,807	990,900	14,926,542,554

Source: Comision Regional Del Platano, *ESTADISTICAS*, 1986, Santa Cruz de Tenerife.

TABLE 7   UK BANANA SOURCES (THOUSANDS TONNES)

	Jamaica	Windward	EEC/Lome	Dollar	Other	Total
1963	137.6	115.4	63.1	0.6		316.7
1964	147.1	129.4	22.8	9.5		308.8
1965	168.6	158.1	9.4	1.0		337.1
1966	181.9	150.3	6.2	1.0		339.4
1967	177.6	148.6	2.3	1.2		329.7
1968	151.7	166.3	1.1	6.3		325.4
1969	148.7	181.7	1.7	6.0		338.1
1970	136.0	138.9	29.4	8.7		313.0
1971	122.1	121.0	49.4	11.7		304.2
1972	118.9	115.1	55.7	16.0		305.7
1973	109.4	89.1	50.6	48.3		297.4
1974	72.0	100.3	65.0	62.2		299.5
1975	68.1	89.3	72.7	70.1		300.2
1976	75.2	115.1	70.2	40.6		301.1
1977	76.6	107.3	61.5	47.1		292.5
1978	73.6	128.2	51.5	58.0		311.3
1979	66.5	98.2	47.0	87.9		299.6
1980	34.3	67.3	51.5	154.3		307.4
1981	17.1	102.0	44.7	156.8		320.6
1982	20.7	101.6	36.9	154.5		313.7
1983	23.3	115.7	48.3	115.5		302.8
1984	11.1	133.3	48.0	111.3	0.6	304.3
1985	12.4	144.4	46.1	105.1	2.2	310.2
1986	20.1	195.6	54.6	56.8	0.9	328.0
1987	32.3	174.3	58.3	73.9		338.8
1988	29.2	229.8	61.2	57.4	0.3	377.8

Data sources:
1963–71 Commonwealth Secretariat's Fruit Review No. 19 page 117
1972–88 Fyffes' volume reports

T ABLE 8 F LEET L IST

Ship	Gross tons	Type of engine	Builders H: hull E: engine	Date compl.	Remarks
1 Appomattox	3338	Steam 3 expansion	H: Furness Withy & Co. W. Hartlepool E: T. Richardson & Sons	1893	Purchased 1902 from Chesapeake & Ohio S.S. Co. Sold 1909
2 Chickahominy	3354	Steam 3 expansion	H: Furness Withy & Co. W. Hartlepool E: Central Marine Engine Works	1893	Purchased 1902 from Chesapeake & Ohio S.S. Co. Sold to breakers 1910
3 Greenbrier	3332	Steam 3 expansion	H: Furness Withy & Co. W. Hartlepool E: T. Richardson & Sons	1893	Purchased 1902 from Chesapeake & Ohio S.S. Co. Sold to Tropical Fruit S.S. Ltd. 1910
4 Oracabessa	3459	Steam 3 expansion	H & E: W. Doxford & Sons Ltd., Sunderland	1894	Purchased 1903 from Furness Withy & Co. Sold to W. Garthwaite 1909
5 Matina	3872	Steam 3 expansion	H: Swan Hunter & Wigham Richardson Ltd., Newcastle E: Wallsend Slipway Co.	1904	Sold to breakers 1928
6 Miami	3762	Steam 3 expansion	H & E: Barclay Curle & Co., Glasgow	1904	Torpedoed and sunk 22 June 1917
7 Manistee	3869	Steam 3 expansion	H: Swan Hunter & Wigham Richardson Ltd., Newcastle E: Wallsend Slipway Co.	1904	Torpedoed and sunk 26 June 1917

TABLE 8 continued

8 Nicoya	3911	Steam 3 expansion	H & E: Alex. Stephen & Sons, Glasgow	1905	Sold to breakers 1928
9 Pacuare	3891	Steam 3 expansion	H & E: Workman Clark & Co., Belfast	1905	Sold to breakers 1936
10 Zent	3890	Steam 3 expansion	H & E: Workman Clark & Co., Belfast	1905	Torpedoed and sunk 5 April 1916
11 Barranca	4124	Steam 3 expansion	H & E: Alex. Stephen & Sons, Glasgow	1906	Sold to breakers 1936
12 Chirripo	4126	Steam 3 expansion	H & E: Workman Clark & Co., Belfast	1906	Mined and sunk 28 Dec. 1917
13 Reventazon	4042	Steam 3 expansion	H & E: Workman Clark & Co., Belfast	1906	Torpedoed and sunk 5 Oct. 1918
14 Tortuguero	4161	Steam 3 expansion	H & E: Alex. Stephen & Sons, Glasgow	1909	Torpedoed and sunk 26 June 1918
15 Aracataca	4154	Steam 3 expansion	H & E: Workman Clark & Co., Belfast	1911	Lost after collision 18 April 1917
16 Manzanares	4094	Steam 3 expansion	H & E: Alex. Stephen & Sons, Glasgow	1911	Sold to Union Handels, Germany 1936
17 Chagres	5288	2 steam 3 expansion	H & E: Alex. Stephen & Sons, Glasgow	1912	Twin screw Torpedoed and sunk 10 March 1918
18 Patia	6103	2 Steam 3 expansion	H & E: Workman Clark & Co., Belfast	1913	Twin screw Torpedoed and sunk 13 June 1918

TABLE 8 continued

19 Bayano	5948	2 Steam 3 expansion	H & E: Alex. Stephen & Sons, Glasgow	1913	Twin screw Torpedoed and sunk 11 March 1915
20 Patuca	6103	2 Steam 3 expansion	H & E: Workman Clark & Co., Belfast	1913	Twin screw Sold to breakers 1935
21 Motagua	5977	2 Steam 3 expansion	H: Swan Hunter & Wigham Richardson Ltd., Newcastle E: Wallsend Slipway Co.	1912	Twin screw Purchased from Hamburg Amerika Line 1914 Sold to breakers 1933
22 Changuinola	5978	2 Steam 3 expansion	H: Swan Hunter & Wigham Richardson Ltd., Newcastle E: Wallsend Slipway Co.	1912	Twin screw Purchased from Hamburg Amerika Line 1914 Sold to breakers 1933
23 Cavina	6539	2 Steam 3 expansion	H & E: Workman Clark & Co., Belfast	1915	Twin screw Torpedoed and sunk 1 June 1917
24 Coronado	6539	2 Steam 3 expansion	H & E: Workman Clark & Co., Belfast	1915	Twin screw Sold to breakers 1935
25 Camito	6611	2 Steam 3 expansion	H & E: Alex. Stephen & Sons, Glasgow	1915	Twin screw Torpedoed and sunk 6 May 1941
26 Bayano II	6788	2 Steam 3 expansion	H & E: Alex. Stephen & Sons, Glasgow	1917	Twin screw Sold to breakers 1956

Table 8 continued

27 Chirripo II	5356	Steam 3 expansion	H & E: Workman Clark & Co., Belfast	1920	Sold Union Handels 1936. Seized and sailed for Honduras subs. 1941/6. Returned E & F 1946. Sold to breakers 1952
28 Zent II	5362	Steam 3 expansion	H & E: Cammell Laird & Co., Birkenhead	1920	Sold Union Handels, Germany, 1936
29 Miami II	4727	Steam 3 expansion	H & E: J. C. Tecklenborg, Geestemunde	1915	Purchased from Allied Shipping Controller 1921. Sold Midgard, Germany 1933
30 Greenbrier II	4798	Steam 3 expansion	H & E: J. C. Tecklenborg, Geestemunde	1914	Purchased from Allied Shipping Controller 1921. Sold Midgard, Germany 1933
31 Reventazon II	5394	Steam 3 expansion	H & E: Workman Clark & Co., Belfast	1921	Sold Union Handels, Germany 1936
32 Manistee II	5360	Steam 3 expansion	H & E: Cammell Laird & Co., Birkenhead	1921	Torpedoed and sunk 23 February 1941
33 Tortuguero II	5285	Steam 3 expansion	H & E: Alex. Stephen & Sons, Glasgow	1921	Sold to breakers 1958
34 Patia II	5355	Steam 3 expansion	H & E: Cammell Laird & Co., Birkenhead	1922	Sunk by air attack after conversion to R. N. catapult ship 27 April 1941
35 Cavina II	6907	2 steam 3 expansion	H & E: Stephen & Sons, Glasgow	1924	Twin screw. Sold to Barkston Shipping Co., 1957

TABLE 8 continued

36 Casanare	5376	Steam 3 expansion	H & E: Cammell Laird & Co., Birkenhead	1925	Torpedoed and sunk 3 Nov. 1940
37 Aracataca II	5378	Steam 3 expansion	H & E: Cammell Laird & Co., Birkenhead	1925	Torpedoed and sunk 29 Nov. 1940
38 Carare	6878	2 Steam 3 expansion	H & E: Cammell Laird & Co., Birkenhead	1925	Twin screw Mined and sunk 28 May 1940
39 Cristales	5389	Steam 3 expansion	H & E: Cammell Laird & Co., Birkenhead	1926	Torpedoed and sunk 12 May 1942
40 Sulaco	5389	Steam 3 expansion	H & E: Cammell Laird & Co., Birkenhead	1926	Torpedoed and sunk 19 Oct. 1940
41 Tucurinca	5412	Steam 3 expansion	H & E: Alex. Stephen & Sons, Glasgow	1926	Torpedoed and sunk 10 March 1943
42 Tetela	5389	Steam 3 expansion	H & E: Cammell Laird & Co., Birkenhead	1926	Sold to breakers 1959
43 Ariguani	6746	2 Steam 3 expansion	H & E: Alex. Stephen & Sons, Glasgow	1926	Twin screw Sold to breakers 1956
44 Telde	2519	Steam 3 expansion	H & E: Alex. Stephen & Sons, Glasgow	1927	Sold to Empresa Hond. de Vapores 1934
45 Argual	2496	Steam 3 expansion	H & E: Cammell Laird & Co., Birkenhead	1927	Sold to Empresa Hondurena de Vapores 1934
46 Orotava	2517	Steam 3 expansion	H & E: Alex. Stephen & Sons, Glasgow	1927	Sold to Empresa Hondurena de Vapores 1934
47 Samala	5390	Steam 3 expansion	H & E: Cammell Laird & Co., Birkenhead	1928	Torpedoed and sunk 30 Sept. 1940

TABLE 8 continued

48 Chagres II	5406	Steam 3 expansion	H & E: Alex. Stephen & Sons, Glasgow	1928	Mined and sunk 9 Feb. 1940
49 Tilapa	5392	Steam 3 expansion	H & E: Cammell Laird & Co., Birkenhead	1928	Sold to breakers 1959
50 Matina II	5389	Steam 3 expansion	H & E: Cammell Laird & Co., Birkenhead	1929	Torpedoed and sunk 26 Oct. 1940
51 Nicoya II	5364	Steam 3 expansion	H & E: Alex. Stephen & Sons, Glasgow	1929	Torpedoed and sunk 12 May 1942
52 Mopan	5389	Steam 3 expansion	H & E: Cammell Laird & Co., Birkenhead	1929	Sunk by 'Admiral Scheer' 5 Nov. 1940
53 Corrales	5363	Steam 3 expansion	H & E: Alex. Stephen & Sons, Glasgow	1930	Sold to breakers 1961
54 Aztec	5502	Steam 3 expansion	H & E: Barclay Curle & Co., Glasgow	1929	Acquired 1931. Sold to P. A. Jensen, Denmark 1938
55 Mazatec	5502	Steam 3 expansion	H & E: Barclay Curle & Co., Glasgow	1929	Acquired 1931. Sold to P. A. Jensen, Denmark 1938
56 Toltec	5501	Steam 3 expansion	H & E: Barclay Curle & Co., Glasgow	1929	Acquired 1931. Sold to P. A. Jensen, Denmark 1938
57 Zent III	3248	9 cyl. B & W Diesel	H: Oresundsvarvet, Landskrona E: Burmeister & Wain Copenhagen	1938	Purchased from MOWT 1946. Sold to breakers 1962
58 Matina III	6801	Geared steam turbines	H & E: Alex. Stephen & Sons, Glasgow	1946	Sold to breakers 1968
59 Reventazon III	4876	6 cyl. MAN Diesel	H: Deutsche Werft, Hamburg E: M.A.N., Augsburg	1939	Purchased from MOWT 1946. Sold to Jade Co. Inc. 1963

TABLE 8 continued

60 Manistee III	5824	Steam 3 exp. & supp. elec. drive	H: Workman Clark & Co. Belfast E: Workman Clark & Metro. Vickers	1932	Purchased from Standard Fruit Co., 1947. Sold to breakers 1960
61 Pacuare II	3675	5 cyl. MAN Diesel	H & E: Bremer Vulkan, Vegesack	1934	Purchased from MOWT 1947. Sold to breakers 1959
62 Nicoya III	3843	5 cyl. MAN Diesel	H & E: Bremer Vulkan Vegesack	1935	Purchased from MOWT 1947. Sold to breakers 1959
63 Golfito	8736	2 sets geared steam turbines	H & E: Alex. Stephen & Sons, Glasgow	1949	Twin screw. Sold to breakers 31 Dec. 1971
64 Camito II	8687	2 sets geared steam turbines	H & E: Alex. Stephen & Sons, Glasgow	1956	Twin screw. Sold to breakers 5 April 1973
65 Changuinola II	6283	Geared steam turbines	H & E: Alex. Stephen & Sons, Glasgow	1957	Sold to Empresa Hond. de Vapores 1970
66 Chiripo III	6283	Geared steam turbines	H & E: Alex. Stephen & Sons, Glasgow	1957	Sold to Empresa Hond. de Vapores 1969
67 Chicanoa	6283	Geared steam turbines	H & E: Alex. Stephen & Sons, Glasgow	1958	Sold to Empresa Hondurena de Vapores 1970
68 Sulaco II	7602	Steam turbo-electric (2 sets)	H: Newport News S.B. Co. Newport News, Va. E: G. E. C. Schenectady	1931	Twin screw Acquired from U. F. Co. 1958. Sold to breakers 1964
69 Sinaloa	7513	Steam turbo-electric (2 sets)	H: Bethlehem S. B. Corp. Quincy, Mass. E: G. E. C. Shenectady	1932	Twin screw Acquired from U. F. Co. 1958. Sold to breakers 1964

271

TABLE 8 continued

Name	Tonnage	Machinery	Builders	Year	Notes
70 Samala II	7479	Steam turbo-electric (2 sets)	H: Bethlehem S. B. Corp. Quincy, Mass. E: G. E. C. Schenectady	1932	Twin screw Acquired from U. F. Co. 1958. Sold to breakers 1964
71 Chuscal	6282	Geared steam turbines	H & E: Alex. Stephen & Sons, Glasgow	1961	Sold to Greek owners 1972
72 Pacuare III	5168	Geared steam turbines	H & E: Bethlehem Steel Co., Sparrows Point, Md.	1948	Acquired from U. F. Co. 1968. Sold to breakers 1972
73 Rio Cobre	6845	2 sets Geared steam turbines	H: Gulf S. B. Corp., Chickasaw, Ala. E: De Laval, Trenton, N. J.	1945	Twin screw. Acquired from U. F. Co. 1968. Sold to breakers 1975
74 Roatan	6845	2 sets Geared steam turbines	H: Gulf S. B. Corp., Chickasaw, Ala. E: De Laval, Trenton, N. J.	1946	Twin screw. Acquired from U. F. Co. 1969. Sold to breakers 1975
75 Matina IV	6351	10 cyl. M.A.N. Diesel	H & E: Kawasaki Heavy Industries Ltd., Kobe	1969	Sold to Saudi Arabian owners 1983
76 Morant	6348	10 cyl. M.A.N. Diesel	H & E: Kawasaki Heavy Industries Ltd., Kobe	1970	Sold to Saudi Arabian owners 1983
77 Patia III	5168	Geared steam turbines	H & E: Bethlehem Steel Co., Sparrows Point, Md.	1947	Acquired from U. F. Co. 1970. Sold to breakers 1972
78 Patuca II	5168	Geared steam turbines	H & E: Bethlehem Steel Co., Sparrows Point, Md.	1947	Acquired from U. F. Co. 1970. Sold to breakers 1978
79 Pecos	5168	Geared steam turbines	H & E: Bethlehem Steel Co., Sparrows Point, Md.	1948	Acquired from U. F. Co. 1970. Sold to breakers 1972

TABLE 8 continued

80 Ronde	6845	2 sets Geared steam turbines	H: Gulf S. B. Corp., Chickasaw, Ala. E: De Laval, Trenton N. J.	1945	Twin screw Acquired from U. F. Co. 1970. Sold to breakers 1975
81 Motagua II	6348	10 cyl. M.A.N. Diesel	H & E: Kawasaki Heavy Industries Ltd., Kobe	1970	Sold to Saudi Arabian owners 1983
82 Musa	6510	10 cyl. M.A.N. Diesel	H & E: Kawasaki Heavy Industries Ltd., Kobe	1971	Sold to Saudi Arabian owners 1983
83 Barranca II	4087	2 sets medium speed geared Diesel	H & E: Hijos de J. Barreras S. A., Vigo	1972	Twin screw – refrig. container ship. Sold to breakers 1985
84 Bayano III	4087	2 sets medium speed geared Diesel	H & E: Hijos de J. Barreras S. A., Vigo	1972	Twin screw – refrig. container ship. Sold to breakers 1985
85 Manistee IV	6513	10 cyl. M.A.N. Diesel	H & E: Kawasaki Heavy Industries Ltd., Kobe	1972	Sold to Fleetway Ltd., Hong Kong 1984
86 Mazatec II	6513	10 cyl. M.A.N. Diesel	H & E: Kawasaki Heavy Industries Ltd., Kobe	1972	Sold to Skyrama Ltd., Hong Kong 1984
87 Magdalena	6513	10 cyl. M.A.N. Diesel	H & E: Kawasaki Heavy Industries Ltd., Kobe	1973	Sold to Bluestream Ltd. Hong Kong 1984
88 Manzanares II	6513	10 cyl. M.A.N. Diesel	H & E: Kawasaki Heavy Industries Ltd., Kobe	1973	Sold to Barrydale Sg. Ltd., Hong Kong
89 Darien	4970	9 cyl. M.A.N. Diesel	H: Deutschwerft, Hamburg E: M.A.N., Hamburg	1964	Purchased 1973. Sold to Greek owners 1981

APPENDIXES

TABLE 8 continued

90 Davao	4851	9 cyl. M.A.N. Diesel	H & E: Blohm & Voss, Hamburg	1964	Purchased 1974. Sold to Greek owners 1981
91 Almirante	1967	m.v.	Formerly *Ea*	1978	1979 from Empresa Hondurena de Vapores. (United Brands subsidiary)

Ships managed for Surrey Shipping Coy., Ltd., Bermuda

1 Box Hill	3346	2 M.A.N. Diesel	H & E: Bremer Vulkan, Bremen-Vegesack	1952	Twin screw. Acquired by Surrey S. Co. 1959. To Empresa Hondurena de Vapores 1966
2 Leith Hill	3351	2 M.A.N. Diesel	H & E: Bremer Vulkan, Bremen-Vegesack	1952	Twin screw. Acquired by Surrey S. Co. 1959. To Empresa Hondurena de Vapores 1966
3 Tenadores	6738	Geared steam turbines	H: Bremer Vulkan, E: De Lavals Angturbin, Stockholm	1960	To Empresa Hondurena de Vapores 1966
4 Tetela	6738	Geared steam turbines	H: Bremer Vulkan, E: De Lavals Angturbin, Stockholm	1960	To Empresa Hondurena de Vapores 1966
5 Turrialba	6738	Geared steam turbines	H: Bremer Vulkan, E: De Lavals Angturbin, Stockholm	1960	To Balboa S.S. Co., 1977
6 Tilapa	6738	Geared steam turbines	H: Bremer Vulkan, E: De Lavals Angturbin, Stockholm	1961	To Empresa Hondurena de Vapores 1973
7 Telde	6738	Geared steam turbines	H: Bremer Vulkan, E: De Lavals Angturbin, Stockholm	1961	To Empresa Hondurena de Vapores 1973
8 Tucurinca	6738	Geared steam turbines	H: Bremer Vulkan, E: De Lavals Angturbin, Stockholm	1962	To Empresa Hondurena de Vapores 1977

TABLE 8 continued

Vessels currently (1988) operating in the Company's service

Almirante 1967 gross tons.

Nickerie 4233 gross tons
Built by the Hayashikane Shipping & Engineering Co., Nagasaki in 1985

Jarikaba 4238 gross tons
Built by the Hayashikane Shipping & Engineering Co., Nagasaki in 1986

Notes:

During the early years of this century Elders & Fyffes owned several small steam and sailing vessels in the Canary Islands amongst which were the *Ajax, Esperanza, Golden Eagle, Guanche, Mariposa, Taora* and, later, *Colon*. These were later disposed of to local owners but various chartered vessels brought bananas to the main ports from the remoter islands until the 1930s.

Between 1940 and 1946 the following vessels were managed for the Ministry of War Transport: *Bria Thorden, Esther Thorden, Rosenborg, Yildum, Empire Abbey, Empire Balfour, Empire Lady* and *Samstrule*.

Source: This appendix was kindly compiled by Captain Kenneth J. Leslie, a former master with the Fyffes Line.

TABLE 9 ROLL OF HONOUR: 1939–1945

Killed in Action: Name	*Branch*	*Rank*	*Service or Unit*	*Date*
BRIGGS, K. T.	Marine	Midshipman	Royal Naval Reserve	14 May 1940
SLATER, H. C.	High Wycombe	Lieutenant	Royal Naval Reserve	28 May 1940
IRELAND, W. R. D.	Marine	Commander	Royal Naval Reserve	29 Sept. 1940
SLATER, P. H.	Stirling	Pilot Officer	Royal Air Force	26 Oct. 1940
MARSHALL, J.	London	Sub-Lieutenant	Royal Naval Volunteer Reserve (A)	10 Jan. 1941
POCOCK, E. I.	Salisbury	Sergeant Pilot	Royal Air Force	17 Apr. 1941
BAKER, D. M. B., R. D.	Marine	Commander	Royal Naval Reserve	27 Apr. 1941
PRIM, B. K.	Marine	Sub-Lieutenant (E)	Royal Naval Reserve	27 Apr. 1941
GOVE, R. G.	Edinburgh	Sergeant	Royal Air Force	29 Sept. 1941
MAMMEN, D. J.	London	Trooper	Royal Armoured Corps	19 Nov. 1941
OLLIVER, L. E.	Brighton	Able Seaman	Royal Naval Volunteer Reserve	25 Nov. 1941
DANIEL, C. T.	Leicester	Sergeant	Royal Air Force	13 Apr. 1942
CRAIG, K. M.	Brighton	Lieutenant	The Gordon Highlanders	27 Oct. 1942
GOLBY, D. A. D.	Leicester	Sergeant	Royal Air Force	22 Nov. 1942
RISELEY, J. H.	London	Trooper	Royal Armoured Corps	8 Apr. 1943
JOB, F. J.	Exeter	Major	The Devonshire Regiment	6 Feb. 1944
STEAD, E.	Garston	Leading Aircraftman	Royal Air Force	7 Nov. 1944
HALCROW, J. L.	Glasgow Store	Flying Officer	Royal Air Force	26 Mar. 1945
WHALLEY, G. B.	Swindon	Flight Sergeant	Royal Air Force	14 Apr. 1945
WILLIAMS, D.	Swindon	Lance-Corporal	The Queen's Own Royal West Kent Regiment	4 June 1945
Missing – Presumed Killed:				
HAWKINS, J. T.	London	Gunner	Royal Artillery	9 June 1940
ALLISON, J.	Marine	Sub-Lieutenant (E)	Royal Naval Reserve	23 Feb. 1941
COCHRANE, Q. A.	Marine	Sub-Lieutenant (E)	Royal Naval Reserve	Feb. 1941
DUNCAN, J. G.	Marine	Lieutenant-Commander (E)	Royal Naval Reserve	23 Feb. 1941
HARRY, J. H.	Marine	Sub-Lieutenant (E)	Royal Naval Volunteer Reserve	23 Feb. 1941
JENKINS, D. T.	Marine	Chief Steward	Royal Naval Reserve	23 Feb. 1941

276

TABLE 9 continued

WILLIAMS, E.	Marine	Sub-Lieutenant (E)	Royal Naval Reserve	8 May 1941
COX, G.	Marine	Lieutenant	Royal Naval Reserve	June 1941
PICKERING, J. M.	Glasgow Store	Sergeant	Royal Air Force	27 June 1941
KNOWLES, J. P.	Marine	Chief Steward	Royal Naval Reserve	22 Dec. 1941
LAMBERT, H. R.	Southampton	Staff Quarter-master Sergeant	Royal Army Ordnance Corps	5 Feb. 1942
ADDIS, J. H.	Cameroun	Sergeant Pilot	Royal Air Force	25 Mar. 1942
BOUMPHREY, E. H.	London	Sergeant	Royal Air Force	24 July 1942
NASH, G. D.	London	Flight Sergeant	Royal Air Force	15 Oct. 1942
KILBURN, W.	Marine	Chief Steward	Royal Naval Reserve	Apr. 1943
DOWNES, R. F.	Plymouth	Pilot Officer	Royal Air Force	8 Apr. 1943
BAYFORD, F. V.	Somers Town	Sergeant	Royal Air Force	13 Apr. 1943
LOW, J. W.	London	Flight Sergeant	Royal Air Force	4 Aug. 1943
BROWN, J. W.	Manchester	Pilot Officer	Royal Air Force	22 Nov. 1943
BASSAGE, C. T.	Chester	Flight Lieutenant	Royal Air Force	2 Dec. 1943
TYRIE, W. R., D. F. M.	London	Sergeant	Royal Air Force	2 Jan. 1944

Died of Wounds:

BRENDON, P. A.	Marine	Lieutenant	Royal Naval Reserve	29 Mar. 1941
FAIRHURST, J.	Wigan	Lance-Corporal	The Border Regiment	15 May 1944

Died on Active Service:

PARK, J. M.	Marine	Lieutenant-Commander	Royal Naval Regiment	21 Oct. 1940
CLIFFORD, P. J.	London	Trooper	Royal Armoured Corps	13 June 1942
HAWKINS, J. W.	Portsmouth	Driver	Royal Artillery	16 June 1942
LEGGE, A. W., R. D.	Marine	Lieutenant-Commander	Royal Naval Reserve	3 Oct. 1943
NORMAN, J. E.	High Wycombe	Warrant Officer (I)	Royal Air Force	9 Nov. 1943
ROBINSON, I. S.	Newport (Mon.)	Company-Quarter-master-Sergeant	The Royal Irish Fusiliers	30 Sept. 1944
GRAHAM, R. T.	St. Helens	Corporal	Royal Armoured Corps	26 Jan. 1945

Died Whilst Prisoner of War:

CLULEE, L. W. D.	Glasgow Store	Flying Officer	Royal Air Force	14 Dec. 1942
TURNER, T. D.	Portsmouth	Aircraftman (I)	Royal Air Force	19 Aug. 1943
CLAYTON, E.	Manchester	Private	The Manchester Regiment	21 Sept. 1944
EVANS, J. A.	Somers Town	Private	The Middlesex Regiment	1 Mar. 1945

277

TABLE 9 continued

Merchant Navy Casualties (Lost at Sea):

Name	Rank	Ship	Date
ANDERSON, R. W.	2nd Officer	S.S. 'Aracataca'	29 Nov. 1940
BARKER, C. R.	Chief Refrigerating Engineer	S.S. 'Carare'	9 May 1940
BINKS, G. M.	2nd Officer	S.S. 'Samala'	30 Sept. 1940
BOWER, H. C.	Master	S.S. 'Sulaco'	19 Oct. 1940
CHAMBERLAIN, A. G.	Gunlayer	S.S. 'Matina'	24 Oct. 1940
CHANTER, W. G.	Chief Officer	S.S. 'Matina'	24 Oct. 1940
CLINTON, G. J., M. B. E.	3rd Engineer	S.S. 'Tucurinca'	11 Mar. 1943
CONGDON, W. D.	2nd Officer	S.S. 'Sulaco'	19 Oct. 1940
CRANE, W. H.	Chief Engineer	S.S. 'Sulaco'	19 Oct. 1940
CREW, P. L.	Apprentice	S.S. 'Sulaco'	19 Oct. 1940
CROUCH, W.	Chief Refrigerating Engineer	S.S. 'Samala'	30 Sept. 1940
DONALDSON, J. W.	3rd Officer	S.S. 'Aracataca'	29 Nov. 1940
DUNN, K.	Assistant Engineer	S.S. 'Sulaco'	19 Oct. 1940
EKBERY, W. V.	3rd Engineer	S.S. 'Sulaco'	19 Oct. 1940
FORREST, H.	4th Engineer	S.S. 'Aracataca'	29 Nov. 1940
GEORGE, A. J.	Chief Refrigerating Engineer	S.S. 'Matina'	24 Oct. 1940
GRANT, W. E.	Chief Officer	S.S. 'Samala'	30 Sept. 1940
HARPER, F.	Assistant Engineer	S.S. 'Matina'	24 Oct. 1940
HARVEY, A. E.	Master	S.S. 'Samala'	30 Sept. 1940
HAYES, A.	Chief Steward	S.S. 'Samala'	30 Sept. 1940
JACK, D. A.	Master	S.S. 'Matina'	24 Oct. 1940
JOHNSON, T. D. L.	Apprentice	S.S. 'Sulaco'	19 Oct. 1940
JONES, H. B.	4th Engineer	S.S. 'Matina'	24 Oct. 1940
JONES, L. G.	Chief Steward	S.S. 'Aracataca'	29 Nov. 1940
JONES, W.	Assistant Engineer	S.S. 'Samala'	30 Sept. 1940
KENNY, J.	2nd Engineer	S.S. 'Sulaco'	19 Oct. 1940
LEWIS, P. H.	Assistant Engineer	S.S. 'Casanare'	3 Nov. 1940
LEWTHWAITE, J.	Assistant Engineer	S.S. 'Samala'	30 Sept. 1940
LINDSAY, A.	3rd Officer	S.S. 'Matina'	24 Oct. 1940
LLOYD, W. J.	2nd Engineer	S.S. 'Matina'	24 Oct. 1940
McBRIDE, J.	4th Engineer	S.S. 'Samala'	30 Sept. 1940
McCLURE, J.	3rd Engineer	S.S. 'Samala'	30 Sept. 1940
McKENZIE, R.	2nd Engineer	S.S. 'Samala'	30 Sept. 1940
MILLER, E.	Apprentice	S.S. 'Aracataca'	29 Nov. 1940
MOSS, F.	Chief Steward	S.S. 'Matina'	24 Oct. 1940
MURRAY, J. C.	3rd Officer	S.S. 'Sulaco'	19 Oct. 1940
NEWCOMB, J. S.	3rd Engineer	S.S. 'Nicoya'	12 May 1942
NEWTON, K.	Assistant Engineer	S.S. 'Aracataca'	29 Nov. 1940
NIBLETT, D. E.	3rd Officer	S.S. 'Samala'	30 Sept. 1940
ORPIN, F. E.	3rd Engineer	S.S. 'Matina'	24 Oct. 1940
OSBON, A.	Refrigerating Engineer	S.S. 'Sulaco'	19 Oct. 1940
PATERSON, J. D.	Chief Officer	S.S. 'Sulaco'	19 Oct. 1940
PAYNTER, C. A.	4th Engineer	S.S. 'Sulaco'	19 Oct. 1940
PORTEOUS, G. P.	Chief Engineer	S.S. 'Samala'	30 Sept. 1940
PURCELL J. W.	Assistant Engineer	S.S. 'Matina'	24 Oct. 1940
RAWLINSON, T. W.	3rd Engineer	S.S. 'Aracataca'	29 Nov. 1940
SCHOFIELD, A.	Assistant Engineer	S.S. 'Sulaco'	19 Oct. 1940
SMITH, M.	Chief Steward	S.S. 'Sulaco'	19 Oct. 1940
SWALE, E.	2nd Officer	S.S. 'Matina'	24 Oct. 1940
WHITE, A. J.	Chief Engineer	S.S. 'Matina'	24 Oct. 1940

TABLE 9 continued

Civil Defence Casualties:
Killed on duty at 31, Bow Street, London, W.C.2, on 11 January 1941

BURLTON, F. A.	Warden	GODLEY, R. D.	Fire Guard
CRAWFORTH, C.	Decontamination	GRIGGS, E. F.	Fire Guard
DIXON, W.	Fire Guard	LEES, H. E.	Warden
DUTTON, P. J.	Fire Guard	PURCELL, A. H. D.	Decontamination
EDWARDS, J. E.	First Aid	ROBERTS, F. J.	Fire Guard
FATHARLY, W.	First Aid	SMITH, R. F.	Fire Guard
FETCH, F. G. V.	Fire Guard		

Killed on duty at Sea Mills, Bristol, on 30 May 1941
ROWE, W. A.   Warden

TABLE 10 CHIEF EXECUTIVE OFFICERS AND CHAIRMEN OF THE ENTERPRISE, 1888–1988

Chief Executive Officers	*Chairmen*
September 1888 EDWARD WATHEN FYFFE (E. W. Fyffe, Son and Company) (Fyffe, Hudson and Company)	
August 1897 HENRY WOLFSON (Fyffe, Hudson and Company Limited)	EDWARD CECIL BARKER
May 1901 (Elders and Fyffes Limited)* ARTHUR H. STOCKLEY A. ROGER ACKERLEY was appointed Sales and General Manager of the Company in 1904 and later in 1929 referred to as co-founder of the Company.	Sir ALFRED L. JONES, KC, MG
	May 1907 ANDREW W. PRESTON
	April 1924 ROBERT CLARK
May 1930 HENRY (HAL) STOCKLEY, MC	
	August 1940 Sir SAMUEL H. WILSON, GCMS
	May 1946 HENRY (HAL) STOCKLEY, MC
July 1958 Joint Managing Directors Captain JOHN A. MOORE, OBE H. JIM STOCKLEY	Sir JOHN HUGGINS, GCMG
April 1961 Captain JOHN A. MOORE, OBE	
March 1963 Admiral WILLIAM G. COOPER	
	May 1965 Admiral WILLIAM G. COOPER
September 1966 JOHN A. TAYLOR	JOHN A. TAYLOR
May 1969 A. JOHN ELLIS	
	January 1978 SEYMOUR MILSTEIN
	1984 A. JOHN ELLIS, CBE

* Name changed to Fyffes Group Limited in 1969.

Bibliography

Books

Vicente Abad, *Historia de la Naranja*, Comite de la Exportacion de Frutos Citricos, Valencia, 1984.

J. R. Ackerley, *My father and myself*, The Bodley Head, London, 1968

F. U. Adams, *Conquest of the Tropics*, Doubleday, Page and Company, New York, 1914.

Aguayro (ed.) *Primer Centenario del Puerto de la Luz*, Caja Insular de Ahorros, Year 12, No. 146, Las Palmas, March-April 1983.

Patrick Beaver, *Yes! We have some: The story of Fyffes*, Publications for Companies, Stevenage, 1976.

C. V. Black, (ed.) *Jamaica's Banana Industry*, Jamaica Banana Producers Association, Kingston, Jamaica, 1984.

A.. Samler Brown, *Madeira, Canary Islands and Azores*, Simpkin, Marshall, Hamilton, Kent and Company, London, 1922.

T. A. Bushell, *Royal Mail: A Centenary History of the Royal Mail Line, 1839–1939*, Trade and Travel Publications, London, 1939.

Mark Casson *et al. Multinationals and World Trade*, (R. A. Read, *The Banana Industry: Oligopoly and Barriers to Entry*), Allen and Unwin, London.

A. Cioranescu, *The History of Santa Cruz de Tenerife*, vol IV, Santa Cruz, 1979.

Bernabe P. Cobo, *Historia del Nuero Mundo*, Seville, 1890–93.

Tom Cullen, *Autumn of Terror: the Crimes and Times of Jack the Ripper*, London, 1973.

P. N. Davies, *The Trade Makers: Elder Dempster in West Africa, 1852–1972*, George Allen & Unwin, London 1973 (Reissued 1980).

P. N. Davies, *Sir Alfred Lewis Jones, Shipping Entrepreneur Par Excellence*, Europa Publications, London, 1978.

Ralph Davis, *The Rise of the English Shipping Industry*, 2nd Impression, David and Charles, Newton Abbot, 1972.

Charles Edwards, *Rides and Studies in the Canary Islands*, T. Fisher Unwin and Company, London, 1888.

Joaquim Nadal Farreras, *Comercio Exterior Y Subdesarrollo: Espana y Grand Bretanade, 1772–1914*, Institudo de Estudios Fiscales, Madrid, 1978

William Fawcett, *The Banana: its Cultivation, Distribution and Commercial Uses*, Duckworth, 2nd edition, London, 1921.

C. E. Fayle, *A Short History of the World's Shipping Industry*, Oxford University Press, London, 1927.

Gonzales Fernandes de Oviedo Y. Valdes, *Historia general y natural de las Indias, Islas y Tierra Firme del Mar Oceano*, 4 vols, Printing House of the Royal Academy of History, Madrid, 1851–55

J. K. Galbraith, *The Great Crash: 1929*, Penguin Books, Harmondsworth, (revised 1975).

W. J. Gardner, *A History of Jamaica*, Frank Cass, London, 1971.

George Glas, *History of the Canary Islands*, London, 1764.

Basil Greenhill, *The Merchant Schooner*, Conway Maritime Press, London, 1988.

F. Hanington and P. A. Kelly, *The Lady Boats: The Life and Times of Canada's West Indies Merchant Fleet*, published privately in Canada.

S. J. and E. F. Hurwitz, *Jamaica: A Historical Portrait*, Pall Mall Press, London, 1971.

Albert H. Imlah, *Economic elements in the Pax Britannica*, Russell and Russell, New York 1969

A. G. Kenwood and A.L. Lougheed, *The Growth of the International Economy, 1820–1960*, George Allen and Unwin, London, 1971

A. W. Kirkaldy, *British Shipping*, David and Charles Reprints, Newton Abbott, 1970

A. Lewis, *Economic Survey, 1919–1939*, London, 1949

Peter Mathias, *The First Industrial Nation*, Methuen, London, 1969

M. F. Maury, *The Physical Geography of the Sea*, 6th edition, Samson Low, Son and Company, London, 1856

S. May and G. Plaza, *The United Fruit Company in Latin America*, National Planning Association, New York, 1958.

Thomas McCann. *An American Company: The Tragedy of United Fruit*, (ed. Henry Scammell) Crown Publishers Inc., New York, 1977.

M. G. Mulhall, *Dictionary of Statistics*, (4th edition), London, 1898.

Marischal Murray, *Union Castle Chronicle, 1853–1953*, Longmans, Green and Company, London, 1953

Lord Olivier, *Jamaica: The Blessed Island*, Faber and Faber, London.

R. M. Parsons, *The Banana Trade at the Port of Bristol*, published by the City of Bristol Museum and Art Gallery, 1982.

Diana Petre, *The Secret Orchard of Roger Ackerley*, Hamish Hamilton, London, 1975.

Pliny The Elder, *Historia Naturalis*, Lib. xii, cap 12 (6) *The Natural History of Pliny*, (Trans. by John Bostock and H. Riley, 5 Vols, Henry G. Bohn, 1855)

P. K. Reynolds, *The Banana: its History Cultivation and Place among Staple Foods*, Houghton Mifflin Company, Boston, 1927

H. W. Richardson, *Economic Recovery in Britain, 1932–1939*, London, 1967

D. W. Rodriques, *History of the arrival of the banana in Jamaica*, Department of Agriculture, Kingston, Jamaica, 1953

K. T. Rowland, *Steam at Sea: A History of Steam Navigation*, David and Charles, Newton Abbot, 1970.

C. Piazzi-Smith, *Tenerife. An Astronomer's Experiment, or Specialities of a residence above the clouds*, Lowell Reeve, London, 1858

E. C. Smith, *A Short History of Naval and Marine Engineering*, University Press, Cambridge, 1937.

Siegfried Stander, *Tree of Life. The Story of Cape Fruit*, Saayman and Weber, Capetown, 1983.

Roy Stemman, *Geest: 1935–1985*, London, 1986.

W. Stewart, *Keith and Costa Rica*, University of New Mexico Press, Albuquerque, 1964.

A. H. Stockley, *Consciousness of Effort*, printed privately for the author by W.H. Smith and Son, London, 1937.

Olivia M. Stone, *Tenerife and its Six Satellites*, (*The Canaries Past and Present*), Marcus Ward and Company, 2 vols, London, 1887.

Theopharastus, *Enquiry into Plants* ... (trans. by Sir Aruthur Hart,) 2 vols, W. Heineman, London, 1916.

R. Thomson *et al. Greengold*, Latin America Bureau, London, 1987.

Osbert Ward, *The Vale of Orotava*, W. R. Russell and Company, London 1903.

W. R. Wilde, *Narrative of a Voyage to Madeira, Tenerife and along the Shores of the Mediterranean*, William Currey jun. and Company, Dublin, 1858

C. M. Wilson, *Empire in Green and Gold*, Henry Holt and Company, (USA), 1947.

Articles

Interview given by A. L. Jones to the magazine *Great Thoughts* and reproduced under the title of *A Napoleon of Commerce* in the issue of 18 June 1898.

Review of Norman Ball, *The Canary Islands after the Conquest*, (Economic History Review, 2nd series, vol 36, no. 1, Feb. 1983).

R. Bartlett, *Lorenzo Dow Baker: Yankee Entrepreneur in the Caribbean Fruit Trade*, The Log, Mystic Seaport, Spring 1987.

R. S. Best, *The Day of the Sailing 'Fruiter'*, Sea Breezes, May 1972

C. J. M. Carter, *75-Year Link with the Canaries*, Sea Breezes, May 1969.

Capt. H. J. Chubb, *Elders and Fyffes Fleet List*, Marine News, August 1960.

P. N. Davies, *The Development of the Liner Trades*, Ships and Shipbuilding in the North Atlantic Region, Memorial University of Newfoundland, St. John's, 1978.

G. S. Graham, *The Ascendancy of the Sailing Ship, 1850–1885*, Economic History Review; 2nd series, IX, no. 1, August 1956.

Cutcliffe Hyne, *Banana Farming in the Canary Islands*, 1898.

L. Isserlis, *Tramp Shipping, Cargo and Freights*, Journal of the Royal Statistical Society, vol. CI, 1938.

Capt. K. J. Leslie, *Banana Fleet*, Sea Breezes, No. 255, vol. 41, March 1967.

Interview given by Luis Ley, former manager of Elder Dempster's Fruit Department in the Canary Islands and reproduced in the Fruit Trade News, 9 November 1901.

Baron Erland Nordenskiold, *Deductions Suggested by the Geographical Distribution of some Post-Columbian words used by the Indians of S. America*, Comparative Ethnographical Studies, 5, Götoberg, 1922.

D. North, *Ocean Freight Rates and Economic Development 1750–1913*, Journal of Economic History, vol. XVIII, no. 4, Dec. 1958.

E. W. Perry, *Tertiary of Colombia*, American Journal of Science, Series 5, vol. 10, 1925.

R. A. Peters, *Refrigerated Shipping*: Wakefield Lecture presented at the University of Southampton, 1982.

P. K. Reynolds, *Earliest Evidence of Banana Culture*, Supplement to the Journal of the American Oriental Society, no. 12, Dec. 1951.

S. B. Saul, *The Economic Significance of 'Constructive Imperialism,'* Journal of Economic History, vol. XVII, No. 2, June 1957.

Earl B. Shaw, *Banana Trade of Brazil*, Economic Geography, vol. XXIII, 1947.

George F. Stecley, *The Wine Economy of Tenerife in the Seventeenth Century: Anglo-Spanish Partnership in a Luxury Trade*, Economic History Review, 2nd series, vol. 33, no. 3, August 1980.

H. J. Ward, *Bananas and Refrigeration*, Fruit, Flower and Vegetable Trades Journal, 17 October, 1908.

Works of Reference

Crockford's Clerical Directory.
Encyclopaedia Britannica, 11th edition.
Gaceta Agricola Del Ministerio De Fomento, Tomo X, Madrid, 1879.
Kelly's Post Office London Directory.
Kent's London Directory.
Lloyd's Register of Shipping.
Pigot's London Directory.
Robson's London Commercial Directory.
Universal British Directory of Trade, Commerce and Manufacture, London, 1791.
Universal Magazine of Knowledge and Pleasure, London, April 1748.

Government Publications

Commonwealth Secretariat's *Fruit Review*.
House of Commons, *Parliamentary Papers*, 1839, (229) XLVI, 9.
House of Commons, Foreign Affairs Committee, (Session 1981–2) *Caribeean and Central America: Belize*, HMSO, London, 1982.
Foreign Office Miscellaneous Series, No. 246, *Spain: Report on the Social and Economic Conditions of the Canary Islands*, 1892.
Price Commission, Report No. 4, *Prices and Distribution of Bananas*, HMSO, London, 1975.

Newspapers and Periodicals

A.C.T. News
Banana Budget
Covent Garden Gazette and Market Record
Exel Financial Newsletter
Forbes (US magazine)
Fortune (US magazine)
Fruit Grower, Fruiterer, Florist and Market Gardener
Fruit Trade Mail
Fruit Trade News
Fyffes' News
Fyffes' Staff Budget
Greengrocer, Fruiterer and Market Gardener
Hansard
Manchester City News
Surrey Mirror and County Post
The Liverpool Courier
The Horticultural Times
The Stroud Journal
The Times

Primary Sources

A. F. Baillon, unpublished *Memoirs* in the author's possession.
Joseph Chamberlain Mss, held at the Heslop Room at the University of Birmingham Library.
Comision Regional Del Platano *Estadisticas*, (Santa Cruz de Tenerife, 1986).
Elders and Fyffes (later the Fyffes Group) Limited. (File 70123 live at Companies House, London.)
Elders and Fyffes Limited, General Minute Books.
Elders and Fyffes Limited, Minutes of Directors Meetings.
Fruit Distributing Company Limited, (File 75160), official returns held at the Public Record Office, Kew.
Fyffe Family Mss, Archives (B. 59–22–60 and B.59–26–10/11) held at the Sandeman Library, Perth.
Fyffes Limited (File 98506), Canary Islands. Official returns held at the Public Record Office, Kew.
Fyffe Hudson and Company limited, (File 53906). Official returns are held at the Public Record Office, Kew.
Barbara J. Heinzen, *The United Brands Company in Cameroon*, PhD thesis submitted to the School of Oriental and African Studies, University of London, 1980.
Hudson Brothers (London) Limited, (File 59505). Official returns held at the Public Record Office, Kew.

Imperial Direct West India Mail Service Company Limited, (File 72110). Official returns held at the Public Record Office, Kew.

Jamaica Fruit Importing and Trade Company of London Limited, (File 49018). Official returns are held at the Public Record Office, Kew.

Thomas Leyland, *Letterbook, (1786–88)*. This is located in the Local History Department of Liverpool City Library.

Pavillard Mss, Copies of Elder Dempster (Grand Canary) Limited Records, of which the Pavillard Family were the principals, are held by the author.

. A. Philp, *The Winban Agreement*, 1971, (Fyffes internal consultative paper).

Author's Inteviews

(Unless otherwise stated these meetings were all with Fyffes or its associated companies, employees or pensioners.)

Name	Date & Place of Interview	Main Occupation or Area of Interview
A. Baillon	1979 Puerto de la Cruz, Tenerife	Son of A. F. Baillon
J. G. Batten	1981 Angmering-on-Sea	La Compagnie des Bananes
J. A. Benns	1986 London	Head Office
M. R. Blairsey	1982 Santa Cruz de Tenerife	Canary Islands
D. H. Brown	1983 Paris	La Compagnie des Bananes
Capt. T. H. Bull	1981 Carnforth	Fleet
M. Campbell	1985 Glasgow	Malcolm Campbell Ltd
P. R. Caws	1982 Bristol	Bristol
S. Clements	1981 Kirkby Lonsdale	St. Helens
P. J. Cochrane	1988 London	Cameroons and Fernando Po
J. Colville	1981 Adeje, Tenerife	Canary Islands
F. E. Darter	1983 Poole	Head Office
B. Dawson	1989 Liverpool	T. & J. Harrison and Company
Sn. D. M. Diaz	1987 Santa Cruz de Tenerife	CREPE
C. L. M. Dury	1989 London	Head Office
Sn. V. G. Dust	1980 Santa Cruz de Tenerife	Elder Dempster Agent
E. J. Easterbrook	1981 High Wycombe	Hull & London
R. F. Edwards	1981 New Malden	Head Office
Sn. Pepe Escavil	1980 Adeje, Tenerife	Foreman at Hoya Grande

286

Capt. G.L. Foster	1982	Chewton Keynesham	Fleet and Head Office
H. Goodwin	1989	London	Cameroons, Belize & Suriname
F. A. Hall	1989	Elstree	Head Office
H. Hart (& C. V. Black)	1985	Lewes	Jamaica Producers
R. Hilborne	1989	Peterborough	Geest Industries
J. A. Hudson	1981	Chislehurst	Grandson of James Hudson
C. Hughes	1981	Nailsworth	Neighbour of E. W. Fyffe
A. Jeffares	1983	London	JAMCO
S. W. F. Johnson	1985	Bury St Edmunds	Head Office
Capt. J. Kinsley	1983	Stoke Poges	Fleet
W. H. (Angus) Knight	1984	London	Head Office
C. F. H. (Joe) Lees (Secretary of Pensioners Association)	1981	Bury St Edmunds	Continent & Head Office
Capt. K. J. Leslie	1979	Taunton	Fleet
D. G. Martin	1986	London	Head Office
A. (Sandy) Maclaurin	1982	Staines	Cameroons
G. C. Mills	1981	Nailsworth	Neighbour of E. W. Fyffe
Mrs. D. C. Moore	1978	Santa Cruz de Tenerife	Widow of Wilfred Moore
B. Norton-Amor	1984	London	Canary Islands and Head Office
Mrs. B. Norton-Amor	1984	London	Personal Assistant to Wilfred Moore
G. and S. Pavillard	1985	Las Palmas	Elder Dempster Agents
A. C. Penny	1983	London	ex Francis Nichols and Geo. Monro
R. A. Peters	1982	London	Head Office
Mrs. D. Petrie	1983	London	Daughter of A. R. Ackerley
D. A. Philp OBE	1982	London	Cameroons, Tropics and Head Office
C. J. B. Priest	1989	Maidenhead	ex Geo. Jackson
Noel Reid	1980	Puerto de la Cruz, Tenerife	Grandson of Peter Reid
N. T. Ridge	1981	New Malden	Head Office (later joined JAMCO)
G. A. Scott	1983	La Palma	Cameroons and Canary Islands
R. H. Taylor	1982	Bristol	Bristol and Avonmouth

E. Thomas	1989	Southampton	Southampton
A. Wadland	1981	Algarve	Continent
A. J. Walker	1988	London	Head Office
G. Walker	1983	Hull	Canary Islands
S. (Paddy) Watters	1988	Liverpool	Cameroons and Fernando Po
B. Whaley	1983	Wallasey	Garston and Swansea
V. Whiteley	1981	Southampton	Southampton
J. G. Willis	1981	Santa Cruz de Tenerife	Canary Islands

INDEX

289

Cactus, 39
Cadiz, 157
Calabar, 121
Calais, 16
Calcutta, 16
Cameroon, 159–60, 165, 169, 174–5, 177, 179, 182, 187–8, 190, 192–3, 202, 206; Exports, 212
Cameroon Development Corporation, 174–6, 180
Cammell, Laird and Company, 131, 161
Canada, 184
Canada Shipping Company (Beaver Line), 109
Canadian Banana Company, 183, 188
Canadian market, 143, 168
Canadian National Steam Ship Line, 146
Canadian Pacific Railway Company, 109
Canary exports to Spain, 157
Canary Islands, xvi, 8, 21–2, 37–9, 41, 45, 51, 53–4, 57, 60, 64, 69, 75, 83, 86–7, 90–3, 95, 97, 100, 113, 116, 118, 119, 126, 129, 130–1, 154–6, 158, 160, 175, 182, 187–8, 196, 206, 210–12, 217–19, 226, 235
Canary Islands 'Syndicate', 92
Cape Cod, 27
Cape Colony, 65
Cape Town, 65
Capital, 216–17, 219–20, 223, 231, 235
Cardamoms, 81
Cargoes, third party, 176; outward, 177
Caribbean, 22, 24, 78, 116, 130, 154–5, 177, 181, 184, 202, 204, 207–8, 210, 213
Caribbean producers, 214
Caribbean Steamship Agency Limited, 199
Castle Mail Steam Ship Company, 68
Caws, Pat, xvii
Central America, 22, 82, 99, 111, 119, 123, 127, 129, 131, 153–4, 156, 158, 160, 168, 176, 188, 206, 216, 231
Cereals, 20, 40
Chamberlain, Joseph, 82–5, 122, 144
Chandlers Ford, 223
Channel Islands, 227
Cherries, 11, 13
Chestnuts, 21
Chile, 16
China, 55
Chingford, 201
Cifalu, D., 25

Cinnamon, 81
Citrus, 12, 15, 172
City of Dublin Steam Packet Company, 16
Clacton-on-Sea, 227
Clark and Company, 29
Clements, Stan, xvii
Clifford, J., 55, 59
Clifford, Mrs, 137
Clifton School, 49
Clydeside, 194
Coal, 15, 18, 43
Coccus cacti, 39
Cochineal, 39–40, 43
Cochrane, P.J., xvii
Cocoa, 80, 177
Coconuts, 26, 81, 136
Coffee, 20, 80–1, 177
Coisy, A. Limited, 199
Colombia, 34, 82, 126, 144
Colombia Land Company, 35
Colon, 25, 33
Colonial Office, 147
Columbus, Christopher, 78
Colville, John, xvii, 218
Comfit, 45
Commission Agents, 178
Commonwealth producers, 208, 235
Computer, 193
Confederacion Regional de la Exportacion del Platanos, (CREPE), 175, 218–9
Congo, 81
Connolly, L. and Company, 92
Connolly Shaw (Ireland) Limited, 230
Conservative government, 178
Convoys, 168
Cookery exhibitions, 137
Cooper, Admiral Wm. G., 190–1, 198
Copper, 40
Copper sulphate, 177
Cork, 231
Cornwall, 15
Cortes, 221
Costa Rica, 33–4, 103, 107, 116, 123, 126, 144
Cousins, Mr, 83
Covent Garden, 50–1, 57–8, 65, 68, 71, 75, 93, 113, 132, 185, 196, 198–9
Cowling, Frederick, 199
Cowlings Limited, 199
Crawford, J.N., 164
Cricket, 163–4, 228
Cristobal, 125

Natal, 65
Nazi regiéme, 161
Nelson Line, 126, 147
Newbridge, (Midlothian), 223
New Englanders, 30–1
Newhaven, 221, 223
New Jersey, 34
New Malden (Sports Ground), 228
New Orleans, 25, 29, 33–4, 102
Newport, 221
Newsome, William, 123
New York, 16, 24–5, 27–8, 71–2, 126–7, 220
Nicaragua, 34, 127
Nicholls, Francis Welcome, 197
Nigeria, 187
Nordenskiöld, Baron Erland, 23
North America, 64, 88, 95, 105, 143, 171, 199, 234
North of England, 222
Norton-Amor, Mr & Mrs, xvii
Norton, T.L., xviii
Norway, 118, 167, 173
Norwegian timber, 69
Nottingham, 112–13, 195
N.V. Internationale Bananen Maarschappiji, 132, 152

Oidium tuckeri, 38
Oil prices, 219
Onions, 40, 94
Operations, (need for large scale), 214
Oracabessa, 25
Orange juice, 167, 177
Oranges, xvi, 9, 11–13, 15, 21, 64–5, 72, 88, 94, 116, 136, 177, 195–6
Orinoco, 26
Orotarva, 155–6
Oteri, Salvatore, 25
Ottawa Agreement, 153, 156
'Outspan' brand, 196
Over-staffing, 190, 192, 195

Pacific, 33
Pacific Mail Steam Ship Company, xv, 27
Palan, 7
Pacific Steam Navigation Company, 126
Panama, 8, 24–5, 27, 29, 34
Paris, 132; seige of, 57
Pavillard family (especially Mr E.V. and Dr S.S. Pavillard), xvii
Peaches, 68

Pears, 11, 13, 21, 68, 167, 198
Pearsall, John, 24
Peas, 68
P and O Company, 17
Penny, Charles, xvii, 198
Pensions, 162; Elders & Fyffes Staff Provident Fund, 162, 163; Special Benefit Account, 162; Elders and Fyffes Staff Provident Fund, 226; Provisions for Marine Officers, 226; Fyffes Group Pension Scheme, 226; Pensioners Visitors, 227
Perth, 53
Peters, R.A., xvii
Petrograd, 118
Philadelphia, 29, 31–2
Philipps, Sir Owen (Lord Kylsant), 120–2, 176
Philp, David, xvii
Pimento, 80
Pineapples, xvi, 13, 65, 88
Pirrie, Lord, 120, 122
Plantain, 4, 23, 45, 114
Platanos, 8
Plinny, 4
Plums, 11, 13, 167, 198
Pontypridd, 223
Population, 20
Pork, 26
Port Antonio, 25–6, 28–9, 125
Port Glasgow, 150
Port Limon, 102
Port Orotava, 55
Portsmouth, 221–2
Portugal, 11, 16, 65
Portuguese explorers, 8
Potatoes, 9, 11, 40, 185, 198
Poultry, 199
Poupart, T.J. Limited, 146
Pouyat, Jean Francois, 81
Powis, Earl, 12
Pratt, Page, V., 201
Preston, 161
Preston, Andrew Woodbury, 26–8, 30–5, 103, 122
Priest, Frank, 196, 198
Priest, John, xvii
Price Commission Report, 213–4
Price equalization scheme, 135
Price, George, 206
Prime Minister of Belize, 206
Prime Minister of Jamaica, 204
Prime Minister of UK, 204

Shoes, 26

Sicily, 11

Sierra Leone Coaling Company, 120

Singapore, 204

Slaves, 38, 80

Smithfield, 113

Snyder Banana Company, 35

Sorensons: C.H. and Sons, 173

Southampton, 126, 160, 194, 220–1, 223

Southern Fruit Suppliers, 230

South Africa, 66, 197

South African gold fields, 50

South America, 168, 171, 176, 178, 188, 210, 231

Southern Ireland, 136, 209, 230–1, 234

South Wales, 221

South Wales coal mines, 45

Spain, 15, 21, 65, 78, 80, 156, 169, 175, 218; Civil War, 156, 158, 169, 217; Legislation, 218

Spanish explorers, 8

Spanish market, 212, 219

Spanish Nationalist Party, 158

Spanish orange industry, 12, 14

Spalding, 185

Sports grounds: Avonmouth, 164; Liverpool, 164; New Malden, 163

Sports & Social activities, 164

Standard Fruit Corporation, xv, 25, 144, 148, 165, 178, 180, 234

Standard Steam Navigation Company, 28, 30

Steckley, George F., 38

Stems, 192

Stickney, Tim, xvii

Stockley, A.H., 49–50, 54, 58, 60, 70, 75–6, 82–3, 86, 88–90, 93, 95, 97, 99, 100–1, 103, 110, 114, 121–3, 130, 140, 147, 150, 161, 174, 176, 189–90, 226